THE MECCAN REVELATIONS

THE MECCAN

VOLUME I

SELECTED TEXTS OF AL-FUTÛHÂT AL-MAKKIYA ~
PRESENTATIONS AND TRANSLATIONS FROM THE ARABIC
UNDER THE DIRECTION OF
MICHEL CHODKIEWICZ

IN COLLABORATION WITH
WILLIAM C. CHITTICK AND
JAMES W. MORRIS

REVELATIONS

IBN AL 'ARABI

NEW YORK · PIR PRESS · 2002

Pir Press
227 West Broadway
New York, New York 10013

Copyright © 1988 by the Rothko Chapel (edition: Sindbad, Paris)
Copyright © 2002 by Pir Press

All rights reserved. No part of this book may be reproduced or utilized in any form or by any means, electronic or mechanical, including photocopying and recording, or otherwise, without the prior written permission from the publisher. All inquiries should be sent to Pir Press at the above address.

Printed in the United States of America

Note: This edition, the first of two volumes, incorporates all English text and translations from the original 1988 bi-lingual, French-English edition, *Les Illuminations des la Mecque*, published by Sindbad (Paris), and edited by Michel Chodkiewicz. The original (French) introduction by Mr. Chodkiewicz has been replaced with a new one by James W. Morris for this edition. The second volume, forthcoming, will include translations of all of the French portions in the original Sindbad edition.

Text and translation copyright © 1988 by William C. Chittick and James W. Morris
Revised edition: Introduction copyright © 2002 by James W. Morris

ISBN: 1-879708-16-7

CONTENTS

PREFACE *James W. Morris* — 1

INTRODUCTION *James W. Morris* — 3

DIVINE NAMES AND THEOPHANIES *William C. Chittick* — 27

    The Origin of Creation ~ CHAPTER 6 — 29
    The Perfect Man ~ CHAPTER 73 — 43
    The Glories of the Face ~ CHAPTER 73 — 45
    The Beauty of God and the Beauty of the World ~ CHAPTER 73 — 47
    The Breath of the All-Merciful ~ CHAPTER 198 — 50
    The Most Beautiful Names ~ CHAPTER 558 — 57

AT THE END OF TIME *James W. Morris* — 65

    The Mahdi's Helpers ~ CHAPTER 366 — 67

LESSER AND GREATER RESURRECTION *James W. Morris* — 93

    The Soul's Return ~ CHAPTER 302 — 101
    The Voluntary Death ~ CHAPTER 351 — 105
    The Lesser Resurrection and Initiatic Death ~ CHAPTER 369 — 108
    The Presence of the Hour ~ CHAPTER 73 — 112
    The Beatific Vision of the Saints ~ CHAPTER 73 — 116
    The Imaginal Vision of Ordinary People ~ CHAPTER 73 — 122

TOWARD SAINTHOOD: STATES AND STATIONS   *William C. Chittick*   125

    THE STATION OF SERVITUDE ~ CHAPTERS 130-131   130
    THE STATION OF FREEDOM ~ CHAPTERS 140-141   140
    THE TRUE KNOWLEDGE OF UNRULY UTTERANCES ~ CHAPTER 195   150
    ON WITHDRAWAL ~ CHAPTER 205   142
    GATHERING AND ITS MYSTERIES ~ CHAPTER 222   146
    THE WORLD OF IMAGINATION ~ CHAPTER 311   169
    GOD'S SIGN ~ CHAPTER 372   181
    WORSHIP AND ITS SECRETS ~ CHAPTER 470   189

IBN 'ARABI'S SPIRITUAL ASCENSION   *James W. Morris*   199

    "MY VOYAGE WAS ONLY IN MYSELF..." ~ CHAPTER 367   201

NOTES   231
BIBLIOGRAPHY   355
INDEX OF QUR'ANIC REFERENCES   360
GENERAL INDEX ~ GLOSSARY   364

PREFACE

The translations included in this volume have a long history. The guiding intention behind this project, as it was originally conceived by Michel Chodkiewicz (the foremost French student of Ibn 'Arabî, a professor at the École des Hautes Études, and then head of the major French publishing house Éditions du Seuil), was to provide, in a bilingual edition, the first representative overview of Ibn 'Arabî's magnum opus, *Meccan Revelations (al-Futûhât al-Makkiya*[1]*)*. Anyone who has ever attempted to study that immense and utterly unique work—which would require perhaps fifty volumes of this scale to translate in its entirety—will recognize the daunting challenges of selection, translation and adequate explanation actually involved. Fortunately, Mr. Chodkiewicz was quickly able to assemble an international team of scholars to begin work in late 1984, and thanks to the financial support of the Rothko Chapel (and Mme. D. De Menil), as well as the tireless editorial work of our colleague Dr. Martine Gillet, the resulting volume (of some 653 pages), entitled *Les Illuminations de La Mecque,* was published in Paris by Sindbad in late 1988.

The impetus that this project gave to the further study and communication of Ibn 'Arabî's works, and especially the *Futûhât*, went far beyond the publication itself. Professor Chodkiewicz soon published two pioneering, foundational studies of Ibn 'Arabî's works (both now available in English and discussed in the "Further Readings" section of the Introduction to this volume); Professor Denis Gril has continued to publish important editions, translations and studies of Ibn 'Arabî's works; and Professor William Chittick and I have gone on to complete (or should soon publish) several more volumes of English translations and studies of these "Illuminations." As a result, the years since the first appearance of our translations have seen an ongoing worldwide transformation—in the Islamic world at least as much as in Western academic and spiritual circles—in the understanding and appreciation of the nature and wider significance of Ibn 'Arabî's writings.

Unfortunately, the French edition—whose size, cost and foreign publication made access difficult in the English-speaking world from the beginning—soon became entirely inaccessible due to problems at the original publishers. Usually, for the past decade, only those with ready access to university libraries and Islamic research collections have been able to refer directly to these essential translations. Thus we are all immensely grateful to Pir Publications, to its editors, Ann Everds, Sixtina Friedrich and Matthew Brown, to Margot Abel, the copyeditor of this edition, and to the others who contribute to the existence of the press, for their far-sighted initiative in undertaking to publish separately in this first volume the English-language translations that formed more than two-thirds of the original Sindbad edition. (The fourth section of the Introduction that follows outlines the contents and location, in the overall scheme of the *Futûhât*, of those chapters included in the "missing" French sections, which are frequently referred to in cross-references in the English notes and introductory material.) Pir Publications has promised a forthcoming English volume that would include translations of both the original French chapters and Professor Chodkiewicz's original long Introduction to the key themes and opening chapters of the *Futûhât*.

James W. Morris

INTRODUCTION

In assembling this volume, my colleagues and I intended each section to be relatively self-contained and accessible, together with its introductory matter and notes, to readers without previous contact with Ibn 'Arabî's works. In particular, we have chosen passages that are long enough, in most cases, to give readers some taste of the inseparable connection between Ibn 'Arabî's utterly unique style and forms of writing and the process and purposes of realization for which they were designed. For those who are encountering Ibn 'Arabî for the first time, or who would like to pursue their study of his work and teachings, this Introduction will provide helpful background information on the following areas:

> 1. Ibn 'Arabî's life and posterity;
> 2. the origin and distinctive characteristics of his *Meccan Revelations (al-Futûhât al-Makkiya),* in relation to his other works, including both the better known *Bezels of Wisdom (Fusûs al-Hikam)* and the complex Islamic philosophical and poetic traditions that developed from it, as well as the poetic, allusive and highly symbolic works of his Andalusian and North African youth;

3. a summary outline of key assumptions common to all of his writings, which are essential for situating these translated chapters from the *Futûhât;* and of the pedagogical, rhetorical relations between the distinctive style and structure of *The Meccan Revelations* and Ibn 'Arabî's intended audiences, as he himself explains those points in his Introduction to that work;

4. the overall structure of the *Futûhât* and the place of these translated selections—as well as the French translations to appear in a separate companion volume—within that larger structure;

5. and finally, a selection of further English readings in different areas related to Ibn 'Arabî, his works and teachings, and their ongoing influences and inspiration.

However, every reader should pay attention to one absolutely essential point: the notes to these translations—as indeed to any accurate and intelligible translation of Ibn 'Arabî—are an integral and indispensable part of the translation. Since the notes were not published as footnotes, it is necessary to read these translations with a bookmark at the corresponding notes, constantly moving back and forth, and also keeping in mind the ongoing technical sense of terms that are explained only once in a given translation, in a note at their first occurrence. The profusion of notes are necessary here, as with any of Ibn 'Arabî's writings, for the following basic reasons. First, he constantly uses what might otherwise be taken as "normal" Arabic terms, particularly ones drawn from the Islamic scriptural background of the Qur'an and hadith (traditions related from the Prophet), in specifically technical, personal senses (often profoundly based in the etymological roots of the underlying Arabic) that were already unfamiliar, and sometimes intentionally provocative, even to his original readers. To take one recurrent and fundamental example, in most of his writing, the expression *Muhammadan* carries the profound meaning of "spiritually universal" or "spiritually all-inclusive." *Shar'* (which he typically uses instead of the more reified *sharî'a*) refers in many contexts to the universal, ongoing process of spiritual "inspiration" and unveiling that is at the existential core of every human being's uniquely individuated spiritual life, as well as at the ontological Source[1] of the revealed religions. In either of these key cases, modern-day presuppositions (shared by Muslim and non-Muslim readers alike) are likely to suggest diametrically opposite meanings to readers who have not studied the corresponding notes of explanation or otherwise assimilated Ibn 'Arabî's technical terminology.

Second, Ibn 'Arabî—whether in his poetry or prose—constantly plays with the multiple, often very different meanings and registers of key Arabic terms (especially from the Qur'an), which in his writings are normally closer in their polyvalence to musical chords or the symbols of the *I Ching* than to the prosaic "equivalents" of any possible English translation. That semantic reality is what explains the translators' frequent interpolation of transliterations of the underlying Arabic terms, useful at least to those with some familiarity with Sufi and Qur'anic Arabic terminology.

Third, Ibn 'Arabî's usual procedure throughout *The Meccan Revelations* is to shift constantly between multiple registers and references to the terminology, structures and intellectual assumptions of a host of fields of traditional learning that are often unfamiliar to most modern readers.[2]

Finally, *The Meccan Revelations* are replete with allusive *cross-references* to other writings or discussions of related topics elsewhere in the same book, which are absolutely indispensable to understanding the particular passage, symbol or allusion in question.[3] This fundamental structural and stylistic feature is another key reason—as translators are particularly aware—that we still have so few complete translations of any larger sections of this intentionally "sealed" and mysterious work. And at the very least, explanatory notes are essential in such cases to help readers begin to reconstruct the experience of what it would be like to read through the *Futûhât* from the very beginning.

IBN 'ARABÎ'S LIFE AND POSTERITY

An abundance of excellent books intended to introduce Ibn 'Arabî's life, historical context and basic teachings to general audiences have appeared in recent years.[4] Here it may suffice to recall that he was born in present-day Murcia, in Andalusia, in 1165/560; was raised in the great cultural centers of Islamic Spain, where his extraordinary spiritual gifts were already apparent by his adolescence; traveled and encountered innumerable spiritual teachers and "Friends of God" throughout Spain and North Africa in his youth; and left that area definitively for the Hajj, which brought him to Mecca—and the incidents that gave rise to *The Meccan Revelations*—in 1202/598. His years of maturity were spent in travel and teaching (usually privately, and with none of the public charisma and mass following of the more celebrated saints of his day) throughout the narrowing confines of the Islamic East, which was caught between the inroads of the Crusaders and the ongoing conquests of the Mongol hordes. Eventually he settled for a time in Konya (in present-day Turkey) and then in Damascus, where he died on November 9, 1240/638. His place of burial there has been a famous pilgrimage site since Ottoman times.

While all of Ibn 'Arabî's writings—and most especially the *Futûhât*—are replete with autobiographical discussions of his extraordinary inner visionary life and spiritual experiences, everything that is known about him from external sources indicates that in his later years he rigorously lived up to his own ideal of the hidden, "solitary" Friends of God (the *afrâd* or *malâmîya*) as the highest of the spiritual ranks, "invisible" in their outward conformity to the normative practices of the revelation and the ethical and social obligations common to all—carefully avoiding the public, visible "spiritual gifts" *(karamât)* popularly associated with many shaykhs and the then-nascent forms of institutionalized Sufism. Although he was accompanied by a small group of friends and close disciples, who became the eventual vehicles for his later wider influence, Ibn 'Arabî seems to have been best known in his own day as a religious scholar and student of hadith, an impression that could only have been encouraged by his phenomenally prolific literary output of hundreds of works, of which the *Futûhât* was apparently by far the longest and most comprehensive.[5]

Even Ibn 'Arabî's most skeptical biographers have been compelled to note the remarkable way subsequent history has come to confirm his self-conception of his destined role as the "Seal of Muhammadan Sainthood",[6] whose voluminous writings—and more important, the underlying spiritual "Reality" that they are meant to reveal and convey—were specially intended to open up the inner spiritual meanings at the heart of all preceding prophetic revelations (and especially the Qur'an and hadith). At the time of his death, Ibn 'Arabî himself was virtually unknown, in any wider public sense, in that Mongol/Crusader period when Islamic public authority almost vanished for some decades from all but a handful of Arab cities (and permanently from most of his native Andalusia).

Moreover, all of his "books" discussed here existed only in a handful of manuscript copies, left behind in the Maghreb or restricted to the assiduous students and future transmitters of his teachings during his final years in Damascus. Yet within a few centuries, through one of those mysterious developments so familiar to the historian of religions, his writings—foremost among them the *Bezels of Wisdom (Fusûs al-Hikam)* and these *Meccan Revelations*—had come to constitute the constantly cited source of inspiration, and justification (and, as a result, a frequent polemic target) for that vast movement of religious, cultural, social, and literary creativity that brought into being the institutions and masterworks of the Islamic humanities. It was through those creative developments, in a wide gamut of languages, cultures and new institutions, that Islam became a true world religion, with its new cultural and political centers stretching from Southern and Eastern Europe and sub-Saharan Africa across to Central Asia, India and Southeast Asia.[7] Despite the historically quite recent ideological responses to colonialism, the transformations of modernity and the new demands of the nation-state, most Muslims throughout the world have lived for the past six or seven centuries in cultural, spiritual and religious worlds[8] whose accomplished forms would be unimaginable without the profound impact of ideas rooted in and expressed by Ibn 'Arabî. Even his later honorific title, "the greatest Master" *(al-Shaykh al-Akbar)*, does not really begin to suggest the full extent of those influences.

A second, equally mysterious stage in Ibn 'Arabî's ongoing influence has been the ways his writings and concepts have served, over the past century, to inspire contemporary intellectuals and students of religion and spirituality outside traditionally Islamic cultures. Faced with a cosmopolitan, multireligious world not unlike the great Muslim empires of the Ottomans, Safavids and Moguls, these thinkers have increasingly relied on Ibn 'Arabî's works and ideas for the task of creating the common language and subtle conceptual structure required to communicate universal spiritual realities in an increasingly global civilization.[9]

THE ORIGINS OF *THE MECCAN REVELATIONS* AND THEIR CONTRAST WITH OTHER WRITINGS OF IBN 'ARABÎ

The inspirations that gave rise to *The Meccan Revelations*—as its title suggests[10]—took place in the course of Ibn 'Arabî's first pilgrimage in 1202/598. He describes those experiences in a famous passage at the beginning of the book, which has been translated and discussed by each of his recent biographers. As he explains there (I 10), *"The essence of what is included in this work comes from what God inspired in me while I was fulfilling my circumambulations of His Temple* [the *Ka'ba, bayt Allâh*], *or while I was contemplating it while seated in its holy precincts."* However, the actual composition of his first complete version of this immense work, composed during a time of constant travels and the simultaneous production of dozens of other works, lasted until 1231/629. And a few years later, in 1233/632, Ibn 'Arabî began a revision and expansion of the text, which he finished in 1238/636, shortly before his death; the complete autograph manuscript of that final version, preserved by his famous disciple Qûnawî, survives.[11]

Ibn 'Arabî's assertion of a kind of divine inspiration for this work—a point on which his frequent discussions later served as a justification and inspiration for generations of later Muslim poets and creators—in fact extended to virtually all of his writings. As he has noted in another passage at the beginning of the *Futûhât* (I 59), *"Neither this book nor my other books have been composed in the manner of ordinary books, and I do not write in the way authors normally do."* Instead, he affirms more explicitly in a famous later passage (II 456), *"I swear by God, I have not written a single letter of this book that was not in accordance with a divine 'dictation'* [*imlâ' ilâhî*], *a spiritual inbreathing and a 'casting by God'* [*ilqâ' rabbânî*] *in my heart!"* Perhaps just as important, Ibn 'Arabî's remarks suggest the powerful and essentially unique and inimitable ways in which his distinctive language and rhetoric in this work so closely parallels the deeper structures of the Qur'an.[12] Despite the multitude of his later learned and artistic followers and interpreters, no one has really attempted any sort of detailed imitation of that distinctive Arabic literary style, which remains as unique, in its own way, as the equally inimitable Qur'an-inspired structures of Rumi and Hafez.

If the experience and practice of centuries of assiduous and admiring readers lends a certain external "authority" to Ibn 'Arabî's assertions in this domain, this does not at all mean that his books closely resemble each other. In particular, readers approaching the *Meccan Revelations* after having studied Ibn 'Arabî's *Bezels of Wisdom (Fusûs al-Hikam)* and the many traditions of later Islamic (and more recent Western) commentary on them, as we once did, will immediately feel that they are discovering a new continent. The essential guiding ideas are of course the same, but here they are expressed with a constant careful, vivid and enthralling attention to the "living" phenomenology and experiential roots—including, above all, a constant reference to the words and practices of Islamic revelation—underlying the typically ontological and metaphysical formulae of the *Fusûs* tradition. What is often "abstract" or schematic in the highly compressed language of the *Bezels of Wisdom* is expressed here with a profusion of immediate, compelling experiential illustrations: from Ibn 'Arabî's own spiritual life, the experiences of his friends and associates, of earlier Sufis, and the Prophet and Companions. All of these facets highlight the focus of the *Futûhât* on the living process and ends of spiritual realization, which is equally evident in the specific character of its language and structure, discussed in the following sections.

Those distinctive facets of *The Meccan Revelations*, in contrast with the *Fusûs* and its interpreters, help to explain certain of the criteria that guided the selection of chapters and topics for this anthology. Ample treatment is given to illustrations of the autobiographical dimensions of the *Futûhât*, its elaborate phenomenology of spiritual experience and realization, and its constant reference to the inspiration of the equally indispensable metaphysical and practical dimensions of Islamic revelation. A final distinctive characteristic of the *Futûhât*, in the context of Ibn 'Arabî's own writings, is the *relatively* discursive and comprehensible explanatory prose of most of the chapters—a quality that is only apparent, one must admit, when compared with the extremely allusive, poetic and mysteriously symbolic discourse that is more typical of the earlier writings from his North African and Andalusian period.[13]

Assumptions, Intentions and the Rhetoric of Spiritual Pedagogy in *The Meccan Revelations*

This is not the proper place to attempt to summarize the basic teachings of Ibn 'Arabî, a task that has been undertaken, for various audiences, in many recent publications cited or discussed later in this Introduction. Indeed, the single most useful contribution of these (and other) translations from the *Futûhât* may be precisely to *undermine* and call into question—in a particularly constructive and indispensable fashion—many of the notional "doctrines," slogans and ostensible teachings so often connected with the name of Ibn 'Arabî. Whether in later Islamic polemical contexts or Western scholarship, those stereotypes usually reflect the profound influence of his very short and complex later work, the *Bezels of Wisdom (Fusûs al-Hikam)*,[14] the study and interpretation of which has over the centuries both inspired and sometimes antagonized many Islamic philosophic and theological traditions.

The inevitable result of such primarily intellectual (or heresiographical) efforts at "summarizing" Ibn 'Arabî—where he is somehow identified uniquely with a few paradoxical formulae supposedly drawn from the *Fusûs*—is quite similar to what has happened repeatedly over several millenia, in Hellenistic and later Western thought, with attempts to summarize Plato's ostensible "teachings." In both cases, what is lost by neglecting the indispensable role of the unique *dialectical,* dramatic rhetorical forms and underlying intentions of the author is what is in fact most essential to both: the actual transformation of each reader—a process necessarily engaging every dimension of the individual reader's being and particular *concrete* existence—through an active, lifelong process of "spiritual intelligence" (*tahqîq,* discussed below) that both authors understand to be at the very essence of those educational dramas (or "tests," in the language of the Qur'an) that define our life on earth.

In order to appreciate this guiding intention of all of Ibn 'Arabî's writing—which he summarizes or alludes to again and again in a few outwardly simple stories and formulae (usually famous "divine sayings") drawn from the canonical Sunni collections of hadith[15]—one has only to keep in mind what we might call a few "working assumptions." These are not the same as beliefs or teachings that one has to agree with in order to understand and appreciate what is being said. They are on the order of "orientations," or existential possibilities, that each reader needs to be aware of in order to begin to make the indispensable connections between the Shaykh's symbolic language and the universal, experiential realities (themselves in no way dependent on any particular set of beliefs or historical-cultural programming) to which those symbols correspond. Indeed, the necessary effort to rediscover the essential inner connections between those "revealed" symbolic languages and their real existential counterparts is often far *more* difficult for readers deeply imbued with culturally conditioned, inadequate conceptions of the reference points of those symbols.

On an initial, static or schematic level, the first of those fundamental working assumptions, is the profound concordance or correspondence, rooted in the deepest sources of reality, between the three "books" of being[16] or creation; of "revelation" (again, with meanings and domains that go far beyond the usual historicist notions that the word might suggest); and of the human soul.[17] Since each individual soul and its actual surrounding existence are concretely present and unique to that particular person at that unique moment—thanks to what Ibn 'Arabî, following the Qur'an, calls their ever-renewed situation of "constant re-creation" *(tajdîd al-khalq)*—his writings, for all their initial difficulty, are carefully designed to awaken the *particular* spiritual insights and meanings accessible to individual readers in their specific situation and stage of spiritual development.

As the reader of any of his works quickly discovers, Ibn 'Arabî's distinctive language and rhetoric of "allusion" *(ishâra)*—with its repeatedly jarring sudden shifts of perspective, tone, irony, paradox, mystery and (momentary) piety—is marvelously constructed, like its constant model in the Qur'an, to break through each reader's particular unconscious structures of belief and levels of habitual programming in order to make possible an immediate, unitive perception (at once spiritual and intellectual) of "things as they really are,"[18] of immediately inspired "knowing" (*'ilm*, in its Qur'anic sense). Needless to say, this effect presupposes a particular kind of focused, meditative study that resembles prayer or meditation more than what "reading" usually suggests today. What counts, at every stage, is each reader's active intention and willingness to seek and perceive the inner connection between Ibn 'Arabî's words and his or her own corresponding experience and realization.

That ultimate human goal of "immediate knowing" (*'ilm*; or of *'aql*, "divine intelligence"), as Ibn 'Arabî never ceases to remind us, is always a divine gift, the combined outcome of our spiritual intention, preceding experience and very limited efforts of divine "service" (*'ibâda*) with the much larger intangible mysteries of grace, destiny and each soul's intrinsic "preparedness" (*isti'dâd*) and spiritual maturity. The actual practice of spiritual intelligence, in all its equally essential stages and facets, is beautifully summarized in the remarkable Arabic word *tahqîq*, expressing the same process in more dynamic, existential terms: at once the active seeking of what is truly real (that Reality, *al-haqq*, which is the truly divine), the inner process of "realization," and the wider, ongoing ethical and social process of "actualizing" those ethical imperatives[19] that can only be truly and creatively, responsibly grasped in the light of that same spiritual intelligence.

In addition to giving a central role to the scriptural symbolic language of the Qur'an and hadith, Ibn 'Arabî uses a number of different technical "languages" and bodies of symbolism to refer to both of his other working hypotheses: i.e., the plane of "being," or ontology, and the plane of individual spiritual realization, or spiritual epistemology. His most common and all-encompassing symbolic languages in both domains are also drawn from the Qur'an and hadith: i.e., the scriptural discussions and allusions to cosmology and cosmogenesis, including the complex theological language of the divine Names[20]; and the rich, psychologically acute and precise symbolism of eschatology, which is particularly well illustrated in the selections translated below.

Moreover, as is true throughout pre-modern Islamic culture and literatures, Ibn 'Arabî's actual use and understanding of those scriptural languages is inseparable from the elaborate corresponding terminologies of Islamic philosophy, science and theology, on the ontological side; and from the equally complex languages of Islamic ritual and devotional practices and the nascent Sufi tradition, on the side of spiritual realization.

The profusion and initial unfamiliarity of these symbolic languages for most modern readers is a serious obstacle to both the translation and the understanding of Ibn 'Arabî's work, especially since most accessible Western writing on Ibn 'Arabî, until quite recently, has focused on the abstract ontological language and insights associated with his later *Bezels of Wisdom*. What makes this volume of selections from *The Meccan Revelations* still the best available introduction to Ibn 'Arabî's work is precisely the fact that most selections here are intentionally taken from passages that are directly connected with "the language of the soul" and its familiar, immediately apparent realm of experience and transformation: i.e., the Sufi language of spiritual states, stations and inspirations; and the rich spiritual symbolism of Islamic eschatology (as that was developed through earlier centuries of Sufi writers and mystics). Eventually, as each reader becomes more familiar with the actual existential referents—the "realities" *(haqâ'iq)*—underlying Ibn 'Arabî's ontological and cosmological discussions, it will become clear that those discussions are also *equally* phenomenological descriptions of the stages and settings of the larger process of realization.[21] But unprepared readers, with rare exceptions, should find the readings here (together with their notes) far more accessible than many other translations of Ibn 'Arabî's works.[22]

Teaching Ibn 'Arabî's works for decades to a wide range of audiences, almost all without any serious background in Arabic or traditional Islamic learning, has amply confirmed the essential practical reality that Ibn 'Arabî boldly and openly states in his own Introduction to this work: what really counts, in approaching and learning from these 'Meccan Illuminations'—as, no doubt, from their Qur'anic model and inspiration—is each reader's singular aptitude and concentrated intention. What he says there is indispensable in appreciating the different audiences for whom he has written this work, as much today as in his own time:

Introduction to the Book
(of *The Meccan Revelations*)[23]

We said: From time to time it occurred to me that I should place at the very beginning of this book a chapter concerning (theological) creeds, supported by definitive arguments and salient proofs. But then I realized that that would distract the person who is properly prepared and seeking an increase (in spiritual knowledge), who is receptive to the fragrant breaths of (divine) Bounty through the secrets of being. For if the properly prepared person persists in *dhikr* ('remembering' God) and spiritual retreat, emptying the place (of the heart) from thinking, and sitting like a poor beggar who has nothing at the doorstep of their Lord—then God will bestow upon them and give them some of that knowing of Him, of those divine secrets and supernal understandings, which He granted to His servant al-Khadir.[24] For He said (of al-Khadir): *a servant among Our servants to whom We have brought Mercy from Us and to whom We have given Knowledge from what is with Us* [18:65]. And He said: *So be mindful of God, and God will teach you* [2:282]; and *If you are aware of God, He will give you a Criterion* (of spiritual discernment); and *He will give you a light by which you will walk* [57:28].[25]

...Abû Yazîd (al-Bastâmî) said: 'You all took your knowledge like a dead person (receiving it) from another dead person. But we took our knowing from *the Living One who never dies* [25:58]!' So the person with concentrated spiritual intention (*himma*) during their retreat with God may realize through Him—how exalted are His gifts and how prodigious His grace!—(forms of spiritual) knowing that are concealed from every theologian on the face of the earth, and indeed from anyone relying on (purely intellectual) inquiry and proofs, but who lacks that spiritual state. For such knowing is beyond (the grasp of) inquiry with the intellect.

Ibn 'Arabî then goes on to explain more carefully the essential differences between that inspired spiritual "knowing" (*'ilm,* in the Qur'anic sense) and the theoretical "knowledge" of the theologians, scientists, etc., which is acquired and supported by intellectual argument.[26] Having done so, he then offers (in his final version of the *Futûhât*) three successive "creeds," which in fact suggest three different potential audiences who will find these *Meccan Revelations* either incomprehensible, not really needed, or of only limited utility. In particular, these remarks help explain why anyone who approaches the *Futûhât* (as it was actually written, of course, and not through extracts and short selections) without the necessary aptitudes and proper motivating intention will very quickly set it down. First, he explains that he has begun with

> the creed of the uneducated *('awâmm)* among the people of outward submission and unthinking compliance *(taqlîd)*, and the people of (purely intellectual) inquiry *(nazar)*. Next I shall follow it, God willing, with the creed...in which I've alluded to the sources of the (theological) proofs for this religious community....I've named it *'The Treatise Concerning What is Well-Known Among the Beliefs of the People of External Forms* (ahl al-rusûm).' Then I shall follow that with the creed of the elite among the people of God, the 'verifiers' *(muhaqqiqûn)* among the people of the path of God, the people of (spiritual) unveiling and finding....And that completes the Introduction to this book.

In fact, however, that is *not* the end of Ibn 'Arabî's Introduction. For he then goes on to add two essential allusions to the underlying structure and deeper intentions of the work—essential "keys" given to his ideal audience, as it were—which have never ceased to fascinate his serious interpreters:

> But as for presenting the credo of the quintessence (of the spiritual elite), I have not given it in detail in any one place, because of the profundities it contains. Instead *I have given it scattered throughout the chapters of this book,* exhaustively and clearly explained—but in different places, as we've mentioned. So those on whom God has bestowed the understanding of these things will recognize them and distinguish them from other matters. For this is the True Knowing and the Veridical Saying, and there is no goal beyond It. *'The blind and the truly seeing are alike'* in Its regard:[27] It brings together things most far and most near, and conjoins the most high and most low....

And in his final version of *The Meccan Revelations,* completed shortly before his death, he set down this new "last word," which adds one key explanation as to why the full understanding of his writing is so challenging:

> Now this was the credo of the elite among the people of God. But as for the credo of the quintessence of the elite concerning God, that is a matter beyond this one, which we have scattered throughout this book because most intellects, being veiled by their thoughts, fall short of perceiving it due to their lack of spiritual purification.
>
> The Introduction to this book is finished. God speaks the Truth, and He guides on the right Way.

THE STRUCTURE OF *THE MECCAN REVELATIONS* AND THE PLACE OF THESE SELECTIONS

There is every indication that the architectonic structure and detailed outline of the 560 chapters of *The Meccan Revelations,* which is given in full detail (sixty-two pages in the new critical edition) in the elaborate Table of Contents *(fihris)* that precedes Ibn 'Arabî's Introduction, dates from the initial inspiration of this book during the author's first hajj in 1202/598. In reading the following selections—and indeed the many other short passages from the *Futûhât* that are gradually becoming available in Western languages—it is clearly important to have a general idea of the overall structure and the location of particular chapters within it, since each of the six main sections normally has its own distinctive type of writing and organizing substructures, with chapters of radically varying length (some are a few pages long, while others would take several volumes to translate into English). In particular, even a quick glance over the names of the sections should make it clear how central the forms, stages and wider process of spiritual "realization/verification" *(tahqîq)* actually are to the contents and intentions of this work. At the end of a brief discussion of each of the six sections we have indicated the original location of the chapters in this anthology (both the English and the forthcoming translations from the French), as well as the "Part" number (I, II, etc.) and original translator, to facilitate reference from these translations to their original contexts in the *Futûhât.*

The following six sections of *The Meccan Revelations,* with a total of 560 chapters, are preceded not only by Ibn 'Arabî's Introduction and Table of Contents, as already mentioned, but also by two more poetic and highly symbolic shorter passages: Ibn 'Arabî's "Opening Address" *(khutbat al-kitâb),*[28] which has been translated and studied in a number of places, and his introductory "Letter" *(risâla)* to his longtime Tunisian Sufi friend, al-Mahdawî, and other Sufi companions in Tunisia with whom he spent several fruitful months on his way toward Mecca.[29]

I. Section on the fields of [inspired] knowing *(fasl al-ma'ârif)*: Chapters 1-73[30]

This opening section contains chapters of very different lengths introducing, often in abbreviated and initially mysterious form, all the major themes found throughout the rest of the book. For example, the first thirteen chapters develop in a variety of symbolic languages (especially through the symbolic meanings and scriptural correspondences of the letters of the Arabic alphabet) the cosmological "map" of creation and its mirroring in the noetic reality of the "Complete Human Being" *(al-insân al-kâmil)*. Then Ibn 'Arabî turns to a long series of fascinating and eminently readable discussions of the different spiritual types of perfection and realization and the various "Friends of God" who epitomize them, interspersed with further epistemological and cosmological elaborations. Chapters 59-65 (and scattered earlier passages) introduce the scriptural symbols of eschatology in a way that clearly highlights their role as a detailed symbolic map of the process of spiritual realization,[31] while chapters 66-72—one of the most fascinating and potentially valuable sections of the entire *Al-Futûhât*—offer what is almost certainly the most detailed and exacting phenomenology of spiritual experience in the Islamic tradition, presented in terms of an irenic reconciliation of contrasting legal interpretations of the basic ritual practices of Islam (purification, prayer, fasting, etc.). And the lengthy chapter 73 (numerous parts of which are translated in this volume) includes both an elaborate discussion of the types of spiritually realized "saints" *(awliyâ')* and Ibn 'Arabî's famous responses to Hakîm Tirmidhî's marvelous "spiritual questionnaire," or inventory of symbolic expressions that can only be understood by purely spiritual inspiration.[32]

In this anthology: chapters 6 ("Divine Names and Theophanies", Chittick) and 73 (sections in "Divine Names and Theophanies", and "Lesser and Greater Resurrection", Morris); in the French sections of Sindbad edition: chapters 2 (Part VIII, Gril) and 73 (Part VI, Gril).

II. Section on (proper) modes of action *(fasl al-mu'âmalât)*: Chapters 74-189

Although the title of this section initially (and no doubt intentionally) evokes the usual second half of Islamic books of hadith and *fiqh* (normally following the purely individual "acts of devotion," *'ibâdât*), which deals with all of the ethical dimensions of social life (marriage, inheritance, proper behavior, trade, etc.), Ibn 'Arabî turns his attention here to the very different "interactions" between each soul and its Source, framed in terms of the spiritual "stations" *(maqâm)* that traditionally constitute the essential stages of the spiritual path of realization. Many of the 116 chapters in this section appear in pairs of short chapters—well illustrated by the two sets translated in "Towards Sainthood" in this volume—briefly describing each station and then a further stage of "advancement" that goes beyond the initial dualistic distinction of "servant" and "Lord." Indeed, the whole section can be seen as centered around Ibn 'Arabî's most characteristic spiritual ideal of *'ubûdiyya*: the necessity of becoming a "pure servant" whose will has become entirely identified with God's, in an active life of spontaneous, purely voluntary divine service. Each spiritual virtue introduced briefly here is dealt with in increasingly elaborate and subtle ways throughout the rest of the *Futûhât*.

In this anthology: chapters 130-31, and 140-141 ("Towards Sainthood", Chittick); in the French sections of the Sindbad edition: chapters 88, (IV, C. Chodkiewicz); and 161 (VI, Gril).

III. Section on spiritual states *(fasl al-ahwâl)*: Chapters 190-269

The eighty chapters of this section take up the classical Sufi distinctions of these passing spiritual states, but typically with an approach—well illustrated in the selections translated here—quite distinctive to Ibn 'Arabî. As in much of the *Futûhât* and his other writings, what he tries to do here can appear as a sort "*ontological* commentary" on the vast earlier literature and practical traditions of Sufi spiritual commentary, which he usually assumes to be quite familiar to his readers. Each earlier "phenomenological" expression or category—often poetic, vague and even potentially dangerous in its original formulation—is presented and analyzed in its wider contexts (both ontological and epistemological), highlighting its particular role, and simultaneous limits and dangers, in the larger process of spiritual realization.

In this anthology: chapters 195, 205, 222 ("Towards Sainthood", Chittick); 198 ("Divine Names and Theophanies", Chittick).

IV. Section on spiritual "points of descent" *(fasl al-manâzil)*: Chapters 270-383

Many of the most celebrated and lastingly influential passages of the *Futûhât*, including chapters 366, 377 and others partially translated here, are to be found in this section. The familiar Sufi term for the spiritual pilgrim's "waystation" (*manzil*: taken from pre-Islamic Arabic poetry) here has a very specific and uniquely "Akbarian" meaning: *"The place in which God descends to you, or where you descend upon Him"* (II 577). The 114 dense and often lengthy chapters of this section correspond, in inverse order, to the inner meanings of each Sura of the Qur'an, and each *manzil* is explicitly (albeit mysteriously) related as well to one or more of the spiritual "Realities" of Muhammad, Jesus and Moses. Finally, and even more mysteriously, each chapter concludes with a long but highly enigmatic catalogue of the various spiritual gifts and insights that are "given" in connection with this divine encounter, often connected with particular details of the corresponding Sura. Without exaggeration, an adequate explanation and translation of many of these individual chapters would require a small book.[33]

In this anthology: chapters 302, 351, 369 ("Lesser and Greater Resurrection", Morris); 366 ("At the End of Time", Morris); 367 ("Ibn 'Arabî's Spiritual Ascension", Morris); 311 and 372 ("Towards Sainthood", Chittick). In the French sections of the Sindbad edition, chapters 318 and 344 (IV, C. Chodkiewicz).

V. Section on spiritual "mutual points of encounter (of Lord and servant) (*fasl al-munâzalât*): Chapters 384–461

The seventy-eight chapters of this section are truly "Illuminations," complex series of reflections and flashes of insight ("commentary" is far too pedestrian a term!) initially connected with a single key passage or symbolic phrase from the Qur'an or other divine sayings.

In the French sections of the Sindbad edition: chapters 420 (VI, Gril); 437 (IV, C. Chodkiewicz).

VI. Section on spiritual stations (*fasl al-maqâmât*): Chapters 462–560

Apart from the final three chapters of *The Meccan Revelations*, most of the ninety-nine chapters[34] in this vast section (itself a quarter of the entire *Al-Futûhât*) are devoted to Ibn 'Arabî's personal identification[35] of a long series of spiritual "Poles" (here in the wider sense of the emblematic "chief" of a particular spiritual type, station or mode of realization) and the profound inner spiritual realization of a particular spiritual "motto" (*hijjîr*: often familiar Qur'anic verses, divine Names or other traditional formulas of *dhikr* and invocation) that becomes fully "illuminated" for those participating in that spiritual station. As with the preceding section, these chapters are usually too rich and complex in their contents to be summarized in any meaningful fashion.

Each of the final three chapters of this section is a long "recapitulation," in different domains, of the contents of the book as a whole. Thus chapter 558 (partly translated in this anthology) is an immense discussion of the influences and underlying realities of each of the ninety-nine divine Names. Chapter 559 is devoted to an enigmatic summary of the divine "secrets" concealed in each of the preceding chapters. And the vast concluding chapter of "spiritual advice," frequently copied and reprinted as a separate volume, brings together a host of selections of practical ethical and spiritual advice, drawn from scriptural sources, earlier prophets, Companions and saints, and other (not specifically religious) ethical writers. What lends it all its power and lasting importance is the way all the preceding "illuminations" will have radically transformed, for readers who have faithfully followed Ibn 'Arabî up to this point, their inner awareness and appreciation of the actual, unimaginable complex of meanings, intentions and spiritual realizations which are in fact encapsulated and briefly expressed in each of those particular bits of spiritual advice. In the larger context of the classical schemas of spiritual "journeys," it is also an eloquent reminder of Ibn 'Arabî's characteristic insistence that the final, unending journey, for the fully realized soul, is always the "Return": "from and with God, to the creatures." It is an elaborate reminder of the ultimate finality and responsibilities of spiritual realization, which are never far from Ibn 'Arabî's sight and intention.

In this anthology: chapters 470 ("Toward Sainthood", Chittick) and 558 ("Divine Names and Theophanies", Chittick).

SUGGESTIONS FOR FURTHER READING

The relative profusion of translations, biographies and studies of Ibn 'Arabî and his writings in recent years has created something of a fortunate dilemma for those readers, new to his work, who might want to explore the perspectives opened up by this anthology. In addition to works already mentioned in earlier notes, the following suggestions, for those without any prior background in Ibn 'Arabî or the Islamic spiritual and philosophic traditions, are limited to English language books (partly because many of the most important recent French studies have been well translated into English). However, readers at home in Spanish will now find a number of important recent translations by Pablo Beneito, Victor Palleja and others, a happy sign of increasing interest in this native son who (like his near-contemporary Moses de Leon) must surely be counted among the enduring contributors to world civilization and religious understanding.

For Ibn 'Arabî's life, immediate historical context and a basic summary of his central teachings, one can now readily recommend S. Hirtenstein's *The Unlimited Mercifier: The Spiritual Life and Thought of Ibn 'Arabî* (Oxford, Anqa/White Cloud Press, 1999), which is the first volume explicitly designed to introduce these points to a general, nonacademic English-speaking audience. The numerous photographs of the cities and sites where Ibn 'Arabî lived, taught and prayed are especially helpful for anyone unfamiliar with these cultural centers of the Islamic world. C. Addas's *Quest for the Red Sulphur: The Life of Ibn 'Arabî* (Cambridge, Islamic Texts Society, 1993), ably translated into English, is a longer, slightly more academic introduction to the same subjects, giving greater detail on Ibn 'Arabî's own teachers and cultural roots in different fields of medieval Islamic scholarship. Her *Ibn 'Arabî: The Voyage of No Return* (Cambridge, Islamic Texts Society, 2000) is a shorter, more accessible introduction to Ibn 'Arabî's life and teachings. For Ibn 'Arabî's own vivid depiction of his earliest Spanish and North African teachers, companions and friends on the Sufi path, R. Austin's *Sufis of Andalusia* (London, Allen & Unwin, 1971) remains an indispensable and endlessly fascinating source.[36] Finally, William Chittick's *The Sufi Path of Knowledge: Ibn al-'Arabî's Metaphysics of the Imagination* (Albany, SUNY, 1989), offers a voluminously illustrated, detailed, and clearly structured introduction (based on hundreds of shorter translations from the *Futûhât*) to virtually all the key facets of Ibn 'Arabî's teaching.

For the *Bezels of Wisdom (Fusûs al-Hikam)* and the subsequent Islamic traditions of commentary, probably the most readable (and certainly the most comprehensible and clearly explained) introduction remains T. Izutsu's pioneering *A Comparative Study of the Key Philosophical Concepts in Sufism and Taoism: Ibn 'Arabî and Lao-Tzū, Chuang-Tzū* (Tokyo, Keio Institute, 1966),[14] despite its reliance on the more Avicennan philosophic commentary tradition of al-Kâshânî. For the novice in this field, the English translation of T. Burckhardt's original French version of a few key selected chapters of the *Fusûs, The Wisdom of the Prophets* (Oxford, Beshara, 1975) is considerably more approachable than R. Austin's complete translation, *Ibn al 'Arabî: The Bezels of Wisdom* (New York, Paulist Press, 1980)—which has long, helpful prefaces to each chapter.

An ever-increasing number of recent studies have elaborated the far-reaching influences of this work and its commentators throughout later Islamic culture and religious life, from the Balkans to China and Indonesia. See, among others, the voluminous anthology of related texts from many key figures in the later Islamic humanities (though the subtitle might suggest something quite different) included in S. Murata's *The Tao of Islam: A Sourcebook on Gender*

Relationships in Islamic Thought (Albany, SUNY, 1992); the four-volume version of later Turkish commentaries on the *Fusûs,* translated as *Ismail Hakki Bursevi's translation of and commentary on Fusûs al-Hikam...* (Oxford, MIAS, 1986); and perhaps most fascinating, S. Murata's recent far-reaching study of several Neo-Confucian Chinese Muslim thinkers profoundly influenced by Ibn 'Arabî, *Chinese Gleams of Sufi Light...* (Albany, SUNY, 2000).

On a more widely accessible level, M. Sells's *Stations of Desire: Love Elegies From Ibn 'Arabî...* (Jerusalem, Ibis, 2000) should now replace R. Nicholson's frequently cited versions *(The Tarjuman al-Ashwaq: A Collection of Mystical Odes)* as a superb introduction to the central poetic dimension of Ibn 'Arabî's work, which is of course quite evident in the "keynote" poems that introduce virtually every chapter of *The Meccan Revelations.* The even more recent translations of Ibn 'Arabî's prayers by S. Hirtenstein and P. Beneito, *The Seven Days of the Heart* (Oxford, Anqa, 2001) suggest something of the profound spiritual and devotional *practice* underlying and always assumed in Ibn 'Arabî's writings; the translators' introduction is especially helpful in that regard. And our forthcoming volume of Ibn 'Arabî's powerful shorter writings on practical spirituality, *Spiritual Practice and Discernment,* should make this central dimension of Ibn 'Arabî's work more widely accessible.

A more demanding, but absolutely fundamental and groundbreaking work on Ibn 'Arabî's understanding of "Sainthood" *(walâya)*—a study that has become indispensable for understanding the spiritual and conceptual underpinnings of this central feature of popular Islamic devotion and piety in every corner of the Islamic world, even today—is M. Chodkiewicz's *The Seal of the Saints: Prophethood and Sainthood in the doctrine of Ibn 'Arabî* (Cambridge, Islamic Texts Society, 1993), ably translated but still to be studied in the original if at all possible. Finally, G. Elmore's recent study and translation of Ibn 'Arabî's early *'Anqâ' Mughrib, Islamic Sainthood in the Fulness of Time: Ibn al-'Arabî's "Book of the Fabulous Gryphon"* (Leiden, Brill, 2000) illustrates the many challenges of deciphering, much less translating, the extraordinarily cryptic poetic and symbolic writings from Andalusia and North Africa that preceded the composition of *The Meccan Revelations.*

The most extensive translations of the *Futûhât* to appear since the original publication of this anthology are certainly William

Chittick's two massive volumes, the above-mentioned *The Sufi Path of Knowledge* and *The Self-Disclosure of God: Principles of Ibn al-'Arabî's Cosmology* (Albany, SUNY, 1998); they are to be followed by an equally long volume of translations on related areas of cosmogony and ontology. Complementary to those translations—in that they focus on the humanly immediate, active dimensions of eschatology, spiritual realization and Ibn 'Arabî's phenomenology of spiritual life—are a series of volumes on the *Futûhât*, including many translations and studies originally delivered (and sometimes published) as public lectures and conference papers over the past decade, which we plan to publish in book form in the near future. These include the translations of the eschatological chapters 59–65 and 271 (plus related passages from other chapters), already promised in the original notes to this book *(Ibn 'Arabî's "Divine Comedy": An Introduction to Islamic Eschatology)*; *The Traveler and the Way: "Wandering" and the Spiritual Journey* (a translation and commentary on the *Risâlat al-Isfâr*, plus several chapters on the same theme from the *Futûhât*); and at least two volumes of thematic explorations of Ibn 'Arabî's treatment of spiritual topics in the *Futûhât*, accompanied by full translations of key corresponding chapters. Indeed the level of scholarly understanding and worldwide interest in the *Futûhât* has approached the point where the possibility of a serious, collective effort to begin to translate at least the opening *Fasl* (more than a quarter of the entire work) is now being seriously considered. Such a task should be realizable within the next decades.

Anyone wishing to keep up with translations and studies of Ibn 'Arabî, and more particularly with the dramatic unfolding of worldwide academic research into his profound influences in all aspects of later Islamic religion and the Islamic humanities, should refer to past and present issues of the *Journal of the Muhyiddîn Ibn 'Arabî Society* (Oxford, now in its third decade). With contributions that have often been delivered first by world-renowned scholars, increasingly from all regions of the Islamic world, at the two international symposia sponsored by the Ibn 'Arabî Society each year (at Oxford and Berkeley), the journal has helped to create an active worldwide network of scholars, students and translators whose impact is increasingly evident in, among other fields, the number of international conferences now devoted to the "Greatest Master" and his later Muslim interpreters each year. This worldwide collective effort to rediscover the profound influences of Ibn 'Arabî and his teachings on central dimensions of Islamic culture from West Africa to China and Indonesia is not just an academic project of historical archeology: those involved, in each country and region concerned, are well aware of the contemporary and future significance of Ibn 'Arabî's understanding of the roots of Islamic spirituality and tradition for any lasting effort of renewal and revivification within a global civilization.

Finally, the truly great books in this field, as in any other, do not age, but only become more apparent with the passage of time. The following two classic volumes—both originally published in French, although fortunately available in reliable English translations[15]— were certainly not intended for beginners, in the sense we introduced earlier. Both are the mature, richly evocative and moving fruits of an intensely personal, life-long reflection on the central issues and perspectives of all of Ibn 'Arabî's accessible writings, with visions and emphases that are radically different, yet ultimately astonishingly complementary. The first is Henry Corbin's *Creative Imagination in the Sufism of Ibn 'Arabî*;[16] the second is Michel Chodkiewicz's *An Ocean Without Shore: Ibn 'Arabî, the Book and the Law* (Albany, SUNY, 1993). One could readily apply to both of these remarkable works what Ibn 'Arabî says of *The Meccan Revelations* and his ideal readers in his Introduction, quoted above: the "preparedness" such works require is not simply, or even essentially, academic. Reading them gives some sense of how diverse, yet powerfully transforming, the influences of Ibn 'Arabî have been and will continue to be.

James Winston Morris
University of Exeter

DIVINE NAMES
AND THEOPHANIES

William C. Chittick

THE ORIGIN OF CREATION
CHAPTER 6[1]

This is the first major chapter of the Futûhât to deal in summary fashion with Ibn al-'Arabî's overall cosmological perspective. He begins by answering briefly and without elaboration the questions posed in the title of the chapter, which is: "On the True Knowledge of the Origin *[bad']* of the Spiritual Creation *[al-khalq al-rûhânî]*, and On Who is the First Existent *[awwal mawjûd]* Within It? From What Did [the spiritual creation] Come into Existence? Within What Did It Come into Existence? In What Likeness *[mithâl]* Did It Come into Existence? Why Did It Come into Existence? What Is its Goal *[ghâya]*? [And on] the True Knowledge of the Spheres *[aflâk]* of the Great and the Small Worlds *[al-'âlam al-akbar wa'l-asghar]*." In answering the question "Why did the spiritual creation come into existence?" he mentions the "divine realities," thereby alluding to the importance of the Divine Names—a topic which he has discussed in detail in previous chapters (and which is dealt with in the present work, especially in the translations of Chapter 73, Question 118; and Chapter 558). In the first half of the chapter Ibn al-'Arabî classifies everything that can be known into four broad categories or "objects of knowledge," thus outlining the contents of his own teachings. Then he turns to an exposition of the structure of the world, the third "object of knowledge," by answering each of the questions posed *in the title. At the end he enumerates some of the correspondences that can be observed between the microcosm and the macrocosm. In the beginning section, "A Concise Exposition," a number of terms are mentioned which are explained later on in the text and hence are not footnoted at the first occurrence.*

A Concise Exposition
Through a Kind of Summation
(ijmâl)

I 118.4   The "origin of creation" is the Dust *(al-habâ')*[2]. The "first existent within it" is the Muhammadan Reality pertaining to the All-Merciful *(al-haqîqa al-muhammadiyya al-rahmâniyya)*, [a Reality] which is not restricted by position, since it is not spatially confined *(li 'adam al-tahayyuz)*. "From what did [creation] come into existence?" From the Known Reality which is described neither by existence nor nonexistence. "Within what did it come into existence?" Within the Dust. "In what likeness did it come into existence?" The form *(sûra)* known within God's Self *(nafs al-haqq)*. "Why did it come into existence?" To make manifest the divine realities *(al-haqâ'iq al-ilâhiyya)*.[3] "What is its goal?" Deliverance from mixture *(mazja)*, so that each world *('âlam)* may know its share *(hazz)* from its Producer *(munshi')*. So its goal is to make manifest its own realities. The "true knowledge of the spheres of the Greater World"—which is everything other than man *(mâ 'adâ al-insân)* in the technical terminology of the [Sufi] Community *(istilâh al-jamâ'a)*—"and of the Smaller World," i.e., man, has to do with the spirit, cause, and occasion of the world. The world's "spheres" are its stations *(maqâmât)*, its movements *(harakât)*, and the differentiation of its strata *(tafsîl tabaqâtihi)*. This is everything contained in the present chapter.

118.9   Just as man is small by way of his body, so he is paltry by way of his temporal origination *(hudûth)*. But his theomorphism *(ta'alluh)*[4] is a fact, since he is the vicegerent of God in the world, while the world is subjected *(musakhkhar)* to him and a vassal of God *(ma'lûh)*, in the same way that man is a vassal of God.[5]

118.10 Know that man's most perfect plane *(nash'a)* is in this world *(al-dunyâ)*. As for the next world *(al-âkhira)*, the state of each person of the two groups[6] will be one half, though not his knowledge, since each group has knowledge of the opposite state. For [in this world] man is nothing if not faithful and infidel at once: felicity and wretchedness, bliss and chastisement, blissful and chastised. Hence knowledge *(ma'rifa)* in this world is more complete *(atamm)*, while theophany *(tajallî)*[7] in the next world is more elevated *(a'lâ)*. So understand, and open this lock! For those who understand, we have composed an intimation; though its words are repulsive and loathsome, its meaning is marvelous.:

The spirit of the Great Existence is this small existence.
If not for him, He would not say, "I am the Great, the Powerful."
Let not my temporal origination veil you, nor my annihilation and resurrection.
For I—if you regard me closely—am the All-Encompassing, the Great.
In my essence I belong to the Eternal, though I am manifest in the newly arisen.
God is the Solitary, the Eternal, afflicted by no incapacity.
Engendered existence *(al-kawn)* is a "new creation" *(khalq jadîd)*,[8] imprisoned in His two hands *(qabdatayh)*.[9]
It follows from this that I am the paltry existence,
And that every existence turns round about my existence.
For there is no night like my night, no light like my light.
He who calls me servant—I am the poor servant.
If he says that I am existence—I am the All-Aware Existence.
So call me a king—and find me such—or the rabble: you will not go wrong.
Oh you who are ignorant of my worth! Are you the All-Knowing, the All-Seeing?
Inform my existence about me, though words are both true and false.
Say to your people that I am the All-Compassionate, the All-Forgiving;
Say that my chastisement is the ruinous chastisement.
And say that I am weak, incapable, a prisoner,
So how should anyone attain blessing or ruin at my hand?

Expansion and Exposition
of the Chapter
—God gives confirmation and aid!—

118.33   Know that the objects of knowledge *(al-ma'lûmât)* are four. [The first is] God, who is described by Nondelimited Being *(al-wujûd al-mutlaq)*, for He is neither the effect *(ma'lûl)* nor the cause *('illa)* of anything. On the contrary, He exists through His very Essence. Knowledge of Him consists of knowledge that He exists, and His existence is not other than His Essence, though His Essence remains unknown; rather, the Attributes that are attributed to Him are known, i.e., the Attributes of Meanings *(sifât al-ma'ânî)*, which are the Attributes of Perfection *(sifât al-kamâl)*.[10]

118.35   As for knowledge of the Essence's reality *(haqîqat al-dhât)*, that is prohibited. It cannot be known through logical proof *(dalîl)* or rational demonstration *(burhân 'aqlî)*, nor can definition *(hadd)* grasp it. For He—glory be to Him—is not similar to anything, nor is anything similar to Him. So how should he who is similar to things know Him to whom nothing is similar and Who is similar to nothing? So your knowledge of Him is only that "*Nothing is like Him*" (Qur'an 42:10) and *"God warns you of His Self"* (Qur'an 3:27).[11] Moreover, the Law *(al-shar')* has prohibited meditation upon the Essence of God.[12]

119.3   A second object of knowledge is the Universal Reality *(al-haqîqat al-kulliyya)* that belongs to God and the world.[13] It is qualified neither by existence nor nonexistence, temporal origination nor eternity *(al-qidam)*. This reality is eternal when the Eternal is described by it, but temporally originated when the temporally originated is described by it. No objects of knowledge—whether eternal or temporally originated—are known until this reality is known, but this reality does not exist until those things described by it exist. If something exists without a precedent nonexistence *('adam mutaqaddim)*, as, for example, the Being of God and His Attributes, one says about this reality: it is an eternal existent, because God is qualified by it. But if something exists after nonexistence, as, for example, the existence of everything other than God *(mâ siwâ Allâh)*, i.e., the temporally originated thing that exists by means of something other than itself, then this reality is said to be temporally originated. But in every existent it maintains its own reality, for it does not accept division *(tajazzi')*, since it has neither whole nor part. It cannot be known disengaged from form *(mujarrada 'an al-sûra)* through logical proof or demonstration. In short, the world has come into existence by means of God *(bi wasâtat al-haqq)* from this reality; but it is not an existent, such that God might have brought us into existence from an eternal existent and we should be established as eternal.

119.9   You should also know that this reality is not qualified by precedence *(taqaddum)* in relation to the world, nor the world with subsequence *(ta'akhkhur)* in relation to this reality. Rather, it is the root *(asl)* of all existents, the root of substance *(al-jawhar)*, the Sphere of Life *(falak al-hayât)*, the "Truth through which creation takes place" *(al-haqq al-makhlûq bihî)*,[14] and so forth. It is the All-Encompassing Intelligible Sphere *(al-falak al-muhît al-ma'qûl)*. If you say that it is the world, you have spoken the truth; and if [you say] that it is not the world, you have spoken the truth. [If you say] that it is God or that it is not God, you have spoken the truth. It receives all of this, while it becomes plural through the plurality *(ta'addud)* of the world's individuals *(ashkhâs)* and is considered incomparable through God's Incomparability *(tanzîh)*.

119.13   If you want a likeness of this reality in order to understand it better, look upon the quality of being wood in a timber, a chair, an inkwell, a pulpit, and a coffin; or upon such things as rectangularity of shape, for example, in everything that is a rectangle, like a room, a coffin, and a sheet of paper. Rectangularity and woodness lie within the realities of every one of these things. It is the same way with colors—[e.g.,] the whiteness of cloth, pearls, paper, flour, and fat. The whiteness understood from the cloth, without being characterized as being a piece of whiteness within the cloth—but rather, as the reality of whiteness—becomes manifest in the cloth just as it becomes manifest in paper. The same holds true for knowledge, power, will, hearing, and sight, and for each and every thing. Thus have I explained to you this [second] object of knowledge; we have spoken about it in great detail in our book named *Inshâ' al-jadâwil wa'l-dawâ'ir.*[15]

119.17 The third object of knowledge is the entire world: the angels, the spheres and the worlds they contain, and the air and the earth and everything of the world contained by these two. This is the Greater Kingdom *(al-mulk al-akbar)*.

119.18 The fourth object of knowledge is man, the vicegerent whom God placed within this world, which is subdued under his subjection *(taskhîr)*. God says, *"And He has subjected to you what is in the heavens and what is in the earth, all together, from Him"* (Qur'an 45:12).

119.19 He who knows these [four] objects of knowledge has no other object of knowledge to seek, for among them is that of whom we only know the existence—i.e., God—and whose Acts and Attributes are known through various kinds of likenesses *(mithâl)*; among them is that which is only known through likeness, such as knowledge of the Universal Reality, and among them is that which is known in these two manners as well as through quiddity *(mâhiyya)* and quality *(kayfiyya)*, and these are the world and man.[16]

Subsection

119.21 [The Prophet said,] *"God was, and nothing was with Him."* Then into this saying was incorporated the sentence, *"And He is now as He was."*[17] When God brings the world into existence, no Attribute that He did not possess comes to be ascribed to Him. On the contrary, before His creation He is described and named in Himself by the Names by which His creatures call Him. So when He desired the existence of the world and when He originated it in accordance with His Knowledge of it within His Knowledge of Himself, there arose from that sacred Desire *(al-irâdat al-muqaddasa)*—through one kind of theophany of Incomparability directed toward the Universal Reality—a reality called the Dust. It can be compared to the plaster that a builder throws down in order to mold within it whatever shapes and forms he desires; it is the first existent in the world and has been mentioned by 'Alî ibn Abî Tâlib,[18] Sahl ibn 'Abdallâh,[19] and others of the People of Verification, the People of Unveiling and Finding.[20]

119.26 Then God manifested Himself in theophany through His Light to that Dust, which is called by the People of Reflection *(ashâb al-afkâr)*[21] "Universal Hylé" *(al-hayûlâ al-kull)*; within the Dust was the entire world in potentiality *(quwwa)* and readiness *(salâhiyya)*. Each thing in the Dust received from His Light in accordance with its own preparedness *(isti'dâd)* and potentiality, just as the corners of a room receive the light of a lamp and, to the degree of their proximity to that light, increase in brightness and reception *(qabûl)*. God says, *"The likeness of His Light is as a niche within which is a lamp"* (Qur'an 24:35). Thus He compared His Light to a lamp.

119.29 Within the Dust nothing is nearer to the Light in reception than the Reality of Muhammad, which is called the Intellect. So he is the lord of the world in its entirety and the first thing to become manifest within existence. Hence his existence derives from the Divine Light, the Dust, and the Universal Reality, while his entity *('ayn)* comes into existence within the Dust; then the entity of the world stems from his theophany. The nearest of mankind to him is 'Alî ibn Abî Tâlib and the inmost consciousnesses *(asrâr)* of the prophets.[22]

119.32 As for the likeness in which the world—the whole of it without differentiation—came into existence, that is the Knowledge subsistent in God's Self *(al-'ilm al-qâ'im bi nafs al-haqq)*. For He knows us through His Knowledge of Himself and brings us into existence in accordance with His Knowledge of us, so we are upon the shape entified *(al-shakl al-mu'ayyan)* in His Knowledge. If this were not the case, this shape would have been assumed by chance *(bi hukm al-ittifâq)*, not by intention *(al-qasd)*, since He would not have known it. But it is impossible for a form to come into existence by chance. Hence, if this entified shape were not known to God and desired by Him, He would not have brought us into existence upon it. Nor is this shape taken over from "other than He," since it has been established that *"He was, and nothing was with Him."* So the shape can only be the form that emerges within Himself *(mâ baraza 'alayhi fî nafsihi min al-sûra)*. Hence His Knowledge of Himself is His Knowledge of us from eternity without beginning *(al-azal)*, not after our nonexistence, so His Knowledge of us is the same [as His Knowledge of Himself]. Hence our likeness—which is identical with His Knowledge of us—is eternal through God's eternity, since it is one of His Attributes and since temporally originated things do not subsist in His Self—God is far greater than that![23]

120.2   As for our questions, "Why did [creation] come into existence?" and "What is its goal?" [the answer is as follows]: God says, *"I did not create jinn and men except to serve Me"* (Qur'an 51:56). Thus He made explicit why He brought us—and likewise the entire world—into existence, while He singled out us and the jinn for mention.

120.4   Here by *jinn* is meant everything hidden,[24] including the angels and other things. God said in respect of the heavens and the earth, *"'Come willingly or unwillingly.' They said, 'We come willingly'"* (Qur'an 41:11). In the same way He said, *"[We offered the Trust to the heavens and the earth and the mountains], but they refused to carry it"* (Qur'an 33:72). That was because it was an "offer." If it had been a command, they would have obeyed and carried it, since disobedience from them is inconceivable; they were created in [obedience]—but the fiery jinn and men were not created so.

120.6   Likewise with *men*. The People of Reflection, those who occupy themselves with speculation *(nazar)* and proofs restricted to the senses and to necessary and self-evident matters, maintain that the person for whom [a command] is prescribed must be intelligent so as to understand what is addressed to him, and they are correct. Such is the situation in our view also: The whole world is intelligent, living, and speaking[25]—in respect of the unveiling that breaks the customary views *(kharq al-'âda)* of people; that is, in respect of the knowledge that we attain in this way. But the People of Reflection say, "This is an inanimate object *(jamâd)*; it has no intelligence." They stop with what their eyesight gives to them, while we consider the situation differently. Thus, when it is reported that a stone, or the shoulder of a lamb, or the stump of a date palm, or a wild animal spoke to a prophet,[26] these people say that God created life and knowledge within that thing at this time. But we do not see the situation like that. On the contrary, the mystery of life fills the entire world: *"Everyone, wet or dry, who hears the muezzin, gives witness to him,"*[27] and his giving witness is based only on knowledge. This comes to us from unveiling, not from a deduction *(istinbât)* based upon considering what is demanded by the outward meaning of a hadith, nor from anything else. If a person wants to understand this, let him follow the path of Men *(al-rijâl)* and persevere in spiritual retreats *(khalwa)* and invocation *(dhikr)*; then God will give him direct news of all this, and he will know that people are blind to the perception of these realities.

120.13   So He brought the world into existence to make manifest the authority *(sultân)* of the Names, since power without an object, generosity without bestowal, a provider without one provided for, a helper without someone helped, and a possessor of compassion without an object of compassion would be realities whose effects are nullified *(mu'attalat al-ta'thîr)*.

120.15   God made the world, in the present world, a mixture: He mixed the two handfuls into dough, then He differentiated individuals from it. Hence something of the one entered into the other—from each handful into its sister—and the situation became confused. It is here that some of the men of knowledge *(al-'ulamâ')* become preferred over others *(tafâdul)* in respect of their extracting the corrupt from the good and the good from the corrupt. The goal in all this is deliverance *(takhlîs)* from this mixture and the separation of the two handfuls, so that each may be isolated in its own world, just as God says: *"[And the infidels will be mustered into Gehenna], that God may separate the corrupt from the good, and place the corrupt one upon another, and so heap them up altogether, and put them in Gehenna"* (Qur'an 8:37).

120.18   When some of that mixture remains in a person until he dies with it, he will not be mustered on the Day of Resurrection among the Secure.[28] Some of these people will be delivered from the mixture at the Reckoning *(al-hisâb)*. Some will not be delivered from it except in Gehenna, out of which a person will be taken as soon as he is delivered from mixture; these are the people of intercession *(al-shafâ'a)*. As for him who is separated here into one of the two handfuls, in reality he will be transferred from his grave into the next abode, into bliss or chastisement and hellfire, for he has already been delivered [from mixture].

120.21   So this is the goal of the world. And these two [handfuls] are two realities that go back to Attributes that God possesses in His Essence. This is why we say that the People of the Fire see Him as Chastiser and the People of the Garden as Bliss-giver. This is a noble mystery; perhaps you will come to understand it in the next abode during contemplation, God willing. But the Verifiers have already attained to it in this abode.

120.23   As for our words in this chapter, "The knowledge of the spheres of the Greater World and the Smaller, i.e., man," I mean by these spheres the realms *('awâlim)* of the world's universal things, its kinds *(ajnâs)*, and its commanders *(umarâ')*, those who exercise effects in other than themselves. I made these spheres correspond; the one is a transcription *(nuskha)* of the other. We drew circles for them in the forms and arrangement of the spheres in the book *Inshâ' al-dawâ'ir wa'l-jadâwil,* whose composition we began in Tunis at the place of the Imam Abû Muhammad 'Abd al-'Azîz,[29] our friend and executor—may God have mercy upon him! We will set forth from this book in this chapter what is appropriate for this brief exposition. Hence we say:

120.27   The worlds are four: the highest world, which is the world of subsistence *(al-baqâ')*; then the world of transmutation *(al-istihâla)*, which is the world of annihilation *(al-fanâ')*; then the world of inhabitation *(al-ta'mîr)*, which is the world of subsistence and annihilation; then the world of relations *(al-nisab)*. These worlds are in two locations *(mawtinayn)*: in the Greater World, which is everything outside man, and the Smaller World, which is man.

120.28   As for the Highest World, that is the Muhammadan Reality, whose sphere is Life. Its equivalent *(nazîr)* in man is the subtle reality *(al-latîfa)*, the holy spirit *(al-rûh al-qudsî)*. Included within this world is the All-Encompassing Throne *(al-'arsh al-muhît)*, whose equivalent in man is the body. Of this world is the Footstool *(al-kursî)*, whose equivalent in man is the soul. Of it is the Inhabited House *(al-bayt al-ma'mûr)*, whose equivalent in man is the heart.[30] Of it are the angels, whose equivalents in man are the spirits and faculties within him. Of it are Saturn and its sphere, whose equivalent in man are the cognitive faculty *(al-quwwat al-'ilmiyya)* and the breath. Of it are Jupiter and its sphere, whose equivalents are the faculty of memory *(al-quwwat al-dhâkira)* and the back of the brain. Of it are Mars and its sphere, whose equivalents are the intellective faculty *(al-quwwat al-'âqila)* and the crown of the head. Of it are the sun and its sphere, whose equivalents are the reflective faculty *(al-quwwat al-mufakkira)* and the middle of the brain. Then Venus and its sphere, whose equivalents are the estimative faculty *(al-quwwat al-wahmiyya)* and the animal spirit; then Mercury and its sphere, whose equivalents are the imaginal faculty *(al-quwwat al-khayâliyya)* and the front of the brain; then the moon and its sphere, whose equivalents are the sensory faculty *(al-quwwat al-hissiyya)* and the organs *(al-jawârih)* that possess sensation. These then are the strata *(tabaqât)* of the Highest World and their equivalents in man.

120.35 As for the World of Transmutation, some of it is the sphere *(kura)* of ether, whose spirit is heat and dryness; it is the sphere of fire. Its equivalent [in man] is yellow bile *(al-safrâ)*, whose spirit is the digestive faculty *(al-quwwat al-hâdima)*. Of it is air, whose spirit is heat and wetness; its equivalent is blood, whose spirit is the attractive *(jâdhiba)* faculty. Of it is water, whose spirit is cold and wetness; its equivalent is phlegm, whose spirit is the expulsive *(dâfi'a)* faculty. Of it is earth *(al-turâb)*, whose spirit is cold and dryness; its equivalent is black bile *(al-sawdâ)*, whose spirit is the retentive *(mâsika)* faculty. As for the earth *(al-ard)*, it has seven strata: black, brown, red, yellow, white, blue, and green. The equivalents of these seven in man are in his body: skin, fat, flesh, veins, nerves, muscles, and bones.

121.6 As for the World of Inhabitation, among [the "inhabitants" *(al-'ummâr)*] are the Spirituals *(al-rûhâniyyûn)*, whose equivalents are the faculties in man. Among them is the world of animals, whose equivalent in man is that which has sensation. Among them is the world of plants, whose equivalent is that of man which grows. And among them is the world of inanimate things, whose equivalent in man is that which has no sensation.

121.8 As for the World of Relations:[31] among them are accidents *(a'râd)*, whose equivalents are black, white, the colors, and engendered events *(al-akwân)*. Then quality *(kayf)*, whose equivalent is states like healthy and sick. Then quantity *(kam)*, whose equivalent is that the leg is longer than the arm. Then location *(ayn)*, whose equivalent is that the neck is the place of the head, and the leg the place of the thigh. Then time *(zamân)*, whose equivalent is "I moved my head when I put my hand into motion." Then relation *(idâfa)*, whose equivalent is "This is my father, so I am his son." Then position *(wad')*, whose equivalent is my language and accent. Then activity *(an yaf'al)*, whose equivalent is "I ate." Then passivity *(an yanfa'il)*, whose equivalent is "I became satiated." Among the relations is the diversity of forms in the three kingdoms *(al-ummahât)*, such as elephant, donkey, lion, and cockroach. The equivalent of this is that human faculty which receives forms related to blameworthy *(madhmûm)* and praiseworthy *(mahmûd)* meanings: this one is clever, so he is an elephant; that one is stupid, so he is a donkey; this one is brave, so he is a lion; that one is timid, so he is a cockroach. "And God speaks the truth and guides on the way" (Qur'an 33:4).

Answers to Tirmidhî's questions / Chapter 73

This chapter, one of the longest in the Futûhât, *comprises 138 pages at the beginning of volume II. In the first 38 pages Ibn al-'Arabî enumerates and describes the various kinds of saints. Then he turns to answering the 157 (155, according to his own count) questions posed more than 300 years earlier by al-Hakîm al-Tirmidhî in the work* Khatm al-awliyâ' *("The Seal of the Saints") in order to illustrate the kinds of sciences known only to the saints and unapproachable by means of the speculative and rational powers of the mind.*[32]

The three questions translated here are typical in style and content, though the answers are particularly significant in throwing light on three of Ibn al-'Arabî's basic themes: the Perfect Man, the Divine Names, and the nature of the theophany that is the world.

Question 108 deals very briefly with the Perfect Man as the exemplar of the human state. Human beings were created in the form of the Divine Name Allah, the Name that comprehends within itself the realities of all other Names. But in most people, these Names remain as virtualities, or some Names are actualized to a certain degree but not others. Only those human beings who have attained to perfection have actualized all God's Names in their fullness. Hence every Perfect Man is the outward form (sûra *or* zâhir) *of an inner meaning* (mâ'na *or* bâtin) *that is Allah Himself.*

Question 115, on the Glories of the Face, divides the Names into two fundamental kinds, those that relate to God's Similarity (tashbîh) *with the creatures, and those that relate to His Incomparability* (tanzîh). *The contrast between these two types of Names, or kinds of relationship which God possesses with creation, is one of the key topics in Ibn al-'Arabî's writings. It might best be summed up in the expression "He/not He"* (huwa lâ huwa), *or simply "yes and no," which is the basic answer to most questions asked about the world's status in relation to God. In other terms, the world always remains in an ambiguous situation, half way between Being and nothingness. If in respect to Being one thing can be said about it, in respect to nothingness the opposite can be said. The perception of this ambiguity is one source of the "bewilderment"* (hayra) *which Ibn al-'Arabî considers one of the highest of spiritual stations (see Chapter 558).*

In the third question Ibn al-'Arabî speaks about the manifestation of God's Beauty within the world. This topic brings up the relationship of God's Acts (the creatures) to both His Attributes (e.g., Beauty) and His Essence and leads to an affirmation of the Oneness of Being. The true knowledge of these things, Ibn al-'Arabî concludes in typical fashion, can only be achieved by the lifting of the veil between man and God (kashf).

THE PERFECT MAN

CHAPTER 73 / QUESTION 108[33]

What is the Crown of the King (tâj al-malik)*?*

II 104.28   *Answer:* The Crown of the King is the sign of the king, while the "crowning" *(tatwîj)*[34] of the royal document is the sultan's signature upon it.

104.29   Existence is *"an inscribed writing, witnessed by those brought nigh"* (Qur'an 83:20-21), but ignored by those who have not been brought nigh. The "crowning" of this writing can only take place through him who gathers together all realities, which are the mark *('alâma)* of Him who gave him existence. Hence, the Perfect Man—who denotes his Lord by his very essence in an a priori manner *(min awwal al-badîha)*—and only the Perfect Man, is the Crown of the King. He is referred to in the Prophet's words, *"God created Adam upon His own form."*[35] Now *"He is the First, the Last, the Manifest, and the Nonmanifest"* (Qur'an 57:3). The Divine Perfection *(al-kamâl al-ilâhî)* does not become manifest except in composite things *(al-murakkab)*, since they comprise the noncomposite things *(al-basît)*, while the noncomposite do not comprise the composite.[36] So the Perfect Man is the "first" in intention, the "last" in actuality, the "manifest" through the letter, and the "nonmanifest" in meaning.[37] He gathers together nature *(al-tab')* and intellect *(al-'aql)*, so within him are the grossest *(akthaf)* and subtlest *(altaf)* of compositions in respect of his nature, and within him is disengagement *(al-tajarrud)* from substrata *(al-mawâdd)* and the faculties *(al-quwâ)* that govern bodies.[38] No other creature possesses that, and this explains why he was singled out for the knowledge of all the Names and the All-Comprehensive Words:[39] God has not informed us that He has given this to anyone other than the Perfect Man.

104.35 There is no level *(martaba)* of creature above man except that of the angels, and they were his students when he taught them the Names.[40] This does not mean that he is better *(khayr)* than the angels, but it does mean that his plane *(nash'a)* is more perfect *(akmal)* than theirs.[41]

105.2 In conclusion, since he is the locus of theophany *(majlâ)* for the Divine Names, it is correct to say that he is for this writing like a crown, since he is the noblest adornment through which it is adorned. Through the "crowning" the effects of a king's commands become manifest in the kingdom; in the same way, through the Perfect Man the Divine Judgment *(al-hukm al-ilâhî)* concerning reward and punishment in the world becomes manifest. Through him the order *(al-nizâm* [i.e., of the universe]) is established and overthrown; in him God decrees, determines, and judges.

THE GLORIES OF THE FACE

CHAPTER 73 / QUESTION 115[42]

What are the Glories of the Face (subuhât al-wajh)?[43]

110.25 *Answer:* The "face" of a thing is its essence *(dhât)* and reality *(haqîqa)*. So the "Glories of the Face" are Lights pertaining to the Essence *(anwâr dhâtiyya)*; between us and them are the veils *(hujub)*—the Divine Names. That is why He says, *"Everything is perishing except His Face"* (Qur'an 28:88), in one of the interpretations of this "face."[44]

110.26 Generally speaking, these Glories are the lights of the profession of God's Incomparability *(anwâr al-tanzîh)*, which is the negation *(salb)* from Him of everything that is not worthy of Him, i.e., all properties pertaining to nonexistence *(ahkâm 'adamiyya)*, since in reality it is nonexistence that is unworthy of the Essence. Here bewilderment *(hayra)* sets in, since He is Being Itself, so He is not declared incomparable with any ontological thing *(amr wujûdî)*. For this reason the Divine Names are relations[45]—if you understand—relations that have been occasioned *(ihdâth)* by the entities of the possible things because of the states that the things have acquired *(iktisâb)* from the Essence, since every state *(hâl)* pronounces a Name which it denotes in respect to itself, either by negation *(salb)* or affirmation *(ithbât)* or by both together.

110.30   These Names are of two kinds.[46] One kind is totally lights; these are the Names that denote ontological things. Another kind is totally darkness *(zulam)*; these are the Names that denote Incomparability. The Prophet said, *"God has seventy"—or "seventy thousand"—"veils of light and darkness; were they to be removed, the Glories of His Face would incinerate everything perceived by the creatures' eyes."*[47] For if the Divine Names were to be taken away, the veils would be lifted; and if the veils—which are the Names—were to be lifted, the Unity *(ahadiyya)* of the Essence would become manifest. Because of Its Unity, no entity would remain qualified by existence. Hence Unity would erase the existence of the entities of the possible things, and they would cease being described by existence, since they only become qualified by existence through the Names. They do not become qualified by any of their own properties—in the view of both reason and the Law *('aqlan wa shar'an)*—except through the Names. So the possible things are behind those veils that lie adjacent to the Presence of Possibility *(hadrat al-imkân)*, since possibility is a theophany of the Essence that causes the possible things to become qualified by existence from beyond the veils of the Divine Names. Hence the entities of the possible things gain no knowledge of God except in respect of the Names, whether by intellect or unveiling.

THE BEAUTY GOD AND THE BEAUTY OF THE WORLD

CHAPTER 73 / QUESTION 118[48]

From whence (min ayn)?

114.8 *Answer:* From His theophany in His Name the Beautiful.

The Prophet said, *"God is beautiful and He loves beauty"*; this is an established hadith.[49] So He described Himself as loving beauty, and He loves the world,[50] so there is no thing more beautiful than the world. And He is beautiful, while beauty is intrinsically lovable; hence all the world loves God. The beauty of His Making *(sun')* permeates His creation, while the world is His loci of manifestation *(mazâhir)*. So the love of the different parts of the world for each other derives from God's love for Himself. This is because love is an attribute of the existent thing *(al-mawjûd)*, and there is nothing in existence except God.[51]

114.11 Majesty *(jalâl)* and Beauty *(jamâl)* are intrinsic Attributes of God in His own Self and in His Making, while awe *(hayba)*, which is an effect of Beauty, and intimacy *(uns)*, which is an effect of Majesty, are two attributes of created things, not of the Creator nor of that by which He is described.[52] Nothing that is not existent becomes the object of awe or intimacy, and there is no existent but God, since the effect *(athar)* is the same as the Attribute, and the Attribute is not different from the object to which it belongs *(al-mawsûf)* in the state of its being qualified by it; on the contrary, the Attribute is identical with that to which it belongs, even if you understand this only in the second place. Hence there is no lover and no beloved except God, so there is nothing in existence except the Divine Presence *(al-hadrat al-ilâhiyya)*, which is His Essence, His Attributes, and His Acts.

114.14   In the same way you say: God's Speech *(kalâm)* is His Knowledge, and His Knowledge is His Essence, since it is impossible for there to subsist within His Essence a superadded thing *(amr zâ'id)* or a superadded entity that is not His Essence and that bestows upon It a property which otherwise It could not possess and through which It possesses Its perfection in Divinity, or rather, without which It could not be the Divinity.[53] [His Knowledge] is the fact that He knows all things; He mentioned that concerning Himself by way of lauding His own Essence,[54] and it is established by rational proofs. It is impossible for His Essence to possess Its Perfection through something that is not Itself; then He would have acquired excellence *(sharaf)* through something other than His own Essence.

114.18   Those who know God come to know concerning Him through His Knowledge of His own Essence that which intellects cannot know in respect of their own sound reflections. This is the knowledge about which the Tribe[55] says that it lies beyond the stage of the intellect *(warâ' tawr al-'aql)*. God says concerning His servant Khidr, *"We taught him a knowledge from us"* (Qur'an 18:64); and He says, *"[He created man] and taught him the explanation"* (Qur'an 55:4); so He attributed the teaching to Himself, not to reflection *(al-fikr)*. Hence we know that there is a station beyond reflection that bestows upon the servant knowledge of various things.

114.20   Among these things, some can be perceived by reflection; some are allowed by reflection, even though the intellect cannot actualize *(husûl)* them through reflection; some are allowed by reflection, even though it is impossible for reflection to determine *(ta'yîn)* them; and some are considered impossible by reflection, while the intellect accepts from reflection that they cannot exist.

The intellect cannot accept them because of the proof of their impossibility, so it comes to know them from God through a sound Incident *(wâqi'a)*,[56] which is not impossible. But the name and property of impossibility do not disappear from them in respect to the intellect.

114.24 The Prophet said, *"There is a knowledge that has the guise of the Hidden* [hay'at al-maknûn]; *none knows it but those who have knowledge of God. When they speak of it, none denies it but those who are deluded about God."*[57] Such is the situation, yet this is a knowledge that can be spoken about. So what do you think about their knowledge that cannot be spoken about? For not every knowledge can be expressed. These kinds of knowledge [that cannot be expressed] are all sciences of Tastings *('ulûm al-adhwâq)*.

114.26 So there is none more knowledgeable than the intellect, and none more ignorant, for the intellect never ceases acquiring *(mustafîd)*. Hence it is the knowing one whose knowledge is not known and the ignorant one whose ignorance has no end.

THE BREATH OF THE ALL-MERCIFUL

CHAPTER 198

This chapter, entitled "On the True Knowledge of the Breath (al-nafas)" and covering eighty-one pages, is one of the longer chapters of the Futûhât. *It deals mostly with cosmology, i.e., the engendering of the universe through the Breath of the All-Merciful, and includes detailed accounts of the influence of twenty-eight specific Divine Names on the world. Why it should have been included in Section 3, which is dedicated to the "states" (ahwâl), is not particularly clear.*

We have selected two short subsections of the chapter. Section 11 summarizes in a manner that is unusually free of digressions Ibn al-'Arabî's cosmological scheme, beginning with the distinction between Absolute Being and absolute nonexistence. The world of possible existence, which lies between these two in the ambiguous situation of being neither the one nor the other, is full of dualities which point to the domination of either Being or nonexistence, depending on the situation. Central to the passage is the idea of "preparedness" (isti'dâd), according to which each thing shares in existence to the measure of its capacity. Differences in preparedness account for the different degrees, levels, and worlds manifested within existence. But in all situations, various sorts of dualities and plays of complementary forces are at work based upon the original distinction between Being and nonexistence.

Section 46 discusses the immutable reality of the world and its multiplicity, a reality that makes it necessary to rely upon the world. Here again Ibn al-'Arabî points out the ambiguous situation of all created things, an ambiguity that is demanded by the fact that God is both Incomparable and Similar. Since God is Incomparable with the world, it cannot denote Him, so it can only denote that in Him which allows for His Similarity, i.e., the meanings that are fixed forever in Him and are known as the Divine Names and the immutable entities (al-a'yân al-thâbita). *These in turn become manifest within the world in respect to a given individual in succession, a fact which demands the constant transformation of the world its "new creation" at each instant. The great saints are those who dwell in this constant flux in the station of bewilderment and variegation* (talwîn).

A Clarification *(ifsâh)* of the Entire
Affair's Situation
(bi mâ huwa'l-amr 'alayh)
Section 11[58]

II 426.27 Know that the entire affair *(al-amr)* is God *(al-haqq)* and creation *(al-khalq)*. It is Sheer Being *(al-wujud al-mahd)* without beginning and end, sheer possibility *(al-imkân al-mahd)* without beginning and end, and sheer nonexistence *(al-'adam al-mahd)* without beginning and end. Sheer Being never receives *(qabûl)* nonexistence for all eternity, sheer nonexistence never receives existence for all eternity, and sheer possibility receives existence for a reason *(sabab)* and nonexistence for a reason for all eternity. Sheer Being is God *(Allah)*, nothing else; sheer nonexistence is that whose existence is impossible *(al-muhâl al-wujûd)*, nothing else; and sheer possibility is the world, nothing else. The [ontological] level *(martaba)* of possibility lies between Sheer Being and sheer nonexistence; through that of it which gazes *(nazar)* upon nonexistence, it receives nonexistence, and through that of it which gazes upon Being, it receives existence. It consists of both darkness *(zulma)*, i.e., nature *(tabî'a)*,[59] and light *(nûr)*, i.e., the All-Merciful Breath *(al-nafas al-rahmânî)*, which bestows existence upon the possible things.

426.32   So the world is both carrier *(hâmil)* and carried *(mahmûl)*. As carrier, it is form *(sûra)*, body *(jism)*, and active *(fâ'il)*; as carried it is meaning *(ma'nâ)*, spirit *(rûh)*, and passive *(munfa'il)*. There is no form sensory *(mahsûs)*, imaginal *(khayâlî)*, or spiritual *(ma'nawî)*[60] that is not shaped *(taswiya)* and balanced *(ta'dîl)*[61] by God in a manner appropriate to it and to its station and its state; and this takes place before composition *(tarkîb)*, i.e., its combination *(ijtimâ')* with what it carries. So when the Lord shapes it as He desires through word, hand, two hands, or hands[62]—and there is nothing more than these four, since existence stands upon quaternity *(tarbî')*[63]—and He balances it, which is to give it the readiness *(tahayyu')* and preparedness *(isti'dâd)* for composition and carrying *(haml)*, it is delivered over to the All-Merciful. He turns His Breath toward it, the Breath which is the Spirit of God mentioned in His words, *"When I have shaped him and breathed of My Spirit into him"* (Qur'an 15:29), a Spirit which is identical with the Breath received by the form.[64] The forms are diverse in their reception in keeping with their preparedness.[65] If the form is elemental *('unsurî)*,[66] and if its wick ignites through that Breath, it is called an animal at ignition; but if no ignition becomes manifest from it, but its entity manifests movement *(haraka)*, it is called a plant. If neither ignition nor movement appears, i.e., to sense perception *(fi'l-hiss)*, it is called a mineral *(ma'dan)* or an inanimate object *(jamâd)*.

427.4   If the form is passive toward a celestial *(falakî)* movement, it is called a pillar *(rukn)*, of which there are four levels.[67] The passivity of these pillars produces a shaped and balanced form called heaven *(samâ')*, which has seven strata *(tabaqât)*. So the All-Merciful turns His Breath toward these forms and they come alive through a life not perceived by the senses, though not denied by faith *(îmân)* or the soul; hence they do not receive ignition. Each place *(mawdi')* within the heavens that accepts ignition is called a star *(najm)*. So the stars become manifest and their spheres come into movement through them. Hence [heaven] is like the animals in that of it which ignites, and like the plants in that of it which moves.

427.8   If the form is engendered from a spiritual *(ma'nawî)* movement, an active faculty, and an attentiveness *(tawajjuh)* of the Breath, it is called Universal Body, Throne, Footstool, and sphere—the sphere of the constellations *(burj)* and the sphere of the mansions *(manâzil)*. The All-Merciful turns the attentiveness of His Breath toward these forms; those of them that receive ignition are called stars and are like the pupils *(hadaq)* in a man's face; those which do not receive ignition are called spheres.

427.10   If the form is intellective *('aqliyya)*, it arises inherently *(inbi'âth dhâtî)* from a disengaged intellect *('aql mujarrad)* and seeks through its preparedness that which the attentiveness of the All-Merciful will make it carry through His Breath when the Lord shapes it. That of it which ignites is called a light of knowledge *(nûr 'ilm)*, that which moves but does not ignite is called a work *('amal)*, and the essence that carries these two faculties[68] is called a soul *(nafs)*.

427.12   If the form is divine, it must be either all-comprehensive *(jâmi'a)*, i.e., the form of man, or not all-comprehensive, i.e., the form of the Intellect. So when the Lord shapes the intellective form with His Command or gives form *(taswîr)* to the human form with His two hands, the All-Merciful turns His attentiveness toward the two through His Breath and breathes into them a spirit from His Command. As for the form of the Intellect, through that breathing it is made to carry all the knowledge *('ulûm)* of engendered existence until the Day of Resurrection. He makes it the root of the existence of the world and bestows upon it primacy *(awwaliyya)* in possible existence *(al-wujûd al-imkânî)*.[69] And as for the form of the First Man, created with two hands,[70] through that breathing he is made to carry the knowledge of the Divine Names, which are not carried by the form of the Intellect. So man emerges upon the form of God; in him the property of the Breath comes to its end—since there is nothing more perfect than the form of God—the world inscribes a circle, and possible existence becomes manifest between light and darkness, nature and spirit, unseen *(ghayb)* and visible *(shahâda)*, concealing *(satr)* and unveiling *(kashf)*.

427.18   Of everything that we have mentioned, that which is adjacent *(mâ waliya)* to Sheer Being is light and spirit; and of everything that we have mentioned, that which is adjacent to sheer nonexistence is darkness and body. Through the combined totality *(al-majmû')* a form is engendered. If you look upon the world in respect of the Breath of the All-Merciful, you will say, "It is nothing but God." But if you look upon it in respect of the fact that it is shaped and balanced, you will say, "creatures." *"You did not throw"* in respect of being a creature *"when you threw"* in respect of being God, *"but God threw"* (Qur'an 8:17), since He is God.[71]

427.21   Through the Breath the whole world is breathed *(mutanaffas)*, the Breath making it manifest. The Breath is nonmanifest *(bâtin)* in God and manifest *(zâhir)* in creation. So the nonmanifest of God is the manifest of creation, and the nonmanifest of creation is the manifest of God. Through the combined totality engendered existence is realized, and in abandoning this totality one says "God" and "creation." So God belongs to Sheer Being and creation to sheer possibility. When something of the world becomes nonexistent and its form disappears, it pertains to the side of nonexistence; when something subsists and cannot become nonexistent, it pertains to the side of existence.

427.24   These two affairs *(amrân* [i.e., existence and nonexistence]) continue to display their properties in the world forever. Hence creation is renewed at every breath,[72] in this world and the next. The Breath of the All-Merciful is forever turning its attentiveness, and nature is forever undergoing generation as the forms of this Breath, so that the Divine Command may never be rendered ineffectual, since ineffectuality *(ta'tîl)* is impossible. So forms are temporally originated and become manifest in accordance with their preparedness to receive the Breath.

427.26   Thus have I explained that which can be explained concerning the origination *(ibdâ')* of the world. *"And God speaks the truth and guides on the way"* (Qur'an 33:4).

Concerning Reliance *(al-i'timâd)* on the World
Section 46[73]

The entire title is: "Concerning Reliance *(al-i'timâd)* on the World in Respect of the World's Being a Writing Inscribed *(kitâb mastûr)* on the Parchment of Existence *(raqq al-wujûd)* Unrolled Within the World of Bodily Things *(ajrâm)* and Engendered from the Name of God the 'Manifest' *(al-zâhir)*."

II 473.32 Know that this reliance *(i'timâd)* cannot be possessed by someone who has not received his knowledge by a divine instruction *(ta'rîf ilâhî)*.[74] It is as follows: We refer to the "world" *(al-'âlam)* by this word only to show that it has been made a "mark" *('alâma)*. It has been established that Being is God Himself *('ayn al-haqq)* and that the constant variation *(tanawwu')* in the forms manifested within it is a mark of the properties of the immutable entities of the possible things *(a'yân al-mumkinât al-thâbita)*. It follows that those forms that are manifest through their properties within God Himself—like writing manifested on a parchment—are named the "world." They are made manifest by the Divine Name the Manifest, or rather, this Name is manifested through them. Here God is distinguished from the creation. Though the forms display variation, they have no effect upon the Self *(al-'ayn)* manifest within them, just as substance *(jawhar)* does not cease being substance because of the states and accidents that become manifest through it; for what becomes manifest is the property of the hidden meaning *(al-ma'nâ al-mabtûn)* that has no existence save through the property in the eye of the beholder *(fî 'ayn nâzir)*. So its properties are neither existent nor nonexistent, even though they are immutable.

474.2 So the world is relied upon inasmuch as it is a mark, not of God—*"For God is independent of the worlds"* (Qur'an 3:92)—but of the immutability of the meanings that possess these properties which are manifest in God Himself. Hence the world is a mark of itself, as is every single thing. Nothing denotes a thing better than itself, for the thing itself is a denotation that does not disappear, while extraneous denotations *(al-dalâlât al-gharîba)* disappear and are not immutable.

474.5   He who relies upon the world in this respect has relied upon something sound and unchanging. In reality, only it can be relied upon in this respect, for God is *"each day upon some task"* (Qur'an 55:29),[75] so one does not know what this task is. One cannot rely upon something that is not known in itself.

474.7   So the perfect one among the Folk of Allah undergoes variation because of the variation of the "tasks," for God does not become manifest in existence except in the form of the tasks. The reliance of this person is a divine reliance; in other words, he is qualified by it through God's attribute of acting as a receptacle for the tasks through which the world becomes manifest.

474.8   This [section] pertains to the knowledge that is withheld from those unworthy of it *(al-madnûn li ghayr ahlihî)*. So know that! *"And God speaks the truth and guides on the way"* (Qur'an 33:4).

THE MOST BEAUTIFUL NAMES

CHAPTER 558[76]

The complete title of this chapter is: "On the True Knowledge of the Most Beautiful Names (*al-asmâ' al-husnâ*) Possessed by the Lord of Might (*rabb al-'izza*) and on Those Which May and May Not be Literally (*lafzan*) Ascribed to Him." *It is one of the* Futûhât's *longest chapters, covering 131 pages and divided into 101 subsections, including an introduction, one section for each of the ninety-nine Most Beautiful Names, and a conclusion called "The Presence of Presences, Comprehending the Most Beautiful Names." In effect this chapter is a major book on the Divine Names, far longer than, for example, al-Ghazâlî's* Al-Maqsad al-asnâ *or Fakhr al-Dîn al-Râzî's* Lawâmi' al-bayyinât. *Translated below are the introduction and the first subsection, on the Divine Name "Allah."*

In the introduction Ibn al-'Arabî provides a succinct explanation of the "Oneness of Being," employing theological language: the Divine Presence—that is, the sphere of existence dominated by the Name "Allah"—embraces the Essence, the Attributes, and the Acts or creatures. So everything that may be said to exist in whatever mode is denoted by the Name "Allah." In completing the introduction Ibn al-'Arabî turns to a linguistic discussion of how various words may be considered as Divine Names in order to explain why he has limited himself in the present chapter to a discussion of only the Most Beautiful Names. In the translated subsection he returns to a discussion of the Oneness of Being by showing that all things in the universe come under the sway of this all-comprehensive Name; he then classifies in a theological manner the various kinds of names that it embraces. Finally he turns to the proper and true human response to this name: bewilderment, worship, and the profession of Incomparability.

I see the ladder of the Names, rising and falling, through it blowing a wind from south and north.
I wonder—how to reach safety? For blindness is the brother of guidance and affairs are not separate.
Do you not see that in the Fire God is Just? That in the Garden of Firdaws He favors and obliges?
If you say, "This one is an infidel," I say, "God is Just." If you say, "This one a man of faith," I say, "He gives preference."
Here is proof that my Lord is one: God appoints and removes whom He will.
So our entities are His Names, they are nothing other, for in His own Self he decrees and differentiates affairs.

IV 196.10 God says, *"To God belong the Most Beautiful Names"* (Qur'an 7:180). These are none other than the Divine Presences *(al-hadarât al-ilâhiyya)* that are sought and entified by the properties of the possible things *(ahkâm al-mumkinât)*.[77] And these properties are none other than the forms manifest within True Being *(al-wujûd al-haqq)*. Hence "Divine Presence" is a name belonging to an Essence, Attributes, and Acts; or, if you like, you can say: to the Attributes of Acts *(sifa fi'l)* and the Attributes of Incomparability *(sifa tanzîh)*.[78]

196.12 The Acts derive from the Attributes. No doubt the Acts are Names, but some of the Names He ascribes *(itlâq)* to Himself, while others He does not ascribe, though they have come in words [indicating] Acts, such as, *"[They deceived] and God deceived"* (Qur'an 3:54); *"God derides [them]"* (Qur'an 9:79); *"[They scheme a scheme] and I scheme a scheme"* (Qur'an 86:16); *"God mocks them"* (Qur'an 2:15). In these cases it is not impossible for an active noun *(ism fâ'il)* to be built from the words.[79]

196.14   A similar case is provided by indirect expressions *(kinâyât)*, such as, *"[He has appointed for you] shirts to protect you from the heat"* (Qur'an 16:81). In fact He is the Protector, while the shirt here is the deputy. And so on with other verses.

196.15   There are also pronouns, whether referring to the first, third, or second person, or to all things *('âmm),*[80] as in God's words, *"Oh people, you are the poor toward Allah"* (Qur'an 35:15), where He is named by everything toward which people are poor. Hence, everything toward which someone is poor is a Name of God, since [as stated in this verse] there is no poverty except toward Him; though no word is ascribed to Him here, we take into account the meanings given us by the sciences.[81]

196.17   As for prohibition *(tahjîr)* and lack of it in the ascription [of Names] to Him, that depends on God. Hence, if He has restricted Himself to certain words in ascription, we also restrict ourselves, since we only name Him by what He has named Himself. Those Names which are forbidden, we forbid, out of courtesy *(adab)* toward God.[82] For we are in Him and we belong to Him. Hence in this chapter we will mention, Presence by Presence, the Divine Presences that God has alluded to as the Most Beautiful Names. We will restrict ourselves to one hundred Presences. Then we will follow that with sections, each of which will refer back to this chapter. Among the Presences is:

The Divine Presence, that is, The Name "Allah"

Allah, Allah, Allah—His signs *(âyât)* have passed judgment that He is Allah.
Glory be to Him!—He is greater than that any of the servants should win Him, for there is no god but He.
He alone possesses a Name not shared by any other: that is the speaker's word, "Allah."

This is the Presence that comprehends *(jâmi')* all Presences. Hence no worshipper of God worships anything but this Presence. God judges *(hukm)* this in His words, *"Thy Lord has decreed that you shall not worship any but Him"* (Qur'an 17:23), and His words,

"You are the poor toward Allah."[83]

To God belongs what is hidden, to God belongs what appears,
How excellent is that which is God, that which is none other than He.

196.28   You should know that since the power *(quwwa)* of the Name Allah contains, according to the original coinage *(al-wad' al-awwal)*, every Divine Name, or rather, every Name having an effect *(athar)* within engendered existence, it takes, on behalf of what it names, the place of every Name of God.[84] So when someone says, "Oh Allah," look at the state which incited him to make this call and consider which Divine Name is specifically connected to that state. That specific Name *(al-ism al-khâss)* is what the caller is calling with his words, "Oh Allah." For the Name Allah, by its original coinage, names the Essence of God Itself, *"in whose hand is the dominion of everything"* (Qur'an 36:83). That is why the Name which refers specifically to the Essence takes the place of every Divine Name.[85]

196.31   To the One who is named by this Name, in respect of the fact that *"To Him the whole matter will be returned"* (Qur'an 11:123), belongs the name of every named thing toward which there is poverty, whether mineral, plant, animal, man, celestial sphere, angel, or any such thing, whatever name is applied to it, that of a creature *(makhlûq)* or an originated thing *(mubda')*.[86] Hence He is named by every name which is possessed by a named thing in the world and which has an effect within engendered existence *(al-kawn)*; and there is nothing that does not have an effect in engendered existence.

196.35   As for the fact that the Name Allah includes the Names of Incomparability, the source for this is near at hand: though every Divine Name is the same in respect of denoting the Essence of God, nevertheless, since every Name other than Allah while denoting the Essence of God also denotes—because of its derivation *(ishtiqâq)* [from a specific root having a specific meaning]—a meaning of negation *(salb)* or affirmation *(ithbât)*, it cannot be as strong as this Name in the unity of its denotation *(ahadiyyat al-dalâla)* of the Essence; such is the case with the All-Merciful *(al-rahmân)* and others of the Most Beautiful Names. It is true that in the Qur'an God says to the Prophet, commanding him, *"Say: 'Call upon Allah or call upon the All-Merciful; whichever you call upon, to Him belong the Most Beautiful Names'"* (Qur'an 17:110), but the pronoun "Him" refers back to Him who is called upon, since He who is originally named, outside of derivation, is but One Self *('ayn wâhid)*.

197.5   God has preserved this proper name *(ism 'alam)* from naming any but the Essence of God. Therefore God says, as an argument against those who had ascribed divinity to something other than this Named One, *"[They ascribe to Allah associates.] Say: 'Name them!'"* (Qur'an 13:33), and those who had held such a view were rendered speechless, for if they had named that thing, they would have named it by other than the Name Allah.

197.7   As for the all-comprehensiveness *(jam'iyya)* of this Name, that is because the objects denoted *(madlûlât)* by the Names, which are superadded *(zâ'id)* to what is understood *(mafhûm)* by the "Essence," are multiple and diverse. We do not have any pure proper name for the Essence except the Name Allah, since the Name Allah denotes the Essence by exact congruence *(bi hukm mutâbaqa)*, in the same way that proper names denote the objects they name.

197.8   There are Names which denote Incomparability.

197.9   There are Names which denote the affirmation of the entities of the Attributes, though the Essence of God does not allow that numbers should subsist *(qiyâm al-'adad)*.[87] These are the Names that make known *(i'tâ')* the entities of the affirmative Attributes of the Essence *(a'yân al-sifât al-thubûtiyyat al-dhâtiyya)*, such as the Knower, the Powerful, the Willing, the Hearing, the Seeing, the Living, the Responder, and the Thankful; the Names that make known descriptions *(nu'ût)*,[88] so that nothing is understood from their ascription except relations *(nisab)* and correlations *(idâfât)*, like the First and the Last, the Manifest and the Nonmanifest; and the Names that make known Acts, such as Creator, Provider, Author, Shaper, etc.

197.12   In this way everything has been classified. All the Divine Names, as many as there may be, can be reduced to one of these kinds, or to more than one; while everyone of them must unquestionably denote the Essence.

197.14   So this Presence contains all the Presences. He who knows Allah knows all things. But he does not know Allah who does not know one thing, whatever named possible thing it might be, since the property of one of these things is the property of them all in denoting knowledge of God, in respect to the specific fact that He is God over the world. Then when you receive unveiling *(kashf)* in respect to works set down in the Law *(al-'amal al-mashrû')*, you will see that you did not know Him except through Him. The denotation *(dalîl)* is identical to what is denoted through that denotation and denoter.

197.17   Though this Presence comprehends all realities, the states which pertain to it most specifically are bewilderment *(ḥayra)*, worship *('ibâda)*, and the profession of Incomparability *(tanzîh)*. As for Incomparability, which is the fact that He stands high above similarity *(tashabbuh)* with His creatures, it leads to bewilderment in Him and also to worship. God gave us the power of reflection *(quwwat al-fikr)* so that we might speculate *(nazar)*[89] upon what we know of ourselves and of Him. The property of this power demands that there be no likeness *(mumâthala)* between us and Him in any respect, except specifically our dependence *(istinâd)* upon Him for the bestowal of existence upon our entities. The most that the profession of Incomparability gives is the affirmation of relations *(nisab)* that He possesses toward us, because of what the concomitants of our entities' existence demands. These relations are called Attributes.

197.21   If we say that these relations are things superadded to His Essence, that they are ontological *(wujûdî)*, and that He possesses no perfection except through them—even were He not to have them—this would mean that He is imperfect in essence but perfect through the superadded ontological thing.[90]

197.22   If we say, "They [the relations] are neither He nor other than He,"[91] this would be a contradictory statement *(khulf min al-*

kalâm), words with no life that denote a deficiency of intelligence and a lack of speculative power in the speaker far more than they denote God's Incomparability.

197.24 If I say that they are not He, that they have no existence, and that they are only relations, while relations are nonexistent things *(umûr 'adamiyya)*, then we would have given nonexistence an effect within existence, while the relations are multiple because of the multiplicity of the properties bestowed by the entities of the possible things.

197.25 If we say none of this whatsoever, we will have rendered the speculative power ineffectual *(mu'attal)*.

197.25 If we say that nothing has any reality, that things are illusions *(awhâm)* and sophistry *(safsata)* and of no avail, and that no one can trust any of them, whether [they are known] by way of sense perception or rational reflection—then if this position is correct and known, what is the proof *(dalîl)* that can have led us to it? If it is not correct, how can we know that it is not correct?

197.28 Since the intellect is incapable of reaching knowledge of any of these matters, we return to the Law *(al-shar')*, but we only accept it through the intellect. The Law is a branch *(far')* of a root *(asl)* that we know through the Lawgiver *(shâri')*. But through which attribute has the existence of the Law reached us, when we are incapable of knowing the root? So we are even more incapable of [knowing] and affirming the branch. If we pretend to be blind and accept the Lawgiver's words through faith in something self-evident *(darûrî)* within ourselves which we cannot repel, we will hear him attributing to God things depreciated by speculative proofs. No matter which proof we grasp hold of, another stands opposed to it. If we interpret *(ta'awwul)* what he has brought, we will be taking it back to rational speculation. Hence we will have worshipped our own intellects and based His Being upon our existence; but He cannot be perceived by reasoning *(qiyâs)*. So the fact that we have professed God's Incomparability has taken us to bewilderment, since all the paths are muddled *(tashawwush)*. Both intellectual and Law-inspired speculation lead to a single center, which is bewilderment.[92]

197.33   As for worship: In respect of its being directed at the Essence it is nothing but the possible thing's poverty *(iftiqâr)* toward Him who gives preponderance *(al-murajjih* [i.e., to existence over nonexistence]). I mean by worship only prescription *(taklîf)*; no one can have prescriptions made for him unless he has power over the acts that are prescribed for him and over the prohibited things from which he must hold himself back. In one respect, we negate acts from created things and give them back to Him who has made the prescriptions; but a thing cannot prescribe for itself, so there must be a locus that receives the address *(khitâb)* for it to be correct. In another respect we affirm acts for created things because of what the wisdom in prescription demands. But negation stands opposed to affirmation, so this view throws us into bewilderment, as did the profession of Incomparability. But bewilderment yields nothing.

198.2   So rational speculation leads to bewilderment and theophany leads to bewilderment. There is nothing but a bewildered one. There is nothing exercising properties but bewilderment. There is nothing but Allah.

198.3   When one of them was faced in his inmost consciousness *(sirr)* with all these conflicting properties, he used to say, "Oh bewilderment! Oh confusion! Oh conflagration that cannot be fathomed!" This property does not belong to any Presence but the Presence of the Name Allah.

AT THE END OF TIME

James W. Morris

THE MAHDI'S HELPERS[1]
CHAPTER 366

The title of Chapter 366 of the Futûhât is "Concerning inner knowledge of the stage of the Helpers of the Mahdi appearing at the end of time...." The primary focus of this chapter is the distinctive set of spiritual qualities and capacities marking a particular spiritual stage (manzil)—*characteristics which Ibn 'Arabî finds symbolized in the various hadith concerning the eschatological role of the Mahdi and his "Helpers" or "Ministers,"[2] but which he insists are already realized by those saints* (awliyâ') *who have attained this degree of spiritual realization, who have already reached the "end of time." In a broader metaphysical perspective, as he indicates allusively in the poem introducing this chapter, all those characteristics are in fact essential aspects of the ongoing divine governance of this world in its microcosmic, individual human dimensions, especially in the spiritual judgment or authority* (walâya) *of the saints as it is realized inwardly or, more rarely, manifested outwardly and officially in the functions of religious judges or in the case of the Prophet (who preeminently combined the roles of the Mahdi and his Helpers). The two principal, complementary aspects of Ibn 'Arabî's treatment of this stage and its associated functions are clearly relevant to the spiritual life of every individual. The first is the question of divine "communication" (in all its manifestations, but with special attention to the central role of the Qur'an and the "heritage" of the Prophet Muhammad) and the decisive role of each person's unique and radically varying receptivity or sensitivity to that deeper dimension of reality. The second is the "application" of that communication—which, for Ibn 'Arabî, obviously includes, but is by no means limited to, the familiar external forms of Islamic law and tradition—in guiding our spiritual and communal life. Especially striking, in regard to this latter point, are the Shaykh's recurrent, sometimes pointed allusions to the distance separating the historical, limited conception of the Sharia[3] shared by many of the 'ulamâ' in the popular sense of that term (i.e., the Islamic jurists and theologians) and the deeper, more challenging perennial reality of its demands and presuppositions as understood by the awliyâ', whom Ibn 'Arabî consistently regards as the true "knowers" and "authorities" (wulât) of the Community.*

The treatment of these questions in this chapter is often subtle and highly allusive, no doubt partly because of the potentially controversial nature of Ibn 'Arabî's broader understanding—largely only implicit in this chapter—of the relations between the inspiration and spiritual authority underlying the "judgments" of the Prophet, saints, and the mass of jurists and theologians "learned in the external forms" ('ulamâ' al-rusûm). As a result, it provides a remarkable illustration of his typical methods of esoteric writing, in which each reader's perceptions of the apparent content, aims and unifying structure of the work will necessarily differ radically according to his own particular intentions and sensitivities. At the same time, it constitutes an excellent introduction to the principles underlying Ibn 'Arabî's complex understanding of the practical interrelations between spiritual realization and the historical forms of Islamic tradition—a perspective which clearly transcends the usual stereotyped (and often polemic or apologetic) conceptions of those questions.[4]

There should be no need to stress the wider significance of each of these issues throughout Ibn 'Arabî's writings. But what lends this chapter its special impact and dramatic interest are its primary focus on the experiential sources of Ibn 'Arabî's key insights, his frequent autobiographical remarks (including a number of references to his own self-conception of his role as the unique "Seal of Muhammadan Sainthood") and colorful anecdotes based on his encounters with other Sufis—illustrative materials that provide an essential phenomenological complement to the better-known metaphysical and doctrinal aspects of his teaching, while at the same time pointing to some of its indispensable practical presuppositions.

The Relation between the *Mahdi* and His Helpers[5]

...Know—may God support us!—that God has a viceregent *(khalîfa)* who will come forth when the earth has become filled with injustice and oppression, and will then fill it with justice and equity. Even if there were only one day left for this world, God would lengthen it so that he [i.e., the Mahdi] could rule....[6] He will wipe out injustice and its people and uphold Religion *(al-Dîn)*, and he will breathe the spirit back into Islam. He will reinvigorate Islam after its degradation and bring it back to life after its death. He will levy the poll tax[7] and call [mankind] to God with the sword, so that whoever refuses will be killed, and whoever opposes him will be forsaken.

He will manifest Religion as it [really] is in Itself, the Religion by which the Messenger of God would judge and rule if he were there. He will eliminate the different schools [of religious law] so that only the *Pure Religion* (Qur'an 39:3) remains,[8] and his enemies will be those who follow blindly the *'ulamâ'*, the people of *ijtihâd*,[9] because they will see the Mahdi judging differently from the way followed by their imams [i.e., the historical founders of the schools of Islamic law]. So they will only accept the Mahdi's authority grudgingly and against their will, because of their fear of his sword and his strength, and because they covet [the power and wealth] that he possesses. But the common people of the Muslims and the greater part of the elite among them will rejoice in him, while the true Knowers of God among the People of the [spiritual] Realities will pledge allegiance to him because of God's directly informing them [of the Mahdi's true nature and mission], through [inner] unveiling and immediate witnessing.

He will have divine men upholding his call [to the true Religion] and aiding him in his victory; they are the Helpers *(wuzarâ')*. They will bear the burdens of [his] government and help him to carry out all the details of [the duty] God has imposed on him.

[...[10]] God will appoint as His ministers a group [of spiritual men] whom He has kept hidden for him in the secret recesses of His Unseen [i.e., the spiritual world]. God has acquainted [these Helpers], through unveiling and immediate witnessing, with the [Divine] Realities and the contents of God's Command concerning His servants. So the Mahdi makes his decisions and judgments on the basis of consultation with them, since they are the true Knowers, who really know what is There [in the Divine Reality]. As for the Mahdi himself, he has a sword [in the service of the] Truth and a [divinely inspired] political policy *(siyâsa)*, [since] he knows from God the exact extent of what is required by his rank and station; for he is a rightly guided Viceregent [of God], one who understands the language of animals, whose justice extends to both men and jinn.[11]

Among the secrets of the knowledge of the Mahdi's Helpers whom God has appointed as ministers for Him is His saying: *"The victorious support of the men of faith is obligatory for Us"* (Qur'an 30:47),[12] for they follow in the footsteps of those men among the Companions [of the Prophet] who sincerely fulfilled what they had pledged to God. These Helpers are from the non-Arab peoples; none of them is Arab, although they speak only Arabic. And they have a guardian, not of their kind, who never disobeys God at all,[13] he is the most elect of the Helpers and the most excellent of [the Mahdi's] Trusted Ones.

Now in this verse (Qur'an 30:47)—which the Helpers take as their constant prayer[14] [by day] and their inseparable companion at night—God has given them the most excellent knowledge of true sincerity *(sidq)*, as their inner state and direct experience. So they know that true sincerity is God's sword on earth: God always gives His victorious support *(nasr)* to whoever stands up for someone [in the divine cause] while being distinguished by this true sincerity....

The long following passage (III 328.18-329.25) is devoted to a detailed analysis, at once psychological and metaphysical, of this inner condition of sidq *or pure spiritual intention* (himma), *which Ibn 'Arabî sees as one of the distinguishing signs of the highest forms of true faith in God, and to its natural effect of divine "victorious support"* (nasr). *Thus "the truly faithful person whose faith is perfect is forever divinely supported (mansûr), which is why no prophet or saint is ever defeated" (III 329.9). To be sure, for Ibn 'Arabî this divine support and triumph flows from the saint's inner realization of pure and unquestioning identification with what is required by the divine Will and purpose, not necessarily with what might be considered a worldly "victory" from external, less enlightened points of view.*

...Now since the rightly guided Imam *(Mahdî)*[15] knows this [i.e., the victorious divine support flowing from the sincerity of perfect faith], he acts accordingly and is the most truly sincere of the people of his time. So his Helpers are the guides *(al-hudât)*, while he is the rightly guided one *(al-mahdî)*. And this is the extent of what the Mahdi attains of the knowledge of God, with the aid of his Helpers.

But as for the Seal of Muhammadan Sainthood, of all the creatures he is the one who knows God best: there is no one in his own time nor after his time who better knows God and the details of His Judgment *(mawâqi' al-hukm minhu)*.[16] For he and the *Qur'ân* are brothers,[17] just as the Mahdi and the sword are brothers.

[...[18]] You should know that I am uncertain about the length of this Mahdi's rule, because as far as this world is concerned I have not sought God's verification of that, nor have I asked Him to specify that or any other temporal happening among the engendered realities [of this world]—except for whatever God happens to teach me spontaneously, without my seeking it. For I am afraid that during the time when I am asking God to inform me about some engendered or temporal thing I will miss out on some portion of my awareness of Him. So instead I have surrendered my affair to God in His kingdom *(mulk,* i.e., in this world), letting Him do with me as He pleases. And indeed I have seen a number of the people of God (i.e., the Sufis) seeking to obtain from Him the knowledge of temporal, engendered happenings, and especially trying to become acquainted with the Imam of [this] time.[19] But I was ashamed to do that, and afraid that [my lower, bodily] nature would rob me [of my knowledge of God] if I were to associate with them while they were in that state.

So I asked God only that He grant me stability in a single sort[20] of knowledge of Him, even though I be constantly transformed in my [inner] states. And He did not refuse me....

Ibn 'Arabî concludes this section by recapitulating, in a beautiful poetic "dialogue with God" too long to translate in its entirety here, his discovery of one of the central spiritual insights of his work: the paradoxical fact that this continual transformation of the Heart (fully perceived only by the true Knowers) is itself the perpetually renewed theophany of the noetic "Realities," in no way contradicting the transcendent Unity of the divine Essence. "So when I asked [God] that question [about the apparent conflict between the divine Unity and the multiplicity of theophanies in our experience], He showed me my ignorance and said to me: 'Are you not content that you are like Me?!'"

The Characteristics of the Spiritual Station of the "Helpers"[21]

Now I do know what [spiritual qualities] are needed by the Mahdi's Helper. So if there is only one Helper, then everything he needs is united in that one person, and if they are more than one, then there are not more than nine of them, since that was the limit of the uncertainty the Messenger of God expressed in his saying concerning the rule of the Mahdi, that it was *"for five, seven, or nine years."*[22] And the totality of what he needs to have performed for him by his Helpers are nine things; there is not a tenth, nor can they be any fewer....

Ibn 'Arabî then briefly enumerates the nine characteristics described in detail in the rest of this chapter (using the phrases given in quotation marks at the beginning of each section), and again insists that all nine of these qualities are required by the Helpers, no matter what their exact number may be. However, the Helpers themselves are not mentioned in the rest of the chapter, where these spiritual attributes are instead attributed directly to the "Imam," "Imam of the Age," "Rightly guided Imam," etc.—or else to the saints or accomplished Sufis more generally.

1. As for "penetrating vision," that is so that his praying[23] to God may be *"with [clear] inward vision"* (Qur'an 12:108) concerning what he requests in his prayer, not Him to whom the prayer is addressed. So he regards the inner essence *('ayn)* of each [Divine Reality or Name][24] to Whom he is praying and sees what is possible for Him to do in response to his prayer, and then he prays to Him for that, even if it be by way of special pleading.[25]

As for those things where he sees that [God] will not [ordinarily] respond to his prayer, he prays to Him, without any special pleading, to carry out [for him] the divine Argument *(hujja)* in this special case,[26] since the Mahdi is God's Argument for the people of his time, and that (i.e., his function as *hujja*) is part of the rank of the prophets and participates in that rank. God said: *"[Say: 'This is my path:] I pray to God with inward vision, I and whoever follows me'"* (Qur'an 12:108). [God] reported that [to us] through His Prophet, and the Mahdi is among "those who follow him," because the Prophet does not err in his praying to God, nor does the person who follows him,[27] since he follows the trace of [the Prophet's] footsteps. And that is what appears in the [hadith] report describing the Mahdi, that the Prophet said: *"He follows in the trace of my footsteps, and he does not err."*[28] This is the [inner state of] immunity from error *('isma)* in praying to God, and it is attained by many of the saints, or indeed by all of them.[29]

Among the attributes of this "penetrating vision" are that the person possessing it sees the luminous and fiery spirits [i.e., the angels and the jinn] without those spirits themselves wanting to appear or take on a form [for that person]....

Ibn 'Arabî illustrates this ability with a story about Ibn 'Abbâs and 'A'isha, who both saw a stranger conversing with the Prophet and subsequently learned that they had actually seen the angel Gabriel.

Likewise [as a result of this special vision] they perceive the men of the Unseen[30] even when they want to be veiled and not to appear to [ordinary human] vision. And it is also [characteristic] of this penetrating vision that if the spiritual meanings *(ma'ânî)* take on bodily form, then they recognize [the underlying realities] in those very forms, and they know without any hesitation which spiritual meaning it is that became embodied [in that particular form].[31]

2. Now as for "understanding the divine address when it is delivered,"[32] this is [summarized] in His saying: *"And it was not for any mortal man that God should speak to him except through inspiration or from behind a veil or He sends a messenger"* (Qur'an 42:51).

So as for the divine address "through inspiration" *(wahy)*[33] that is what He delivers to their hearts as something newly reported [to them],[34] so that through this they gain knowledge of some particular matter, i.e., of what is contained in that new report. But if it does not happen in that way [i.e., as something received from outside oneself], then it is not a [divine] inspiration or address. For instance, some people [may] find in their hearts the knowledge of something of the necessary forms of knowledge[35] among people in general. That is genuine knowledge, but it is not obtained from a [particular divine] address *(khitâb)*, and our discussion is only concerned with that form of divine address which is called "inspiration" *(wahy)*....[36]

And as for His saying *"or from behind a veil,"* that is a divine address delivered to the [person's] hearing and not to the heart, so that the person to whom it is delivered perceives it and then understands from that what was intended by the One Who caused him to hear it. Sometimes that happens through the forms of theophany, in which case that [particular] divine form addresses the person, and that form itself is the veil. Then [the person having this condition of spiritual insight] understands from that divine address the knowledge of what it indicates, and he knows that [this theophanic form] is a veil and that the Speaker [i.e., God] is behind that veil.

Of course, not everyone who perceives a form of the divine theophany realizes that that form is God. For the person possessing this state [of spiritual insight] is only distinguished from other men by the fact that he recognizes that that form, although it is a "veil," is itself precisely God's theophany for him.[37]

And as for His saying, *"or He sends a messenger,"* that is [the divine address] He sends down with an angel or that is brought to us by the mortal human messenger when either sort of messenger conveys "God's Speech" in this particular way [i.e., perceived as an individual "address" coming directly from God]....[38] But if either sort of messenger [simply] conveys or gives expression to knowledge that he found [already] in his soul [and not as a distinct message given him by God], then that is not Divine Speech [in this particular sense].

Now it may happen that the messenger and the form [of the message] occur together, as in the very act of writing [the revealed Book]. For the Book is a messenger, and it is also the veil over the Speaker [i.e., God], so that it causes you to understand what It brought. But that [i.e., the divinely revealed nature of the Book] would not be so if the messenger wrote on the basis of his own knowledge: it is only the case if the messenger wrote on the basis of a [divine] report *(hadîth)* addressed to him in those very words he writes down, and when it is not like that then it is not [divine] speech. This is the general rule....

So all of this [i.e., all three forms of theophanic perception] is part of the divine address directed to the person who possesses this [spiritual] station.[39]

3. As for "the knowledge of how to translate from God," that belongs to every person to whom God speaks through inspiration *(wahy)* or the delivery [of a particular divine address, *ilqâ'*], since [in such cases] the translator is the one who creates the forms of the spoken or written letters he brings into existence, while the *spirit* of those forms is God's Speech and nothing else.[40] But if someone "translates"[into words] from [their own, non-inspired] knowledge, then they are inevitably not a "translator" [in this inspired sense]....

Ibn 'Arabî goes on (333.1-10) to distinguish carefully between this state of inspired vision which is typical of the perception of the saints and "people of inner unveiling" (ahl al-kashf), *on the one hand, and the purely theoretical references by "those who are learned in the outward appearances"* ('ulamâ' al-rusûm) *to the "language of states"* (lisân al-hâl) *in their interpretations of Qur'anic references to the "speech" of what we ordinarily call inanimate objects, such as minerals. The former group, who directly experience the living, theophanic nature of all beings, are able to see for themselves that* "everything other than God really is alive and speaking, in the very nature of things," *while the latter group* "are veiled by the thickest of veils."

...Thus there is nothing in the world but translator,[41] if it is translated from divine Speaking. So understand that.

4. As for "appointing the [various] ranks of the holders of authority,"[42] that is the knowledge of what each rank [of judge or administrator of the religious law] rightfully requires [in order to assure the] kinds of welfare for which it was created. The person possessing this knowledge looks at the soul of the person whom he wants to place in a position of authority and weighs the appropriateness of that person for that rank. If he sees that there is the right equilibrium between the person and the post, without any excess or deficiency, then he gives him that authority, and if the person is overqualified there is no harm in that. But if the person is inadequate to the position he does not entrust him with that authority, because he lacks the knowledge that would qualify him for that rank, so that he would inevitably commit injustice.

For this [inner ignorance of the true reality of the Sharia] is the root of all injustice in the holders of authority, since we hold it to be impossible that someone could [truly] know [a particular divine command] and then deviate from the judgment [required by] his knowledge all at once. This is something that is considered possible by those learned in the external forms,[43] although we ourselves consider that this "possible" thing never actually occurs in reality; it is indeed a difficult question.

Now it is because of this [inner knowledge of men's souls and the true divine commands] that the Mahdi *"fills the world with justice and equity,"* just as *"it was filled with injustice and oppression."*[44] Because in our view [true spiritual] knowledge necessarily and inevitably implies action [in accordance with it], and if it does not do so, then it is not really knowledge, even if it appears in the [outward] form of knowledge....[45]

Ibn 'Arabî goes on to discuss at some length the importance for the Mahdi as for any wise ruler—to appoint judges and authorities who not only have the right [formal] knowledge of the appropriate provisions of the religious law, but in whom that knowledge also fully controls their own personal prejudices,[46] *so that they will always act according to their knowledge.*

5. As for "mercy in anger," that is only in the *divinely* prescribed penalties *(al-hudûd al-mashrû'a)* and punishment, since in everything else [i.e., in merely human affairs] there is anger without any mercy at all.... For if a human being gets angry of his own accord, his anger does not contain mercy in any respect; but if he becomes angry for God's sake [i.e., in fulfilling the divine commandments], then his anger is God's Anger and God's Anger is never free from being mixed with divine Mercy....Because (God's) *Mercy*, since it preceded [His] Anger, entirely covers all engendered being and *extends to every thing* (Qur'an 7:156)....[47]

Therefore this Mahdi does not become angry except for God's sake, so that his anger does not go beyond [what is required in] upholding God's limits[48] that He has prescribed; this is just the opposite of the [ordinary] person who becomes angry because of his own desires for [something happening] contrary to his own personal aims. And likewise the person who becomes angry [only] for God's sake can only be just and equitable, not tyrannical and unjust.

Now a sign of whoever [rightfully] lays claim to this spiritual station is that if he becomes angry for God's sake while acting in judgment and upholding the [divinely prescribed] penalty against the person with whom he is angry, then his anger disappears once he has finished fulfilling [that religious duty]—[to the extent that] sometimes he may even go up to the [condemned] person and embrace him and be friendly with him, saying to him "Praise be to God Who has purified you!" and openly showing his happiness and pleasure with him. And sometimes [the condemned man] also becomes friendly with [his judge] after that, for this [inner fulfillment and realization of the divine commands] is God's Scale [of Justice], and all of [God's Mercy] comes back to that condemned man....[49]

Ibn 'Arabi proceeds to illustrate this phenomenon with the story (III 334.2-8) *of a personal acquaintance who frequented the same masters of hadith in the city of Ceuta, a highly respected and unusually modest religious judge* (qâdî) *who was famous for his rare charismatic ability* (baraka) *to establish peace among*

78 • MECCAN REVELATIONS

feuding parties or tribes—an ability Ibn 'Arabî attributes to his extreme conscientiousness and concern for maintaining only a disinterested, "divine point of view" in his inner relation to his legal duties. This leads him to take up the broader divine standards of judgment (ahkâm) *regarding all of our actions, especially their inner spiritual aspect.*

This [necessary attention to the spiritual sources and repercussions of all our actions] is also [expressed] in God's saying: *"... and then We test your records* [of your actions]*"* (Qur'an 47:31). For first of all He tests [mankind] with regard to the obligations He has imposed on them [i.e., according to the first half of the same verse: *"And surely We test you until We know those of you who make every effort and are patient..."*]; and if they have acted [in accordance with the divine commands], then their actions are tested as to whether they have acted for the sake of the Truth *(al-Haqq)* or instead for some other end. Likewise it is this [inner spiritual judgment that is expressed] in God's saying: *"On the Day when the innermost selves are tested"* (Qur'an 86:9). For the people of inner unveiling hold this [i.e., the judgment of each soul's innermost being, the *sarîra*] to be *God's* Scale [of Justice]. Therefore the judge,[50] whenever he is carrying out the [divine] penalties, must not forget to examine his own soul in order to guard against the feelings of vengeance and aggression that happen to souls [in such situations]....

Here Ibn 'Arabî continues to explain how the above-mentioned qâdî *in Ceuta was always careful to examine his conscience in this way, even when his emotions of anger or vengeance did not derive directly from the case actually before him. In fact, he concludes, the moral and spiritual factors involved in each case are so complex that the responsibility of judgment—in the ultimate, all-inclusive sense of that term—can only belong to God or those rare individuals divinely "appointed" for this role.*[51]

So you must know that God has not appointed anyone but the judge to carry out the penalty against [the guilty person]. Therefore no one [else] should be angry with the person who transgresses God's limits, since that [i.e., the responsibility of anger in imposing the divine penalties] only belongs to the judges in particular, and to God's Messenger insofar as he is a judge. For if [the Messenger] were only communicating [the divine Message][52] and not judging, then he would not carry out the [divine] Anger against those who reject his call. That matter [i.e., their response, insofar as he is simply a Messenger] does not involve him at all, and he *is not responsible for their being rightly guided* (Qur'an 2:272).

Thus God says to the Messenger concerning this matter: *"You are only responsible for communicating* [the divine Message]" (Qur'an 42:48, etc.). So [the Prophet] communicated, and God caused whomever He wished to listen (Qur'an 8:23, etc.) and caused whomever He wished to be deaf (Qur'an 47:23), and they—that is, the prophets—are the most self-restrained of men.[53] For [even] if the [prophetic] caller were [fully] revealed to the person whom God has made deaf to his call, that person would still not hear the call and would not be changed because of that. And if the [prophet who is] calling out brought together those thus deafened, so that they knew that they did not hear his cry, that would still not help him [to convince them], and he would acknowledge their excuse.

Therefore if the Messenger acted as judge *(hâkim)*, that was [only because] he was made specifically responsible for the judgment that God had specified for him in that case. And this is a sublime knowledge required by everyone on earth who has authority over [this] world.[54]

6-a. As for "the forms of [spiritual] sustenance *(arzâq)* needed by the ruler,"[55] this [requires] that he know the kinds of worlds, which are only two—i.e., by "world" I mean the worlds in which this Imam's influence *(hukm)* is effective, which are the world of [physical] forms and the world of the souls[56] governing those forms with regard to their physical movements and activities. As for what is beyond those two kinds [i.e., the worlds of the angelic spirits and the jinn], he has no influence over them except for those, such as [individuals in] the world of the jinn, who wish for him to have influence over their souls.[57]

But as for the luminous world [of the angelic spirits],[58] they are beyond this mortal human world's having any authority over them, for each individual among them has a *known station* (Qur'an 37:163) determined for him by his Lord, so that he does not *descend* [to this earth] *except with the permission of his Lord* (Qur'an 97:4). Thus whoever wants one of them to be sent down to him must turn to his Lord [in praying] for that, and his Lord [may] order [that angel] and give him permission to do that, in compliance with that person's request—or He may send down an angel of His own accord.

As for the "travelers" among the angels, their *station is known* (Qur'an 37:163), since they are constantly traveling around seeking the sessions of *dhikr*.[59] So "when they find the people of *dhikr*"— who are the people of the *Qur'ân,* those who are [truly] recalling the *Qur'ân*[60]—they do not give precedence to anyone from the sessions of *dhikr* of those who are recalling [something] other than the *Qur'ân.* But if they do not find people recalling the *Qur'ân* and they do find people recalling God—not just reciting—then they come to sit with them and "they call out to each other:'Come quickly to what you all desire!'" because that [remembrance of God] is their sustenance; through it they flourish and in it they have their life.

Now since the Imam knows that, he always keeps a group of people *reciting the Signs*[61] *of God throughout the night* (Qur'an 3:113) and the day. And we ourselves, when we were in Fez in the lands of the Maghreb, used to follow this practice, thanks to the agreement of companions favored by God, who listened to us and readily followed our counsel.[62] But when we no longer had them [with us] we thereby lost this pure [spiritual] work, which is the noblest and most sublime of the forms of [spiritual] sustenance.

So when we no longer had [companions] like those men, we began to take up the diffusion of knowledge,[63] because of those [angelic] spirits whose food is [spiritual] knowledge. And we saw that there was not a single thing we set forth that did not spring from this Source that is sought by this spiritual kind [of angels], which is the *Qur'ân.* Hence everything about which we speak, both in my [teaching] sessions and in my writings, comes only from the presence of the *Qur'ân* and Its treasures.[64] I was given the keys of Its understanding and divine support *(imdâd)* from It—all of this so that we might not swerve from It.[65]

For this is the loftiest [spiritual knowledge] that can be bestowed on one, and no one can know its full worth except for the person who has actually tasted it in experience and directly witnessed its rank as a [spiritual] state within himself, the person to whom the True One *(al-Haqq)* has spoken it in his innermost being *(sirr)*. For when it is the True One Who speaks to His servant in his innermost being after all the intermediaries have been lifted away[66]—then the understanding is immediate and inseparable from His speaking to you, so that the [divine] speaking itself *is* identical with your understanding of it. The understanding does not follow after it—and if it does come after it, then that is not God's speaking.

Thus whoever does not find this [immediate spiritual understanding within himself] does not have [true] knowledge of God's speaking to His servants. And if God should speak to him through the veil of a form—whether with the tongue of a prophet or whoever else in the world He may wish—then the understanding of that [divine] speech may accompany it or it may come later.[67] So this is the difference between the two [i.e., between direct divine inspiration and its mediated transmission].

 6-b. *The role of the Mahdi—or rather of the "Imam of the Time"*[68]*—with regard to "the sensible forms of divine sustenance" concerns his unique, divinely inspired ability (resembling that of the Prophet) to decide what material goods of this world should rightfully "belong" to each believer, since individuals can only be at best the temporary "owners" (or more properly speaking, "custodians") of those earthly goods.* "Since everything in the world is divine sustenance and part of 'What God has left,'[69] the Imam judges with regard to (allocating) it in accordance with the judgment *(hukm)* God sends down to him concerning it." *In the meanwhile, Ibn 'Arabî advises, we should act* "according to the divine commandment which the divinely prescribed law *(shar')* has conveyed to us," *while abstaining from judgment in all other cases.*

7. As for the "knowledge of the interpenetration of things"...,[70] that [reality] inwardly penetrates and informs all the practical and intellectual crafts.[71] Therefore if the Imam knows this, he will not be bothered by doubt and uncertainty in his judgments. For this [precise inner awareness of the interpenetration of spiritual and manifest reality] is the Scale [of divine justice] in the world, both in sensible things and in the inner spiritual meanings *(ma'ânî)*. So the

rational, responsible person[72] behaves according to that Scale in both worlds—and indeed in every matter where he has control over his actions.

But as for those who judge in accordance with the divine inspiration *(wahy)* that [God] has sent down, those to whom [that inspiration] has been delivered *(ahl al-ilqâ')*[73] among the [prophetic] Messengers and those like them [i.e., the saints], they did not depart from [their inner awareness of] this interpenetration [of spiritual and material being]. Thus God made them the receptacle (of revelation) for that part of His judgment concerning His servants which he delivered to them, [as] He said: *"The Faithful Spirit brought down (the revelation) upon your heart"* (Qur'an 26:193-94), and *"He sends down the angels with the Spirit from His Command upon whomever He wishes among His servants"* (Qur'an 16:2).

Therefore every judgment [or command: *hukm*] concerning the world that is made manifest through a [divine] Messenger is the outcome of a "spiritual marriage";[74] this [essential spiritual inspiration underlying the judgment] is not in the textual indications and not in those who judge on the basis of analogy *(qiyâs)*.[75] Hence it is incumbent on the Imam that he know what is [learned] through being sent down by God [through divine inspiration] and what is [ordinarily supposed] through analogy. However the Mahdi does not know this—I mean the knowledge acquired by analogy—in order to pass judgment according to it, but only so that he can *avoid* it! For the Mahdi only judges according to what the angel delivers to him *from what is with God* (Qur'an 2:89, etc.), [the inspiration] God has sent him in order to guide him rightly.

So that is the *true* Muhammadan *Shar'*[76]—the one such that Muhammad, if he were alive [on earth] and that particular case were presented to him, would pass judgment on it in exactly the same way as this Imam. For God will teach him [by inspiration] that this is the Muhammadan *Shar'* and will therefore forbid him [to follow judgments arrived at by] analogical reasoning, despite the existence of the textual indications[77] God has bestowed on him. And this is why God's Messenger said, in describing the Mahdi, that "He follows in the trace of my footsteps, and he makes no mistake." Through this he informed us that [the Mahdi] is a follower [of the Prophet], not one who is followed [i.e., not a Messenger with a new revealed Law], and that he is [divinely] protected from error *(ma'sûm)*[78]—since the only [possible] meaning of someone's being protected from error is that they do not make mistakes. Thus if the Messenger [i.e., Muhammad] pronounced a judgment [in some matter], no mistake is ascribed to him, since *"he does not speak from passion, but it is only an inspiration* [wahy] *inspired in him"* (Qur'an 53:3-4); and likewise analogical reasoning is not permissible in a place where the Messenger is to be found.

Now the Prophet *does* exist and *is* to be found [here and now] with the People of Unveiling, and therefore they only take their [inspired understanding of the appropriate divine] judgment from him. This is the reason why the truthful and sincere *faqîr*[79] doesn't depend on any [legal] school: he is *with* the Messenger [i.e., Muhammad] alone, whom he directly witnesses, just as the Messenger is with the divine inspiration *(wahy)* that is sent down to him. Thus the notification of the [appropriate divine] judgment concerning the particular events and cases is sent down from God to the hearts of the truthful and sincere true knowers, [informing them] that this is the judgment of the *Shar'* that was sent with the Messenger of God.

But those adhering to knowledge of the external forms [of religious tradition][80] do not have this [spiritual] rank, because of their having devoted themselves to their love for [prominent social] position, the domination of others, [furthering] their precedence over God's servants[81] and [insuring that] the common people need them. Hence *they do not prosper* (Qur'an 16:16) with regard to their souls,[82] nor shall one prosper through [following] them. This is the [inner] condition of the jurists *(fuqahâ')* of [our] time, those who desire to be appointed to posts as judges, notaries, inspectors or professors. As for those of them who cunningly hide themselves in [the guise of] Religion *(al-dîn)*—those who hunch their shoulders and look at people furtively, with a pretense of humility; who move their lips as though in *dhikr,*[83] so that the person looking at them will know they are performing *dhikr;* who speak obscurely and in an affected manner—they are dominated by the weaknesses of the carnal self and "their hearts are the hearts of wolves," [so that] *God does not [speak to them nor] look at them* (Qur'an 3:77-78).[84] This is the condition of those among them who make a show of religion—not those who are the companions of Satan (Qur'an 4:38; 43:36). These [outwardly pious hypocrites] "dressed up for the people in the skins of gentle sheep"[85]: [they are] brothers outwardly and enemies inwardly and secretly. But God will examine them and *take them by their forelocks* (Qur'an 55:41; 96:15-16) to that [level of Hell] which contains their happiness.[86]

Thus when the Mahdi comes forth [to establish justice in the world] he has no *open enemy* (Qur'an 2:188, etc.) except for the jurists in particular. For then they will no longer have any power of domination and will not be distinguished from the mass of common people, and they will only keep a slight knowledge of [the divine] commandment, since the differences concerning the commandments will be eliminated in this world because of the existence of this Imam.

However, if the Mahdi did not have the sword [of worldly authority] in his hand, then the jurists would all deliver legal opinions [demanding] that he be killed. But instead [as stated in the hadith] "God will bring him forth with the sword and noble character" and they will be greedy [for his support] and fearful, so that they will [outwardly] accept his judgment without having any faith in it; indeed they will grudgingly conceal their disagreement, just as do [the two legal schools of] the Hanafites and Shafiites concerning those matters where they disagree. For in fact it has been reported to us that the followers of these two schools in the lands of the non-Arabs [i.e., Iran and Transoxiana] are constantly fighting one another and that a great many people of both groups have died—that [they go to such extremes that] they even break the fast during the month of Ramadan in order to be stronger for their battles.[87]

So people like this, if the Imam-Mahdi did not conquer with the sword, would not pay any attention to him and would not obey him [even] in their outward actions, just as they do not obey him in their hearts. In fact what they [really] believe about him if he makes a judgment involving them that is contrary to their school, is that he has gone astray with regard to that judgment, because they believe that the period of the people of *ijtihâd*[88] has ended [long ago], that there remains no *mujtahid* in the world and that after the death of their [founding] imams God has not brought anyone into existence in the world with the rank of *ijtihâd.*

And as for the person who claims to be divinely informed about the judgments prescribed by the *Shar'*, for [these jurists] such a person is a madman whose imagination has gone wild, and they would pay no attention to him. But if such a person happens to possess wealth and worldly power *(sultân)*, then they will submit to him outwardly because of their coveting his wealth and their fear of his power, although inwardly they have no faith in him at all.

8. Now as for "striving to one's utmost and going to any length to satisfy the needs of mankind" that is especially incumbent upon the Imam in particular, even more than [it is] for the rest of the people. For God only gave him precedence over His [other] creatures and appointed him as their Imam so that he could strive to achieve what is beneficial for them. This striving and what results from it are both prodigious....

In the intervening passage (III 336.16-25) *Ibn 'Arabî illustrates the essential theme of this section—that it is above all by striving for the welfare of others, in the midst of the responsibilities of "ordinary" life, and not in seeking to obtain what one imagines to be special powers or experiences for oneself, that the individual is most likely to reach the highest spiritual stages*[89]*—with the Qur'anic account* (28:29ff.) *of Moses' having unintentionally discovered God, without consciously looking for Him, precisely in the theophanic form of the burning bush he was seeking in order to warm his family. For Ibn 'Arabî, who repeatedly insists on the fact that Moses was only seeking to fulfill the needs of his family,* "this verse constitutes an admonition from God *[tanbîh min al-Haqq]* concerning the value of this [spiritual virtue] for God."[90]

Now the activities of all of the just Imams are only for the sake of others, not for their own sake. Hence if you see a ruler busying himself with something other than his subjects and their needs, then you should know that his [high] rank has cut him off from this activity [of true leadership], so that there is no [real] difference between him and the mass of common people *(al-'âmma)*....[91]

And Khadir...[92] was also like this. He was in an army, and the commander of the army sent him to explore for water for them, since they were in need of water. That was how he fell into the Fountain of Life and drank from it, so that he has remained living up until now, for he was not aware [before setting out on his search] of that Life through which God distinguishes the person who drinks of that Water...,[93] since this Fountain of Life [is] Water through which God distinguishes with [spiritual] Life the person who drinks that Water. Then he returned to his companions and told them about the water, and all the people rushed off toward that place in order to drink from it. But God turned their sight away from it so that they were not capable of [attaining] it. And this is what resulted for him from his striving for the sake of others.

...Thus no one knows what is their rank[94] with God, because absolutely all of their actions are for the sake of God, not for their own sake, since they prefer God to what their [bodily and psychic] nature demands.

9. As for "possessing the knowledge of the Unseen *('ilm al-ghayb)* that he requires for [rightly governing] this engendered world in particular during a particular period of time," this is the ninth matter which the Imam requires for his leadership, and there are no [others] besides these.

This is because God informed [us] concerning Himself that *"every Day He is in an affair"* (Qur'an 55:29), and that "affair"[95] is whatever the state of the world is that day.

Now obviously when that "affair" becomes manifest in [external] existence [everyone] recognizes that it is known by whoever witnesses it. But this Imam, because of this matter [i.e., his inspired foreknowledge of events], is well-informed by God *(al-Haqq)* concerning those affairs which He wishes to bring into temporal being *before* they actually occur in [external] existence. For he is informed about that affair on the "day" *before* it occurs. So if that affair contains something beneficial for his subjects he thanks God and remains silent about it. But if it contains a punishment [in the form of] the sending down of some widespread affliction or one aimed at certain specific persons, then he implores God on their behalf, intercedes [with Him] and begs [Him]. So God, in His Mercy and Bounty, averts that affliction from them [before it actually happens] and answers [the Mahdi's] prayer and petition.[96]

This is why God (first of all) informs him about [each event] before it occurs to his fellows in actual existence. Then after that God informs him, with regard to those "affairs," about the [particular] events that will occur to [specific] individuals and specifies for him those individuals with all their outward particularities, so that if he should see those individuals [in the material world] he would not doubt that they were exactly the one he saw [in this inspired vision]. And finally God informs him about the divinely prescribed judgment appropriate for that event, the [same standard of] judgment which God prescribed for His Prophet Muhammad to apply in judging that event.[97] Hence he only judges according to that [divinely inspired] judgment, so that [in the words of the hadith] "he never makes a mistake."

Thus if God does not show [the Mahdi] the judgment regarding certain events and he does not experience any inner unveiling [of that divine judgment], then God's aim was to include those events [or "cases"] in the judgment of what is [religiously] permissible,[98] so that he knows from the absence of any [divine] specification [of a particular judgment] that this is the judgment of the divinely prescribed Law *(shar')* concerning that event. Thus he is divinely protected *(ma'sûm)* from personal opinion *(ra'y)* and analogy *(qiyâs)* in Religion.

For [the use of] analogy [to extend the law beyond God's explicit commandments] by whoever is not a prophet amounts to passing judgment on God concerning *the Religion of God* (Qur'an 3:83, etc.)[99] on the basis of something that person does not [really] know. This is because analogy [involves] extending a [hypothetical] "reason" [underlying a particular judgment to all other "analogous" cases].[100] *But what makes you know?—perhaps* (Qur'an 80:3)[101] God does not want to extend that reason; for if He had wanted to do that He would have clearly stated it through the voice of His Messenger and would have ordered this extension, if indeed the [underlying] "reason" were among what was specifically ordained by the divinely prescribed Law *(shar')* in a particular [legal] case. So what do you suppose [is the validity] of the "reason" that the jurist extracts [from an action or saying of the Prophet] all by himself and through his own reasoning, without its having been mentioned by the divinely prescribed Law in any specific textual stipulation concerning that? [Or about the jurist who] then, having deduced this "reason," extends it generally [to what he arbitrarily assumes to be the "analogous" cases]? Indeed this is one arbitrary judgment on top of another judgment concerning a "divine law" *(shar')* *of which God is unaware*[102] (Qur'an 52:21)!

So this is what prevents the Mahdi from speaking on the basis of [this sort of factitious] analogy[103] concerning the *Religion of God*—all the more so because he also knows that the intention of the Prophet was to lighten the burden of [religious] obligation *(taklîf)* on his community.[104] That was why the Prophet used to say, *"Leave me alone [i.e., without requesting any further religious precepts] so long as I leave you alone,"*[105] and why he used to dislike being questioned about religion, out of fear of [unnecessarily] increasing the [divine] commandments *(ahkâm)*.

Therefore in everything about which nothing is said to him [by God] and concerning which he is not informed [by God] about a specific, definite judgment, he establishes the [divine] judgment concerning it, in natural consequence, [to be] the primordial judgment.[106] And every [judgment] of which God informs him through inner unveiling and [an inspired] "notification" *(ta'rîf)* is the judgment of the [eternal] Muhammadan *shar'*[107] concerning that matter.

...Therefore the Mahdi is a mercy, just as God's Messenger was a mercy, (as) God said: *"And We only sent you as a mercy to the worlds"* (Qur'an 21:107).

...Now these nine things are not combined all together for any Imam among the leaders of Religion and the viceregents of God and His Prophet until the Day of the Rising, except for this Rightly guided Imam *(al-Imâm al-Mahdî)*....[108]

The Forms of Knowledge Typifying This Spiritual Stage[109]

Each of the 114 chapters concerning the spiritual "stages" (fasl al-manâzil, chapters 270-383) concludes with a long list of the forms of spiritual knowledge or awareness "belonging" to that stage, usually described in a series of cryptic expressions that may relate symbolically to the corresponding Sura of the Qur'an (al-Khaf in this case). Although in most cases the exact inner connection between those descriptions and the rest of the chapter (or its corresponding Sura) is not readily apparent, a few of the longer descriptions in this chapter clearly do illuminate some of the preceding discussions. And quite apart from those internal connections, the immediacy of the first three descriptions in particular—whose poignant contrast between our ordinary ways of perceiving the world and the touchstone of certain rarer moments of epiphany may find an echo in each reader's experience—should suggest something of the deeper practical relevance of Ibn 'Arabî's spiritual insights here.

...In this [spiritual stage] there is a knowledge which removes the burden of anguish from the soul of the person who knows it.[110] For when one looks at what is ordinarily the case with [men's] souls, the way that all the things happening to them cause them such anguish and distress, [it is enough] to make a person want to kill himself[111] because of what he sees. This knowledge is called the "knowledge of blissful repose" *('ilm al-râha)*, because it is the knowledge of the People of the Garden [of Paradise] in particular. So whenever God reveals this knowledge to one of the people of this world [already] in this world,[112] that person has received in advance the blissful repose of eternity—although the person with this quality [in this world] still continues to respect the appropriate courtesy[113] [towards God] concerning the commandment of what is right and the prohibition of what is wrong, according to his rank.

And in this stage is the knowledge that what God made manifest to [men's] vision in the bodies [of all things in this world] is an adornment for those bodies; [the knowledge] of why it is that some of what is manifest seems ugly to a particular person when he regards it as ugly; and [the knowledge] of *which* eye it is that a person sees with when he sees the whole world as beautiful,[114] when he does see it, so that he responds to it spontaneously with beautiful actions.[115] Now this knowledge is one of the most beautiful [or "best"] and most beneficial forms of knowledge about the world, and it [corresponds to] what some of the theologians say about this, that "there is no Actor but God, and all of His Acts are beautiful".[116] Therefore these people [i.e., those who "see things as they really are"] do not consider ugly any of God's Acts except for what God [calls or makes] ugly and that is up to Him [to decide], not to them, since if they did not consider ugly what God has called so they would be disputing with God.[117]

This stage also includes knowledge of what God has placed in the world as [an object for] marvel and the "marvelous" [as men usually understand it] is only what breaks with the habitual [course of things].[118] But for those who comprehend things from the divine perspective, *every* thing in this "habitual" course is itself an object of marvel, whereas the "people of habits" only wonder at what departs from that habitual course.

...And in this stage there is a kind of knowledge among the things known [only] by inner unveiling. This is that the person experiencing this "unveiling" knows that every person or group, however large or small, inevitably has with them one of the men of the Unseen[119] whenever they are speaking. Then that individual [among the men of the Unseen] spreads reports about those persons in the rest of the world so that people discover those things in their own souls, [for example] when a group is gathered together in [spiritual] retreat or when a man says something to himself that [presumably] only God knows. Then that man or that group [who have discovered these reports in this mysterious fashion] go out and tell people about it so that [soon] people are all talking about it.

Ibn 'Arabî goes on, in a long excursus (338.35-339.19) to cite two personal experiences illustrating this phenomenon. The first (in the year 590)[120] *was when he ran into a man in Seville who recited to him several verses that Ibn 'Arabî himself had composed, but never committed to writing, at a particular place in Tunis one night several months before. Not knowing Ibn 'Arabî's identity, the man went on to explain that he had learned the poem in a Sufi gathering outside Seville, on the very night Ibn 'Arabî had composed them, from a mysterious stranger* "whom we did not know, as though he were one of the 'Travelers.'" [121] *After teaching his companions those verses, the mysterious stranger went on to tell them the full name of the author and even to give them the name and exact location of the particular quarter in Tunis where he had heard them—which was precisely where Ibn 'Arabî had been staying that same night. On the second occasion, also in Seville, Ibn 'Arabî was listening to a Sufi friend praising* "one of the greatest of the people of the [Sufi] Path, whom he had met in Khorasan" *(in Persia), when he noticed a stranger nearby who remained invisible to the rest of the group and who said to him:* "I am that very person whom this man who met with us in Khorasan is describing to you." *Then Ibn ʿArabî began describing this otherwise invisible stranger—who continued to sit there beside them—to his friend, who confirmed the exactitude of his description of the Persian master.*

And this stage includes the knowledge of what sort of arguing [concerning the practice and principles of religion] is praiseworthy and what sort is to be condemned.[122] Someone who has [truly] surrendered [to God] among those who depend on God[123] should not argue except concerning what he has had confirmed and realized [through God] by way of inner unveiling *(kashf)*, not on the basis of [his own] thinking and inquiry. So if he has actually witnessed [as a direct inspiration from God] that about which they are arguing, then in that event it is incumbent on him to argue about it *using that which is better* (Qur'an 29:46)[124]—provided that he has been specifically ordered to do so by a divine command. But if he does not have a divine command to do so, then the choice is up to him.

Thus if the task of helping the other person [by convincing him of] that [revealed insight] has been assigned to him [by God], then he has been entrusted with that mission for him. But if he despairs of his listeners' ever accepting what he has to say, then he should shut up and not argue. For if he should argue [with no real hope of affecting his listeners], then he is [really] striving to bring about their perdition with God.[125]

LESSER AND GREATER RESURRECTION

James W. Morris

LESSER AND GREATER RESURRECTION

AN INTRODUCTION

If all of Ibn 'Arabî's writing (and the Futûhât in particular) can best be seen as a single vast commentary on the spiritual dimensions of the Qur'an and hadith, nowhere is this more obviously the case than in his treatment of the elaborate eschatological symbolism to be found throughout those scriptures.[1] But the role of those "last" or ultimate things, especially in the Qur'an, is so fundamental and all-pervasive that even the most apparently mundane aspects of this worldly life are always viewed from within that eschatological perspective, in the light of man's Source and ultimate spiritual destiny: the eschaton (al-âkhira), is presented not simply as some other, "later" series of "events," but rather as the ever-present divine framework and context at once Source and destination of man's life in this "nearer" or "lower" world (al-dunyâ).[2] For that life, truly perceived, is nothing else but man's "return" to a full and awakened awareness of his primordial reality: thus "true faith in God and the Last Day" are repeatedly mentioned as the two essential and inextricable aspects of man's awareness of this comprehensive reality that already defines and constitutes each individual's metaphysical situation. The hundreds of Qur'anic verses alluding more specifically and vividly to the Day of Resurrection, the Gardens of Paradise, or the hellfires, and other torments of Gehenna are themselves only *more particular reminders of this all-encompassing eschatological dimension of man's being.*

The extent to which this comprehensive, metaphysically determinate eschatological perspective is also shared by Ibn 'Arabî, whose understanding of this aspect of the Qur'anic message of course builds on many generations of earlier Sufi (and other, less mystical) interpreters,[3] is perhaps most clearly revealed in the following key passage from one of his most accessible short treatises, the Risâlat al-Anwâr,[4] *in which the Shaykh outlines the fundamental "realms of being" or spiritual and ontological "homelands"* (mawâtin) *that together constitute the total field of being and experience of the Perfect Man*[5]:

"Now these [ontological] realms, although they are [quite] numerous, come down to six: the first is the realm of *'Am I not your Lord?'*[6] (Qur'an 7:172), and we have already become separated from it; the second is the realm of the 'lower world' *(al-dunyâ)* in which we are right now; the third is the realm of the *barzakh* (Qur'an 23:100) to which we go after the lesser and greater deaths[7]; the fourth is the realm of the Raising [of the dead] on the 'Earth of the Awakening' (Qur'an 79:14) and 'the return to the Original State' (Qur'an 79:10)[8]; the fifth is the realm of the Garden [of Paradise] and the Fire [of Hell][9]; and the sixth is the realm of the Dune [of the 'Visit' and beatific vision of God], outside the Garden."[10]

Thus these last four "eschatological" realms, for Ibn 'Arabî, in fact constitute by far the greater part of manifest reality and potential experience. And for him, their full spiritual apprehension—not as a theory or system of concepts, but through the profound inner "realization" of their living presence accomplished by those rare saints (and prophets) who have followed the spiritual path through to its end—is no doubt the most essential part of any true, comprehensive understanding of the nature of God and man. So it is not surprising if his initial "systematic" discussions of each of those realms (in chapters 61–65, and all of them together in the long chapter 371), far from being exhaustive, are in reality only a sort of preamble outlining the full range of scriptural indications and his personal principles of interpretation insights that are subsequently actually applied (and implied) throughout the Futûhât. In fact, as readers can easily verify even within this anthology, almost every chapter of that work contains numerous allusions to the "eschatological" realities and dimensions of existence; and indeed Ibn 'Arabî is often much more explicit about the personal, experiential aspects of his own eschatological insights and interpretations precisely in such otherwise unexpected contexts.[11]

Because the adequate translation and commentary of those few chapters alone would require a good-sized book,[12] we have limited ourselves here to a representative selection of several shorter passages that do bring out quite clearly some of the essential themes and interpretive principles that appear and are applied in virtually all of Ibn 'Arabî's discussions of eschatological questions. In addition, given the importance of the "other world" and afterlife in the Qur'an and hadith as a whole, these readings likewise offer a superb illustration of Ibn 'Arabî's distinctive approach to understanding and interpreting Islamic scripture more generally. And finally, in light of the highly enigmatic character of many of those scriptural symbols in themselves combined with the even more problematic character (for the wider public, at least) of any claims to know the true nature of the other world and what lies beyond the grave—Ibn 'Arabî's treatment of these eschatological questions raises to the greatest possible degree those complex issues of the saints' spiritual realization of these divine "secrets" ('ilm al-asrâr) and their problematic written expression which he evoked in a critical passage of his introduction to the Futûhât as a whole.[13]

Now there are three equally fundamental aspects or "levels" of Ibn 'Arabî's understanding of the scriptural symbols of Islamic eschatology (both from the Qur'an and hadith): 1. the "literal" scriptural expressions and descriptions of those realities; 2. the "microcosmic" aspect of their immediate experiential realization by each individual, whether in the initiatic "voluntary return," the "lesser death," or in the "obligatory return" shared by all men; and 3. the more complex "macrocosmic" dimensions of that reality in terms of the other essential cosmological and metaphysical principles of Ibn 'Arabî's—thought principles which, for him, are themselves likewise grounded both in revealed scriptural indications and in their *corresponding personal spiritual realization and verification* (tahqîq). *But although these three basic interpretive dimensions can be described or analyzed separately—and indeed must be, for modern readers who are likely to be equally unacquainted with each of these perspectives—it is also true that in Ibn 'Arabî's own thought they are ultimately inseparable aspects of a single unified vision, corresponding to the essential unity of the Reality in question. However, as we shall see below, that comprehensive eschatological vision is intentionally set forth in such a way, throughout the* Futûhât, *that its unity and inner integrity can only become fully apparent to those devoted readers who are willing and able to undertake the difficult practical and intellectual efforts required to retrace the author's own footsteps.*

To begin with, it must be stressed that Ibn 'Arabî's distinctive "spiritual literalism" in his understanding of the language of the Qur'an and hadith—whether with regard to eschatology or any other subject—is something quite different from those widespread (and often largely "fictional") popular narrative and interpretive assumptions that underlie what are commonly taken to be the "literal" meanings of these verses.[14] *For Ibn 'Arabî, the literal terms of the Qur'an (or hadith) precisely are the fullest, most appropriate possible expression of the spiritual realities or intentions in question.*[15] *As a result, his typical procedure of scriptural interpretation almost always assumes the closest possible attention to the exact Arabic language and precise context of the verse in question—to such a degree that (as can be seen throughout this anthology) extensive background commentary is usually required to elucidate those specific linguistic and contextual elements in each interpretation. Thus, although the popular, narrative connection and sequence of the eschatological "events" and "places" is assumed throughout chapters 61-65, that outline only provides the framework for further detailed discussions of particular verses and symbols scattered throughout the* Futûhât *(including the shorter passages translated below). Still another consequence of this approach is Ibn 'Arabî's strict focus on the Qur'an and hadith, to the exclusion of the further legendary embellishments and spectacular imagery that tended to predominate in the more popular later accounts.*[16] *And finally, an equally essential facet of Ibn 'Arabî's approach to scripture is his consistent focus on the profound spiritual and metaphysical dimensions of the eschatological reality—dimensions that are often obscured by the more obvious "moralizing" and ethical aims that are the usual focus of attention in the popular depictions of Paradise and Hell (whether in Islam or other religious traditions). A frequent consequence of this characteristic spiritual perspective is that it brings out the fundamental "eschatological" meaning and import of many Qur'anic verses and incidents that would not ordinarily be seen in that light, at least in the popular imagination.*[17]

The second essential aspect of Ibn 'Arabî's approach to Islamic eschatology, and one in which he of course builds on the insights and experience of many generations of earlier Sufis and Islamic thinkers, is his reliance on the personal realization of these "eschatological" dimensions of reality by the saints and "people of unveiling" already in this life. This microcosmic "lesser death" (and concomitant spiritual rebirth) or "voluntary return" is, at the very least, a powerful prefiguration and confirmation of that "Lesser Resurrection" (al-qiyâmat al-sughrâ) *which otherwise begins with each person's physical, "obligatory" death.*[18] *The passages of the* Futûhât *selected below (from chapters 73, 302, 351 and 369) all tend to bring out this fundamental experiential focus of Ibn 'Arabî's eschatological thought. Of course Ibn 'Arabî himself constantly refers as well to the many hadith and Qur'anic verses (e.g., 44:56-57; 39:42; 2:154; etc.) which provided the classical justification for (and exhortation to) this more direct approach to the inner meaning of the symbols of the Last Day.*[19]

The third—and probably the most mysterious and complex—governing dimension of Ibn 'Arabî's understanding of Islamic eschatology is its "macrocosmic" integration within the larger schema of his cosmological and metaphysical conceptions.[20] *Since his spiritual cosmology is itself likewise closely based on both the scriptural indications of Qur'an and hadith and a corresponding experiential realization, but in this case expressed in terms of the accepted astronomical and cosmological theories of his day, it is often especially difficult for the modern reader to tell, in any given context, which one of those planes of reference is primarily in question—or in other words, whether allusions to that cosmology (e.g., topics involving various astrological or cosmic "cycles" of time) are meant to be taken mainly as symbols (i.e., of some corresponding* spiritual reality and experience) or as "science." The ambiguities and uncertainties this creates become especially evident when one tries to reconcile or integrate what Ibn 'Arabî describes from this macrocosmic point of view with the relatively more familiar microcosmic perspective and experience of the individual human being. And in some cases, at least, the resulting ambiguities are almost certainly intentional.[21]

In the selections translated below, for example, this interpretive problem is posed most frequently by Ibn 'Arabî's recurring contrast between the "Lesser Resurrection" of the individual (following immediately upon either his physical death or spiritual rebirth), which is the primary subject of those passages, and what he variously calls without any further clarification here the "Greater" Resurrection, Gathering, Hour, Reviewing, Visit, etc.[22] Now in the popular, "exoteric" understanding of these Qur'anic symbols, such expressions would present no real problem: the "Lesser Resurrection" would be the period each individual spends in the "tomb" (or the barzakh, etc.) until the Day (and "Hour") of the "Greater," universal Resurrection when all men are brought together before God in judgment. This relatively straightforward temporal conception of the sequence of eschatological "events," as we have indicated, is also largely assumed throughout the initial presentation of the scriptural descriptions of the eschatological realms in chapters 61-65. But elsewhere—most notably in his encounters with Adam and Idrîs during the autobiographical spiritual Ascension described in chapter 367 (sections IV-B and IV-E of our translation here)—Ibn 'Arabî indirectly suggests another, rather different way of conceiving this relationship. There Idrîs openly states that "I do not know any period at the close of which the universe as a whole comes to an end"; and he likewise indicates that since "the abode of Being is one: it does not become 'nearer' [dunyâ] except through you, and the 'other world' [al-âkhira] is not distinguished from it except through you," the "Hour" has perhaps already "drawn near" to man ever since the very creation of Adam.[23]

From this perspective, then, the relation of the "Lesser" and "Greater" Resurrections is not that of two different sorts of reality, but rather of the range of individual movements or partial perspectives within a much larger, all-encompassing Whole. This *possibility, which was of course expressed more openly by other Sufi (and philosophic) writers, could be further corroborated by Ibn 'Arabî's many remarks, in other contexts, concerning the different meanings—psychic, spiritual, cosmic, etc.—of "time" (zamân).*[24] *However, this conception of the full range of eschatological reality as being potentially in direct relation to each soul is in itself less an "answer" than a further opening, a point of view suggesting any number of possible conceptions of man's destiny, the true "sites" of Heaven and Hell, and so on. Ibn 'Arabî's relative reluctance to more openly evoke those possibilities (or realities) could be interpreted in several ways: as a realistic avowal of man's ignorance and uncertainty concerning such ultimate things; as a prudent concession to more orthodox opinion; or as the intentional concealment of those "divine secrets," surpassing ordinary understanding and therefore reserved for the "quintessence of the elite," which he mentions so pointedly at the very beginning of the* Futûhât.[25]

In any case, Ibn 'Arabî clearly indicates to his more discerning readers that any satisfactory "answer" to these further questions, any lasting resolution of this truly ultimate uncertainty, is not to be found on the plane of concepts (nor, a fortiori, in an attitude of blind acceptance of traditional beliefs), but rather in that rare condition of inner openness and constant spiritual attention and practical effort which (as he describes it in selection V below) is the distinguishing mark of the true "Knowers of God," those who have already "visited the graves."[26] *That insistent openness to spiritual experience (in each soul's ongoing inner dialogue with belief and the forms of revelation), so beautifully illustrated in each of the passages translated below, is one of the most characteristic features of Ibn 'Arabî's writing more generally—and a trait which at the same time strikingly distinguishes his work from that of so many of his commentators and predecessors (whether they be Sufis, philosophers or* mutakallimûn*).*

THE SOUL'S RETURN

CHAPTER 302

The first half of chapter 302 is concerned with the proper understanding of the metaphysical relations of the worlds of ghayb *and* shahâda: *the "visible" world must be understood in its true condition as the manifestation of the "unseen," governed by its spiritual forms and continuously "returning" to its creative Source in the spiritual realm. The passage translated here is immediately preceded by an illustration of one aspect of this broader reality: the relations of the human "spirits" to their physical forms in the visible world. There Ibn 'Arabî strongly denies that men's individual spiritual forms are determined by their physical "constitution"* (mizâj); *instead, "the spirits are distinguished by their (own individual) forms" before they are joined with their bodies.*[27] *This discussion inevitably leads, in the passage translated here, to the question of the eschatological "return" of those spirits after the separation from their earthly bodies.*

After passing in review some alternative conceptions (which would tend to minimize the spiritual responsibility of each individual and the full reality of the Last Judgment and other scriptural promises), Ibn 'Arabî alludes to his own characteristic understanding of the individual's ongoing spiritual development, until the universal "greater Resurrection," in the intermediate, imaginal world (the barzakh)—*a conception that is amply illustrated elsewhere in his numerous descriptions of personal encounters with the souls or spiritual entities of prophets, saints and others in that realm. In fact, as he goes on to point out (following a number of famous hadith already mentioned in our introduction), the inner realities of the "unseen," spiritual world—including Paradise and Hell—are always present and already visible to the people of unveiling* (ahl al-kashf), *those who have awakened their spiritual senses. He concludes with scriptural citations that forcefully emphasize the full universality of this situation—and at the same time suggest the corresponding aims of revelation:*

…God's Messenger said: "If…there were no confusion in your hearts, then you would see what I see and hear what I hear." [For] God said: *"[…We sent down to you the Reminder] so that you might make clear to the people what was sent down to them (already)"* (Qur'an 16:44). Now what could be more straightforward than this clear declaration [i.e., through the Qur'an and the Prophet]? But where is the person who opens up the place [of his heart in order] to receive the influences of his Lord…? Such a one is rare indeed![28]

Translation:[29]

As for when the spirits are separated from these material supports [of their physical bodies], one group of our fellows say that the spirits become completely separate from these materials and return to their Source, just as the sun's rays [that happen to be] reflected by a polished mirror return to the sun [i.e., do not disappear] if the mirror becomes tarnished. But these people had two different ways of conceiving this. One group of them said that the spirits were not [individually] distinguishable after their separation from their bodies, any more than the water in jars along the banks of a river can be distinguished from the water of the river once those jars have broken and their water has returned to the river. So (men's) bodies are [like] those containers, and the river water that filled them is like [their] spirits in relation to the Universal Spirit.

Now another group of them said that, on the contrary, these spirits do acquire good or bad dispositions through their proximity to the body, so that they continue to be distinguished by those dispositions when they are separated from their bodies. It is as though those jars contained things that changed that water from its [original] condition with regard to its color, taste or smell, so that when it is removed from those jars it still retains in itself the color, taste or smell it acquired: similarly God preserves those acquired dispositions in the spirits. And in this respect this group were in agreement with some of the philosophers.[30]

Another group said that the governing spirits never cease governing in this world,[31] so when they are transferred to the intermediate world *(barzakh)* they continue to govern bodies in that world—and these are [like] the form in which a person sees himself in dreams. Hence death is also like that, and this is what is symbolized by the "Trumpet."[32] Then the spirits are raised up on the day of Resurrection in their physical bodies, as they were in this world.

This is the extent of the disagreement among our fellows concerning the spirits after their separation [from the physical body]. As for the different views concerning this matter of those who are not our fellows, they are numerous—but our purpose is not to mention [all] the sayings of those who are not on our path.

Know, my brother—may God guide and protect you with His mercy—that the Garden which is attained by those who are among its people in the other world is [already] visible to you *today* with respect to its place, though not its form. So you are *in* the Garden, transformed, in whatever state you happen to be, but you don't *know* you are in it, because you are veiled from it by the form in which it manifests itself to you! Now the people of unveiling, who perceive what is unseen by ordinary men, do see that place: if it is the Garden [of paradise], then they see a green meadow; or if it is Gehenna, then they see it according to the traits of its bitter cold, burning winds, and the other things God has prepared in it.[33] And most of the people of unveiling see this at the beginning of the path.

Now the Revelation *(al-shar')* alluded to that in [Muhammad's] saying: *"Between my grave and this pulpit is one of the meadows of the Garden."*[34] So the people of unveiling see it as a meadow, just as he said; and they see the Nile, Euphrates, Sayhan and Jayhan as the rivers of honey, water, wine and milk in the Garden (Qur'an 47:15), as [Muhammad] said, since the Prophet reported that these rivers are part of the Garden.[35] But the person whose vision has not been unveiled by God, who remains blinded by his veil, cannot perceive that.[36] He is like a blind man in a park: he is not at all absent from it, yet he does not see it. But the fact that he does not see it does not imply that he is not in it; on the contrary, he really *is* in it.

The same is true of the places that God's Messenger mentioned as being part of the Fire [of hell], such as the valley of Muhassir at Mina and others; that is why he prescribed to his community that they should hurry when they leave there.[37] For he sees what they cannot see, and he witnesses what they do not. And some people share with him this unveiling, while others do not, depending on what God has willed concerning that, according to the wisdom He concealed in His creation. Do you not notice, for example, that when God protects persons of scrupulous piety from eating something [that is not outwardly] illicit, one of the signs warning them that that food is illicit is that in their vision it changes into the form of something [clearly] forbidden, such as blood or pork, for example, so that they find it impossible to eat it. Then when they inquire as to how that food was obtained they discover that it was not acquired in the [divinely] prescribed manner.[38]

Thus the people of God have eyes with which they see, ears with which they hear, hearts with which they understand, and tongues with which they speak, and all of them are different from the form of these [ordinary] eyes and ears and hearts and tongues. So it is with those eyes that they witness, with those ears that they listen, with those hearts that they understand, and with those tongues that they speak—and their words hit the mark. *For it is not the eyes that are blind* to the Truth and unable to grasp It, *but the hearts that are in their breasts* (Qur'an 22:46). They are *deaf, dumb, blind, so they do not take their understanding* (Qur'an 2:171) from God, *and so they do not return* (Qur'an 2:18) to God. By God, their eyes are in their faces, their hearing in their ears and their tongues in their mouths, but divine providence did not favor them, nor *were they destined for the Best Outcome* (Qur'an 21:101). So praise be to God in thankfulness for His having given us life through these hearts and tongues and eyes and ears![39]

THE VOLUNTARY DEATH

CHAPTER 351

The numerous Qur'anic verses and hadith underlying Ibn 'Arabî's conception of the "voluntary death" (mawt irâdî) and corresponding spiritual awakening or "rebirth" of the saints have already been mentioned in the introduction to these eschatological selections.[40] *As mentioned there, the many scattered references in the* Futûhât *to such experiences (and to the broader ontological perspective they presuppose) offer the most accessible —although often still extremely ambiguous—key to his understanding of the profound spiritual meaning and intentions of the complex symbols of Islamic eschatology. Nowhere is that distinctive approach more openly and personally stated than in the following (partially autobiographical) brief remarks from chapter 351.*

Translation:[41]

The voluntary return to God is something for which the servant is most thankful. God said: *"The whole affair is returned to Him"* (Qur'an 11:123). So since you know that, return to Him willingly and you will not be returned to Him by compulsion. For there is no escaping your return to Him, and you will surely have to meet Him, either willingly or against your will. For He meets you in [the form of] your attributes, nothing else but that—so examine your self, my friend! [The Prophet] said: *"Whoever loves to meet God, God loves to meet him; and whoever is averse to meeting God, God is averse to meeting him...."*[42]

Now since we knew that our meeting with God can only be through death,[43] and because we knew the inner meaning of death, we sought to bring it about sooner, in the life of this world. Hence we died, in the very Source of our life,[44] to all of our concerns and activities and desires, so that when death overcame us in the midst of that Life which never passes from us—inasmuch as we *are* that [Life] with which our selves and our limbs and every part of us glorifies and praises [God][45]—we met God and He met us. And ours was the case [mentioned in the hadith above] of "those who meet Him while loving to meet Him" [so that He loves to meet us].

Thus when there comes what is commonly known as death, and *the veil* of this body *is removed from* us (Qur'an 50:22), our state will not change and our certainty will not be any greater than what we already experience now. For we *tasted no death but the first death,* which we died during our life in this world, because our Lord *protected us from the torment of hell as a bounty from your Lord; that is the Supreme Achievement* (Qur'an 44:56-57). [As the Imam] 'Alî said: "Even if the veil were removed, I would not be any more certain."[46]

So the person who returns to God in this way is among the blessed, and he does not even feel the inevitable, compulsory return [of physical] death, because it only comes to him when he is already there with God. The most that what is [ordinarily] known as death can mean for him is that his soul, which is with God, is kept from governing this body that it used to govern, so that the soul remains with God, in its same condition, while that body reverts to its origin, *the dust* from which it was formed (Qur'an 3:59, etc.). For it was a house whose occupant has traveled away; then *the King* established that person *with Him in a firm position* (Qur'an 54:55) *until the Day they are raised* (Qur'an 23:100, etc.). And his condition when he is raised up will be just like that: it will not change insofar as his being with God is concerned, nor with regard to what God gives him at every instant.[47]

It is also like this in the general Gathering (*al-hashr al-'âmm* [on the Day of Resurrection]) and in the Gardens [of Paradise] which are this person's residence and dwelling place, and in the realm [of being *(nash'a)*] which he inhabits. For there he sees a realm created without any [fixed] pattern, a realm that provides him in its outward manifestation what the realm of this world provides in its inner [psychic and spiritual] dimension *(bâtin)* and its imagination *(khayâl)*. So this is the way he freely controls the outward dimension *(zâhir)* of the realm of the other world. He enjoys all that he possesses in a single instant. Nothing that belongs to him, whether his wives or other things, is ever separated from him, nor is he ever separated from them; he is among them [simply] through his being desired, and they are in him through their being desired.[48]

For the other world is an abode of swift reaction, without any delay, [where external appearances constantly change] just as is the case with passing thoughts *(khawâtir)* in the inner dimension of the realm of this world. Except that for man the planes are reversed in the other world, so that his inward dimension permanently maintains a single form—just as his outward dimension does here—while the forms of his outward dimension undergo rapid transformations like those of his inner dimension here. [God] said: *"... by what a reversal they will be transformed!"* (Qur'an 26:227), yet when we have undergone our transformation, nothing will have been added to the way we were. So understand...

THE LESSER RESSURECTION AND INITIATIC DEATH

CHAPTER 369

Few passages in Ibn 'Arabî's writing more richly and succinctly illustrate his characteristic combination of scriptural interpretation, metaphysical penetration, and subtle allusion to the fruits and pathways of spiritual realization than this short section from chapter 369, which evokes in a few lines the most central insights and principles of his thought and their indispensable practical foundations. On that level of realization (tahqîq), *this whole passage can be seen as an extended commentary on the famous verses of Sûra 102* ("The proliferation of things distracted you, until you visited the graves...*"*),[49] *although it is only at the end of it that he openly underlines his particular understanding of the traditional Sufi distinction of the three levels of spiritual "certainty"* (yaqîn) *based on that Sûra. The "tombs" in this case are man's ordinary, unenlightened existence in this world, and the "death" that primarily interests Ibn 'Arabî here (as in the preceding selections) is the "lesser Resurrection"* (al-qiyâmat al-sughrâ), *the transformed awareness and immediate vision* (ru'ya) *of the true reality of the Self (summed up here in the famous hadith, "He who knows his self knows his Lord") and its undying Life that is the constant center of his rhetoric and reflection.*

But here this reawakened recognition of the full spiritual and imaginal dimensions of man's being and relation to God does not at all lead to some "gnostic" rejection of the world and the complexities of this life, to an illusory escape into the bliss of fanâ'. Instead—and this point is one of the most crucial and distinctive features of Ibn 'Arabî's spiritual perspective, throughout all his work—it is precisely the mystic's "return" to those bodily "graves" (and the concomitant awareness that our passage through this world is indeed only a "visit") that completes his spiritual knowledge and certainty, while at the same time fully revealing man's unique position and responsibility (amâna), *as God's "deputy" with regard to all the realms of being. The necessary fulfillment of that ontological "comprehensiveness"—with all the perplexing suffering, sin and distraction (the full range of manifold distractions* [takâthur]*) that it implies—is precisely what distinguishes the unique (and unavoidable) role of the completely human being* (al-insân al-kâmil) *in Ibn 'Arabî's understanding of this "divine comedy." Nowhere is that comprehensive vision of man's destiny and true stature more succinctly and strikingly stated than at the end of this section, in his transformed interpretation of the familiar gnostic symbol of the "pearl" of the soul.*

Translation:[50]

The final outcome of the affair *(al-amr)* is the return from the many to the One, for both the man of faith and the polytheist *(mushrik)*. This is because the man of faith who is granted the unveiling of "things as they really are"[51] is granted [the immediate vision of] this, as He said: *"Now We have removed from you your veil, so your vision today is keen"* (Qur'an 50:22). And this is *before* he leaves this world. For everyone who is taken [by physical death] is in [a state of spiritual] "unveiling" at the moment he is taken, so that at that point he inclines toward God *(al-Haqq)* and toward faith in Him and [the true awareness of] divine Unity. Hence the person who attains this certainty *before* being brought into the presence [of God at the time of physical "death"] is absolutely sure of his felicity and his conjunction with [that condition of blessedness]. For the certainty which comes from sound [rational] inquiry and unambiguous [experiential] unveiling prevents him from straying from the Truly Real, since he has *"a clear* *proof"*⁵² (Qur'an 6:57, etc.) in the matter and *"discerning inner vision"* (Qur'an 12:108).

But the person who attains this certainty [only] when he is brought into the presence [of death] is subject to the [ineluctable] divine Will.⁵³ And although the final outcome is [also] felicity,⁵⁴ however that is only *after* the imposition of torments and afflictions with respect to the person who is punished for his sins. For one is only "brought into the presence [of death]" after having witnessed that *(al-amr)* to which the creatures *(al-khalq)* are transferred [after death]. So long as he has not witnessed that, *death* has not *come near him* (Qur'an 4:18; etc.), nor is that [what we mean here by] "being brought into [its] presence."⁵⁵

...Now God has brought two Resurrections into existence, the lesser Resurrection and the greater Resurrection. The lesser Resurrection is the transferring of the servant from the life of this world to the life of the intermediate world *(barzakh)* in the imaginal body, as in [the Prophet's] saying: "When someone dies, his Resurrection has already begun."⁵⁶ Thus whoever is among the People of Vision⁵⁷ actually sees his Lord. For [as] God's Messenger says, in warning his community about the Antichrist: "No one sees God until he dies."⁵⁸ The greater Resurrection is the Resurrection of the Raising *(ba'th)* [of all men from their graves] and the supreme Gathering *(al-hashr al-a'zam)* in which all men are joined...⁵⁹

Know that these bodies are the coffins of the spirits and what beclouds them; they are what veil them so that they do not witness [the spiritual world] and are not witnessed. So the spirits do not see, nor are they seen, except through being parted from these [bodily] tombs (cf. Qur'an 102:2)—by becoming oblivious *(fanâ')* to them [in their absorption in spiritual things], not through [physical] separation. Therefore since they have inner vision, when they become oblivious to witnessing the bodies then they witness the One Who gives them Being in the very act of witnessing themselves.⁶⁰

So "he who knows his self knows his Lord."⁶¹ Likewise he who witnesses his self witnesses his Lord, and thereby moves from the "certainty of knowledge" to the "certainty of seeing." Then when he is returned to his [bodily] tomb he is returned to [the highest stage of] "true certainty" *(yaqîn haqq)*, not to the "certainty of knowledge."⁶² This is how man learns the [inner] differentiation of the Truly Real *(al-Haqq)*, through His informing [us] of the true saying concerning *the true reality of certainty* (Qur'an 56:95), *the seeing of certainty* and *the knowing of certainty* (cf. Qur'an 103:3-7).[63] So for [the person who reaches this stage] every property [of reality] becomes firmly established in its proper rank, and things are not confused for him (cf. Qur'an 2:42; 3:71). And he knows that the [prophetic] announcements did not mislead him (cf. Qur'an 6:5, etc.).

Therefore whoever truly knows God in this way has truly known and understood the wisdom [underlying] the formation *(takwîn)* of the pearl in its shell from *fresh sweet* [water] in *salty bitter* [water] (Qur'an 25:53)[64]: the shell is its body and its saltiness is its [physical] nature. So the influence of nature predominates in its shell, but the salt is [also] its whiteness—and that is like the Light which is revealed through it. So realize [what is meant by] this sign!

THE PRESENCE OF THE HOUR

CHAPTER 73 / QUESTION 62

Chapter 73 of the Futûhât, *the conclusion of the opening* fasl al-ma'ârif *(chapters 1-73) and one of the longest chapters of the entire work, begins with a detailed and highly important discussion of the different ranks and types of "saints"* (awliyâ') *in the spiritual hierarchy* (II 1-39) *and concludes* (II 39-139) *with Ibn 'Arabî's responses to 155 "spiritual questions" originally posed by the influential Sufi thinker al-Hakîm al-Tirmidhî (d. after 295/902).*[65] *Tirmidhî's questions, as Ibn 'Arabî explains at the beginning of his response* (II 39-40), *were designed as a sort of "test" to separate the true "Verifiers"* (muhaqqiqûn) *from the many pretenders to such wisdom who exist in every age:*

"The answers to them can only be truly known by someone who knows them by immediate experiencing *(dhawq)* and inspiration, not through discursive thinking or on [purely] rational bases;...they can only be attained through a divine Theophany *(tajalli ilâhî)* in the Presence of the Unseen [spiritual world], through one of the [divine] Self-manifestations *(mazâhir)*...whether bodily...or spiritual."

Among these questions, numbers 59-74 (II 80-87) *all involve events or symbols traditionally associated with the scriptural descriptions of the Resurrection and Paradise, descriptions which were already outlined, following the popular, relatively "exoteric" understanding of their sequence and location, in chapters 64 and 65. But here, in keeping with the special requirements of Tirmidhî's questionnaire, Ibn 'Arabî's discussions are much more openly focused on his understanding of the inner spiritual significance of those eschatological symbols. This is especially true for his responses concerning the different types of beatific vision* (ru'ya) *of God in the other world, some of which are translated in our final two selections below.*

In this particular question (no. 62), however, Ibn 'Arabî alludes to two points which are perhaps of even broader importance for his spiritual conception of these eschatological symbols in general. The first of these insights—in response to a question concerning the "Hour" of Resurrection—suggests his deeper understanding of the relations between the "microcosmic" Lesser Resurrection (al-Qiyâmat al-Sughrâ) *and the "macrocosmic" Greater Resurrection; the problematic role of "time" in these interpretations has already been evoked several times in our introduction and the preceding selections.*[66] *The second critical point is his allusion—illustrated here in the form of an intriguing anecdote—to the central role of the "eye of Imagination"* ('ayn al-khayâl) *in the realization of the "events" of the other world and indeed in man's spiritual life much more generally; again these insights are developed in greater detail in the earlier chapter 63 on the* barzakh, *or imaginal realm of being, which is also the "site" of man's Lesser Resurrection.*

[How is it that] *The affair of the Hour is* [only] *like a twinkling of the eye or It is even nearer* [Qur'an 16:77]?[67]
Question 62

The answer is that the Hour [of Resurrection] is called an "hour" (*sâ'a*) because it "hastens" toward us *(tas'a)*[68] by passing through these moments of time and breaths,[69] not by traversing distances. So "when someone dies" his Hour has reached him and "his Resurrection has already begun,"[70] until the Day of the Greater Hour (*al-sâ'at al-kubrâ*), which is related to the [continually re-created] "Hours" of the breaths as the year is related to the totality of its days particularized by the seasons with their differing qualities.[71] *So the affair of the Hour* and its role *(sha'n)* in the world is *closer than the twinkling of an eye* (Qur'an 16:77). For its arrival is itself identical with its judgment, its judgment is the same as its execution in the one who is judged, its execution is the same as its coming to pass, and its coming to pass is precisely the peopling of the two Abodes,[72] *a group in the Garden and a group in the Flame* (Qur'an 42:7).

Now no one is truly aware of this "nearness" but the person who is aware of God's power [as manifested] in the existence *(wujûd)* of the Imagination *(al-khayâl)* in the natural world, who is aware of the vast extent of the matters that are found, in a single breath or blink of the eye, by someone who knows [God's power manifested in] the Imagination. Then [such a person actually] *sees* the effect of that in sense perception, with the eye of the Imagination,[73] so that he is truly aware of this nearness and the "folding up" of years into the smallest instant of the time of the life of this world. Whoever has come across the story of Jawharî[74] has seen a marvelous thing that illustrates this sort [of phenomenon].

Now if you should ask "But what is the story of Jawharî?," we may say that he mentioned that he left his house [one day] with some dough to take to the baker's oven, while he happened to be in a state of ritual impurity. So [after dropping off the dough at the baker's] he came to the bank of the Nile to do his ablutions, and there, while he was standing in the water, he saw himself, in the way a dreamer sees things, as though he were in

Baghdad. He had married, lived with the woman for six years and had had several children—I forget the exact number—with her there. Then he was returned to himself [i.e., in his ordinary consciousness], while he was still standing in the water, so he finished his ablutions, got out of the water and put on his clothes, went off to the baker's oven, picked up his bread, came back to his house and told his family about what he had seen during that visionary incident.[75] However, after several months had passed, the woman [from Baghdad] with whom he had seen himself married during that experience came [to Jawharî's town in Egypt] and asked directions to his house. So when she met him, he recognized her and the children, and he did not deny that they were his. And when she was asked, "When did you get married?" she replied, "Six years ago, and these are his children with me." Thus what happened in the Imagination emerged [concretely] in sense-perception. This is one of the six topics [mentioned by] Dhû al-Nûn al-Misrî[76] which [ordinary] intellects consider to be impossible.

But *God is Omnipotent* (Qur'an 22:74)[77] in the world: He created it with [a wide range of] diverse properties, just as the property of the intellect among ordinary people is different from the properties of sight, hearing, taste and the other powers [of perception] among the usual run of men *('âmmat al-nâss)*. Thus God singled out His saints by bestowing [special spiritual] powers with [unique] properties like these,[78] powers that are only denied by someone who is ignorant of the [unimaginable] power and ability that is appropriate to the divine Proximity. There is sufficient [illustration] of this matter in the Ascension[79] of the Messenger of God, with those immense distances he traversed in a short period of time.

THE BEATIFIC VISION OF THE SAINTS

CHAPTER 73 / QUESTION 67

One of the central features of Ibn 'Arabî's understanding of the eschatological symbols in the Qur'an and hadîth, in which he generally follows the approach of earlier Sufis, is his consistent distinction between, on the one hand, those "Gardens" (and levels of the "Fire" or Gehenna) corresponding to the recompense (or punishment and purification) of men's actions in this world and, on the other hand, certain symbols—especially in a number of hadith concerning the "vision of God" (ru'yat Allâh)— that he takes to refer to men's different degrees of spiritual realization or inner "knowledge" of God ('ilm, in the Qur'anic sense). These distinctions are developed in their full complexity in Ibn 'Arabî's integral accounts of the eschatological "events" and "locations" in chapters 61-65 and 371 of the Futûhât, *while his responses to Tirmidhî's questions, as already indicated, focus more exclusively on the purely spiritual dimensions of these problems. This is especially true of questions 67-72, all of which concern the vision of God among different groups of men at the "Day of the Visit" (yawm al-zawr) briefly described in certain hadith.*[80]

Two of those hadith are especially important in providing the symbolic framework assumed in the selections translated below. At the same time, since these particular sayings also offer an excellent illustration of the subtle expression of profound spiritual insights—which in this case are clearly by no means the "invention" of Ibn 'Arabî—in this still little-known literature, it may be helpful to provide a translation of certain key passages. The first of these, known as the "hadith of the Dune" (kathîb) or of the "Market of Paradise" (sûq al-janna), is the Prophet's response to Abû Hurayra's question concerning this mysterious "Market"[81]:

"When the people of the Garden [of Paradise] enter it they settle down in it according to the excellence of their actions. After that, during the period [corresponding to] the Day of Reunion[82] among the days of this world, they are called [to prayer] and they visit their Lord: He shows them His Throne, and He manifests Himself to them in one of the meadows of the Garden. Then there are set up for them platforms of Light and [of five other precious stones and metals, corresponding to the ranks discussed below]..., while the lower ones of them and those among them who are ignoble[83] take their seats on dunes of musk and camphor. And [those sitting down] do not realize ['see'] that those who are on the pedestals have more excellent seats than them.[84] [Then Abû Hurayra asks the Messenger of God: "Do we see our Lord?" And Muhammad replies:] Yes indeed! Do you have any doubt about [your] seeing the sun and the moon when it is full?... Likewise you will not have any doubt about your seeing your Lord, and there will not remain a single man in that gathering but that God is present with him so intimately [that He knows the smallest detail of each person's life]..."[85]

The second hadith being commented, as it were, in the following passages is the famous "hadith of the transformations," perhaps the most frequently cited hadith (usually in the form of implicit allusions) in all of Ibn 'Arabî's work,[86] *which describes the testing of mankind with regard to their objects of worship* (ma'bûdât) *on the Day of the Gathering. According to this account, God will present Himself to this [Muhammadan] community "in a form other than what they know, and will say to them:* 'I am your Lord!'" *But the "hypocrites" among them—who, for Ibn 'Arabî, are ultimately all of mankind with the exception of the handful of "friends" and "true servants" of God described in the following selection—will fail to recognize Him until He appears in the form they already knew and expected, according to their beliefs in this world. This hadith stands behind Ibn 'Arabî's contrasting discussions of the highest rank of the "true knowers of 'God' " (al-'ulamâ' bi-llâh) in the following passage and throughout his writings.*[87]

"How are the saints and
the prophets ranked on the Day of the Visit"?[88]
Question 67

While the main subject of this translated section is the comprehensive spiritual understanding of the true "Friends of God" (awliyâ' Allâh), that discussion assumes an acquaintance with Ibn 'Arabî's ranking of the beatific vision of the saints and prophets and his technical terms for describing them at the beginning of this section (II 84.27-85.1). There, in his initial response to Tirmidhî's question, he distinguishes four main ranks: 1. the small number of "Messengers" (rusul) who have brought the publicly revealed divine paths (the sharâ'i'); *2. the "prophets [who received other, personal] revealed paths"* (anbiyâ' al-sharâ'i')[89]; *3. the "prophets who are followers [of a particular Messenger]"* (al-anbiyâ' al-atbâ'); *and 4. the saints, including both a) those who are likewise "followers" of particular prophets or Messengers* (al-awliyâ' al-atbâ') *and b) those who have lived in periods or places without direct contact with the revealed religious paths* (awliyâ' al-fatarât)....[90]

Now the full explanation of this matter is that the vision [of God] on the Day of the Visit is according to [men's] beliefs in this world. Thus the person who believes concerning his Lord what was given to him by intellectual reflection *(nazar)*, and by immediate "unveiling" *(kashf)*, and by imitating *(taqlîd)* his Messenger *(rasûl)* sees his Lord in the form of the aspect of each belief he held concerning Him, except that in his [outward] imitation of his prophet he sees his Lord in the form of his prophet, with regard to what that Messenger taught him from what was revealed to him in his inner knowledge of his Lord.[91] So such a person receives three theophanies, with three [different] "eyes," at the same instant. And similarly with the condition of the person [whose belief is based] solely on intellectual inquiry, or the person [who follows] only immediate unveiling, or the person [who accepts] only imitation [i.e., their vision of God is limited to that particular sort of theophany]. So the ranks of the saints who are followers [of only a particular prophet] on the Day of the Visit are distinguished [from those of the prophets they follow] by the precedence of the prophets.

But the two levels who are not prophets [with a *Sharia*] or [prophetic] followers are *the close friends of God* (Qur'an 10:62-64),[92] *who are not* governed by any [particular spiritual] *station* (Qur'an 33:12).[93] They are distinguished from all of [the ordinary believers below them] by their integral relationship to their Lord.[94]

However, the people of intellectual reasoning *(nazar)* among them are in a rank lower than the people of immediate unveiling *(kashf)*, because in their vision the veil of their thinking[95] stands between them and God (*al-Haqq* [the Truly Real]). Whenever they want to lift that veil they are not able to do so. And likewise the followers of the prophets [i.e., by way of outward imitation *(taqlîd)*], however much they may desire to raise the veils of the prophets from themselves so that they can see God without that intermediary *(wâsita)*, are still unable to do so. Therefore absolutely pure and flawless [spiritual] vision belongs in particular only to the Messengers *(rusul)* among the prophets, those who bring the divinely prescribed Paths *(sharâ'i')*,[96] and to the people of immediate unveiling. And whoever happens to attain this station, whether he be a follower [of a particular prophet] or of intellectual reflection, still participates in this to the extent of what he has realized—even if he be on [any of] a thousand paths!

But as for those true men[97] who concur with the belief held by each individual with regard to [their inner awareness of] what led him to that belief, taught it to him and confirmed him in it, on the Day of the Visit such people see their Lord with the eye of *every* belief. Hence the person who means to do well by his soul must necessarily seek out, during his [life in] this world, *all* the things that are professed[98] concerning that [i.e., the ultimate divine

Reality], and he must come to know why each individual professing a [particular] position affirms what he professes. So when [one of these "true men"] has realized in himself the particular aspect of that profession which gives it its validity for the person holding it and because of which that person professes it with regard to what he believes, so that [the true Knower] does not deny or reject it, [only] then will he reap the fruit of that profession on the Day of the Visit, whatever that credo (*aqîda*) may be. For this is the *"All encompassing"* divine Knowledge (cf. Qur'an 2:115; etc.).[99]

Now the principle underlying the validity of what we have just mentioned is that each person who looks at[100] God is under the influence of one of the Names of God, so that that Name is what manifests Itself to him in theophany and gives him that [particular] belief by Its appearing to him, without his being aware of this. And the relations of all of the divine Names to the Truly Real (*al-Haqq*) are sound, so therefore his vision [of God] in every belief is sound, despite their differences, and there is not the slightest error in it. This is what is given by the most complete [spiritual] unveiling (*al-kashf al-atamm:* cf. Qur'an 66:8).

Thus the gaze of [every] person who looks never leaves God, nor is it even possible for it to do so.[101] It is only that most people are veiled from the Truly Real by the Truly Real, because of the [omnipresent] clarity of the Truly Real.[102] But this group [i.e., the true "friends of God"], who have this special kind of [comprehensive] knowledge of God, are in a separate row on the Day of the Visit. So when they [i.e., most of the ordinary believers in the other Gardens of Paradise] return from the Visit, everyone of them who holds a [particular] belief imagines that [the saint, or true "friend of God"] belongs to their [group alone] because he sees that the [saint's] form of his belief during the Visit is like his own form [of belief].[103] So the person who is like this [i.e., who realizes the underlying truth in every individual's inner form of belief] is beloved by *all* the groups—and it was [already] that way in this world!

Now what we have just mentioned is only truly understood by the most outstanding and accomplished representatives of the people of [spiritual] unveiling and [true] being.[104] But as for the people of intellectual reasoning and inquiry, they have not caught even a whiff of its fragrance. So pay heed to what we have just mentioned and act accordingly: give the Divinity *(al-ulûhîya)* its rightful due, so that you may be among those who treat their Lord equitably in their knowledge of Him. For *God is far too exalted* (Qur'an 6:100, etc.) to be bound by any sort of delimitation or to be restricted to one form to the exclusion of [all] others. In this way you may come to know for yourself the universality of the felicity of all God's creation and the vast extent of that *Mercy which encompasses every thing* (Qur'an 40:7).[105]

THE IMAGINAL VISION OF ORDINARY PEOPLE

CHAPTER 73 / QUESTION 71

Needless to say, the spiritual example of the saints and the true "Friends of God" evoked in the preceding selection always remains a more or less distant ideal for the vast majority of men. In briefly evoking the divine "vision" of the mass of ordinary believers (the 'âmma),[106] *Ibn 'Arabî alludes here to four fundamental themes or principles of his religious and metaphysical thought that constantly recur throughout the* Futûhât *(including most of the chapters in this anthology). The first of these is the indispensable but also highly ambivalent function of the* 'ulamâ' *(i.e., the learned religious authorities in the popular sense of the term) as the guardians and transmitters of the external forms of the* Sharia.[107] *Closely related to this are his assumptions concerning the complex types and hierarchies of spiritual and psycho-intellectual "aptitudes" or predispositions that inevitably color men's conceptions of those forms (and of reality more generally). And following from this is his understanding of the reasons why each Sharia (including, in Islam, both the Qur'an and hadith) primarily employs the methods of* tashbîh, *of symbolic or "imaginal" representation, in its descriptions of God and of man's destiny and in its prescriptions for worship and right action more generally. Finally, underlying all of these points is Ibn 'Arabî's distinctive conception of the fundamental role of* khayâl *(inadequately translated as "Imagination")—in its manifold ontological and epistemological aspects—with regard both to the realities of the afterlife and to man's spiritual experience in general.*[108]

<blockquote>
What share do ordinary people
(al-'âmma) have in contemplating Him
[on the Day of the Visit]?[109]
Question 71
</blockquote>

The answer [is that] the shares of ordinary people in their contemplation of Him are according to the extent of what they have understood of what they have [outwardly and formally] taken over and imitated[110] from the learned, according to their different ranks.[111] Now among them there are those who have received from their learned authority [the formal knowledge] he possesses [with nothing added]; and among them are those who have received from their learned authority to the extent of what he learned on the basis of his [limited] intellect and receptivity.[112] For the natural dispositions[113] are different and of various ranks, depending on what God has placed in them; they are divisions [of psychic and intellectual types] whose source is in the constitution *(mizâj)* on which God mounted [their spirits].[114] That is the cause of the differences of outlook among the learned in their thoughts about intellectual matters *(ma'qûlât)*.

Thus the share [of ordinary people] in the pleasure of contemplating [God] is their share in what has been presented to them in images *(tukhuyyilat lahum)*, because the shares of the common people are imaginal and they are not able to transcend material [forms] in [their perception of] the spiritual realities *(al-ma'ânî)* in all those things which they enjoy in this world, the intermediate world and the other world. Indeed, very few of the learned can even conceive of the total transcendence *(tajrîd)* of material [forms]. This is why most of the *Sharia* came according to the understanding of ordinary people, although it also brings allusions intended for the elect, such as His saying: *"There is nothing like Him"* (Qur'an 42:11), and *"May your Lord be glorified, the Lord of Might, beyond [all] that they describe!"* (Qur'an 37:180).[115]

[To summarize][116]...Every individual's share in [the vision of] his Lord is according to the extent of his knowledge and the extent of what he believes among the ranks of beliefs, their differences and their greater or lesser number, as has already been established in these sections. So know that, and *God is the Guide* (cf. Qur'an 22:54, etc.). And in the "market of Paradise"[117] is the knowledge of that to which we have alluded [here].

TOWARDS SAINTHOOD: STATES AND STATIONS

William C. Chittick

THE STATION OF SERVITUDE

INTRODUCTION TO CHAPTERS 130 AND 131

These two chapters deal with one of thirty-seven pairs of terms discussed in seventy-four chapters of Section II of the Futûhât (interspersed with another forty-nine chapters in the same section). Most of these pairs take the form, "The Station of x" and "The Abandonment (tark) of the Station of x." Since, in Ibn al-'Arabî's view, the saints and Perfect Men undergo constant transformation in this world and the next, no station—except perhaps variegation (talwîn) *and* bewilderment (hayra)—*can be said to be their permanent abode. Every station and state that is acquired by the traveler must also be abandoned by him when he assumes another mode of existence or when his situation is viewed from a different point of view. Can we affirm that X is a station of the saints? Invariably the answer is "yes and no."*

In Chapter 130 Ibn al-'Arabî begins by explaining the significance of servanthood, one of the highest conceivable attributes in Islamic parlance, since God's servants ('abd) *are constantly praised in the Qur'an and since the Prophet Muhammad, by universal consent the most perfect of human beings, was first God's servant, then His messenger ('abduhu wa rasûluhu). Servant* is the opposite of "Lord," *so true servanthood entails abandoning any claim to possess existence or the attributes of existence, all of which are God's. In the text of the* Futûhât, *Ibn al-'Arabî discusses servanthood, along with the closely related concepts "worship" ('ibâda, a word derived from the same root) and poverty (faqr, iftiqâr), as much as any other human attribute.*[1] *In his view the station of the greatest saints is utter servanthood* (al-'ubûdiyyat al-mahda; II 627.2), *and it is this station which he invites people to achieve* (II 118.30). "The highest station with God is that God should preserve in His servant the contemplation of his servanthood, whether or not He should have clothed him in one of the robes of Lordship *[rubûbiyya]*" (II 132.9). *In the last analysis, only the Perfect Man is able to actualize servanthood:*

"Utter servanthood, untainted by any lordship whatsoever, can belong only to the Perfect Man, while Lordship totally untainted by servitude can only belong to God. So here the Perfect Man is in the form of God in respect of his incomparability and his being too holy *(taqdîs)* for any taints *(shawb)* in his reality. Hence he is the absolute divine vassal *(al-ma'luh al-mutlaq)*, while God is the Absolute Divinity *(al-ilâh al-mutlaq)*.... The Perfect Man stands apart from the nonperfect only through a single subtle meaning *(raqîqa)*, and that is that his servanthood is not stained by any lordship whatsoever" (II 603.14).

In searching for the root of servanthood in the Divine Reality, Ibn al-'Arabî turns to the nature of the existence ascribed to the creatures. Toward the end of Chapter 130 and at the beginning of Chapter 131 he touches on this question in a manner that typifies the way he expresses the "Oneness of Being" (wahdat al-wujûd), *a term which he himself never employs, here or elsewhere. In this passage he mentions two key concepts,* mazhar *or "locus of manifestation" and* 'ayn *or "entity," the latter of which is synonymous with "object of [God's] knowledge"* (ma'lûm). *The first is connected to the divine Name the Manifest* (al-zâhir). *That which appears within the world by means of God's Self-manifestation* (zuhûr) *or theophany* (tajallî) *is God Himself—Being—but colored by the locus within which He appears. The locus in turn is determined by the immutable entity* ('ayn thâbita), *i.e., God's Knowledge of how Being will become manifest in that particular situation. The two basic ideas here are Being, which is One by definition, and the Divine Knowledge, which carries within it the principle of multi-*

plicity, *since it knows all the infinite possible forms of Self-manifestation possessed by Being; these forms themselves become the "existent things" or the "loci of manifestation" when God chooses to make them manifest. It is interesting to note that Sa'îd al-Dîn al-Farghânî (d. circa 700/1300), disciple of Sadr al-Dîn al-Qûnawî (himself disciple of Ibn al-'Arabî), was the first to use the term "Oneness of Being" in a systematic fashion, and in so doing he contrasted it with the "manyness of [God's] knowledge" (kathrat al-'ilm).[2] This distinction between Oneness and manyness goes back to Ibn al-'Arabî's distinction between the two points of view of Incomparability, or the nature of the Divine Essence which is Absolutely One, and Similarity, or the manifestation of the Divine Names in all their manyness (cf. the translation of Chapter 558, note 87).*

In discussing the entities, which are the objects of God's knowledge (ma'lûmât), *Ibn al-'Arabî is drawn into a consideration of plurality, which of course has a positive reality since it derives from the Divine Names. Ibn al-'Arabî also examines that existence which, in the language of the philosophers, is said to be "acquired" by the created things, mentioning in the process the views of various Sufis.*

CONCERNING THE STATION OF SERVITUDE *('ubûda)*

CHAPTER 130[3]

I am ascribed to myself, for I know that our ascription to God is defective.
That He should be a cause *('illa)* for creation is problematic, unknown because of the elevation of His rank.
He is the Independent absolutely: He has no poverty—this the All-Merciful has revealed.
That which I have said the Qur'an explains.[4] Study it: in study you will see a detailed explanation.

214.5   "Servanthood" *('ubûdiyya)* is [grammatically] an ascription *(nasab)* to "servitude" *('ubûda)*; "servitude" is pure, without ascription, neither to God nor to itself, since it does not accept ascription. Hence the word does not have the suffix *iyy*.

214.6   The lowest of the low *(adhall al-adhillâ')* is that which is ascribed to something low which boasts *(iftikhâr)* over it. Hence it is said about the earth, "the very lowly" *(dhalûl;* Qur'an 67:15) in a word form [i.e., *fa'ûl*] that indicates exaggeration in lowliness; for the lowly walk upon it, so it is more tremendous in its lowliness than they.

214.7   The station of servanthood is a station of lowliness and poverty *(iftiqâr)*; it is not a divine attribute *(na't ilâhî)*. Abû Yazîd al-Bistâmî[5] found no cause *(sabab)* by which he could gain proximity *(taqarrub)* to God, since he saw that the Divinity *(al-ulûhiyya)* entered into every attribute by which proximity was gained. When he found himself incapable he said, "Oh Lord, by what shall I gain proximity to Thee?" God said to him in the way that He has customarily addressed His friends *(awliyâ')*: "Gain proximity to Me through that which I do not possess: Lowliness and poverty...."

214.13   The meaning of "servant" *('abd)* is "lowly" *(dhalîl)*. It is said, "earth made into a servant" *(ard mu'abbad)*, i.e., "made lowly" *(mudhallal)*. God says, *"I created jinn and men only to serve Me"* (Qur'an 51:56).[6] He said this only concerning these two kinds, since none claimed divinity, none believed divinity was in other than God and none was proud *(takabbur)* over God's creatures except these two kinds. Hence God mentioned them specifically without the other creatures. Ibn 'Abbâs[7] said, "The meaning of the words 'to serve Me' is 'to know Me.'" So he did not explain *(tafsîr)* [this verse] in terms of what is given by the reality of the word's denotation *(dalâla)*. Its explanation can only be: "to be lowly toward Me"; but none is lowly toward Him unless he knows Him, so it is necessary first to know Him and then to know the fact that He is the Possessor of Mightiness *('izza)* before which the mighty are lowly. Hence Ibn 'Abbâs turned in his explanation of "service" to knowledge. This is the opinion *(zann)* concerning him.[8]

214.17   No one has realized *(tahaqquq)* this station to its perfection like the Messenger of God, for he was an utter servant *('abd mahd)* who renounced *(zâhid)* those states which would have removed him from the level of servanthood. God gives witness that he was a servant of Him both in respect of His He-ness and His All-Comprehensive Name.[9] He says concerning His Name, *"When the servant of Allah stood calling on Him"* (Qur'an 72:19); and He says concerning His He-ness, *"Glory be to Him who carried His servant by night"* (Qur'an 17:1). So *He* carried him by night as a servant.

214.20   When he was commanded to instruct concerning his station on the Day of Resurrection, he qualified that, for he said, "I am the lord of the children of Adam, without boasting," reading *fakhr* with an *r*.[10] In other words, "I do not aim to boast before you about my lordship; on the contrary, I wish to instruct you as good news to you, since you are commanded to follow me." This has also been read as *fakhz* with a *z*, i.e., "without bluffing": "I do not say this by way of bluffing; I am not like that," for *fakhz* is to boast of a falsehood as if it were true.

214.23   The relationship of the servant with God in the state of servanthood is like that of a shadow with the person [who throws it] before a lamp: the closer he moves toward the lamp, the greater is the shadow; there is no proximity to God except through that which is more specifically *(akhass)* your attribute, not His. The more the person moves away from the lamp, the smaller the shadow becomes; for nothing moves you away from God except your leaving aside those attributes of which you are worthy and your coveting His Attributes. *"Even so does God set a seal on every proud* (mutakabbir) *and tyrannical* (jabbâr) *heart"* (Qur'an 40:35); these are two Attributes that belong to God.[11] *"Taste: you are the mighty* ('azîz), *the generous* (karîm)" (Qur'an 44:49).[12] This [situation] is [referred to in] the Prophet's words: *"I seek refuge in Thee from Thee."*[13]

214.26   This station does not leave you with any attribute which belongs exclusively and solely to God and in which sharing *(ishtirâk)* cannot be achieved—i.e., [it leaves you with none of] the affirmative *(thubûtî)*, not the negative *(salbî)* or correlative *(idâfî)* attributes[14]—without this being known specifically by the possessor of this station. But its possessor's Tasting *(dhawq)*[15] is rare; for when you realize and stand alone in your most specific attributes *(al-wasf al-akhass)*, and when you enter upon God through them, He faces *(muqâbala)* you only with His most specific Attributes, to which you have no access. But when you come with the shared attributes, He appears in theophany to you with the [same] shared attributes; so you come to know the mystery of His relation *(nisba)* to you through your relation to Him. This is an astonishing science; you will find few who taste it. Yet it lies below the first, which is the most specific for you. So know this and realize this station, for this will be given to you by the station of servanthood.

214.31   As for the station of servitude, you will not know the sciences that you actualize through it, for within it you annihilate ascription to Him and to engendered existence.[16] This is an extremely rare station, for the Tribe cannot allow that engendered existence should subsist in its possibility without ascription, since it is inherently *(bi'l-dhât)* "necessary through the Other" *(wâjib bi'l-ghayr)*.[17] That which alerts one to this station is the fact that, within the locus of manifestation *(mazhar)*, the Manifest *(al-zâhir)* is described by the attribute of the servant,[18] for the Manifest becomes colored by the reality of the locus of manifestation, whatever this may be. But the Manifest does not trace its origin to servanthood, for there is nothing lower than the latter, and that which traces its origin to something must be lower in level than that thing. But the Manifest only traces its origin to that thing to which it is ascribed, since the effect *(athar)* given to the Manifest by the entity of the locus of manifestation is nothing other than the Manifest; "There is no goal beyond God."[19] But a thing cannot be ascribed to itself. Hence "servitude" does not have the *iyy* of ascription. It is said, "A man between servanthood and servitude,"[20] i.e., his essence is manifest but his ascription is unknown, so he is not ascribed, since there is no "to so-and-so." So he is a servant/nonservant *('abd lâ 'abd)*.

CONCERNING THE STATION OF ABANDONING SERVANTHOOD (tark al-'ubûdiyya)

CHAPTER 131[21]

If you trace your origin to an effect to which you belong—you belong to God, not creation, so consider yourself rebuked!
We are loci of manifestation, and the Worshipped One is He who makes us manifest; the engendered existent's locus of manifestation is his very entity—so take heed!
He did not bring me in vain, but in order that I should worship Him as God—such is the judgment of Law and reason.
But I do not worship Him except through His form, for He is the God within whom man is concealed.
So what is God's decree—if you realize our form? And what are control, judgments, and destiny?
All are admonitions—if you possess reason. He who applies the admonitions will never go wrong.

II 215.9   No one can abandon servanthood unless he sees that the entities of the possible things remain in their original state of nonexistence and that they are the loci of manifestation for God, who is Manifest within them. So none has existence but God, and none has effects *(athar)* but the entities; by their very essences they impart to the existence of the Manifest that through which limitations *(al-hudûd)* occur within the entity of every manifest thing. So the entities are the things most similar to number *(al-'adad)*, for they are intelligible *(ma'qûl)* but have no existence.[22] The properties of number permeate and are established within the countable things *(al-ma'dûdât)*, which are nothing but the forms of the existents, whatever they may be. As for the existents, the cause *(sabab)* of their manyness *(kathra)* is the entities of the possible things, which also cause the diversity *(ikhtilâf)* of the forms of the existents.[23] So the property of number precedes *(muqaddam)* the property of everything that displays a property *(hukm kull hâkim)*.

215.13 When I reached number and the countable things at the beginning of this chapter in this copy, I slept, and I saw the Messenger of God in a dream, while I was seated before him. Someone had asked me, "What is the smallest plural number?" I had answered, "According to the jurists *[al-fuqahâ']* it is two, but according to the grammarians *[al-nahwîyîn]* it is three." The Prophet said, "Both these and those are mistaken." I said to him, "Oh Messenger of God, what should I say?" He replied, "Numbers are even and odd. God says, *'By the even and the odd!'* [Qur'an 89:2]; though both are numbers, He distinguished between them." Then he took out five dirhams with his blessed hand and threw them down on the mat upon which we were seated. Throwing two in one place and three in another he said to me, "He who is asked this question should say to the questioner, 'Of which number do you speak? Of the number called "even"? Or of the number called "odd"?'" Then he placed his hand upon the two dirhams and said, "This is the least plural of the even numbers." He placed his hand on the three and said, "This is the least plural of the odd numbers. In this manner should he who is asked this question answer. This is how it is with us."

215.20 I awoke and wrote down my dream in this chapter just as I had seen it when I awoke. But I have not mentioned many questions between me and him that pertain to matters unrelated to this chapter. I was in extreme joy and happiness from seeing him, and I found in my mind once I awoke the correctness of the prohibition of the single cycle prayer,[24] for he spoke in this manner. I have never seen a teacher better than he.

215.22 Then I went back to writing this book. So I return and say: the property of number precedes the property of everything that displays a property. Hence the manyness of the possible things imposes manyness upon them, while the diversities of their preparednesses impose manyness upon the Manifest within them, in spite of Its Unity *(ahadiyya)*. So Its manyness is that of the possible things. Since this is the case, it is impossible for servanthood to possess an entity;[25] because of this station, one may uphold the "abandonment of servanthood."

215.25 The property of number and the power of its permeation *(sarayân)*, even though it possesses no existence, led to God's saying, *"Three men conspire not secretly together, but He is the fourth of them, neither five men, but He is the sixth of them, neither fewer than that,"* i.e., two, which confirms our vision mentioned above, *"neither more, but He is with them, wherever they may be"* (Qur'an 58:8) within the levels demanded by numbers; hence the property of number applies to them. There is also the saying of the Prophet, *"God possesses ninety-nine Names, one hundred less one"*[26]; this shows the property of number.

215.28 God says, *"They are infidels who say, 'God is the third of three'"* (Qur'an 5:77), but he is not an infidel who says that God is the fourth of three. This is because, if He were the third of three or the fourth of four, as is conspired by those who speak such words, He would be of the same kind *(jins)* as the possible things. But He—high exalted is He—is not of the same kind as the possible things, so it cannot be said concerning Him that He is one of them, since He is One eternally for every manyness and group, without becoming one of their kind. Hence He is the fourth of three, so He is One; the fifth of four, so He is One; and so on indefinitely.

215.31 This is what is called "Allah." Though He is the existence manifest in whatever forms are possessed by the loci of manifestation, He is not of their kind, for He is Necessary Being in His Essence, while they are necessary nonexistence *(wâjibat al-'adam)* in their essences eternally. They possess properties in that which clothes itself within them, just as ornaments possess properties in him who adorns himself with them. Hence the relation of the possible things to the Manifest is the relation of knowledge and power to the knowledgeable and the powerful[27]: there is no existent entity that bestows the properties of being knowledgeable and powerful upon the object of the attribution *(al-mawsûf)*; hence we say that it is knowledgeable and powerful in its essence. Thus also are the realities.

215.35   So number bestows properties by its very essence *(hâkim li dhâtihî)* upon countable things, though it has no existence; and the loci of manifestation bestow properties upon the forms of the Manifest and upon the manyness of these forms within the Reality of the One *('ayn al-wâhid)*, though they have no existence.

216.1   In our view there is no issue *(mas'ala)* in theology *(al-'ilm al-ilâhî)* more obscure than this. For everyone *(al-jamâ'a)* maintains that the possible things acquire *(istifâda)* nothing from God but existence. But no one knows the meaning of the words, "acquire nothing but existence," except him whose insight has been unveiled by God; those who use this expression do not understand its true meaning.

216.3   There is no existent but God, while the possible things remain in the state of nonexistence. Now this "acquired existence" *(al-wujûd al-mustafâd)* either must be existent, while being neither God nor the possible thing, or it must consist of the Being of God. But if something is superadded *(zâ'id)*, then it is neither God nor the entities of the possible things. So there remains only that this existence be existent; hence it is described by itself, and this is God, since it has been proven that there is no existence from eternity without beginning except that of God, since He is the Necessary Being in Himself. So it is established that there is no existent through itself but God. Hence the entities of the possible things receive the Being of God through their realities, since there is no other Being. This is indicated by His words, *"We created not the heavens and the earth and all that is between them save through the Truth"* (Qur'an 15:85), which is Sheer Being[28]; so to It came to be ascribed everything that is bestowed by the realities of the entities. In this way limitations are occasioned, measurements become manifest, and judgment and decree are exercised; the high, the low, and the middle, diverse and parallel things, and the classes, genera, kinds, individuals, states, and properties of the existents all become manifest within One Reality, since shapes *(al-ashkâl)* become distinguished within It. The Names of God become manifest, possessing effects *(athar)* within that which becomes manifest in existence, out of [divine] jealousy *(ghayra)*, lest those effects be attributed to the entities of the possible things within the Manifest within them. Since the effects belong to the Divine Names, and the Name is the Named *(al-musammâ)*, there is nothing in existence but God.[29] So He displays properties and He receives them, since He is *"Receiver of penitence"* (Qur'an 40:2), and thus has described Himself by "reception" *(qabûl)*.

216.12   In spite of all this, the clear formulation of this issue is exceedingly difficult, since verbal expression *(al-'ibâra)* is inadequate for it, nor does conceptualization *(tasawwur)* capture it, since it quickly escapes and its properties are contradictory. For [this issue] is like His words, *"You did not throw,"* so He negated, *"when you threw,"* so He affirmed, *"but God threw"* (Qur'an 8:17), so He negated the engendered existence *(kawn)* of Muhammad and affirmed Himself as identical to Muhammad, giving to him the Name Allah.[30] This is the property of this issue, or rather, this is the issue itself for him who verifies. This then is the meaning of the abandonment of servanthood for the elite knowers of God *(khusûs al-'ulamâ' bi'llâh)*.

216.15   As for him who does not attain to their degree, he maintains that servanthood cannot be abandoned inwardly, because of the existence of poverty *(al-iftiqâr)*,[31] which no temporally originated thing *(muhdath)* denies from himself. His poverty will necessarily lower him, and this lowliness *(dhilla)* is identical with servanthood; [he will remain in this station of servanthood] unless he is taken from knowledge of himself [e.g., by an ecstatic state].

216.17   As for man's abandonment of servanthood through knowledge, that takes place as follows: When you look at the servant in respect of his self-control *(tasarruf)*, not in respect of his being a possible thing, and when you ascribe to him the name of servanthood in this respect, then it is possible for him to abandon servanthood through knowledge—in respect of self-control, not in respect of his possibility. The reason for this is that the reality of servanthood is to attend to the commands of one's master. Here none is commanded except him to whom can be ascribed acts in accordance with the commands. Now acts *(al-af'âl)* are God's creation, so He is the commander and the commanded. So where is true self-control, through which the servant is called either a servant upholding the commands of his master or one who contends with him, thus being qualified as a runaway *(al-ibâq)*?

216.20 Hence during the manifestation of the divine Power and the occurrence of Acts in his outward and inward, he who is named "servant" remains either in conformity *(muwâfaqa)* with the command or in opposition *(mukhâlafa)* to it. If this is the case, there is no servanthood of self-control, so the servant is an existent without a property. This is the station of verifying *(tahqîq)* the abandonment of servanthood for all the men of knowledge through Tasting *('ulamâ' al-dhawq)*, the People of God, except for one tribe of our companions—and others who are not of us—who hold a different view.[32] [They maintain] that the possible thing possesses acts and that God has entrusted *(tafwîd)* His servants with the performance of certain possible acts. Hence He prescribed the performance of these acts, since He said, *"Perform the prayer and pay the alms"* (Qur'an 22:78), *"Fulfill the Pilgrimage and the Visitation unto God"* (Qur'an 2:192), *"Struggle for God"* (Qur'an 22:77), and so forth. Since they affirm that the servant possesses acts, they cannot abandon the servanthood of self-control.

216.25 As for the servanthood of possibility, they concur that there is such a thing and that its abandonment is inconceivable, for it belongs to the very essence of the possible thing.

216.26 Some of our companions take into account in the abandonment of servanthood God's being the faculties and organs of the servant,[33] for in this state he is absent from servanthood, but this is the abandonment of a state, not of a reality.

THE STATION OF FREEDOM
INTRODUCTION TO CHAPTERS 140 AND 141

In the Qur'an and the Hadîth the term "free" (hurr) *along with certain derivatives refers to the status of someone who is free as opposed to someone who is the property of another person. But the term* 'abd, *slave or servant, denotes not only being owned by someone but also the proper human situation before God, as was indicated in the introduction to Chapters 130 and 131; one may not be owned by another human being, but one can hardly be free before God. In Sufism, freedom was early considered a high spiritual station, not of course in opposition to being God's slave, but as another side of the same reality. Abû Nasr al-Sarrâj (d. 378/988-89) writes,* "'Freedom' is an allusion to the fullest degree of the realization *[tahaqquq]* of servanthood. It is that you should not be owned by any engendered or other kind of thing, so that you are free, since you are God's slave *['abd].* Hence Bishr [al-Hâfî] said to Sarî [al-Saqatî] concerning the words of the Prophet, 'God created you free, so be as you were created!': 'Do not take into account your family when at home or your companions when traveling. Do everything for God, and leave people aside.' Junayd said, 'The final station of the knower is freedom.' Another said, 'The servant is not a true servant as long as he is in bondage to anything other than God.'"[34]

In his usual manner, Ibn al-'Arabî has in mind the sayings of earlier masters as the background for what he wants to explain, but he then takes the concept of freedom back to its deepest meaning in the divine realities. The themes he covers, which are among the most recurrent in the Futûhât, *include the contrast between the Essence as such (Incomparability) and the properties of the Names (Similarity) and the station of the highest saints (i.e., the Blameworthy, though they are not mentioned by name), those who have fully actualized servanthood and put all things in their proper places by acting in accordance with the demands of the Names within creation.*

CONCERNING THE KNOWLEDGE OF THE STATION OF FREEDOM (hurriyya) AND ITS MYSTERIES

CHAPTER 140[35]

This is a chapter of danger.

The servant of self-will has run away from his Master's kingdom, but he cannot go outside of it, so he wanders aimlessly.
The free man is he who owns all engendered things and is not owned by any property or position.
Were he to resist engendered existence, he would nullify his root in his Master's kingdom.

II 226.23   Know—God give you success—that freedom is a station of the Essence *(maqâm dhâtî)*, not of the Divinity *(ilâhî)*.[36] It cannot be delivered over to the servant absolutely, since he is God's servant through a servanthood that does not accept emancipation. We have considered freedom impossible for God *(al-haqq)* in respect of His being a divinity *(ilâh)* because of His relationship *(irtibât)* to divinity's vassal *(ma'lûh)*, a relationship corresponding to that of the lord to the existence of the servant, the owner to the property, and the king to the kingdom. Consider God's words, *"If He will, He can put you away and bring another people."*[37] He gives news of bringing another people in respect of this relationship, for the reality of correlation *(idâfa)* demands, both rationally and ontologically, the concept of two correlative terms. So there can be no freedom with correlation, while Lordship *(rubûbiyya)* and Divinity are correlations.

226.25 But since there is no correspondence *(munâsaba)* or correlation between God and creation *(al-khalq)*—on the contrary, He is *"Independent of the worlds"* (Qur'an 3:92), and this belongs to no existent essence except the Essence of God—no engendered existent is related to Him, no eye perceives Him, no limitation encompasses Him, and no demonstration found to be necessary *(darûrî)* by the intellect gives knowledge of Him, just as the negation of the attributes of interdependence *(ta'alluq)* that would bring Him under delimitation is but speculation.[38]

226.28 So when the servant desires the realization *(tahaqquq)* of this station—for it is one of realization, not of the assumption of traits *(takhalluq)*[39]—and he considers that this can only come about through the disappearance of the poverty *(iftiqâr)* that accompanies him because of his possibility,[40] and he also sees that the Divine Jealousy *(al-ghayrat al-ilâhiyya)* demands that none be qualified by existence except God—because of the claims *(da'wâ)* existence entails—he knows through these considerations that the ascription of existence to the possible thing is impossible, since Jealousy is a limitation that prevents it.[41] Hence he looks at his own entity and sees that it is nonexistent, possessing no existence, and that nonexistence is its intrinsic attribute *(wasf nafsî)*. So no thought of existence occurs to him, poverty disappears, and he remains free in the state of possessing nonexistence, like the freedom of the Essence in Its Being.

226.31 Then the servant desires to know what corresponds to the Divine Names that belong to the Essence within the essence of the nonexistent possible thing. He sees that the entity of every possible thing possesses a preparedness *(isti'dâd)*[42] not possessed by any other, in order that the entities may become distinct *(tamyîz)*. Hence, what separates the essence of the possible thing and the Essence of God pertains to the Necessary Being of God and the necessary nonexistence *(al-wâjib al-'adam)* of the possible thing. So the servant gives the preparednesses of the possible things a status corresponding to that of the Names of God, while the existence of the possible entities belongs to God. So when He becomes manifest to Himself in the entity of a possible thing through one of the Divine Names, the preparedness of the entity bestows upon Him a temporally originated Name *(ism hâdith)* by which He is then called. It is said that this is a Throne, this an Intellect, this a Pen, a Tablet, a Footstool, a celestial sphere, an angel, fire, air, water, earth, an inanimate thing, a plant, an animal, and a man, in all kinds and species. Then this Reality permeates the individuals and it is said that this is Zayd, 'Amr, this horse, this stone, this tree. All of this is bestowed by the preparedness of the entities of the possible things. Hence you infer *(istidlâl)* from the effects *(âthâr)* of the entities in existence what realities they comprise in their essence, just as you infer from the effects of the Names in existence the Divine Names, though the Named *(al-musammâ)* possesses no entity that is perceived.

227.4   Hence when the possible thing clings to its own entity, it is free, with no servanthood; but when it clings to its preparedness, it is a poor servant. So we possess no station in nondelimited freedom *(al-hurriyyat al-mutlaqa)* in what we have mentioned. So do not allow yourself to maintain anything but this.

227.6   He who does not contemplate this station will never know the sense of God's words, *"God is independent of the worlds"* (Qur'an 3:92), which mean that He is independent of denotation *(al-dalâla 'alayhî)*. For, if He had brought the world into existence that it might denote Him, He could not be independent of it. So know this truth! Who made the world a denotation and whom does it denote? For He is more manifest and apparent than that His denotation should be sought from something else or that He could be delimited by an "other" *(siwâ)*. If this were the situation, the denotation would possess a certain authority *(saltana)* and boasting *(fakhr)* over that which it denotes. If the object of denotation made the denotation a denotation, the latter would never be separated from the level of vainglory *(zahûw)*, because it would be giving to its object something that the object could not attain alone. As a result Independence and Freedom would be nullified, but these two are established for God. Hence He did not make the denotations refer to Himself, rather to His [ontological] level *(martaba)*, so that it might be known that there is no god but He.[43] This is the tongue of the elite *(al-khusûs)* concerning freedom.

227.11   As for the tongue of the generality *(al-'umûm)* of the Sufis *(al-qawm)*, "freedom" belongs to him who is not enslaved by any engendered existent, only by God. Hence he is free from everything other than God. So freedom is a verified servanthood of God; its possessor is not the servant of anything but God, who created him to serve Him.[44] Hence he fulfills that for which he was created, and it is said concerning him, *"How excellent a servant—indeed he is constantly returning"* (Qur'an 38:44), i.e., constantly coming back to the servanthood for which he was created—since he was created in need of everything in existence. There is nothing in existence that does not call to him in the tongue of his poverty: "I am that toward which you are poor, so return to me."

227.24   If he has knowledge of the true situation, he knows that God is with that phenomenon *(sabab)* that calls him, and that he is poor toward it because he has the preparedness for poverty toward it, so he is poor in his very reality.[45] Then he will look at the bestower of that toward which he has need in this phenomenon and he will see it as the Divine Name. So he is only poor toward God in respect of His Name, and he is only poor through his own self from the effect of his preparedness. Hence he knows what poverty is, who it is that is poor, and toward whom he is poor. That is why the Prophet was commanded to say, *"My Lord, increase me in knowledge"* (Qur'an 20:113).

224.27   Thus have I sufficiently apprised you of freedom and its mysteries, things that you will not find in other books, the writings of anyone else.

CONCERNING THE STATION OF ABANDONING FREEDOM (tark al-hurriyya)

CHAPTER 141[46]

How should he who never becomes separate from his needs be free while his needs are seeking him?
Hence he is poor toward all things: poverty is his doctrine, poverty his earnings.[47]
God became named for us within the entities of the engendered things so that His religion might be distinguished for us through speech.
None is free in engendered existence, for He seeks us from every direction—and from every direction we seek Him.

II 227.24 Know—God give you success—that the abandonment of freedom is pure and utter servitude; the possessor of this station is enslaved by phenomena *(asbâb)*, for he has attained to the realization of the knowledge of the wisdom *(hikma)* in their establishment *(wad')*.[48] So he is lowly before their authority. The possessor of this station is like the earth: both the pious and the wicked tread upon it, and it bestows its benefits on both the man of faith and the infidel. Phenomena affect him just as supplication *(du'â')* on the part of engendered things affect God in that He answers them; he attains the realization of his Master, for he sees that this station accompanies Him in spite of the Independence *(ghinâ)* attributed to Him. So what is the state of him whose mount *(markab)* becomes hungry, naked, thirsty, and is slaughtered, while he is commanded to preserve it and to watch over its situation and over that which makes it prosper? God placed him in charge of it and made him a vicegerent within it; it is not within his power to take care of its rights *(huqûq)* unless phenomena enable him to do so. So he must humble himself in acquiring phenomena so that he can fulfill God's right upon him directed toward his mount. For God says to him, "Thy self *(nafs)* has a right upon thee, thy eye *('ayn)* has a right upon thee, and thy guest *(zawr)* has a right upon thee."[49] How can a person faced with rights possess freedom?

So every engendered thing has a right upon him: he is slave to that right.
He is not free—so be knowledgeable and aware of him, like him who has attained realization.
Be not like him who rejects the command of his Master once he enters creation.
God is Lord and you are His servant. So be a servant! This has priority.
I say this while He is my hearing and He is my words while I speak.[50]
He who is like what I say is the man of knowledge who has been given success.

228.1　So he is the servant of his self as long as it demands its right from him, the servant of his eye as long as it demands its right from him, and the servant of his guest as long as he demands his right from him. Divine blessings demand that he give thanks to Him who blessed him with them, and religious prescriptions *(taklîf)* are in effect. Compulsion *(idtirâr)* is unavoidable; if he desires to repel it, it cannot be repelled. Praise and laudation exercise effects upon him, so he says, "Praise belongs to God, the Benefactor, the Bestower." Blame, harshness, and annoyance master him, so he says, "Praise belongs to God in every state."[51] So his praise changes with the change in states; were the states to change with the change in praise, he would be free of them.

228.4　The Messenger of God said to Abû Bakr al-Siddîq,[52] "What has brought you out?" He answered, "Oh Messenger of God, hunger." The Messenger of God said, "I too have been brought out by hunger." So he went with those Companions who were with him to the house of al-Haytham ibn Abî al-Tîhân, who sacrificed for them and fed them. So the only thing that brought them out was He who delivered a verdict in favor of that thing—i.e., hunger—which faced them with a right. Hunger is a thing of nonexistence *(amr 'adamî)*. So if an existent is acted upon by a nonexistent thing, what should be its state in face of an existent thing? Moreover, people such as these mentioned here have been seen to possess freedom. But because of this tasting *(dhawq)* they came out to seek the fulfillment of the rights their selves had upon them. Hence hunger enslaved them. If they had not come out but remained in their places, they would have been under the coercion *(qahr)* of patience *(sabr)* and everything that it demands. So the ultimate ascription of excellence *(fadl)* to them is that they came out, as we said, seeking to fulfill the rights of their selves through striving *(sa'y)* for them, since they had the ability to do this. There is nothing higher than this, for if they had sat back while possessing the ability, they would have been described by wrongdoing *(zulm)* and ignorance of the divine decree *(al-hukm al-ilâhî)*.

228.10 How can we conceive of freedom in someone whose attributes are such [as the above] in both this world and the next? In this world, such is the actual situation and a person cannot deny it. He may refuse it and disclaim it for himself, but if he does not depend and rely upon phenomena, the most he can do is rely upon God in employing them, so he is then a defective servant *('abd ma'lûl)*, since this is a specific attentiveness.[53] Likewise in the next world he is the servant of his passion *(shahwa)*,[54] since he is under its authority and it rules over him; and servanthood has no meaning other than this: his entrance under properties and the bondage *(riqq)* of phenomena.

228.13 When the knower *(al-'ârif)* discerns this for himself, he knows that "freedom" is the talk of the ego *(hadîth nafs)* and an accidental state with no permanence in sobriety *(sahw)*. Then [he knows] that the abandonment of freedom is a divine attribute *(na't ilâhî)*. So how can he not abandon it? Its ultimate limit is that in his abandonment of freedom he should be in the form of the God who requests supplication and seeks repentance and the asking of forgiveness from His servants and who blames them if they do not come to what He has requested from them. He even says, "If you did not sin, God would bring a people who do sin, then repent, so that He might forgive them."[55]

228.16   Thus have I apprised you of the mysteries of this station. If you cling to them, you will know your self and you will know your Lord, and you will not go beyond your own measure. Though freedom has degrees among God's servants, God considers the not-free *(ghayr al-ahrâr)* as greater in degree and more perfect in description. The root is with them: a Protector who protects them in the abandonment of freedom and in enslavement to that which Wisdom demands.

THE TRUE KNOWLEDGE OF
UNWORTHY UTTERANCES

CHAPTER 195[56]

Unruly utterances, which are usually known by such terms as "theopathic locutions" *(Massignon) or* "inspired paradoxes" *(Corbin), have exercised a certain fascination over Western scholars, though the only book-length study devoted to clarifying their place in Sufism does not take Ibn al-'Arabî's views into account.*[57] *The outstanding feature of these utterances is their apparent blasphemy or at least contradiction of the letter and spirit of the Law. The most famous examples are Hallâj's* "I am the Truth" *and Abû Yazîd's* "Glory be to me," *though the Sufis wrote long compilations on the topic.*

In translating the term, we have tried to approach the literal meaning rather than interpret the content of the sayings. According to Abû Nasr Sarrâj, the term in its original sense implies a strong movement; it is employed in describing the water of a stream which has gone out of control and overflowed its banks. In the same way, a Sufi overcome by ecstasy may say things that overflow the boundaries of reason and the Law.[58] *Ibn al-'Arabî certainly has the negative implications of the term in mind when discussing it. However, he acknowledges that such expressions will be justified if, and only if, God has commanded the person to speak them, as in the case of certain sayings of the prophets. As one example he offers an interesting commentary on a long*

Qur'anic passage that quotes the words of Jesus, words which would have been "unruly utterances" if spoken without the divine command.

At the end of the passage Ibn al-'Arabî turns to emphasizing the fact that the greatest saints—the Verifiers or the Blameworthy —never make unruly utterances, since they have fully actualized the station of servanthood. He also refers in passing to miracles and their similarity to certain phenomena that can be brought about by magicians.

An unruly utterance is the soul's claim through nature because of a remnant of the effects of self-will within it.
This is when the unruly words are true, have not been commanded, and are spoken by a master of understanding.

Know—God confirm you—that an "unruly utterance" is a justified claim *(da'wâ bi'l-haqq)* which expresses the speaker's position with God bestowed upon him by God but which [is made] without a divine command and by way of boasting *(fakhr)*. If the speaker is commanded to utter the claim, then he expresses through it a communication *(ta'rîf)* by divine command without intending any boast. The Prophet said, "I am the lord of the children of Adam, without boasting."[59] In other words, "I do not intend to boast before you through this communication, but rather to give you news through it of certain things to your benefit and to let you know of God's favor to you through your prophet's rank with Him". Unruly utterances are the slips *(zalla)* of the Verifiers *(al-muhaqqiqûn)* when they are not commanded to speak the words as the Prophet was. Hence he clarified [his words] by saying, "without boasting"; in other words, "I know that I am God's servant, just as you are God's servants, and the servant does not boast before the servant when their master is the same."

387.15 The words of Jesus were similar. He began with servanthood, which corresponds to the Prophet's words, "without boasting." In order to exonerate his mother and because he knew through the light of prophecy within his own preparedness that he would certainly be called the son of God, he said to his people, *"Lo, I am God's servant"* (Qur'an 19:31). Hence at the outset of his communication and testimony he began with a state about which those like him ordinarily do not speak. He meant: I am not the son of any man, and my mother is pure, a virgin. Nor am I the son of God; just as He does not accept a consort, He does not accept a son. Rather, I am God's servant like you. *"God gave me the Book and made me a Prophet"* (Qur'an 19:31). Hence Jesus articulated his prophecy at its time in his own eyes, but at other than its time in the eyes of those present, since there is no doubt that he would have to announce his prophecy at its time, as was God's custom with the prophets before him. So the prophets are commanded in everything that becomes manifest through and from them, i.e., in the true claims that denote their position of proximity [with God] and their distinction from their equals and likes because of their exemplary rank with God.

387.21 *"And He made me blessed,"* i.e., a locus and mark of increase in good for you, *"wherever I was"* (Qur'an 19:32), i.e., in every state; this blessedness for you because of me does not pertain to some states rather than others. Jesus spoke all of this in the past tense, but he meant the present and the future. What pertains to the present is his words in testimony concerning the innocence of his mother and in admonition and instruction to those who wanted to call him the son of God. Hence he declared God incomparable *(tanzîh)* [i.e., in respect to such an ascription], and this is equivalent to his exoneration of his mother from what they were ascribing to her. So his words are a declaration of Incomparability for God and an exoneration for his mother. The past tense in his words *"wherever I was"* shows that this was a communication of this fact to him from God, just as in the case of Muhammad when he said, *"I was a prophet when Adam was between water and clay"*[60]; so he knew his rank with God when Adam's bodily form had not yet come into existence.

387.26 Jesus also announced with the past tense that God gave him the Book and enjoined him to pray and give alms as long as he is in the world of [religious] prescription *(taklîf)* and Law-giving *(tashrî')*, a point expressed by his words, *"so long as I remained alive"* (Qur'an 19:32). This obviously means, for those who are his listeners, his living under prescription. For us it means this, but it also means something else, i.e., [it refers to] His words concerning

Jesus that he is the *"Word of God"* (Qur'an 4:169). A "word" is a collection of letters—the science of letters will come in the chapter on the Breath.[61] So God announced that He gave Jesus the Book, meaning the Gospel and meaning also the station of his existence in respect to the fact he is a Word. A "book" is a combination of written letters for the sake of making words manifest, or it is the combination of meaning and the forms of the letters that denote it[62]. So there must be composition *(tarkîb)*. Hence Jesus mentioned that God gave him the book, a statement similar to His words, *"He gave each thing its creation"* (Qur'an 20:52).

387.31 Jesus meant by *"enjoining prayer and alms"* (Qur'an 19:32) worship *(al-'ibâda)*.[63] These words denote these [specific] works *(al-'amal)*, but they denote worship even more, since they are in no need of explanation because they are worship. If the works were meant, it would have been necessary to specify them and explain their form, so that the person for whom they are prescribed may perform them. Since the meaning is worship, this shows that Jesus will continue to live wherever he is. Even if he departs from the body *(haykal)* through death, life will accompany him, since it is his intrinsic attribute, all the more so since he was made the "Spirit" of God (Qur'an 4:169)[64].

387.34 Then Jesus mentioned that he is dutiful to his mother (Qur'an 19:33), i.e., he does good *(muhsin)* toward her; the first of his good-doing was that he exonerated her from what was being ascribed to her while he was in a state where his listeners could not doubt that his communication was true.

387.35 Then he completed his words by saying, *"He did not make me mighty"* (Qur'an 19:33), for mightiness *(jabarût)*, which is tremendousness *('azama)*, contradicts servanthood, which was spelled out by his words that he is God's servant. By "might" he means: I do not exercise mightiness over the community to which I have been sent with the Book, prayer, and alms. I am only delivering a message from God, nothing else. I am not their guardian *(musaytir)* that I should be mighty and exercise mightiness over them. I deliver a message, as God said, *"O Messenger, deliver the message that has been sent down to thee"* (Qur'an 5:71); *"It is only for the messenger to deliver the message"* (5:99); *"Thou art only a reminder; thou art not their guardian"* (88:21-22). God's word is "reminder", and someone can only remind a person who is in a forgetful state. If this were not the case, he would be a teacher *(mu'allim)*, not a reminder. This shows that he is only reminding them of the state of their acknowledgment of God's Lordship over them when He took Adam's progeny from his reins at the First Covenant (Qur'an 7:172).

388.5   Then Jesus said, *"And safety* (salâm [i.e., "peace"]) *be upon me, the day I was born"* (Qur'an 19:34), when I spoke to you about the fact that I am God's servant, and thus was safe from the attribution of my existence to fornication or marriage, *"and the day I die"* (Qur'an 34:34), and I become safe from the slaying that will be attributed to me by those who think that they slew me. This refers to the words of the Children of Israel, *"We slew the Messiah, Jesus son of Mary"* (Qur'an 4:156). God declared them liars with His words, *"They did not slay him, neither crucified him, but it seemed so to them"* (Qur'an 4:156). So Jesus said to them that safety was upon him on the day that he died, safe from being slain. For if he had been slain, he would have been slain in martyrdom, and the martyr is alive, not dead, just as we have been prohibited from saying that,[65] a command that still remains [in effect]. So Jesus gave news that he died and was not slain, since he mentioned safety upon him on the day he died.

388.9   Then he mentioned that safety is upon him on the day that he is raised up alive (Qur'an 19:34), i.e., at the resurrection, which is the abode of safety for those who are free of every evil, like the prophets and other people of grace *('inâya)*. So Jesus possesses safety in all these places. Nor is there a third abode; there is only life in this world and life in the next, and between the two death.[66]

388.11   All these [words of Jesus], if they had not derived from the Divine Command, would have been unruly utterances on the part of their speaker, for they are words that show his degree with God by way of boasting of it before his equals and likes. But far be it from the Folk of Allah[67] to distinguish themselves from their likes or to boast! Hence unruly utterances are a frivolity of the self *(ru'ûna nafs)*; they never issue from a Verifier, for he has no object of contemplation but his Lord, and he does not boast before his Lord, nor does he make claims. On the contrary, he clings to his own servanthood, ready for the commands that come to him. He hastens to obey them, and he looks upon everything in engendered existence in this manner. So if he makes an unruly utterance, he has been veiled from that for which he has been created and is ignorant of himself and his Lord. Even if he possesses every power *(quwwa)* that he claims, so that he gives life and death and appoints and dismisses, still he has no [special] place with God; on the contrary, he is like a purgative or costive medicine. He acts by the specific characteristic of his state, not by his position with God, just as a sorcerer acts by the specific characteristic of his art for the eyes of the beholders.[68] He snatches their eyes away from seeing the truth *(al-haqq)* in what they see.

388.18 Everyone who makes an unruly utterance does so out of forgetfulness *(ghafla)*. We have never seen nor heard of a saint *(walî)* from whom an unruly utterance has issued because of the frivolity of the self while he was a saint of God, except that he demonstrated his poverty, became abased, and returned to his original state, so that the vainglory which assailed him disappeared.

388.19 Such is the situation of unruly utterances if they are justified, when they are still blameworthy. So what if they should issue from a liar *(kâdhib)*? If it is asked: How can he be a liar in an unruly utterance if he displays acts and effects? We reply: How excellent a question! As for the answer: The Folk of Allah, if they are Folk of Allah, produce effects only through veracious [spiritual] states *(al-hâl al-sâdiq)*. They name this [effect, when expressed verbally], an unruly utterance if it is not connected to a divine command that commands it, as is realized in the case of the prophets. But there are people who know the specific properties of the [Divine] Names *(khawâss al-asmâ')*, through which they display marvelous effects and correct influences. But a person like this never says, "This takes place through some Names that I know." He makes it appear to those present that it derives from the strength of his state, his position with God, and true sanctity, but he is a liar in all that. This is not called an unruly utterance, nor is its owner said to possess such a thing. On the contrary, this is sheer and hateful falsehood.

388.25   So unruly utterances are true words that issue from the frivolity of a self that still possesses the remnants of nature *(al-tab')*.[69] They testify that their possessor is distant from God in that state. And this much is sufficient concerning the state of the true knowledge of unruly utterances.

ON WITHDRAWAL
CHAPTER 205 [70]

This is one of the ninety-nine chapters that make up Section III of the Futûhât, *on the "[spiritual] states"* (ahwâl). *The term* takhallî *is the fifth verbal form of the root* kh.l.w., *from which also comes* khalwa *or "[spiritual] retreat." The root meaning is to be empty or vacant. Hence "withdrawal" signifies entering into a retreat or, more literally, to empty oneself, i.e., of that which distracts from God and ultimately of everything other than God. Withdrawal is often discussed along with two rhyming terms,* tahallî, *or "adornment," and* tajallî, *or "theophany," the subjects of Chapters 204 and 206. Ibn al-'Arabî says that the Sufis generally define adornment as* "making one's states similar to those who are truthful *[al-sâdiqîn]* in word and deed" (II 483.21), *whereas in his own view it is* "to take on the embellishment of the Divine Names as defined by the Law" (II 483.23). *He relates withdrawal to theophany by saying,* "Withdrawal is to choose the retreat and to turn away from everything that distracts from God in seeking theophany…, which is the unseen lights that are unveiled to hearts" (II 132.7; cf. *Istilâhât* 9).

The spiritual retreat, to which Ibn al-'Arabî devotes Chapters 78 and 79, is one of the mainstays of Sufi practice. The purpose of making retreats is "to empty the heart from thoughts connected to the various parts of engendered existence and actualized through directing the senses toward sensory objects. The treasury of the imagination *[khizânat al-khayâl]* becomes filled [with images derived from the sensory world], and the form-giving faculty *[al-quwwat al-musawwira]* then chooses out those forms with which it is enamored *[ta'ashshuq]*. Then these forms act as a barrier between the person and the Divine Level. Hence he [the spiritual traveler] inclines toward retreats and toward invocations *[adhkâr]* in praise of Him *"in whose hand is the Dominion"* (Qur'an 36:83). Then, when the soul becomes purified and the veil of nature that stands between him and the World of the Dominion *['âlam al-malakût]* is lifted, all the sciences imprinted within the forms of the World of the Dominion come to be reflected in the mirror of the soul" (II 48.20).

Once the veil has been lifted, the traveler has no more need of retreats. "The retreat is only correct for him who is veiled *[al-mahjûb]*. As for the People of Unveiling, the retreat is never correct for them, since they contemplate the higher spirits *[al-arwâh al-'ulwiyya]* and the fiery spirits *[al-arwâh al-nâriyya]* and see the engendered things speaking..." (II 151.26).

For Ibn al-'Arabî the retreat is a necessary stage on the path, but the elect will eventually reach the point where there will be no difference for them between being in a retreat (khalwa) *and being in "society"* (jalwa, *literally: the unveiling of a bride, but defined technically as leaving the retreat* [tark al-khalwa, II 152.22] *and closely connected in meaning to "theophany," which is derived from the same root).*

In discussing withdrawal, Ibn al-'Arabî follows his usual pattern of referring to a term's outward meaning, and then pointing out the root phenomenon in the divine things (ilâhiyyât). *Withdrawal is not retreat from the everyday world to God, but from our mistaken perception that our existence is real, to the true knowledge that we have no existence and that Being belongs to God alone. The subject of the chapter is not so much the spiritual state of withdrawal, which is to leave aside everything that distracts from God, as the root of this spiritual state in the Oneness of Being: There is nothing other than God, since none possesses Being but He. The things or entities remain eternally nonexistent. They cannot "acquire existence" as the philosophers maintain because "realities do not change"* (al-haqâ'iq lâ tatabaddal).

What appears to be the acquisition of existence by the things is in fact God disclosing Himself to us under the guise of His name the "Manifest" (al-zâhir), though His Self-disclosure is colored by the properties and effects of the things. Thus it is impossible to "withdraw" from acquired existence, since none has been acquired; the spiritual traveler must withdraw from his ignorance of the true situation.

Were it not for the levels set down in the Law, God's realities would not become manifest, though the entities give witness to Him.[71]
How should there be "withdrawal"? For there is no one in engendered existence save Him—and He it is whom we worship in engendered existence.
This prevents us from delimiting Him, so sometimes we make Him nonexistent, and sometimes we bring Him into existence.
For according to our creeds God brings every accident in engendered existence into existence.
So if you possess an eye and true knowledge, contemplate Him in all things and in the fact that things fail to find Him.

484.18   Know that for the Tribe "withdrawal" is to choose the retreat and to turn away *(i'râd)* from everything that distracts from God. But for us withdrawal takes place in relation to acquired existence *(al-wujûd al-mustafâd)*, since the creed *(al-i'tiqâd)* holds this to be so; and in reality *(fî nafs al-amr)* there is none but True Being *(al-wujûd al-haqq)*. That which is described as having acquired existence remains with its root *('alâ aslih)*: It does not pass from its possible existence *(imkân)*. Its property [of nonexistence] remains while its entity is immutable.

484.20   God is Witness *(shâhid)* and Witnessed *(mashhûd)*. For it is not proper that He should swear by that which is not He, since that by which He swears must possess tremendousness *('azama)*. Hence He did not swear by anything that is not He. We have mentioned this in the chapter on Breath.[72] Among the things by which He has sworn, are [those things mentioned in the verse], *"By a Witness and a Witnessed"* (Qur'an 85:3). So He is the Witness and the Witnessed, and He is that which acquires existence; or rather, He is the Existent *(al-mawjûd)*.

484.22   If you ask: Who then is ignorant of this, that you should teach him about it? For only that which is existent can be given knowledge. We reply: Your question is answered by your own creed, since you have faith that He said to the thing, *"Be!"*[73] He only addresses and commands that which hears, yet you hold that it has no existence when it is addressed; so that which has no existence is able to hear. Hence it is He who teaches the thing what it does not know, and it comes to know it; in the state of its nonexistence it receives teaching, just as—according to you—it hears God's address and then receives engendered existence *(qabûl al-takwîn)*. But in our view, contrary to your view, this is not its receiving engendered existence. Its "receiving engendered existence" is that it becomes a locus of manifestation *(mazhar)* for God.[74] This is the meaning of *"And it is"* (Qur'an 36:82). This does not mean that it acquires existence; it only acquires the property of being a locus of manifestation. So, it can be taught just as it can hear; there is no difference.

484.27   If you have paid attention and understood, I have apprised you of something tremendous. He is identical *('ayn)* to all things in manifestation *(zuhûr)*, but not identical to them in their essences *(dhawât)*—Glory be to Him and high exalted is He [above that]! No, He is He, and the things are the things. But when you see the properties of certain loci of manifestation in the Manifest, you imagine that their entities have become qualified by "acquired existence."

484.29   Then, when we came to know that among the possible entities there are people who are in this manner ignorant of the situation, it became incumbent upon us—though we remain immutable in our state of nonexistence—to teach the real situation to those of our fellow humans who do not know it. This is all the more so since we are qualified *(ittisâf)* as being a locus of manifestation, and we have been given the power through this relation *(nisba)* to teach him who does not know. Hence we gave him what he does not have, and he accepted it. Among the things I have taught him is that by being a locus of manifestation he does not acquire existence. So he "withdrew" from this belief, not from acquired existence, since there is none. That is why, in [the discussion of] withdrawal, we have turned away from [the position] that it is withdrawal from acquired existence.

484.33 Those People of Wayfaring *(ahl al-sulûk)* without knowledge of this, not knowing who is the Manifest and the Witnessed and who is the world, have chosen retreat *(khalwa)* in order to be isolated *(infirâd)* with God. Since the manyness *(kathra)* witnessed in existence veils them from God, they have inclined to withdrawal [through retreat]. This is one of the things that should show you that they have not renounced things in respect of the forms of the things, for they are not able to do that. In their retreat they must witness forms; in it they do not withdraw from the walls, door, roof, and furnishings which make up the retreat room, nor from carpet and curtain, food and drink. So the person in retreat is not able to withdraw from forms. There only remains that he has fled *(harb)* from the comprehensible speech *(al-kalâm al-mafhûm)* that arises from forms, not from Acts *(al-af'âl* [i.e., created things]). If there were animals with him, he would still be in retreat and would not be distracted from his purpose unless he feared being harmed by them; in a similar way [he would be distracted from his purpose] if the walls were leaning, for he would fear that they might fall on him. Hence he sought out withdrawal only because of the words that people speak. But if he were to understand the words that people speak in the mode *(wajh)* in which God places them within them, his knowledge would increase through something that he had not known. If someone were to pray a single prayer—I mean a single cycle *(rak'a)*—the person in retreat would not seek withdrawal from it, for when he hears the servant [performing the prayer] say, "God hears him who praises Him," and [knows] that these are the words of God,[75] then Reality permeates everything he hears.

485.7 Hence everything that people say imparts knowledge of God to the knowers. That is why one of the charismatic gifts *(karâmât)* of the Wholesome *(al-sâlihûn)* is that God allows them to hear the speech of things.[76] If this not did impart knowledge to them, it would not be a gift *(ikrâm)* from God to them.

485.9 For him whom God has given understanding, retreat *(khalwa)* and society *(jalwa)* are the same. Rather, it may be that society is more complete for a person and greater in benefit, since through it at every instant he increases in sciences about God that he did not possess.

GATHERING AND ITS MYSTERIES
CHAPTER 222[77]

This chapter, "Concerning the True Knowledge of Gathering *[jam']* and its Mysteries," *part of Section III on the states, is followed immediately by a complementary chapter dealing with the opposite of gathering, i.e., dispersion* (tafriqa). *Ibn al-'Arabî begins the present chapter by mentioning a few of the sayings of the Sufis concerning gathering and its more intense form, "gathering of gathering"* (jam' al-jam'). *He explains that in his own view, gathering is to make a clear distinction between God and creation, while gathering of gathering is to realize that, creation too, is but the manifestation of God. He alludes to his fundamental position on the Oneness of Being: The entities are forever nonexistent, while their properties bestow specific colors upon Being, the Manifest. The profession of God's Incomparability means that nothing else exists, so nothing can be found to which He might be compared. Oneness is the property of God, while multiplicity and manyness stem from the properties of the possible things (i.e., from the Divine Names, or the level of Similarity). Finally Ibn al-'Arabî turns to interpreting the sayings that he quoted at the beginning of the passage.*

If you should hear or see through God—He is the All-Hearing, the All-Seeing, the One, the Unique.

You are not in Him, while the entities subsist: soul, intellect, spirit, and body.
But if you enter into gathering of gathering, you will accompany Him through Him. Here you are the eternally subsistent Lord.
If you come to know this and become qualified by it in your state, you will knit together the whole affair.

Know that gathering for one of the Tribe is the allusion of him who alludes to God without creation.[78]

Abû 'Alî Daqqâq[79] said, "Gathering is what is negated from you." A tribe of them said, "Gathering is the Act of God through you which He truly lets you contemplate."

Some people said, "Gathering is the contemplation of true knowledge; its proof is, *'From Thee alone we seek help'* (Qur'an 1:5)."[80]

One of them said, "Gathering is the affirmation of creatures subsisting through God, while gathering of gathering is annihilation *(fanâ')* from the contemplation of anything but God."[81]

One of them said, "Gathering is the contemplation of others *(al-aghyâr)* through God, while gathering of gathering is total absorption *(al-istihlâk)* and the annihilation of the sensation *(ihsâs)* of everything other than God in the overpowering waves of Reality."[82]

One of them said, "Gathering is the contemplation of God's control *(tasrîf)* over all."[83]

Among the poetry written by the People on gathering and dispersion *(farq)* is the line:

Having been gathered in Him, I was dispersed from myself: single in union, two in number.[84]

516.21 Thus have I mentioned some of the sayings that have reached us concerning gathering and gathering of gathering. In our own view, gathering is that you gather in Him His Attributes and Names that you have attributed to yourself, and you gather in yourself your attributes and names that God has attributed to Himself, so that you are you and He is He. Gathering of gathering is that you gather in Him what belongs to Him and what belongs to you, and you return all of it to Him. *"To Him will be returned the whole affair"* (Qur'an 11:123). *"Surely unto God all things come home"* (Qur'an 42:53).

516.23 So there is nothing in engendered existence but His Names and Attributes, though the creatures have claimed some of them for themselves and God has gone along with their claim *(da'wâ)*.[85] So He addresses them according to what they claim. Some of them claim Names that are specific to Him in common usage *(al-'urf)*. Others have claimed that as well as attributes which have come in the Law and which, according to the exoteric authorities *('ulamâ' al-rusûm)*, are only worthy of temporally originated things.

516.26 As for our own path, we do not claim any of that whatsoever. However, we let it be known that the Names are the property of the effects of the preparedness of the entities of the possible things within Him. This is a hidden mystery, known only by him who knows that God is identical with Being *('ayn al-wujûd)* and that the entities of the possible things remain in their state: nothing of them changes in their entities.

516.28 For the person of sound intelligence, the expression "gathering" is sufficient, since it is a word that announces manyness *(kathra)* and distinction *(tamyîz)* among many entities. Hence, in respect of distinction, gathering is the same as dispersion *(tafriqa)*, though dispersion is not the same as gathering, except in the case of the dispersion of similar individuals *(ashkhâs al-amthâl)*, which is both gathering and dispersion together and the definition and reality of which is the gathering of similar things. Take for example "humanity" *(al-insâniyya)*. The individuals of this kind are qualified by dispersion, since Zayd is not 'Amr, even though both are human beings. It is the same with all similar things and individuals of a single kind.

516.31 God says, *"There is nothing like Him"* (Qur'an 42:11) in many senses *(wujûh)*; He already knows how every exegete *(muta'awwil)* will interpret this verse.[86] The highest of these senses is: There is nothing in existence that resembles God or is a likeness of God, since Being/existence[87] is nothing but God Himself *('ayn al-haqq)*. So there is nothing in existence other than He that might be His likeness *(mithl)* or opposite *(khilâf)*. This is inconceivable.

516.34   If you say, "Here we have an observed manyness," we will reply: Manyness is the relations *(nisab)* of the properties of the preparednesses of the possible things within God Himself, who is Being. Now relations are not entities or things *(ashyâ')*; they are matters of nonexistence *(umûr 'adamiyya)* in respect to the realities of the relations.[88] So, since there is nothing in existence but He, nothing is like Him, because nothing is there. So understand and verify what we have alluded to! For the entities of the possible things have not acquired *(istifâda)* anything but existence, and existence is nothing but God Himself, since it is impossible for it to be a superadded thing *(amr zâ'id)* that is not God, as is shown by clear proofs.[89] So nothing becomes manifest in existence through existence except God, since existence/Being is God, and He is One. So there is nothing that is His likeness, since there cannot be two diverse or similar Beings.

517.3   So in reality, as we have explained, gathering is that you gather within Him existence, since He is existence itself, and that you gather within the entities of the possible things the properties of number and dispersion that become manifest, since these are their very preparednesses.[90] Once you have come to know this, you have come to know the meaning of gathering, of gathering of gathering, and of the existence of manyness. You have attached things to their roots, distinguished among the realities, and given everything its own property, just as God *"gave everything its own creation"* (Qur'an 20:52). If you do not understand gathering as I have mentioned it, you know nothing of it.

517.7   As for the allusions of the Tribe which we quoted, they all had their own aims, which I will mention, God willing, along with their knowledge of our own position, or the knowledge of the great ones among them.

517.8   As for the saying, "Gathering is God without creation." that is what we maintain, i.e., that God is identical with Being/existence. However, the speaker did not turn his attention to what the preparednesses of the entities of the possible things bestow upon the Being of God, so that It becomes qualified by that by which It becomes qualified.

517.9   As for the saying of al-Daqqâq on gathering, that it is "what is negated from you", his station demands that he mean the negation of that concerning which you make claims, while it belongs to Him, as, for example, assuming the traits *(takhalluq)* of the Most Beautiful Names or attributing acts to yourself while they belong to Him. This [explanation] is given by al-Daqqâq's state *(ḥâl)*, not his words; if someone else had said them, he might have meant by "what is negated from you" existence itself, for that is what is negated from you since God is existence itself.

517.12   As for the next saying—"Gathering is the Act of God through you which He truly lets you contemplate"—it means that you are the locus *(maḥall)* for the accomplishment *(jarayân)* of His Acts, though in reality the situation is the reverse; in fact He is described by the property of the effects of the preparednesses of the possible entities within Him. But the speaker may mean by his words, "the Act of God through you," that the Act becomes manifest through you. He did not undertake to mention in whom the effect becomes manifest, so he may mean this, which is the position that we maintain and that the realities bestow. If we knew who is the author of this saying, we would judge it by his state, as we judged al-Daqqâq through our knowledge of his station and state.

517.16   As for the saying of him who said, "Gathering is the contemplation of true knowledge," you should know that true knowledge *(ma'rifa)* of God demands that the servant possess a sound relationship *(nisba)* with works *('amal)*, a relationship affirmed by God—hence He prescribed *(taklîf)* works for him—and that God possesses a relationship with works that is affirmed by God for Himself. God laid down in the Law that the servant should say in his works, *"From Thee alone we seek help"* (Qur'an 1:5). The messengers of God are more knowledgeable of Him than all other creatures; Moses, to whom God spoke directly,[91] said to his people, *"Seek help from God and be patient"* (7:125); and for us there is no difference in correctness or in attribution to God between what God says and what a messenger of God says as described by Him. God says, *"I have divided the canonical prayer between Me and My servant."*[92] Then He differentiated, explaining what the servant says and what God says. So the words are attributed to the servant with a sound attribution. Words are a work, and the servant seeks help from God in his work. So it is correct to say that the work is shared *(musbâraka)*. Thus have I gathered God and the servant together in the work, and this is the meaning of gathering.

517.21   I have already explained that the entity of the servant is a locus of manifestation *(mazhar)*, that the Manifest is God Himself *('ayn al-ḥaqq)*, and that God is identical with the attribute of the servant. Through the attribute the work comes into existence, while the Manifest is the Worker. So the work belongs only and specifically to God. This we said. When we explained what we just mentioned, we also explained that the entity of the servant possesses a specific preparedness which exercises an effect upon the Manifest. It is this which gives rise to the diversity of forms within the Manifest, which is God Himself. This preparedness made the Manifest say, *"From Thee alone we seek help."* The Manifest, through the effect of the preparedness of the praying entity, addresses the property of the Name the Helper *(al-mu'în)*, asking it to help it in its work; for if the preparedness of the entity of the possible thing should bestow incapacity or weakness, its property would appear in the Manifest. So the speech of the Manifest is the tongue of the entity of the possible thing; or rather, it is the speech of the possible thing in the tongue of the Manifest. In the same way God gives news that He says with the tongue of His servant, *"God hears him who praises Him."*[93]

517.27   Hence true knowledge demands that you should gather works in their Worker, because of the claims that take place as the result of the views of those speculative thinkers *(ashâb al-nazar)* who maintain that acts are attributed to the servant exclusively and those who maintain that they are attributed to God exclusively.[94] But the truth is between the two tribes, i.e., between the two opinions. So the servant possesses a relationship to the work as we have described it, i.e., as the effect of the preparedness of the entity of the possible thing within the Manifest; and God possesses a relationship to the work as we have described it, i.e., as the reception by the Manifest of the effectivity *(ta'thîr)* of the entity within it. For the servant says in the tongue of his effect within the Manifest, *"Thee alone we worship, and from Thee alone we seek help"* (Qur'an I:5).

517.31 This is our position *(madhhab)* on gathering. If the possessor of the saying on gathering means that it is the "contemplation of true knowledge," and if he knows the meaning of the contemplation of true knowledge, then he maintains what we said. For we have only been speaking of the contemplation of true knowledge, not of the station of the speaker; this saying has senses below that which we have maintained in explaining it, since we have explained it in its most complete and most perfect sense, which describes the entire affair as it is in itself. Because of some of these senses we have objected to the speaker of this saying in the synopsis of this book.[95]

517.34 All the sayings that we mentioned and related at the beginning of this chapter go back to what we have explained and upheld. *"And God speaks the truth and guides on the way"* (Qur'an 33:4).

THE WORLD OF IMAGINATION
CHAPTER 311[96]

This chapter, entitled "Concerning the Waystation of Arisings from the Unseen through Designation *[al-nawâshî al-ikhtisâsiyyat al-ghaybiyya]* From the Muhammadan Presence," *is one of 114 chapters in Section IV of the* Futûhât *on the waystations* (manâzil). *The term "designation"* (ikhtisâs) *relates the discussion to the long-standing debate between theologians and philosophers as to whether prophecy must be designated by God or can be earned* (iktisâb). *Briefly, in Ibn al-'Arabî's view, everything comes into being through designation, since all is determined by the immutable entities. As for the term "arisings," it calls to mind a number of Qur'anic terms from the same root, especially "plane"* (nash'a); *the connection with the main topic of the discussion becomes clear toward the end of the passage, where Ibn al-'Arabî quotes the verse,* "Then We made man arise as another creation" (Qur'an 23:13). *The first part of the chapter concerns observations on the meanings of these terms, while the major portion deals with the World of Imagination, which represents a single one of the sciences (from among a large number of possibilities)*[97] *perceived by the traveler when he dwells in this waystation.*

Ibn al-'Arabî discusses imagination in this chapter not so much in its cosmological function, but as a distinct world accessible to adepts in their spiritual journeys. In the process he tells a long anecdote about the power of "imaginalization"—the ability to assume any form desired—possessed by one of the shaykhs of Awhad al-Dîn Kirmânî. He also refers to the difference between utilizing the World of Imagination through various states of sanctity and through magic. Much of the rest of the chapter concerns man's special place among the creatures because of his power of imaginalization. Finally, there is an allusion to eschatology, since all the events in the next world take place in an imaginal realm.

41.23   Know that on the night that I wrote down this chapter I had a dream which filled me with joy. I awoke and composed a verse that I had previously worked on in my mind. It is a verse of boasting *(fakhr)*:

Every age has one person through whom it soars:
For the rest of the age, I am that one.

This is because to my knowledge there is no one today who has realized *(tahaqquq)* the station of servanthood *('ubûdiyya)* more than I, though there may be my equal *(mithlî)*. For I have reached the utmost limit *(ghâya)* of servanthood, since I am the pure and utter servant who knows no taste of lordship *(rubûbiyya)*.[98]

41.27   One day 'Utbat al-Ghulâm was seen strutting like a haughty and conceited man.[99] Someone said, "'Utba, what is this haughtiness you show? Nothing like this was known from you before today." He replied, "A person like me has a right to be haughty. How should I not be? For He has become my master, and I His servant."

41.29   Know that in every time there must be an outstanding person in each level *(martaba)*—even among artisans—and in each science *('ilm)*. Were any time to be studied, the situation would be found to be as we say. "Servanthood" is one of the levels, and Allah has bestowed it upon me as a gift *(hiba)*. I did not reach it through works *('amal)*, but through a divine designation *(ikhtisâs ilâhî)*. I ask God to keep me firmly fixed within it and not to separate me from it until I meet Him in it. *"In that let them rejoice; it is better than what they gather together [through works]"* (Qur'an 10:59).

41.32   Know that this waystation is that of Arisings through Designation *(al-nawâshi' al-ikhtisâsiyya)*; these consist of the beginning and outset of every station and state. God says, *"And We will make you arise within that which you do not know"* (Qur'an 56:61). If this were the return *(i'âda)* of our spirits to our bodies in this specific constitution which we know in the plane[100] of this world, it would not be correct for Him to say, *"within that which you do not know."* For He has said, *"You have known the first plane, so why will you not remember?"* (Qur'an 56:62). He has also said, *"As He originated you, so you will return"* (Qur'an 7:28), i.e., in the plane of the next world, since it is similar to the plane of this world in not having an exemplar *(mithâl)*, since God brought it into existence without a precedent exemplar.[101] So also He will cause us to arise [in the next world] without a precedent exemplar.

42.1   If someone objects that then there is no point to His words, *"You will return,"* we will reply: He is addressing human spirits. They will return to the governance of bodies *(tadbîr al-ajsâm)* in the next world, as they had governed them in this world in the constitution *(mizâj)* according to which this plane was created. He will bring them out of their burial in the constitution and *"out of the Fire when they grow up like a seed grows up after a flood has passed."*[102] Though He has the power to return their constitution, He does not will to do so. Therefore He suspended *(ta'lîq)* His Will in that, since He says, *"[Then He makes man to die, and buries him], then if He willed, He would raise him"* (Qur'an 80:22), i.e., the constitution which man possessed. If it were exactly the same thing, He would have said, "[Then when He wills], He raises him."

42.5   Let us return to the science of the waystation that we want to explain, the science around which it revolves. We say: The world is two worlds and the presence *(hadra)* two presences, even though a third presence is born between the two from their combination *(majmû')*. The one presence is the Presence of the Unseen *(al-ghayb)*; it has a world called the World of the Unseen. The second presence is the Presence of Sense Perception *(al-hiss)* and of the Visible *(al-shahâda)*; its world is called the World of the Visible. That which perceives *(mudrik)* this world is sight *(basar)*, while that which perceives the World of the Unseen is insight *(basîra)*.

42.8   What is born from the combination of these two presences is a presence and a world. The presence is the Presence of Imagination, the world the World of Imagination. Imagination is the manifestation of meanings *(ma'ânî)* in sensory frames *(qawâlib hissiyya)*, such as knowledge in the form of milk, firmness in religion in the form of a fetter, Islam in the form of a pillar, faith in the form of a handle, and Gabriel in the form of Dihya al-Kalbî, in the form of a Bedouin, and imaginalized *(tamaththul)* to Mary as a man without fault.[103] In the same way a black color appears in the body of gall nuts and vitriol when the two are combined [in the process of making ink], though they did not possess this quality when they were separate.

42.11   This is why the Presence of Imagination is the vastest of presences: it combines the two worlds, the World of the Unseen and the World of the Visible. For the Presence of the Unseen does not embrace the World of the Visible, since no empty space *(khala')* remains in the former[104]; and the same goes for the Presence of the Visible. Hence you know that the Presence of Imagination is the vastest, without doubt.[105]

42.13   You yourself have seen in your sense perception, and in what your plane gives to you, meanings and spiritual beings *(rûhâniyyûn)* appearing in images *(tamaththul)* and imaginal forms (*takhayyul*) within sensory bodies in your vision *(nazar)*, such that if an effect occurs within the imaginal form *(mutasawwar)*, the imaginalized meaning receives the effect in itself. And there is no doubt that you are more entitled *(ahaqq)* to the Presence of Imagination than are meanings and spiritual beings, for within you is the imaginal faculty *(al-quwwat al-mutakhayyila)*, which is one of the faculties which God gave you when He brought you into existence. So you are more entitled to possess *(mulk)* and control *(tasarruf)* imagination than is meaning, since meaning does not have a faculty of imagination; nor do the spiritual beings of the Supreme Assembly *(al-mala' al-a'lâ)* possess in their plane an imaginal faculty, though they can assume distinct identities *(tamayyuz)* in the imaginal presence through appearing in imaginal forms and imaginalization. So you are worthier of appearing in imaginal forms and of imaginalization than they, since you possess this presence in your own reality.

42.18   The common people *(al-'âmma)* do not know imagination or enter into it, except when they dream and their sensory faculties *(al-quwâ al-hassâsa)* return into it. The elite *(al-khawâss)* see it in wakefulness through their power of realizing it. So man's assuming forms *(tasawwur)* within the World of the Unseen in the Presence of Imagination[106] is nearer [to him] and worthier [for him than it is for spiritual beings], especially since in his own plane he possesses an entrance *(dukhûl)* into the World of the Unseen through his spirit, which is his nonmanifest *(bâtin)*; and he possesses an entrance into the World of the Visible through his body, which is his manifest *(zâhir)*. But the spiritual being is not like that; it does not possess an entrance into the World of the Visible except through appearing in imaginal form within the World of Imagination; so sense perception perceives it in imagination as an imaginalized form in sleep or wakefulness.

42.22   If man assumes a distinct identity within the World of the Unseen, this is proper to him, since he assumes a distinct identity in reality—not imaginally—through his spirit, which sense perception does not perceive and which belongs to the World of the Unseen. If he desires to spiritualize *(tarawhun)* his body and become manifest within it in the World of the Unseen, he has something to help him, i.e., the spirit connected to his body's governance. So he is nearer to imaginalization within the World of the Unseen than the spiritual being is to imaginalization within a form of the World of the Visible.

42.24   However, this station is to be earned and acquired, as in the case of Qadîb al-Bân,[107] for he possessed this station. Hence there is something within the power of man that is not within the power of [the inhabitants of] the World of the Unseen. For it is within man's power in respect of his spirit to appear in the World of the Visible in an imaginal form other than his own form. Thus man becomes manifest as he wishes, in any of the forms of the children of Adam like himself, or in the forms of animals, plants, or minerals. This has occurred among the masters.

42.27   I was discussing this issue with one of the shaykhs of the Way of God who in my eyes is a trustworthy and honest man.[108] He said to me: "I will relate to you what I have witnessed in order to confirm your words. I was the companion of a master *(rajul)* who possessed this station, though I was not aware of it. I asked to be his companion from Baghdâd to Mosul in a caravan of pilgrims returning from the *hajj*. He told me, 'If you are determined to come, do not take the initiative with me in any food or drink, but wait until I ask you for it.' I promised him that. He was an old man, so he rode in one half of a *haudah,* while I walked close behind him so that he would not be faced with a need for me.

42.31 "Then he became ill and weak with diarrhea. This was very difficult for me. But he did not take any medicine that would stop it and allow him to rest. I said to him, 'Master, let me go to this man who is the guide of the Sinjâr road and take from the dispensary a costive medicine.' He looked at me as if I were something disagreeable and said, 'Keep to your promise!' and did not answer me.

42.33 "His state became worse and I was not able to keep quiet. The caravan stopped for the night, torches were lit, and people made for the guide on the Sinjâr road. He was a black eunuch and men were posted before him. Those who were sick came to him seeking medicines according to their illnesses. I said, 'My lord, put my heart at ease and comfort me by commanding me to bring you some medicine from this man.' He smiled and said to me, 'Go to him.'

43.1 "I came to him, and he had not known me before that, nor was I in a state or an attire that would demand that he attach importance to me. So I walked to him, fearing that he would reject me or drive me away because he was so busy. I stood before him among the people. When his eyes fell on me, he stood up for me and made me sit down. He greeted me with joy, delight, and cheerfulness and asked me what I needed. I told him about the state of the shaykh and his illness. He asked his assistant to bring the medicine in the best form possible. He excused himself and said, 'I was tired, and have you not been sent to me in that?' I stood up to leave the tent, and he stood up with me and sent a torchbearer ahead of me. I said farewell to him after he had walked a few paces with me, and he commanded the torchbearer to walk in front of me with the light. I told him there was no need, fearing that the shaykh would find it excessive. So the torchbearer returned.

43.6 "I came and found the shaykh as I had left him. He asked me what I had done. I said to him, 'Through your blessing he honored me, though he did not I know me, nor I him.' I described for him what had happened in detail. The shaykh smiled and said, 'Oh Hâmid, I honored you. Without doubt it was not the eunuch who honored you. I saw that you were full of anxiety for me because of my illness and I wanted to ease your mind. So I commanded you to go to him, but I was afraid that he would insult you and reject you as he does with the people. Then you would have returned broken. So I disengaged myself *(tajarrud)* from my bodily frame *(haykal)* and appeared before you in his form through imaginalization. I honored you and treated you with respect and did what you saw until you left. Here is your medicine, which I will not use.

43.11 "I was flabbergasted. He said to me, 'Do not hasten [to believe me]. Return to him and see what he does with you.' So I returned to him and greeted him, but he did not receive me and rejected me. I went away in wonder. I returned to the shaykh and told him what had happened. He said, 'What did I tell you?' I said, 'How astonishing! How did you turn yourself into a black eunuch?' He answered, 'The situation was as you saw it.'"

43.13 Stories like this about the masters *(al-rijâl)* abound. It is similar to the science of *sîmiyâ'*[109] but it is not *sîmiyâ'*. The difference between us in this station and the science of *sîmiyâ'* is that, when you eat something through *sîmiyâ'*, you eat it, but you do not feel full. That which you take to yourself when you take it through this science only occurs in your own vision *(nazar)*. Then when you look for it, you do not find it. The practitioner of this science shows you that you have entered a bath, but when you return to yourself, you do not see any reality to it [what he had shown you]. On the contrary, what you see by way of *sîmiyâ'* is like what a dreamer sees; when he awakens, he finds nothing of what he had seen. The practitioner of *sîmiyâ'* possesses an authority *(sultân)* and control *(tahakkum)* over your imagination through the specific properties of the Names *(khawâss al-asmâ')*, or letters *(hurûf)*, or *qalfatîrât*.[110] For *sîmiyâ'* is of a number of kinds, the crudest *(akthaf)* being *qalfatîrât* and the subtlest *(altaf)* the pronunciation of words through which he snatches the viewer's eyesight away from the sensory world and turns it toward his imagination, so that he sees what a dreamer sees, though he is awake.

43.19   But the station which we mentioned is not like this. For if you eat, you become full, and if you receive something in this station like gold or clothing or whatever, it stays with you in its state without changing. We have found this station within ourselves. We experienced it through tasting *(dhawq)* with the spiritual reality *(rûhâniyya)* of Jesus at the beginning of our wayfaring *(sulûk)*.[111] It explains the Prophet's answer when he forbade fasting through the night during Ramadan and it was said to him, "But you fast through the night": *"I do not have a condition* (hay'a) *like yours; for I am put up for the night while there is with me a Feeder who feeds me and a Cupbearer who gives me to drink,"* or, according to another version, *"My Lord feeds me and gives me to drink."*[112] In the group of people whom he was addressing at the time no one possessed this station, but he did not say, "I do not have a condition like [all] people." So when he ate, he became full and continued in his customary strength; since the eating took place in the Presence of Imagination and not that of Sense Perception, he could fast through the night.

43.24   We saw that Gabriel became manifest within sense perception as a man who is known, such as his manifestation in the form of Dihya, and at another time as a man who is unknown. But it has not reached us that he becomes manifest in the World of the Unseen among the angels in the form of another angel. So Gabriel does not become manifest among the angels in the World of the Unseen in the form of Michael or Seraphiel. Therefore God reported him as saying, *"There is none of us but has a known station"* (Qur'an 37:164). And we saw that human beings possess the power of assuming imaginal forms, so that a person becomes manifest among men in the form of another person, other than his own form. Thus Zayd becomes manifest in the form of 'Amr. But the angels do not possess this in the World of the Unseen.

43.28   Just as Gabriel becomes manifest in human form, so man becomes manifest in the form of any one of the angels that he wishes. Even more marvelous is this: One of the masters from among the lovers *(muḥibbûn)* on this path called on a shaykh, and the shaykh spoke to him about love. Some of those present saw that the man had entered the room. Because of the strength of the lover's realization, the words of that shaykh about love made him keep on melting within himself on the sensory level until he was reduced to a puddle of water in front of the shaykh. Some of those present went into the room and asked where the lover had gone, since they had not seen him leave. The shaykh said, "This water is the lover who was before me." They saw a small amount of water on the mat in front of the shaykh. So look how he returned to the root from which he was created![113] Would that I knew where those parts went!

43.34   Know that in this path man is given a power whereby he becomes manifest in this plane in the same way that he becomes manifest in the plane of the next world, where he becomes manifest in any form he wishes.[114] For this [power] lies within the root of the [human] this-worldly form, but not everyone reaches knowledge of this root. It is [referred to in] God's words, *"[Oh Man! What deceived thee as to thy generous Lord,] who created thee, and shaped thee, and balanced thee,"* i.e., [He gave you] this outwardly manifest plane; then He says, *"and composed thee after whatever form He would?"* (Qur'an 82:6-8). In other words, this shaped and balanced plane is a receptacle for all forms, so God makes it appear in whatever form He wills, since He has told us that this plane has been given receptivity toward any form. Similar are His words, *"Then we made man arise as another creation"* (Qur'an 23:13) after completing the shaping of his outwardly manifest form; so He appointed for him another one of the forms which he had the potentiality and composition to receive.

44.4   When man comes to know through divine unveiling *(al-kashf al-ilâhî)* that his root and reality is such that it receives forms, he should take pains to acquire something through which he can reach true knowledge *(ma'rifa)* of the situation. Once he is given opening *(fatḥ)*[115] in this, he can become manifest within the World of the Visible in any one of its forms that he wishes, and he can become manifest within the World of the Unseen and Dominion[116] in any one of its forms that he wishes.

44.6   Here the difference between us and [the inhabitants of] the World of the Unseen is that when man becomes spiritualized and manifest to spiritual beings in the World of the Unseen, they recognize that he is a body that has become spiritualized. But when people in the World of the Visible see an embodied spirit, they do not know that it is a spirit that has first become embodied *(tajassud)*, so they do not recognize it as such. This is like what the Prophet said when the Faithful Spirit [Gabriel] came before him in the form of a man with intensely white clothing and intensely black hair. The narrator [of the hadith][117] says, "No one among us knew him. [He came forward] until he sat before the Messenger of God and he touched his knees to his knees and placed his hands upon his thighs." Then he mentioned the hadith of his questioning the Prophet about submission *(islâm)*, faith *(îmân)*, and virtue *(ihsân)* and about the hour and its signs *(shurût)*. When he had finished his questioning, he stood up and left. When he had disappeared, the Prophet said to his companions, "Do you know who the man was?"; and in another version, "Bring the man back to me"; he requested, but they could not find him. Then he said, *"That was Gabriel. He came to teach the people their religion."*[118]

44.12   Some people differentiate the spiritual being when it becomes embodied in the outside world *(min khârij)* from men or whatever kind of form in which it becomes manifest. But not everyone recognizes this. They also distinguish between an embodied, supra-formal, spiritual form [in the outside world] and an imaginal form from within *(min dâkhil)* through various signs *('alâmât)* which they know. I have come to know and realize these signs, since I differentiate the spirit when it becomes embodied in the outside or inside world from a true corporeal form. But the common people do not differentiate that.[119]

44.16   All the angels recognize man when he undergoes spiritualization and becomes manifest among them in the form of one of them or in an alien form whose like they have not seen. So they are greater than the common people among humans in this; but they lack the ability to become manifest in their world in the forms of other angels, whereas we—if we possess this station—can become manifest in our world in the form of our own kind. So glory be to the

All-Knowing, the All-Wise, the Determiner of things who is Powerful over them. There is no god but He, the All-Knowing, the All-Powerful.

44.18   Know that in theology *(al-'ilm al-ilâhî)*, the root of the situation that I have been discussing is the divine theophany *(al-tajallî al-ilâhî)*, from which this matter becomes manifest in the Worlds of the Unseen and the Visible. The reason for this is that the form of the world in its totality *(jumla)*, of man in his transcription *(nuskha)*,[120] and of the angel in its power *(quwwa)* is the station of theophany in diverse forms. No one truly knows the reality of these forms within which transmutation *(tahawwul)*[121] takes place except him who possesses the station of transmutation within any form he wishes, even if he does not make this station manifest. This station does not belong to anyone except the pure and utter servant, whose station of servanthood does not allow him to gain similarity *(tashabbuh)*[122] with a single Attribute of his Master. It even happens that as a result of his strength in the realization of servanthood he reaches the point where he is annihilated, oblivious, and destroyed from the knowledge of the power he possesses to undergo transmutation in forms; he does not know that from himself, since he has turned it over to the station of his Master, who describes Himself as possessing it.

44.24   If it were not for the divine root and the fact that God possesses this [transmutation] and owns it in His very Self, this reality would not become engendered in the world, since it is impossible for there to be something in the world which cannot be traced back *(istinâd)* to a divine reality in the very form it possesses. If this were possible, there would be something in existence outside the Knowledge of God. For He does not know the things except through His Knowledge of Himself, and His Self is His Knowledge. We are in His Knowledge like forms in a cloud of dust *(al-habâ')*.

44.27   If you knew, brave youth, who you are, you would know who He is, since none knows God except him who knows himself. The Prophet said, *"He who knows himself knows his Lord."*[123] So God knows you from Himself, and He tells you that you will not know Him except from yourself. He who understands this meaning will come to know what we are saying and to what we are alluding.

44.29 As for the hadith of theophany on the Day of Resurrection, I will include it, God willing, as it is included in the *Sahîh*. [There follows the text of a long hadith from Muslim[124] concerning the divine root of transmutation within forms. In short: on the Day of Resurrection God will appear in various forms and people will deny Him, until finally He shows them a sign they recognize. "Then He will transmute Himself into the form which they saw the first time and will say, 'I am your Lord.' They will answer, 'Indeed, Thou art our Lord.'"]

GOD'S SIGNS
CHAPTER 372[125]

The title of this chapter is "On the True Knowledge of the Waystation of a Mystery and Two Mysteries and of Your Praising *[thinâ']* Yourself for What is Not Yours and God's Answer to You with a Meaning that Ennobles You. From the Muhammadan Presence." *As is often the case, the significance of the title never becomes clear in the text of the chapter, about one-third of which is translated here. Ibn al-'Arabî discusses many of his major themes in the selected passage. Beginning with God's beauty, he turns to its manifestation in the world and the resulting bewilderment that overcomes the knowers* (al-'ârifûn). *The world is nothing but God's signs* (âyât), *but these signs are ranked in degrees, some of them more obvious in their denotation of God than others. And this is only natural, since the signs manifest the Names, and the Names are also ranked in degrees. Expanding on the theme of the signs that manifest God's Names, Ibn al-'Arabî turns to the World of Imagination, one of the greatest of God's signs, and in particular its role in determining the nature of love, whether for something, someone, or God. All who love God love only the images they themselves have constructed; in effect they profess God's Similarity with the creatures, though perfect knowledge of Him demands that they also profess His Incomparability. This discussion brings up the contrast between rational thought, which only perceives God's Incomparability, and revelation, which affirms His Similarity. But again, perfect knowledge demands that we take an intermediary position between Similarity and Incomparability, just as Imagination and the Perfect Man are intermediary states of existence.*

III 449.7   It is reported in the *Sahîh* [of Muslim] that the Messenger of God said, *"God is beautiful and He loves beauty."*[126] It is He who made the world and brought it into existence upon His own form. So the whole world is beautiful in the extreme; there is no ugliness in it. On the contrary, God brought together in it all comeliness *(husn)* and beauty. So there is nothing in possible existence *(imkân)* more beautiful, more wondrous *(abda')*, or more comely than the world.[127] If He were to bring into existence what He brings into existence ad infinitum, it would be like what He has already brought into existence, since the Divine Comeliness and Beauty will have possessed it and become manifest through it. For, as He says, *"He gave everything its creation,"* i.e., its beauty; if it were to lack anything, it would descend from the degree of the perfection of its creation and be ugly; *"then guided"* (Qur'an 20:50),[128] i.e., explained this point to us through His words, *"He gave everything its creation"*....

449.25   The whole world's beauty is inherent *(dhâtî)*; its comeliness is identical to itself *('ayn nafsih)*, since its Maker made it so. That is why the knowers become enraptured by it and the verifiers *(al-mutahaqqiqûn)* realize love for it. And that is why we have said concerning it in some of our explanations of it that it is God's mirror.[129] So the knowers see nothing in it but God's form. He is beautiful, and beauty is inherently lovable. Awe *(hayba)* toward Him is inherent to the hearts of those who gaze upon Him *(al-nâzirîn ilayh)*.[130] So He bestows love and awe.

449.27   The only reason God multiplied the signs in the world and in ourselves[131]—for we are part of the world—was so that we might turn our gaze *(nazar)*[132] toward it with remembrance, reflection, intelligence, faith, knowledge, hearing, sight, understanding, and mind.[133] He created us only to worship and know Him.[134] Hence He turned us over to nothing but gazing upon the world, for He made it identical with the signs and denotations *(dalâlât)* of the knowledge of Him through contemplation *(mushâhada)* and intelligence. So if we gaze, it is upon Him; if we hear, it is from Him; if we employ our intelligence, it is toward Him; if we reflect, it is upon Him; if we know, it is He; and if we have faith, it is in Him. For it is He who is revealed in theophany in every face, sought in every sign, gazed upon by every eye, worshipped in every object of worship *(ma'bûd)*,[135] and pursued in the unseen and the visible. Not a single one of His creatures can fail to find Him in its primordial and original nature *(bi fitratihi wa jibillatihi)*. So the whole world prays to Him, prostrates itself before Him, and glorifies His praise[136]; tongues speak of Him, hearts are enraptured by love for Him, minds are bewildered in Him. The knowers try to separate *(fasl)* Him from the world, but they are unable to do so; they try to make Him identical with the world *('ayn al-'âlam)*, but that does not become verified for them, so they remain impotent. Their understandings become wearied and their intellects bewildered. Their tongues speak about Him in contradictory expressions. At one time they say "He," at another, "Not He," and at still another, "He/not He" *(huwa lâ huwa)*.[137]

449.35   No foot of theirs reaches a firm foundation in Him; no clear path to Him appears for them, since they see Him as identical to the sign and the path. This contemplation stands between them and seeking the end of the path; for paths are traversed to their ends, while the Goal is with them—He is the Kind Companion *(rafîq)*. There is no wayfarer and no way upon which to fare. Allusions disappear: they are nothing but He. Expressions perish: they are only of Him. The knower cannot be rebuked for that part of the world which enraptures him and those waymarks which he presumes.

450.3   Were not the situation as we mentioned it, no prophet or messenger would have loved wife or child, nor would any have preferred one thing over another. This derives from the relative preference *(tafâdul)*[138] of the signs. The world's transformation *(taqallub)* is identical with the signs, which are not other than the "tasks" upon which is God.[139] *"He has raised one of them above another in degree"* (Qur'an 43:32) because through that form He has become manifest in His Names. Thus we know the relative preference of some over others through generality and specificity.[140] For example, [God says], *"He is Independent of the worlds"* (Qur'an 3:97), while He also says, *"I created jinn and men only to worship Me"* (Qur'an 51:56). How can the Creator compare to the Independent? How can the Seizer *(al-qâbid)* and the Preventer *(al-mâni')* compare to the Creator? How can the compass of the Knower be compared to that of the Powerful *(al-qâdir)* and the Triumphant *(al-qâhir)*? And is not all of this exactly what happens in the world?

450.7   Hence no messenger or saint exercised free disposal *(tasarruf)* except in Him. *"But most people do not know"* (Qur'an 7:187), and that is because there are among people those in whose ears is a heaviness (Qur'an 6:25), *"upon whose eyes is a covering"* (Qur'an 45:23), upon whose heart is a lock (Qur'an 47:24), in whose reflection is bewilderment, in whose knowledge is doubt, and in whose hearing is deafness. But, by God, in the knower's view all of this is nothing but excess proximity *(al-qurb al-mufrit)*[141]: *"We are nearer to Him than you, but you do not see"* (Qur'an 56:85); *"We indeed created man; and We know what his soul whispers within him, and We are nearer to him than the jugular vein"* (Qur'an 50:16). How can whispering compare with inspiration *(ilhâm)*? How can the name "man" compare with the Name the "Knower"?

Who are Laylâ, Lubnâ?
   Who are Hind, Bathna?
Who are Qays, Bishr?
   Are they all not He?
I am obsessed with love for Him
   for His engendered existence is mine.
All creatures are my beloved,
   so where, where is He who enraptures me?
He who searches my words
   will find therein a clear explication.

450.14   As for those who cling to accidental beauty and accidental love *(al-hubb al-'aradî)*, that is only a vanishing shadow, an accident on display, and a falling wall, in contrast with what there is for those who have knowledge of God. In the view of the man of God's knowledge, the shadow has prostrated itself before God, the accident has had the preparedness to exist, and the wall does not lean except in worship in order to make manifest what lies beneath it:

the treasures of gnostic sciences *(ma'ârif)* that deliver the aware knower from need. That is why God created Jealousy in the form of Khadir[142] who straightened the reclining wall because he knew there was no aptitude [for knowledge] in its owner at that time, so the treasure would have been used improperly. [He wanted] it to be discovered after some time, for if it had become manifest, it would have been taken uselessly and used wickedly.

450.17 So glory be to Him who lays down decrees, sets up signs, and manifests the beauty of denotations *(dalâlât)*. Among the most beautiful in entity and the most perfect in engendered existence is the World of Imagination *('âlam al-khayâl)*, through which *"God strikes similitudes* (amthâl)"[143] (Qur'an 13:17, etc.). He has explained that He alone has knowledge of it, for He said in prohibition, *"So strike not any similitudes for God; surely God knows, and you know not"* (Qur'an 16:74). He only brought this verse after He struck similitudes for Himself for our sake. Thus the World of Imagination became manifest to engendered existence. This is the introduction.

450.20 Do you not see how dreams *(ru'yâ)*—through the eye of which imagination is perceived—see what will come to be before it exists, what has been, and what there is at the time? Which presence other than the Presence of Imagination possesses such all-comprehensiveness *(jam'iyya)*?

450.21 Everyone who falls in love with something only falls in love with it after actualizing it in his imagination, setting up an image *(mithâl)* for it in his imaginal faculty *(wahm)*,[144] and making his beloved coincide *(tatbîq)* with his image. If this were not the situation, then once the person separated from his connection to his beloved in terms of sight or hearing or other sense faculty, he would also separate from his connection to her person. But we do not find this to be the case. This shows that the beloved exists with the lover in the image of a form *('alâ mithâl sûra)* and that he has brought her forth in his imagination. Hence he clings to contemplating his beloved, his ecstasy *(wajd)* doubles, and his love continues to increase. The image which he formed provokes its former *(musawwir)* to seek her on whose form he formed it. The root [i.e., his beloved] is the spirit of the image, making it subsist and preserving it. The love of the lover intensifies only toward his own making *(san'a)* and act *(fi'l)*, for he himself has made the form with which he has fallen in love in his imagination. So he loves nothing but that which goes back to himself; he attaches himself *(ta'alluq)* to himself, and he praises his own act.

450.26   He who knows this knows God's love for His servants and that His love for them is more intense than their love for Him. Or rather, they do not love Him for Himself *('aynan)* but for His beneficence *(ihsân)*, since His beneficence is what they witness. He who loves Him for Himself only loves an image that he has formed and imagined in himself; such people are none but those who profess Similarity *(al-mushabbiha)* in particular.[145] But if a lover did not profess Similarity, he would not love Him; if not for imagining *(takhayyul)*, he would not attach himself to Him. That is why the Lawgiver *(al-shâri')*[146] placed Him in the servant's *qibla*,[147] made the heart of His servant encompass Him,[148] and made Him like him or like some of his parts as a result of proximity to Him.[149] People of this sort worship Him in images and contemplate Him as actually present *(muhassal)*.

450.30   As for those who profess His Incomparability *(al-munazziha)*, they are bewildered in blindness, striking out in it haphazardly. They find no shadow in its darkness, nor [do they find] the profession of Similarity which proofs *(al-dalîl)* deny to them. There is no faith whose light might outbalance the light of the proofs and within which they might include the proofs. So those who profess Incomparability remain forever grasping at nothing, nor do they actualize anything. They are the People of Severance *(ahl al-batt)*, since their aspiration is dispersed and the imaginal faculty *(wahm)* is far from them. From the perfection of the true knowledge of existence they lack the property of imaginal faculties, which exercise no property except in those Men who are the Perfect *(al-kummal min al-rijâl)*.[150]

450.33   That is why the religions *(al-sharâ'i')* have brought concerning God that which proofs show to be impossible. When the light of a person's faith dominates over the light of his intellect... —in the same way the light of the sun dominates over the light of the other heavenly bodies *(kawâkib)*; it does not take away their lights, it only includes them in its own light, so that the whole world is illuminated by the light of the sun and the light of the heavenly bodies, but people see nothing but the light of the sun, not the light of all. In the same way, when the light of the faith of one of the perfect among the Folk of Allah includes the light of his intellect, he concurs *(taswîb)* with the view of those who profess Incomparability, since it does not go beyond that which their lights unveiled for them. He also concurs with the view of those who profess Similarity, since their view does not go beyond the outward of what the light of their faith gives to them through the similitudes that God has struck for them. So the perfect one knows Him through intellect and faith, thus gaining possession of the degree of perfection.

451.2   In the same way imagination gains possession of the degree of sense perception *(hiss)* and meaning *(ma'nâ)*. Hence it makes the sensory thing subtle *(taltîf)* and the meaning gross *(takthîf)*, thus possessing complete power. That is why Jacob said to his son, *"Relate not thy vision to thy brothers, lest they scheme against thee"* (Qur'an 12:5). He knew what they knew concerning the interpretation of the images God had shown Joseph in his vision. For what he saw and what was shown to him in images was nothing but his brothers and his parents. So imagination had brought forth the forms of his brothers as stars and the forms of his parents as the sun and the moon, though all of them were flesh, blood, veins, and nerves. So look at this passage *(naqla)* from the world of lowness to the world of the spheres and from the darkness of this bodily frame to the light of the stars! Imagination made the gross subtle, then it applied itself to the level of priority *(taqaddum)*, high station, and disengaged *(mujarrad)* meanings. It clothed them in the form of sensory prostration, thus making their subtlety gross; but all the while the vision was one. So if not for the power of this Presence, what happened would not have happened. Were it not in the middle *(wasat)*, it could not exercise its properties over the two sides, for the middle exercises its properties *(hâkim)* upon the two sides, since it is a limit for them, just as the present moment entifies *(ta'yîn)* the past and the future.

451.9   In the same way, God placed the level of the Perfect Man midway between God's being seated upon His Throne and His being located within his heart, which encompasses Him.[151] So he looks upon Him in his heart and sees that He is the Central Point of the Circle *(nuqtat al-dâ'ira)*; and he looks upon Him seated upon His Throne and sees that He is the Circumference *(muhît)*[152] of the Circle. No line becomes manifest from the Center without coming to an end at the Circumference, and no line becomes manifest on the inner side of the Circumference without coming to an end at the Center. These lines are nothing but the world, for *"He is the Circumference of all things"* (Qur'an 51:54), all are His handful,[153] and *"To Him the whole affair shall be returned"* (Qur'an 11:123).

451.12   The "Void" is that which is postulated between the Center and the Circumference.[154] It fills *('amâra)* the world with its entity and engendered existence. Within it become manifest transmutations *(istihâlât)*, from Center to Circumference and from Circumference to Center. So nothing goes outside of Him, nor is there anything outside of the Circumference, since everything enters within His Compass *(ihâta)*. Rather, everything arises from Him and ends up in Him, appears from Him and returns to Him. So His Circumference is His Names, while His Center is His Essence. That is why He is the One/Number *(al-wâhid al-'adad)* and the One/Many *(al-wâhid al-kathîr)*.[155] No eye looks upon Him except the eye of man *('ayn al-insân)*, and were it not for the man of the eye *(insân al-'ayn* [i.e., the pupil]), the eye of man would not gaze. So man looks through man, and God becomes manifest through God.

WORSHIP AND ITS SECRETS

CHAPTER 470[156]

This chapter, entitled "On the State of the Pole Whose Waystation Is 'I Have Not Created Jinn and Mankind Except to Worship Me'" *(Qur'an 51:56), is one in a series of more than ninety in the sixth section of the* Futûhât *(chapters 464ff.) that discuss the stations* (maqâmât) *of the various kinds of "Muhammadan Poles"* (al-aqtâb al-Muhammadiyya) *and the connection of each Pole to a different sacred formula or Qur'anic verse, which is his "constant invocation"* (hijjîr). *It is commonly thought that the Sufis speak of a single Pole* (qutb), *around whom all the affairs of the universe revolve and without whom the universe would cease to exist. Though Ibn al-'Arabî discusses this supreme Pole in many passages,[157] he also points out that there are numerous other Poles, each one of which is the axis or central figure in a particular group of people or in a spiritual station or state. As for the Muhammadan Poles, they are* "those people who have inherited from Muhammad some of the religious laws *[sharâ'i']* and spiritual states *[ahwâl]* that pertain exclusively to him and which were not found in any religion *[shar']* that preceded him, nor in any messenger that came before him. If that which is inherited is something which was in a religion that came before him and is also in his religion, or was in a messenger before him and is also in him, then the inheritor inherits from that specific messenger, but through

Muhammad. So he is related to that messenger, even though he is a member of this community. Hence he is called 'Mûsawî' if he has inherited from Moses, 'Îsawî' if from Jesus, or 'Ibrâhîmî' if from Abraham" (IV 76.27).

Ibn al-'Arabî explains that in this series of chapters he does not mean by "Muhammadan Poles" that type of Pole of whom there is only one in every period. "I will only mention among the Muhammadan Poles everyone around whom revolve the affairs of a group of people in a specific clime or aspect, like the Substitutes *[abdâl]* in the seven climes...; or like the Poles of the towns, since each town *[qarya]* must have a saint of God through which God preserves it, whether it is a believing or unbelieving town... The same thing goes for the possessors of stations. Hence the ascetics *[zuhhâd]* must have a pole, around whom asceticism revolves in the people of his time; and so on with trust, love, knowledge, and the rest of the stations and states" (IV 76.8).

Each of these Muhammadan Poles has a hijjîr *or "constant invocation" specific to himself.* "Know that the *hijjîr* is the invocation *[dhikr]* to which the servant clings *[mulâzama]*, whatever that invocation may be. Each invocation produces a result produced by no other invocation. But when man presents the divine invocations to his own soul, it only receives from them that which his preparedness *[isti'dâd]* allows. The first opening *[fath]* he is given in the invocation is his reception of it. Then he never ceases applying *[muwâzaba]* himself to it with each breath. No breath leaves him in wakefulness or sleep except in invocation, because of his devotion *[istihtâr]* to it. As long as the invoker's state is not like this, he is not the owner of a *hijjîr*" (IV 88.31).

An invocation is not a true hijjîr *until the invoker has been given full "opening." This term, whose meaning is basically the same as* futûh *(of which* Futûhât *is the plural), signifies that God has unveiled* (kashf) *the inward content of the hijjîr to the adept. In some places Ibn al-'Arabî identifies opening with the shining of the divine lights* (al-anwâr al-ilâhiyya) *into the heart (e.g., II 600.3; cf. 626.5). Hence he writes,* "The *hijjîr* yields no profit if its owner has not been given opening. If you see the possessor of a *hijjîr* who does not have opening, you should know that his outward tongue does not harmonize with his inward tongue. Someone like that is not whom we mean by 'possessors of *hijjîrs*' "(IV 127.25).

The hijjîr *of the greatest Poles is the name Allah* (IV 78.8), *which explains why the supreme Pole forever pertains to this name and is called "Abd Allâh"* (II 571.21). *This also explains why* "the Perfect Man is the absolute vassal of the Name Allah *[al-ma'lûh al-mutlaq]*, while God *[al-haqq]* is the Absolute Divinity *[al-ilâh al-mutlaq]*" (II 603.16). *But as for the other Poles, their* hijjîrs *are of a great variety.* "The Poles of the towns, the aspects, and the climes and the shaykhs of different groups have many different kinds of *hijjîr*" (IV 78.9).

In discussing the hijjîrs *of the various kinds of Poles, Ibn al-'Arabî begins with the well-known formulae that are used in prayer and invocation, i.e., "There is no God but God," "God is great," "Glory be to God," and "Praise belongs to God," and then passes on to various Qur'anic verses most of which, even without his commentary, have obvious applications to the spiritual life. If it is true that the* Futûhât *is basically one great commentary on the Qur'an, this is nowhere more apparent than in this sixth section of the work.*

The thrust of the present chapter is to demonstrate the Oneness of Being and the interrelationship of all things as this is expressed in the "worship" ('ibâda) *mentioned in the Qur'anic verse which is the* hijjîr *of the particular Pole in question. The duality perceived in existence between Creator and creature is demanded by the nature of Reality; each side has need of the other, though this does not impinge on the absolute Independence of the Essence. The need, love, and poverty displayed by all creatures toward all sorts of other creatures is in fact their need for God, who manifests Himself within the things of the world, which are His loci of manifestation. All created things worship Him by their very nature (*'ibâda dhâtiyya; *cf. note 160 below). As we saw in Chapter 372,* "He is worshipped in every object of worship" (cf. II 1353.6). *And in the last analysis, God's bestowal of existence upon the creatures is the manifestation of His need for them and "worship" of them.*

Just as He who loves you gave you your creation, so also you should
  give Him that for which you were created.[158]
If you do not give it, yet creation will be given, and He will not have

been shown gratitude.

But it is best to fulfill God's right, my friend—this is a revelation He has given you.[159]

If you attain God's wish as He desires, He will make you attain your wish.

IV 100.33   God says, *"Thy Lord has decreed that you shall not worship any but Him"* (Qur'an 17:23), and His decree cannot be repulsed.[160] We know that the result of the invocation *(dhikr)* [mentioned in the title of this chapter] will be the contemplation of this verse, without doubt.

100.34   God is Being, while the things are the forms of Being. So the entire affair *(al-amr)* is interconnected *(irtibât)* in the same way that matter is interconnected with form. Without doubt worship, in the language in which the Qur'an was sent down, is lowliness *(dhilla)*. When a thing grows up out of an interconnection between two things such that neither of the two can yield that thing without the one's interconnection with the other, then we know that each of the two interconnected things belongs to the love *(hubb)* that arises in each through the manifestation of the third thing and that each of the two seeks the other. Hence there must be seeking *(talab)* in each of them; it is not proper that there be the actual *(al-hâsil)*. So the two things must be qualified as lacking that thing whose existence is desired, and seeking can only be a kind of lowliness *(idhlâl)*.

101.3   *"Your Lord has said, 'Call upon Me and I will answer you'"*(Qur'an 40:60). Hence He seeks calling from His servants, while the servants seek an answer from Him. So everything is seeker and sought. But proofs are established that temporally originated things *(al-hawâdith)* cannot subsist in God. So He cannot assume every seeking in Himself, for seeking by a temporally originated thing is itself temporally originated. So it is impossible for such a seeking to subsist in Him. Hence there must be a seeking of the existence of that through which this temporally originated seeking can subsist. That is His words, *"[The only word We say to a thing] when We desire it [is that We say to it 'Be!' and it is]"* (Qur'an 16:40). Seeking is a desire *(irâda)*, whether He desires you for Himself or He desires you for yourself. But it is not proper for something to be the actual in the respect in which it is sought, since in that respect it is not actual.

101.7 So there cannot be existence *(wujûd)* except from two roots *(asl)*: One root is power *(iqtidâr)*, which is linked to the side of God; the second is reception *(qabûl)*, which is linked to the side of the possible thing. Neither of the two roots is independent *(istiqlâl)* in existence or in the bestowing of existence *(îjâd)*. That which acquires *(al-mustafâd)* existence acquires it only from itself through its reception and from that which influences *(nufûdh)* it through Its power, and that is God. However, that thing does not say concerning itself that it bestowed existence upon itself. Rather, it says that God bestowed existence upon it, while the true situation is as we have mentioned. Hence the possible thing is not equitable *(insâf)* toward itself, but in this manner it prefers *(îthâr)* its Lord. Then, when God comes to know that it has preferred its Lord over itself by attributing the bestowal of existence to Him, He bestows upon it manifestation in His form as a reward. Hence there is none more perfect than the world, since there is none more perfect than God[161]; and existence is not perfected except through the manifestation of the temporally originated thing.

101.12 Since this is the situation in terms of conditionality *(tawaqquf)* and lack of independence on both sides, God called attention to it with His words, *"I have divided the canonical prayer into two halves between Myself and My servant, so one half belongs to Me and one half to My servant."*[162] This division also exists in God's taking the servant as His vicegerent and in God's acting as Guardian *(wakîl)* in that in which the servant was made vicegerent.[163] So Being is Independent, but it is perfected by the temporally originated thing.

101.14 Since God is Jealous lest something else be mentioned along with Him, He manifested Himself in theophany to the world in the form of the temporally originated things.[164] The world's inhabitants come to know Him in them; this is His notification to them that He is *"Independent of the worlds"* (Qur'an 3:97)[165]: You have seen His manifestation in His Essence through theophany in the forms of the temporally originated things—so your manifestation and nonexistence are the same. Thus does He speak to the possible thing. At that the possible thing becomes lowly in itself in actuality *(bi'l fi'l)*. Then there occurs from it that for which God created it [i.e., worship], and there disappears from it the mightiness *('izz)* of possessing the preparedness for reception in the bestowal of existence. When it sees that it is God who is manifest through the entities of the forms which were engendered by its own reception and God's power, [it knows that] there is no need for reception by the possible things. The situation is actualized and His words are correct: *"God is Independent of the worlds."*

101.18 While I was recording this question a divine flash *(bâriqa ilâhiyya)* flashed for me and in it I saw whatever sciences God willed. In a similar way the Prophet struck a stone that had been uncovered in the Trench with a pickax, and when he struck it there flashed forth a flash through which he saw that which God would conquer for his community. He even saw the palaces of Basra like the tusks of an elephant. He saw those things in three strikes, in each of which a flash appeared to him under a specific aspect.[166] I saw this in recording this chapter as a Muhammadan inheritance—praise belongs to God. In it and through it I saw that although God becomes manifest in the forms of the possible things and is qualified by Independence *(ghinâ)*, this does not exclude Him from a lack of independence *(istiqlâl)* in respect to the existence of the temporally originated thing, since there must be reception on its part. But here there occurs debate *(kalâm)*. This is some of what the flash gave to me.

101.23 Since God created the creatures to worship Him, He clothed them in that Attribute of His through which He sought them, and through it they worship Him, for it is not correct that they should worship Him through themselves in respect of [their] independence *(istiqlâl)*. That is why the Law tells them to say *"Thee alone we worship"* and then *"And from Thee alone we seek help"* (Qur'an 1:4), for there is no independence in worship. So it instructs them to seek help in worshipping Him, just as their reception was a help to the Divine Power in creation. If there were not this interconnection, there could be neither worship nor bestowal of existence. Hence bestowal of existence is a worship, but it belongs to God;

while worship is a bestowal of existence, but it is what is sought from the creatures. So they are the worshippers, while He is the worshipped; He bestows existence, while they are the existent things.

101.27 The *lâm* of cause[167] is inherent to both sides; it is what the Law calls a "wisdom" *(hikma)* or an "occasion" *(sabab)*. For God is the Wise, and in each thing He has a manifest wisdom. The People of Unveiling and Finding know what that wisdom is in all things, while the exoteric authorities *(ahl al-rusûm)* know it in prescriptions *(taklîfât)*, which can only be known in respect of the Law, so the wisdom of prescriptions can only be known in respect of the Law; as for example His words, *"In retaliation there is life for you"* (Qur'an 2:179).

101.29 As for the view that prescription has a cause from God's side, this is an opinion *(maznûn)*, not a known fact. But God opened the door of deduction *(istinbât)* for them [i.e., those who hold this opinion] through the causality *(ta'lîl)* He mentioned in the Revelation sent down. So some of it is obvious and some hidden.

101.31 In the same way God has in the things a nonmanifest wisdom known only to Him and those to whom He gives knowledge of it. Therefore He said [in the verse mentioned in the title] *"jinn,"* i.e., that which is hidden,[168] *"and mankind,"* i.e., that which is manifest so that it is known in its essence in respect of its manifestation, *"except to worship Me,"* thereby affirming the cause for creation. So this is the "*lâm* of wisdom and occasion" according to the Law and the "*lâm* of cause" according to the intellect.

101.33 But worship is inherent to the created thing; there is no need for it to be prescribed, since the Creator is necessarily identical with every form the created thing worships, even though form is poor toward *(iftiqâr)* [and in need of] matter. If this were not the case, the worship of the created thing would not be inherent.

101.34 When we limit ourselves to what is called Allah in common language *('urf)*, the created thing worships other than God, for we see that most of the world's inhabitants are only poor toward phenomenal causes *(asbâb)*. How is this? Has not God said, *"Thy*

Lord has decreed that you shall not worship any but Him" (Qur'an 17:23), and *"Oh people! You are the poor toward Allah"* (Qur'an 35:15)?[169] He never mentioned the poverty of a created thing toward other than Allah, nor did He decree that other than Allah be worshipped. Therefore He must be identical *('ayn)* with all things, that is, identical with everything toward which there is poverty and which is worshipped. In the same way He is identical with the worshipper in the case of every worshipper; for He said, *"I am his hearing"*[170] when He addresses him with prescriptions and instruction *(ta'rîf)*. So the servant does not hear His words except through His hearing. And so it is with all of his faculties, through which alone he is able to be a worshipper of God. Hence nothing becomes manifest in the worshipper and the worshipped except His He-ness *(huwiyya)*. Therefore the wisdom, occasion, and cause are nothing but He, while the result and that which is occasioned are nothing but He. So He alone worships and is worshipped. The Prophet said in his address when he was praising his Lord, *"For we [exist] only through Him and for Him."* So He addresses and He listens. This is a situation *(amr)* that cannot be refuted, for He is identical with the situation.

102.6 However, preference *(fadl)* among people takes place through that which some of them contemplate and others declare forbidden. So the knower knows about other than himself what the other does not know about himself, i.e., concerning what the other is in himself. Hence relative preference *(tafâdul)*[171] becomes manifest. But in spite of this manifestation, the created thing does not cease having God as its he-ness, by reason of the relative preference of the Divine Names, which are the Attributes; and they are not other than He.

Not known are the creatures except through Him,
    not known is He except through them.

102.9 As for His being described by "Independence of the world", that is only for him who supposes that God is not identical with the world, who distinguishes between the denotation *(dalîl)* and that which is denoted *(madlûl)*, and who has not realized through speculative thought *(nazar)* that, when the denotation of a thing is the thing itself, it does not oppose itself. So the entire affair is one, though expressions of it are diverse. So He is the knower, knowledge, and the object of knowledge; He is the denotation, the denoter *(dâll)*, and that which is denoted. So through knowledge He knows knowledge; hence knowledge is knowledge's object of knowledge *(al-'ilm ma'lûm li'l-'ilm)*. So He is the object of knowledge and knowledge, while knowledge is inherent to the knower. Here we have the words of the theologian *(mutakallim)*, "It is not other than He," but nothing more. As for the theologian's words, "It is not He" after this, that is because he sees that it [the Attribute] is conceived of *(ma'qûl)* as superadded *(zâ'id)* to what He is.[172] So there remains that it be He. But the theologian is not able to affirm that it is He without a knowledge describing Him thus. So he says, "It is not other than He," since he is bewildered. He speaks in accordance with what his understanding gives him, so he says that God's Attribute is not He, nor is it other than He.

102.14   But when we say something like these words, we do not say them within the limits of the theologian. For he necessarily conceives of the superadded thing, but we do not hold that there is something superadded. Hence the theologian has nothing more to offer than him who says, *"God is poor,"*[173] except in the beauty of the expression. And we seek refuge in God lest we be among the ignorant.

102.16   These are some of the results of this constant invocation.

IBN 'ARABÎ'S
SPIRITUAL ASCENSION

James W. Morris

"MY VOYAGE WAS ONLY IN MYSELF..."

INTRODUCTION TO CHAPTER 367

The initial indications in the Qur'an and hadith concerning the Prophet's Ascension (mi'râj) or nocturnal voyage (isrâ'; Qur'an 17:1) and the revelatory vision in which it culminated (Qur'an 53:1-18) subsequently gave rise to a vast body of interpretations among the many later traditions of Islamic thought and spirituality.[1] Ibn 'Arabî's personal adaptation of that material, in at least four separate longer narratives, reflects both the typical features of his distinctive approach to the Qur'an and hadith and the full range of his metaphysical-theological teachings and practical spiritual concerns. For him, the Prophet's "nocturnal journey"—an expression he prefers both because it is that of the Qur'an and because it is more appropriate to the complete, "circular" nature of the movement in question[2]—is above all an archetypal symbol of the highest, culminating stages in the inner, spiritual journey that must be followed by each of the saints or mystical "knowers" who would participate fully in the heritage of Muhammad,[3] even if the subjective phases and experiences marking that route necessarily appear differently to each individual.[4]

Thus the theme of the Mi'râj provides Ibn 'Arabî with a single unifying symbolic framework for the full range of practical spiritual questions and theoretical issues (ontological, cosmological, *theological, etc.) that are discussed in other contexts throughout the* Futûhât *and his other works.*[5] *If each of his treatments of the Mi'râj approaches those issues from its own particular standpoint and purpose—and with, in addition, very different literary styles and degrees of autobiographical openness—they all do share what is perhaps the most fundamental feature of all of his writing: the continually alternating contrast between the metaphysical (universal and eternal) "divine" point of view*[6] *and the "phenomenological" (personal and experiential) perspective of each individual voyager. The aim of this sort of dialectic, as he pointedly reminds his readers at the very beginning of chapter 367 (section I of the translation below), is quite clear: if the journey in question necessarily appears to move through time and distance, that is not so that we can eventually "reach" God—since* "He is with you wherever you are"—*but rather* "so that He can cause [us] to see His Signs" *(Qur'an 31:31) that are always there,* "on the horizons" *and* "in the souls." *The heavens of this journey, the prophets and angels who populate them, the Temple or the Throne where the final "unveiling" takes place—all of these, he insists, are so many places of the* Heart.[7]

Modern readers who want to understand these narratives on this ultimate and most intimate level, however, must first find their way through an extremely complex set of symbols, and often only implicit references, to what are now largely unfamiliar bodies of knowledge: the task of interpretation is therefore not unlike that facing students of Dante's Divine Comedy *(and more particularly the* Paradiso). *Therefore our annotation to this translation of chapter 367 of the* Futûhât *concentrates on providing that indispensable background in the following areas:* 1. *the actual Islamic source-materials in the Qur'an and hadith which provide the basic structure and key symbols for all of Ibn 'Arabî's Mi'râj narratives*[8]; 2. *the cosmological and astrological presuppositions which he generally shared with other traditions (more or less "scientific") of his time*[9]; 3. *his own personal metaphysical and cosmogonical theories or "doctrines," which are basically those found throughout his other writings; and* 4. *his conception of the particular spiritual "heritages" and distinctive qualities of each of the prophets encountered during the Mi'râj, as they are developed in the* Fusûs al-Hikam *and throughout the* Futûhât.[10]

Finally, since Ibn 'Arabî's four major Mi'râj narratives do share certain common features—and since several are available (at least partially) in French and English translations—it may be helpful, for comparative purposes, to point out some of the more distinctive features of each.

The Other Mi'râj Narratives[11]:
Kitâb al-Isrâ', Risâlat al-Anwâr,
Chapter 167 of the Futûhât

The Kitâb al-Isrâ',[12] *at once the earliest, the longest and the most personally revealing of the works discussed here, was composed in Fez in the year 594, apparently only a relatively short time after certain decisive personal inspirations concerning the ultimate unity of the prophets in the spiritual "station of Muhammad" and the inner meaning of the* Qur'ân *in its full eternal reality that were soon to coalesce in Ibn 'Arabî's conception of his own unique role as "Seal of the Muhammadan Saints."*[13] *In an emotionally fluid and highly expressive Arabic style, drawing on an incredibly dense and allusive symbolic vocabulary*[14] *and combining long poetic interludes with rapidly moving rhymed prose—and culminating in a series of remarkable "intimate conversations"* (munâjât) *with God (pp. 50-82)—he constantly returns to celebrate and elaborate on the twin themes of the eternal Muhammadan Reality (encompassing all the prophets and their teachings) and the metaphysical universality of the Qur'ân as they were inwardly realized and verified in his own mystical experience. Here the passage of this autobiographical "voyager"*[15] *through the heavenly spheres and the higher revelatory stages of the Mi'râj (pp. 11-49) is not so much a means for describing the successive steps of the spiritual path and "progress" of the saints more generally—as it is, to some extent, in all the other Mi'râj narratives—but instead primarily a framework for evoking and clarifying various aspects of the author's own spiritual achievement, as they mirror the even loftier rank of the Prophet (pp. 83-92). What is perhaps most noteworthy about this composition, in a way that reinforces Ibn 'Arabî's repeated assertions that he first received all of this only by divine inspiration (and not through an individual effort of reasoning), is the way the complex systematic metaphysical and ontological framework developed in the* Futûhât *is already entirely present, but for the most part only* implicitly—*expressed instead through an incredibly profuse array of symbols and allusions drawn from the Qur'an and hadith (and whose full explanation is to be sought, for the most part, only in later, more analytical prose works such as the* Futûhât).

Compared to the literary and doctrinal complexities of the preceding work, the *Risâlat al-Anwâr, a relatively brief prose treatise composed at Konya in 602 A.H. (near the beginning of Ibn 'Arabî's long stay in the Muslim East), is stylistically far more accessible and its contents are more readily understandable*—*features which (along with the existence of an excellent commentary by 'Abd al-Karîm Jîlî) no doubt help account for its popularity with modern translators.*[16] *Written in response to a request by a Sufi friend and fellow master, this study, as its full title partly indicates,*[17] *is above all practical in intention and experiential (rather than primarily doctrinal or metaphysical) in its terms of reference and expression; it is aimed at the needs of a reader who, already necessarily possessing a considerable degree of personal accomplishment and experience, is intimately involved with the spiritual direction of disciples at earlier stages of the Path. While the allusions to the Mi'râj proper (pp. 9-13; English tr., pp. 40-46) are very brief*—*mentioning for the most part only the cosmological powers or spiritual qualities traditionally associated with each of the heavenly spheres and the Qur'anic "cosmography" of the Gardens of Paradise, the divine "Throne", "Pen", etc.,*[18] *it does provide an indispensable complement to the other Mi'râj narratives in two critical areas:* 1. *its relatively detailed discussion of the essential practical methods and preliminary stages preparing the way for the inner realization of these more advanced spiritual insights;* 2. *Ibn 'Arabî's repeated emphasis on the fundamental importance of the concluding phase of the saints' "return" to a transformed awareness of the physical and social world (in its immediate relation with God) and to the particular responsibilities and activities*—*whether teaching and spiritual guidance, or the less visible tasks of the representatives of the spiritual hierarchy*—*flowing from that realization.*[19]

Finally, the long chapter 167 of the Futûhât, *"On the Inner Knowledge of the Alchemy of Happiness,"*[20] *uses the framework of the Mi'râj to retrace, in ascending order, the many levels of Ibn 'Arabî's complex cosmology or cosmogony.*[21] *Its primary focus (compared with the other works mentioned here) is on the "objective" metaphysical realities underlying the spiritual insights described in more experiential terms in the other narratives: in this respect it often resembles the* Fusûs al-Hikam, *and the treatment of the various prophets encountered during this heavenly voyage (e.g., Jesus, Aaron or Moses) often closely parallels that found in the corresponding chapters of the* Fusûs. *This feature is further underlined by Ibn 'Arabî's narrative technique of comparison, throughout this ascension, between the initiatic spiritual knowledge granted to the "follower of Muhammad" (representing the methods of the saints and Sufis more generally) and the limited cosmological and theological insights available to his companion, the archetypal "man of reason."*[22] *In general, the full elucidation of many of those complex allusions would require extensive reference to some of the most obscure and unfamiliar aspects of the Shaykh's thought.*

Ibn 'Arabî's Own Mi'râj:
Chapter 367

Ibn 'Arabî's long treatment of the Mi'râj in chapter 367 of the Futûhât *is marked by some distinctive features that make it considerably more accessible (at least for most modern readers) than either chapter 167 or the* Kitâb al-Isrâ'. *To begin with, it is written for the most part in relatively straightforward expository prose; the style does presuppose a profound acquaintance with Ibn 'Arabî's systematic terminology and symbolism (largely drawn from the Qur'an and hadith) as it is to be found throughout the* Futûhât, *but the role of unfamiliar Arabic literary and artistic effects is relatively less important than in the preceding works. Secondly, the focus of this chapter is almost exclusively on the universal spiritual dimensions of the Mi'râj, especially as expressed in the language of the Qur'an and hadith, in a way that should already be familiar to readers of the* Fusûs al-Hikam; *unlike chapter 167, it does not presuppose such extensive acquaintance with the vocabulary and symbolism of other relatively esoteric medieval Islamic sciences (alchemy, astrology, etc.). Similarly, the encounters with the individual prophets associated with each heavenly sphere can often be readily illuminated by comparison with corresponding passages elsewhere in Ibn 'Arabî's writings.*[23] *And finally, as so often in the* Futûhât, *the genuinely autobiographical passages*[24] *especially at the conclusion of Ibn 'Arabî's own spiritual ascent (section IV-I below), add a powerful new dimension of clarity and persuasive force to what otherwise might appear to be simply a complex intellectual and symbolic "system."*

The overall structure of this chapter is quite clear, consisting of four successively broader and more detailed elaborations of the central theme of the inner spiritual meaning of the "nocturnal journey," a theme whose ultimate premises and metaphysical-theological context are briefly evoked in the opening lines (section I), already summarized at the beginning of this introduction. In section II, Ibn 'Arabî takes up the hadith accounts of Muhammad's Mi'râj—which provide the formal framework for the rest of the narrative—and adds his own allusions to many of the key themes developed at greater length in the following sections. In section III, he provides a condensed, still highly abstract schematic outline of the *"spiritual journeys of the saints"* (awliyâ'), *expressed in his own distinctive metaphysical-theological terminology (i.e., "in His Names in their names"). Finally, the greater part of the chapter (section IV) is taken up with Ibn 'Arabî's account, narrated in the first person and closely following the path of the Prophet, of the climactic stages of his own personal spiritual journey.*[25] *If the autobiographical guise at first seems only a sort of didactic literary device, at the end (section IV-I) he does conclude with the description of a decisive personal "revelation", a compelling spiritual experience that seems to have contained—or at least confirmed—virtually all the most distinctive points of his later thought and conviction, the forms of divine knowledge which he goes on to elaborate in a long enumeration of "what he saw" in that culminating "Muhammadan Station."*

The complete title of Chapter 367 is: "Concerning the Inner Knowledge of the Stage *[manzil]* of the Fifth *Tawakkul*, Which None of the People of Realization *[muhaqqiqîn]* Has Discovered, Because of the Rarity of Those Apt to Receive It and the Inadequacy of [Men's] Understandings to Grasp It."[26]

"MY VOYAGE WAS ONLY IN MYSELF..."
CHAPTER 367

I. Introduction:
the Context and Purpose of the
Spiritual Journey

...God said *"There is nothing like His likeness [and He is the All-Hearing, the All-Seeing]"* (Qur'an 42:11),[27] so He described Himself with a description that necessarily belongs only to Him, which is His saying: *"And He is with you wherever you are"* (Qur'an 57:4).[28] Thus He is with us wherever we are, in the state of His "descending to the heaven of this world during the last third of the night,"[29] in the state of His being *mounted upon the Throne* (Qur'an 5:20, etc.),[30] in the state of His being in the "Cloud,"[31] in the state of His being *upon the earth and in heaven* (Qur'an 43:84, etc.),[32] in the state of His being *closer to man than his jugular vein* (Qur'an 50:16)[33]—and all of these are qualifications with which only He can be described.

Hence God does not move a servant from place to place in order that [the servant] might see Him, but rather "so that He might cause him to see of His Signs" (Qur'an 41:53, etc.)[34] those that were unseen by him. He said: *"Glory to Him Who made His servant journey one night from the Sacred Place of Worship to the Furthest Place of Worship, whose surroundings We have blessed, so that We might cause him to see of Our Signs!"* (Qur'an 17:1)[35] And similarly, when God moves [any] servant through his [inner spiritual] states in order also to cause him to see His Signs, He moves him through *His* states.[36] ... [i.e., God] says: "I only made him journey by night in order that he see the Signs, not [to bring him] to Me: because no place can hold Me and the relation of all places to Me is the same. For I am such that [only] 'the heart of My servant, the man of true faith, encompasses Me,'[37] so how could he be 'made to journey to Me' while I am *'with him wherever he is?!'* "(Qur'an 57:4)

II. The Narrative Framework:
the *Mi'râj* of Muhammad and His Many
Spiritual Journeys

The long following section (III 340.32-342.34) combines a virtually complete quotation of one long hadith account of the Prophet's Mi'râj[38]—*whose sequence of events and heavenly encounters with the spirits of earlier prophets provides the narrative framework for all of Ibn 'Arabî's different versions of that voyage—with a number of the Shaykh's personal observations. These brief remarks either foreshadow themes developed at greater length in the rest of the chapter (and in his other treatments of the Mi'râj theme) or else allude to interpretations (e.g., of the drinks offered the Prophet at the beginning of his journey, or of the rivers of Paradise) that he discusses more fully in the other contexts and chapters of the* Futûhât. *However, four of those asides are significant enough to deserve special mention here.*

The first of these is Ibn 'Arabî's understanding of the statement in this hadith that Muhammad "descended from Burâq [his celestial steed] and tied him up with the same halter the [other] prophets had used to tie him." *For the Shaykh,* "all of that was only so as to affirm [the importance and reality of] the secondary causes[39]...although he knew that Burâq was commanded [by God] and would have stayed there even if he had left him without tying the halter."

The second of these parenthetical remarks occurs in the lowest heaven (the one immediately surrounding this sublunar world), when Muhammad is brought face-to-face with all the blessed and the damned among the descendants of Adam.[40] "Then [Muhammad] saw himself among the different individuals belonging to the blessed, at Adam's right hand, and he gave thanks to God. And through that he came to know how it is that man can be in two places [at the same time] while remaining precisely himself and not anyone else: this was for him like the visible [physical] form and the [reflected] forms visible in the mirror and [other] reflected images."[41]

The third such passage is Ibn 'Arabî's statement, in connection with the Prophet's visit to Jesus in the second heaven, that "He was our first master, through whose assistance we returned [to

God]; and he has a tremendous solicitude *('ináya)* for us, so that he does not forget us for a single hour."[42]

The final observation concerns the nature of the Prophet's vision (ru'ya) *of God at the culminating stage of his Ascension, after God—in the words of the hadîth—*"had revealed to him what He revealed."[43] "Then He ordered [Muhammad] to enter; so he entered [the divine Presence], and there he *saw* exactly what he had known and nothing else: the form of his belief did not change."[44] *This question of man's "divine vision" and knowledge is at the heart of Ibn 'Arabî's own long discussion with Moses later in this chapter (IV-F below) and underlies his accounts of his own personal vision at the all-encompassing "Muhammadan Station" (in IV-I below).*

At the end of this section, after pointing out that it was only the Prophet's insistence on the actual bodily—rather than ecstatic or visionary—nature of this ascension that aroused the skepticism and hostility of his contemporaries,[45] *Ibn 'Arabî concludes:* "Now [Muhammad] had thirty-four times[46] in which [God] made him journey at night, and only one of them was a nocturnal journey in his [physical] body, while the others were with his spirit, through a vision which he saw."

III. The Spiritual Journeys of the Saints[47]

As for the saints, they have spiritual journeys in the intermediate world[48] during which they directly witness spiritual realities *(ma'ânî)* embodied in forms that have become sensible for the imagination; these [sensible images] convey knowledge of the spiritual realities contained within those forms. And so they have a [spiritual] journey on the earth and in the air, without their ever having set a sensible foot in the heavens. For what distinguished God's Messenger from all the others [among the saints] was that his *body* was made to journey, so that he passed through the heavens and spheres in a way perceptible by the senses and traversed real, sensible distances. But all of that from the heavens [also belongs] to his heirs,[49] [only] in its spiritual reality *(ma'nâ)*, not its sensible form.

So as for what is above the heavens,[50] let us mention what God made me directly witness in particular of the journey of the People of God. For their journeys are different [in form] because they are embodied spiritual realities, unlike the sensible journey [of the Prophet]. Thus the ascensions *(ma'ârij)* of the saints are the ascensions of [their] spirits and the vision of [their] hearts, [the vision] of forms in the intermediate world and of embodied spiritual realities. And we have already mentioned what we directly witnessed of that in our book called *The Nocturnal Journey*,[51] along with the order of [the stages of] the voyage....

Therefore whenever God wishes to journey with the spirits of whomever He wishes among the heirs of His messengers and His saints, *so that He might cause* them *to see His Signs* (Qur'an 17:1)—for this is a journey to increase [their] knowledge and open the eye of [their] understanding—the modalities of their journey are different [for different individuals]:[52] and among them are those whom He causes to journey *in* Him.

Now this journey [in God] involves the "dissolving" of their composite nature.[53] Through this journey God [first of all] acquaints them with what corresponds to them in each world [of being], by passing with them through the different sorts of worlds, both composite and simple.[54] Then [the spiritual traveler] leaves behind in each world that part of himself which corresponds to it: the form of his leaving it behind is that God sends a barrier between that person and that part of himself he left behind in that sort of world, so that he is not aware of it. But he still has the awareness of what remains with him, until eventually he remains [alone] with the divine Mystery which is the "particular individual aspect"[55] extending from God to Him. So when he alone remains [without any of those other attachments to the world], then God removes from him the barrier of the veil[56] and he remains with God, just as everything else in him remained with [the world] corresponding to it.

Hence throughout this journey the servant remains God and not-God.[57] And since he remains God and not-God, He makes [the servant] travel—with respect to Him, not with respect to [what is] not-Him—*in Him*,[58] in a subtle spiritual *(ma'nawî)* journey....

Ibn 'Arabî goes on (III 343.24–344.4) *to recall the fundamental metaphysical underpinnings of these distinctions in the peculiar nature of the inner correspondence between man and the world (i.e., "not-God"), since both are created—in the words of a famous hadith—"according to the form" of God. Ordinarily however, people think of themselves as simply "parts" of the world, as "things" within it, and it is only at the end of this purifying journey that the saints can realize man's true dignity and spiritual function as the "Perfect Man"* (al-insân al-kâmil) *whose Heart fully mirrors the divine Reality* (al-Haqq), *thereby accomplishing that perfection for which the world itself was created.*[59]

So when the servant has become aware of what we have just explained, so that he knows that he is not [created] according to the form of the world, but only according to the form of God *(al-Haqq)*, then God *makes him journey* through His Names, *in order to cause him to see His Signs* (Qur'an 17:1) within him.[60] Thus [the servant] comes to know that He is what is designated by every divine Name—whether or not that Name is one of those described as "beautiful."[61] It is through those Names that God appears in His servants, and it is through Them that the servant takes on the different "colorings" of his states: for They are Names in God, but "colorings" [of the soul] in us.[62] And they are precisely the "affairs" with which God is "occupied":[63] so it is in us and through us that He acts just as we [only] appear in Him and through Him....[64]

Thus when God makes the saint *(al-walî)* travel through His most beautiful Names to the other Names and [ultimately] all the divine Names, he comes to know the transformations of his states and the states of the whole world.[65] And [he knows] that that transformation is what brings those very Names to be in *us*,[66] just as we know that the transformations of [our] states [manifest] the specific influences *(ahkâm)* of those Names... So there is no Name that God has applied to Himself that He has not also applied to us: through [His Names] we undergo the transformations in our states, and with them we are transformed [by God]....[67]

Now when [the spiritual traveler] has completed his share of the journey through the Names and has come to know the Signs which the Names of God gave him during that journey, then he returns and "reintegrates" his self with a composition different from that initial composite nature,[68] because of the knowledge he has gained which he did not have when he was "dissolved" [in the ascending phase of that journey].[69] Thus he continues to pass through the different sorts of worlds, taking from each world that [aspect of himself] which he had left there and reintegrating it in his self, and he continues to appear in each successive stage [of being] until he arrives back on earth.

So "he awakens among his people" [like the Prophet], and no one knows what happened to occur to him in his innermost being *(sirr)* until he speaks [of his journey]. But then they hear him speaking a language different from the one they are used to recognizing as his; and if one of them says to him "What is this?" he replies that "God made me journey by night and then caused me to see whatever Signs of His He wanted [me to see]." So those who are listening say to him: "You were not gone from us, so you were lying in what you claimed about that."[70]

And the jurist *(faqîh)* among them says: "This fellow is laying claim to prophethood *(nubuwwa)*, or his intellect has become deranged: so either he is a heretic—in which case he ought to be executed—or else he is insane, in which case we have no business talking with him." Thus *"a group of people make fun"* of him (Qur'an 49:11), others *"draw a lesson from"* him (Qur'an 59:2),[71] while others have faith in what he says, and thus it becomes a subject of dispute in the world. But the *faqîh* was unaware of [the true meaning of] His saying: *"We shall show them Our Signs on the horizons and in their souls...*" (Qur'an 41:53),[72] since [God] does not specify one group rather than [any] other.

Therefore whoever God may cause to see something of these Signs in the way we have just mentioned should mention [only] *what* he has seen, but he should not mention the way. For then people will have credence in him and will look into what he says, since they will only deny what he says if he makes a claim about the way [he acquired that knowledge].

Now you should know that [in reality] there is no difference with regard to this journey between ordinary people[73] and the person [distinguished by] this way and this characteristic. That is because [this spiritual journey] is in order to see the [divine] Signs, and the transformations of the states of ordinary people are [likewise] all Signs: they are *in* those Signs, but *"they do not notice"* (Qur'an 23:56, etc.).[74] Hence this sort [of traveler] is only distinguished from the rest of [his fellow] creatures, *those who are veiled* (Qur'an 83:15), by what God has inspired in his innermost being[75] either through his thinking and inquiry with his intellect, or through his preparation, by polishing the mirror of his soul, for the unveiling of these Signs to him by way of inner unveiling and immediate witnessing, direct experience and ecstatic "finding."[76]

Thus ordinary people [when they object to those who speak of this spiritual voyage] are denying precisely That within Which they are and through Which they subsist. So if [the traveler] did not mention the *way* in which he obtained the inner knowledge of these things, no one would deny or dispute him. For all of the [ordinary] people—and I do not exclude a single one of them—are "making up likenesses for God";[77] they have always agreed and cooperated in that, so not one of them criticizes another for doing it. God says: *"Do not make up likenesses for God..."* (Qur'an 16:74)—yet they remain blind to that Sign.[78]

But as for *the friends of God* (Qur'an 10:64-66),[79] they do not make up likenesses for God. For *God* is the One Who *makes up likenesses for the people* (Qur'an 14:25; 24:35), because of His knowledge of the underlying intentions (of those symbols), since *God knows, but we do not know*[80] (see Qur'an 16:74; 3:66; 2:216). Thus the saint [the one truly "close to God"] observes the likenesses God has made, and in that immediate witnessing he actually *sees* precisely what connects the likeness and That Which it symbolizes:

for the likeness is precisely What is symbolized, with respect to that which connects them, but it is different insofar as it is a likeness. So the saint "does not make up likenesses for God"; instead, he truly *knows* what God symbolized with those likenesses....[81]

IV. Ibn ʿArabî's Personal *Miʿrâj*

IV-A. *The Departure From the Elemental World*[82]

So when God wished to "journey with me to cause me to see [some] of His Signs" in His Names among my names[83]—and that was the portion of our inheritance from the [Prophet's] nocturnal journey—He removed me from my place and ascended with me on the Burâq of my contingency.[84] Then He penetrated with me into my [natural] elements....

At this point Ibn ʿArabî allegorically encounters each of the elements constituting the physical, sublunar world, according to the accepted physical theories of his time—i.e., earth, water, air and fire—and leaves behind with each of them the corresponding part of his bodily nature.[85]

So I passed through into the first heaven:[86] nothing remained with me of my bodily nature[87] that I [needed to] depend on or to which I [had to] pay attention.

IV-B. Adam and the First Heaven[88]

As Ibn ʿArabî explains in this section, it was during this encounter with his "father" that he was first given the immediate spiritual awareness of two key themes of his thought: the universality of the divine Mercy which, like the Being that is inseparable from it, "encompasses all things"; and, flowing from this first principle, the temporal, limited nature of the punishments of "Hell" [and the sufferings of the world as a whole], which manifest certain of those Names.[89] *The discovery and awareness of these principles presupposes man's ultimate reality as the "Perfect Man"* (insân kâmil), *the [potentially] complete reflection of the divine Reality at all Its levels of manifestation—i.e., the very foundation of the Shaykh's metaphysical vision which is developed at much greater length in the famous opening chapter on Adam in the* Fusûs.

At the beginning of this encounter Ibn ʿArabî—like Muhammad before him[90]—*suddenly sees his "essential reality"* (ʿayn) *among the souls of the blessed on Adam's right, while at the same time he himself remains standing in front of Adam. Then Adam goes on to inform him that the Qur'anic expressions* "the people of the left hand" *and* "the people of the right" *(Qur'an 56:27, 38, 41, 90, etc.) refer in reality to Adam's hands, since all of mankind are in God's "Right Hand"*—"*the one which destines [them] to happiness*"—"*because both of my Lord's Hands are Right and blessed."*[91]

...Therefore I and my children are [all] in the Right Hand of the Truly Real *(al-Haqq)*, while everything in the world other than us is in the other divine Hand.

I said: "Then we shall not be made to suffer [in Hell]?"

And [Adam] replied: "If [God's] Anger were to continue [forever], then the suffering [of the damned] would continue. But it is happiness that continues forever, although the dwellings are different, because God places in each abode [of Paradise and Gehenna] that which comprises the enjoyment of the people of that abode, which is why both abodes must necessarily be 'filled up' (see Qur'an 11:119, etc.).[92] For the [divine] Anger has already come to an end with the 'Greater Reviewing':[93] [God] ordered that [His] limits be established;[94] so they were established, and when they were established [His] Anger disappeared. [This is] because the sending down of the [divine] Message *(tanzîl al-risâla)* actually *is* precisely the establishment [and application] of [God's] limits for *those with whom He is angry* (Qur'an 1:7), and nothing remains [after that] but [His] Good Will and *Mercy which encompasses every thing* (Qur'an 7:156). So when these 'limits' [and the punishments flowing from them] have come to an end, then the [divine] authority[95] comes back to the universal Mercy with regard to everything."[96]

Thus my father Adam granted me the benefit of this knowledge when I was unaware of it, and that was divine good tidings for me in the life of this world, in anticipation [of its full realization in the hereafter]. Therefore the Resurrection comes to an end with time,[97] as God said: *"[The angels and the Spirit ascend to Him in a Day whose extent is] of fifty thousand years"*[98] (Qur'an 70:4), and this is the period of the establishment [and application] of the [divine] limits.

Ibn 'Arabî goes on to explain that "after this period"—however it is to be understood—only the divine Names "the Merciful" [which encompasses all the "Most Beautiful Names"] and "the Compassionate" will have authority and influence (hukm) *in the world, although the intrinsic, logically necessary "opposition "of the other Names necessarily will remain.*

…Hence the creatures are entirely submerged in [God's] Mercy, and the authority of the [other divine] Names [only] continues in their intrinsic opposition, but *not in us.* So you should know that, for it is a rare and subtle knowledge that [most people] do not realize. Instead, ordinary people are blind to it: there is no one among them who, if you were to ask him "Are you content to have applied to yourself [the influence] of those Names that give you pain?" would not reply "No!" and have the influence of that painful Name applied to someone else in his stead.[99] But such a person is among the most ignorant of people concerning the creatures—and he is even more ignorant of the Truly Real!

So this [experience of] immediate witnessing informed [us] concerning the continuation of the authority *(hukm)* of the Names [i.e., other than those of Mercy] with regard to those Names [in themselves], but not in us. For those Names are *relations* whose realities are intrinsically opposed, so that they [can] never become united [in away that would erase their inherent relational distinctions].[100] But God extends His Mercy to [all] His servants wherever they are, since Being in its entirety *is* Mercy.[101]

IV-C. *Jesus and Yahyâ (John the Baptist) in the Second Heaven*[102]

Ibn 'Arabî next encounters Jesus and his cousin Yahyà (John the Baptist) in the third heaven—the two figures being linked here by their association in the Qur'an with "Life," both "animal" and spiritual. The Shaykh first asks Jesus about his life-giving powers, and is told that they ultimately come from Gabriel (as the Universal Spirit, al-rûh al-kull): "No one who revives the dead revives them except to the extent of what he has inherited from me;[103] so such a person does not occupy my station in regard to that [life-giving power], just as I do not have the station of the one [i.e., Gabriel] who granted me [the power of] reviving the dead."

Ibn 'Arabî then turns to Yahyâ/John, who clarifies a long series of questions involving the references to him (and his relations with Jesus) in the Qur'an and hadith.[104] *Finally, after a brief excursus on the nature of spiritual procreation and marriage in Paradise,*[105] *Yahyâ explains why it is that he moves back and forth between the heaven of Jesus and the sphere of Aaron [where Muhammad met him, and where Ibn 'Arabî will encounter him later (section IV-F)] and sometimes dwells with Joseph and Idrîs as well.*

Most of the themes (such as the interrelations of life, spiritual knowledge, and the divine inspiration of the prophets) mentioned only allusively in this section are treated in greater detail in the chapters of the Fusûs *on Jesus*[106] *and Yahyâ.*

IV-D. *Joseph and the Third Heaven*[107]

This encounter takes the form of a monologue in which Joseph explains to Ibn 'Arabî the true intentions of one of the Prophet's references to him, as well as the meaning of certain verses in the Sûra of Joseph (chapter 12) in the Qur'an. These discussions are the occasion for the following spiritual advice:

This is a lesson for you that your soul does not follow the same course in something where it has no direct experience *(dhawq)* as the person who undergoes that experience.[108] So do not say "If I were in the place of that person when such-and-such was said to him and he said such-and-such, I would not have said that." No, by God, if what happened to him happened to you, you would say what he said, because the stronger state [of direct experience] controls the weaker one [i.e., of whatever you might imagine].[109]

IV-E. *Idrîs and the Fourth Heaven*[110]

Upon his arrival in the fourth and central, pivotal heaven, that of the Sun (and the symbolic "Heart" of the cosmos), Ibn 'Arabî is immediately greeted by Idrîs, who calls him "the Muhammadan inheritor" (al-wârith al-Muhammadî)—*an allusion to the Shaykh's conception of his own unique role as the "Seal of Muhammadan Sainthood."*[111] *Ibn 'Arabî then asks him a series of brief questions which relate to the traditional accounts concerning Idrîs (in one or another of his manifestations) or to his special spiritual function as the perennial "Pole"* (qutb) *and summit of the spiritual hierarchy.*[112]

...I said to him: "It has reached me concerning you that you are a proponent of miracles."[113]

Then he said: "Were it not for miracles, I would not have been *'raised up to a lofty place'"* (Qur'an 19:57).[114]

So I said to him: "Where is your [spiritual] rank in relation to your place [at the center of the universe]?"

And he said: "The outer is a sign of the inner."[115]

I said: "I have heard it said that you only asked *tawhîd*[116] of your people, and nothing else [i.e., no separate revealed Law]."

He said: "And they did not [even] do [that]. Now I was a prophet (*nabî:* see Qur'an 19:56) calling them to the *word* [i.e., the outward profession] of *tawhîd,* not to *tawhîd* [itself]—for no one has ever denied *tawhîd!*"[117]

I said: "This is strange!"

...[Then] I said: "But the differences [of opinion] concerning the Truly Real and the things said concerning Him[118] have become quite numerous."

He said: "It [can] only be like that, since the matter is [perceived differently] according to the constitution [of each individual].[119]

I said: "But I thought[120] that all of you prophets, the whole group of you, did not differ concerning Him?"

So he replied: "That is because we did not say [what we taught concerning God] on the basis of reasoning *(nazar)*; we only said it on the basis of a common direct relationship [with God].[121] So whoever *knows* the realities knows that [the fact that] all of the prophets agree in saying the same thing about God is equivalent to those who follow reasoning [all] saying the same thing.[122]

I said: "And is the matter [i.e., the reality of things] in itself really as it was said to you [by God]? For the signs [followed by] the intellects [of those who rely exclusively on their reasoning] indicate the impossibility of [certain] things you [prophets] brought concerning that."

Then he said: "The matter is as we [prophets] were told—and [at the same time] it is as whatever is said by whoever says [his own inner belief] concerning Him, since 'God is in accordance with the saying of everyone who speaks [of Him].'[123] So that is why we only called the common people to the word [i.e., the verbal profession] of *tawhîd*, not to [the reality of] *tawhîd*."

... I said: "Once, in a visionary experience *(wâqi'a)* I had, I saw an individual circumambulating [the Ka'ba], who told me that he was among my ancestors and gave me his name.[124] Then I asked him about the time of his death, and he told me it was 40,000 years [earlier]. So I proceeded to ask him about Adam, because of what had been established in our chronology concerning his period [i.e., that it was much more recent]. Then he said to me: 'Which Adam are you asking about? About the most recent Adam?'"

[Idrîs] said: "He told the truth. I am a prophet of God [Qur'an 19:56], and I do not know any period at the close of which the universe as a whole stops. However, [I do know] that He never ceases creating [the universe] in its entirety; that [the whole of reality] never ceases to be 'nearer' and 'further';[125] and that the *'appointed times'*[126] apply to the [particular] created things—through the completion of [their] periods [of existence]—and not to the [process of] creation [as a whole], since creation is continually renewed 'with the breaths' [at every instant].[127] Thus we know [only] what He has caused us to *know—And they do not comprehend anything of His Knowledge except for what He wishes"* (Qur'an 2:255).

So I said to him: "Then what remains until the appearance of the 'Hour'?"[128]

And he replied: *"Their reckoning has drawn near to people, but they are in [a state of] heedlessness, turning away"* (Qur'an 21:1).[129]

I said: "Then inform me about one of the conditions of Its 'drawing near.'"

And he replied: "The existence of Adam is among the conditions for the Hour."

I said: "Then was there another abode before this world *(al-dunyâ)*, other than it?"

He replied: "The abode of Being is one: the abode does not become 'nearer' *(dunyâ)* except through you,[130] and the 'other world' *(al-âkhira)* is not distinguished from it except through you! But with regard to bodies [i.e., as opposed to man's inherent spiritual finality and progressive movement of 'return' to his Source], the matter[131] is only engendered states *(akwân)*, transformations and coming and going [of endless material forms]; it has not ceased, and it never will."

I said: "What is *there*?"[132]

He replied: "What we know, and what we do not know." I said: "Then where is error in relation to what is right?"[133] He said: "Error is a relative matter, while what is right is the [unchanging] principle. So whoever truly knows God and the world, knows that what is right is the ever-present Principle, which never ceases [to be], and he knows that error [occurs] through the opposition of the two points of view.[134] But since the opposition [of the two perspectives] is inevitable, then error is also inevitable. So whoever maintains [the real existence of] error [also] maintains [the prior existence and reality of] what is right; and whoever maintains the [ultimate] non-existence of error *speaks what is right* (Qur'an 78:38)[135] and posits error [as deriving] from what is right"....[136]

IV-F. *Aaron and the Fifth Heaven*[137]

Next I alighted to stay with Aaron, and [there] I found Yahyâ, who had already reached him before me. So I said to [Yahyâ]: "I didn't see you on my path: is there some other path there?"

And he replied: "Each person has a path, that no one else but he travels."

I said: "Then where are they, these [different] paths?" Then he answered: "They come to be through the traveling itself."

After Aaron then greets Ibn 'Arabî as "the perfectly accomplished heir [of the Prophet],"[138] he goes on to explain how he became both a prophet (nabî) *and also a lawgiving Messenger* (rasûl) *participating in the revelation* (wahy) *appropriate to that rank, at the request of his brother Moses.*

...I said: "O Aaron, some people among the true Knowers have claimed that the existence [of the external world] disappeared with regard to them, so that they see nothing but God, and so that nothing of the world remains with them that might distract them, in comparison with God. Nor is there any doubt that they [really] are in that [spiritual] rank,[139] as opposed to those like you. Now God has informed us that you said to your brother [Moses] when he was angry [with you for having allowed the Israelites to worship the golden calf]: '... *so do not cause [our] enemies to gloat over me!*' (Qur'an 7:151).[140] Thus you posited their having a certain power [over you in the external world], and this condition is different from the condition of those true Knowers [who experience the 'disappearance' of the external world]."

Then he replied: "They spoke sincerely [about their experience]. However, they did not have any more than what was given them by their immediate experience *(dhawq)*. But look and see—did what disappeared from them [in that state actually] disappear from the world?"

"No," I answered.

He said: "Then they were lacking in the knowledge of the way things are, to the extent of what they missed, since the world was nonexistent for them. So they were lacking the True Reality *(al-Haqq)* to the extent of that [aspect] of the world which was veiled from them. Because the whole world is precisely the Self-manifestation *(tajallî)* of the Truly Real, for whoever really knows the Truly Real. *So where are you going? It is only a reminder to the worlds* (Qur'an 81:26-27) of the way things are!"

Perfection is nothing but its [or 'His'][141] *existence,*
   So whoever misses it is not the perfect one...[142]

IV-G. *Moses and the Sixth Heaven*[143]

Ibn 'Arabî begins his discussion with Moses by thanking him for his having insisted that Muhammad—during the final, descending stage of his Mi'râj—return to ask God to reduce the number of daily prayers prescribed for his community.[144] *Moses replies that* "this is a benefit of knowledge [reached through] direct experience *(dhawq)*,[145] for there is a [spiritual] condition that can only be perceived through immediate contact."

Ibn 'Arabî then mentions that it was Moses' "striving for the sake of others"—*which first led him to the burning bush—that eventually brought him* "all the Good."[146] *Moses responds that* "Man's striving for the sake of others is only a striving for his self, in the truth of things"—*i.e., when he discovers who he really is—and that the thankfulness which flows from this (on the part of all concerned) is one of the highest forms of "remembering" and praising God.*

...After that I said to him:"Surely God has chosen you over the people with His Message and His Word."[147] But you requested the vision [of God],[148] while the Messenger of God said that 'not one of you will see His Lord until he dies'?"[149]

So he said:"And it was just like that: when I asked Him for the vision [of God], He answered me, so that *'I fell down stunned'* (Qur'an 7:143). Then I saw Him in my '[state of] being stunned.'"[150]

I said:"While [you were] dead?"

He replied:"While [I was] dead."

...[51] He said:"...So I did not see God until I had died. It was then that I *'awakened,'* so that I knew *Who* I saw. And it was because of that that I said *'I have returned to you'* (Qur'an 7:143), since I did not return[152] to anyone but Him."

Then I said to him: "You are among the group of 'those who know God,'[153] so what did you consider the vision of God [to be] when you asked Him for it?"

And he said:"[I considered it to be] necessary because of rational necessity."[154] I said:"But then what was it that distinguished you from others?"

He said: "I was seeing Him [all along], and yet I didn't use to *know* that it was Him! But when my 'dwelling'[155] was changed and

I saw Him, then I knew *Who* I saw. Therefore when I 'awoke' I was no longer veiled, and my vision [of God] went on accompanying me throughout all eternity. So this is the difference between us[156] and *those who are veiled* (Qur'an 83:15) from their knowledge [of God] by what they see.[157] Yet when they die they see the Truly Real,[158] since the 'dwelling' [of divine Vision][159] distinguishes Him for them. Therefore if they were returned [to this world as I was], they would say the same thing as we did."

I said: "Then if death were the 'dwelling' of the vision of God, every dead person would see him—but God has described them (Qur'an 83:15) as being *'veiled'* from seeing Him!?"

He said: "Yes, those are *'the ones who are veiled'* from the knowledge that what [they see] *is* God.[160] But what if you yourself had to meet a person with whom you were not personally acquainted, whom you were looking for [simply] by name and because you needed him? You could meet him and exchange greetings with him, along with the whole group of those you encountered, without discovering his identity: then you would have seen him and yet not have seen him, so you would continue looking for him while he was right where you could see him! Hence one cannot rely on anything but knowledge. That is why we [Knowers of God] have said that Knowledge is His very Essence, since if Knowledge were not His very Essence, what was relied on [i.e., our knowledge] would be other than God—for nothing can be relied on but knowledge."

I said: "Now God indicated the mountain to you (Qur'an 7:143) and mentioned about Himself that *'He manifested Himself to the Mountain'* (Qur'an 7:143). [So how do these theophanies differ?]"

Then he replied: "Nothing resists His Self-manifestation; therefore the particular condition *(hâl)* necessarily changes [according to the 'locus' of each theophany]. Hence for the mountain being *'crushed flat'* was like Moses' being *'stunned'*: God says *'Moses'* (Qur'an 7:144), and [He] Who crushed it stunned me."

I said to him: "God has taken charge of teaching me, so I [only] know about Him to the extent of what He bestows on me."

Then he replied: "That is just how He acts with the Knowers of God, so take [your spiritual knowledge] from Him, not from the world.[161] And indeed you will never take [such knowledge] except to the extent of your predisposition *(isti'dâd)*.[162] So do not let yourself be veiled from Him by the likes of us [prophets]! For you will never come to know about Him by means of us anything but what we know about Him through His Self-manifestation.[163] Thus we too only give you [knowledge] about Him to the extent of your predisposition. Hence there is no difference [between learning from us and directly from God], so attach yourself to Him![164] For He only sent us to call you all to *Him,* not to call you to us. [His Message] is *a Word [that is] the same between us and you: that we should worship none but God, and that we should not associate anything with Him, and that some of us should not take others as lords instead of God"* (Qur'an 3:64).

I said: "That is how it came in the *Qur'ân!*"

He said: "And that is how He is."

I said: "With what did you hear 'God's Speech'?"[165]

He said: "With my hearing."

I said: "And what is your 'hearing'?"

He said: "*He* [is]."[166]

I said: "Then by what were you distinguished [from other men]?"

He said: "By an immediate personal experience *[dhawq]* in that regard, which can only be known by the person who actually experiences it."

I said: "So those who possess such immediate experiences are like that?"

"Yes," he said, "and [their] experiences are according to [their spiritual] ranks."

IV-H. *The Seventh Heaven: Abraham and the Temple of the Heart*[167]

Most of Ibn 'Arabî's encounter with Abraham—as earlier with Joseph and John the Baptist—is devoted to questions about certain Qur'anic passages concerning him. Here, for example, Abraham explains that his apparently polytheistic remarks reported at Qur'an 6:74-80 were actually only meant to test the faith of his people, given their limited understanding.

What is of more universal importance for the spiritual journey, however, is Ibn 'Arabî's identification of the celestial Ka'ba, the "House" of Abraham that marks the cosmological transition between the material world and the "paradisiac" realm of the highest spheres, as none other than the Heart of the voyager. For the Heart—as he makes clear in the much longer discussions at this point in his K. al-Isrâ' *and in chapter 167 of the* Futûhât[168]*— is ultimately the "site" of the whole journey.*

...Then I saw the *Inhabited House* (Qur'an 52:4),[169] and suddenly there was my Heart—and there were the angels who "enter It every day"![170] The Truly Real manifests Himself to [the Heart], which [alone] encompasses Him,[171] in "seventy thousand veils of light and darkness."[172] Thus He manifests Himself to the Heart of His servant through those (veils)—for "if He were" to manifest Himself without them, "the radiant splendors of His Face would burn up" the creaturely part[173] of that servant.

IV-I. *The "Lotus of the Limit" and the Culminating Revelation*[174]

So when I had left [the Temple], I came to *the Lotus-Tree of the Limit* (Qur'an 53:14),[175] and I halted amongst its lowest and its loftiest branches.[176] Now *it was enveloped* (Qur'an 53:16) in the lights of [good] actions, and in the shelter of its branches were singing the birds of the spirits of those who perform [those] actions,[177] since it is in the form of Man.[178] As for the four rivers [flowing from its roots, as described in the hadith],[179] they are the four kinds of divine knowledge "granted as a gift" [to man], which we mentioned in a part *(juz')* we called "the levels of the forms of knowledge given freely [by God]."[180]

Next I saw before me the *cushions of the Litters* (Qur'an 55:77) of the [true] Knowers.[181] Then I "was enveloped by the [divine] lights" until all of me became Light, and a robe of honor was bestowed upon me[182] the likes of which I had never seen.

So I said:"O my God, the Signs *âyât* are scattered!" But then 'He sent down upon me'[183] at this moment [His] Saying: *"Say:'We have faith in God and in what He sent down upon Abraham and Ishmael and Isaac and Jacob and the tribes [of Israel], and in what was brought to Moses and Jesus and the prophets from their Lord; we do not separate anyone among them, and we are sur-*

rendered to Him!'" (Qur'an 3:84). Thus He gave me *all* the Signs in this Sign,[184] clarified the matter (i.e., of the eternal Reality of the *"Qur'ân"*) for me,[185] and made this Sign for me the key to *all* knowledge. Henceforth I knew that I *am* the totality of those [prophets] who were mentioned to me [in this verse].

Through this [inspiration] I received the good tidings that I had [been granted] the "Muhammadan station,"[186] that I was among the heirs of Muhammad's comprehensiveness. For he was the last [prophet] to be sent as a messenger, the last to have [the direct Revelation] *descend upon him* (Qur'an 97:4):[187] God "gave him the all-comprehensive Words,"[188] and he was specially favored by six things with which the messenger of no [other] community[189] was specially favored. Therefore [Muhammad's] mission is universal, because of the general nature of his six aspects:[190] from whatever direction you come, you will find only the Light of Muhammad[191] overflowing upon you; no one takes [spiritual knowledge] except from It, and no [divine] messenger has informed [man] except for [what he has taken] from It.[192]

Now when that happened to me I exclaimed: "Enough, enough![193] My [bodily] elements are filled up, and my place cannot contain me!" and through that [inspiration] God removed from me my contingent dimension.[194] Thus I attained in this nocturnal journey the inner realities (*ma'ânî*) of *all* the Names, and I saw them all returning to One Subject[195] and One Entity:[196] that Subject was what I witnessed,[197] and that Entity was my Being. For my voyage was only in myself and only pointed to myself, and through this I came to know that I was a pure "servant,"[198] without a trace of lordship in me at all.

Then the treasures of this station were opened up [for me], and among the kinds of knowledge I *saw* there were....[199]

The list of some sixty-nine kinds of knowledge associated with this particular station differs from the similar listings in each of the other chapters on the fasl al-manâzil *in that it contains a number of Ibn 'Arabî's most fundamental metaphysical theses. The following items may be taken as representative.*[200]

...I saw in it the knowledge of the Return...and that [man] carries this world with him when he is transferred [to the next world]...

I saw in it the knowledge of the interpenetration and [indissoluble] "circularity" (*dawr:* of God and Man), which is that God *(al-Haqq)* can only *be* in [external] reality *(fî al-fi'l)* through the form of the creature *(al-khalq)*, and that the creature can only be there [in reality] through the form of God. So this circularity... is what actually exists *(al-wâqi')* and is the way things are....

... Each community *(umma)* has a messenger... and there is nothing among what exists that is not [part of] a certain community... So the divine message *(risâla)* extends to absolutely all communities, both great and small!...

I saw in it the universality of the divine Gift [of Mercy and Pardon] ... [as] He said concerning the prodigal sinners: "... *Do not despair of God's Mercy; surely God forgives the sins altogether, surely He is the All-Forgiving, the All-Merciful (Qur'an 39:53)."* So nothing could be clearer than this explicit divine declaration concerning the return of [all] the servants to [His] Mercy!...

I saw in it the knowledge that it is God who is worshipped in every object of worship, behind the veil of [the particular] form.

I saw in it the knowledge of the conditions of mankind in the intermediate world *(barzakh)*...

I saw in it the knowledge that this world is a token *('unwân)* of the other world and a symbolization *(darb mithâl)* of it, and that the status *(hukm)* of what is in this world is more complete and more perfect in the other world.

NOTES

Preface
James W. Morris

1. Although the French translation of *al-Futûhât al-Makkíya* was *Les Illuminations de La Mecque*, the American publishers chose the title *The Meccan Revelations* because that is how the work is most commonly known in English. Also note that this edition has kept the system of Arabic transliteration used in the French edition, including in book and article titles. (See also our Introduction n. 10 below on the meaning of the title.)

Introduction
James W. Morris

1. I.e., as distinguished from the various *historically* accrued bodies of interpretation and application in various historical and cultural settings, which may or may not be in accord with that actual Source: hence the *inherently creative* and unavoidably *subversive* potential of Ibn 'Arabî's teachings in any particular historical setting, Islamic or otherwise.

2. This includes the four immense, multidisciplinary fields of the Islamic "religious" sciences, the "intellectual" sciences (all of philosophy, science and logic in their Islamic forms), preceding Sufi tradition, and Arabic poetry and literature. Even in Ibn 'Arabî's day, very few individuals would have been seriously educated in more than one of these complexes of scholarship and learning. This is one of the main reasons that we still have very few *complete* translations of important longer chapters from the *Futûhât*. A particularly dramatic illustration from the

original Sindbad volume, soon to be available in English, is Professor Denis Gril's introduction, translation and commentary on selected key passages explaining the "science of letters" (*'ilm al-hurûf*). Some sixty dense pages of French are necessary to communicate what is little more than a page from the original Arabic text. Fortunately, as can be seen in the rest of these selections, many passages do not require such detailed background explanations.

3. M. Chodkiewicz's *An Ocean Without Shore* (see Introduction, "Suggestions for Further Reading") is the most profound and penetrating discussion of this essential feature of all of Ibn 'Arabî's writings.

4. See Introduction, "Suggestions for Further Reading."

5. See the basic reference in this area, O. Yahia's two-volume *Histoire et classification de l'oeuvre d'Ibn 'Arabî* (Damascus, I.F.D., 1964), which has been supplemented and corrected by several of the recent studies cited in the "Further Reading" section. The English biographies cited in that section also contain helpful summaries and descriptions of many of Ibn 'Arabî's major writings.

6. This topic is well discussed in the biographies cited below, but the best and most extensive treatment is to be found in M. Chodkiewicz's *The Seal of the Saints* (see the "Further Reading" section).

7. See a few key references discussed in the "Further Reading" section, and particularly the *forthcoming* Proceedings of the Kyoto Conference on Ibn 'Arabî's influences in Central and Southeast Asia and China held in January 2001. Perhaps the most emblematic illustration of this infinitely variegated historical process was Ibn 'Arabî's direct inspiration (largely based on chapter 371 of *The Meccan Revelations* and related eschatological interpretations scattered throughout the work) for the form and detailed structures and layout of the Taj Mahal: see W. Begley, "The Myth of the Taj Mahal and a New Theory of Its Symbolic Meaning," in *The Art Bulletin*, LXI:1 (March 1979).

8. Particularly important were his lasting impact on and through later Islamic philosophy, spiritual poetry and music, and the universal spiritual practices associated with veneration of Prophet and saints, as well as specifically Sufi tariqas and their practices. The exploration of the further impact of "Akbarian" ideas, themes and insights during this period on cognate cultural forms in *other* religions and cultural communities living under Muslim rule in Ottoman, Safavid, South and Southeast Asian and Chinese contexts has barely begun. (One might cite here the pioneering efforts of Professor Paul Fenton regarding Jewish spiritual and religious encounters in Ottoman contexts at that time.)

9. In addition to the frequent allusions to this subject in many of the writings of M. Chodkiewicz, see the more detailed references in our essay on *"Ibn 'Arabî in the 'Far West': Spiritual Influences and the Science of Spirituality"* (in the Proceedings of the Kyoto Conference in note 7 above), and the chapter on Ibn 'Arabî in our *Orientations: Islamic Thought in a World Civilisation* (Sarajevo, El-Kalem, 2001).

10. The word *fath* had by Ibn 'Arabî's time taken on the technical sense in Sufi discourse of a sudden, unexpected spiritual "illumination" or "inspiration" appearing without any prior mental preparation; in a literary sense, it also alludes to the "reconquest" of Mecca by the nascent Muslim community of Medina (and subsequent other stages in the expansion of Islam), which is of course the unifying spiritual drama of all the Medinan Suras of the Qur'an and their elaboration in Islamic tradition.

11. Although the critical Arabic edition undertaken by O. Yahya unfortunately remains incomplete, as a result of these very early and fully reliable manuscripts (which were used for the first modern published versions of the *Futûhât*), students of the *Futûhât* do not face the major problems of highly corrupted texts and even entirely apocryphal attributions connected with many of Ibn 'Arabî's other writings. (See detailed discussion of the Arabic sources in M. Chodkiewicz's Introduction to the original Sindbad volume.) One of the major aids to be hoped for from a completion of the critical edition would be the full identification of all the other shorter works which Ibn 'Arabî either inserted and adapted as part of *The Meccan Revelations*, or in some cases may have been extracted and circulated as separate treatises at a later date (either by himself or later students).

12. A few of those features are mentioned in the following section, but the best discussion (still very allusive, and assuming a detailed knowledge of the Qur'an and hadith) is scattered throughout M. Chodkiewicz's *An Ocean Without Shore*. One of the best illustrations of the distinctiveness of Ibn 'Arabî's own style is a rapid comparison with any of the widespread apocryphal works attributed to him (e.g., the famous *R. al-Ahadiyya, al-Shajara al-Ilâhiyya*, or the later commentary on his *K. al-Kunh*, recently translated as "What the Seeker Needs"): see the discussion of various apocrypha in our three-part detailed discussion of *"Ibn Arabî and His Interpreters,"* in *Journal of the American Oriental Society*, 106-7 (1986-87).

13. See the recent study and translation by G. Elmore cited in the "Further Readings" section, or the even more striking example of Ibn 'Arabî's autobiographical *K. al-Isrâ'*. In general, much of Ibn 'Arabî's writing from that period only becomes comprehensible in light of his fuller descriptions and explanations scattered throughout the *Futûhât*.

14. See our discussion and illustration of this subject in the long article cited in note 12 above.

15. One of the most indispensable "tools" or preparations for understanding both the *Futûhât* and the *Fusûs al-Hikam* is a detailed awareness of these core "divine sayings" that are alluded to on virtually every page of both works. Ibn 'Arabî brought most of those hadith together in his own or version of the Islamic tradition of transmitting "forty" *(arba'în)* favorite hadith, the celebrated *Mishkât al-Anwâr* ("Niche for Lights"). A new English translation has been promised, and meanwhile, many of these "divine sayings" are already accessible in English in W. Graham's classic study, *Divine Word and Prophetic Word in Islam*, which was inspired by Ibn 'Arabî's collection. See also the translations and Ibn 'Arabî's discussion of many of those hadith on the "vision" of God in our study *"'Seeking God's Face': Ibn 'Arabî on Right Action and Theophanic Vision,"* JMIAS, XVI-XVII (1994-95).

16. The realms of "being" or creation in question, as any reader of Ibn 'Arabî will quickly discover, are infinitely more extensive than the "lower world" of the physical senses. These ontological and cosmological dimensions of Ibn 'Arabî's writing are the particular focus of a number of the extensive translations by W. Chittick cited in the "Further Reading" section.

17. Later Islamic traditions of interpretation have, for various reasons, tended to emphasize the two corresponding symbol-sets of the "Muhammadan Reality" (in both its existential and scriptural dimensions) and the symbolism of the

"Completely Human Being" ("Perfect Man," etc.: *al-insân al-kâmil*). However—like much of the technical terminology of those later traditions more generally—the unfamiliarity of such language and symbolism (at least in its proper meanings) for most modern audiences can only too easily get in the way of readers' actually perceiving the immediate universality and applicability of the realities to which Ibn 'Arabî is referring.

18. Allusion to the Prophet's prayer,"O my God, cause me to see things as they really are," and to his prayer that Ibn 'Arabî cites even more frequently,"O my Lord, increase me in knowing [of you]"—*rabbî zidnî 'ilman*.

19. An equally essential dimension of *Haqq*, which also means what is 'right' and 'obligatory' in an ultimate sense and perspective.

20. William Chittick's first book on the *Futûhât*, the *Sufi Path of Knowledge* (see "Further Readings") rightly emphasizes the importance (both intellectual and existential) of understanding Ibn 'Arabî's peculiar usage of this theological language, which is so essential that without it most of *The Meccan Revelations* will remain incomprehensible. Sachiko Murata's *The Tao of Islam* (also in "Further Readings") further develops both the Qur'anic roots of this spiritual language and its many elaborations in the later Islamic humanities (poetry, philosophy and Sufi teaching), in a very fruitful comparison with the central themes of Taoist thought.

21. This is often clearly the case in the longer selections from the *Futûhât* translated in W. Chittick's *The Self-Disclosure of God* (see "Further Readings"), which are long enough for their dimensions of realization to become evident, especially in the many discussions of the "imaginal world" *(barzakh)* in the concluding chapter.

22. With the possible exception of his most explicitly "practical" passages on spiritual practice and discernment, many of them translated in our forthcoming book on this subject (see "Further Readings").

23. These key passages of Ibn 'Arabî's *muqaddima* are extracted from our longer overview and more extensive translations from this key opening section: "How to Study the *Futûhât*: Ibn 'Arabî's Own Advice," in *Muhyiddîn Ibn 'Arabî: A Commemorative Volume* (see note 36 below), pages 73-89. Victor Palleja has recently published a more extensive, reliable Spanish translation of much of this complex opening section.

24. The long-lived spiritual guide and archetype of direct divine inspiration—alluded to in the Qur'anic account of Moses' initiation in the following passage from the Sura of the Cave (18:65ff.)—who played an important role in Ibn 'Arabî's own development, as well as in Sufism and popular Islamic spirituality more generally.

25. In each of the translated passages the pronoun *you* is in the *plural*; the mysterious term *al-furqân* ("criterion," "separation") also appears six other times in the Qur'an, usually in reference to a mysterious type or source of revelation or spiritual awareness and divine guidance granted to several prophets. The multifaceted verb translated here as "to be mindful of" God is from the central Qur'anic term *taqwâ*, which refers both to the spiritual condition of awe and reverence of God and to the inner and outer actions of piety and devotion flowing from that state.

26. See the extensive translation of these discussions in our study cited at note 23 above.

27. Here Ibn 'Arabî appears to be playing with the expected Qur'anic *contrast* of the blind and seeing (6:50, etc.): in that light, these final remarks apparently are alluding to the particularly metaphysical, *universal* character of the wisdom in question here.

28. Major autobiographical sections of the *khutba* regarding Ibn 'Arabî's role as "Seal of the Muhammadan Saints" were translated by M. Vâlsan (originally in *Études Traditionnelles,* 1953) and were reprinted under the title *"l'Investiture du cheikh al-Akbar au centre suprême"* in the volume *l'Islam et la fonction de René Guénon* (Paris, 1984), pp. 177-91. A shorter part of that passage has more recently been translated by L. Shamash and S. Hirtenstein as "An Extract from the Preface to the *Futûhât,*" in *Journal of the Muhyiddîn Ibn 'Arabî Society,* IV (1985), pp. 4-6. (See also the more recent Spanish translation by V. Palleja cited above.)

29. Ibn 'Arabî's close friends in Tunisia are presented there as key members of the spiritual hierarchy.

30. See the detailed discussion of the first thirteen chapters of this Section in M. Chodkiewicz's original Introduction to the Sindbad anthology (to be included in the forthcoming translation of the French sections of that book).

31. Fully commented translations of all these chapters, plus the longer chapter 371 which brings them all together in one picture (which later inspired the builders of the Taj Mahal), are included in our forthcoming volume on *Ibn 'Arabî's "Divine Comedy": An Introduction to Islamic Eschatology.*

32. The long section on the different types of "sainthood" here is extensively analyzed, and partially translated, in M. Chodkiewicz's pioneering study *The Seal of the Saints* (see "Further Readings"). Most of the many selections from this chapter included in this anthology were drawn from Ibn 'Arabî's fascinating responses to Tirmidhi's questionnaire.

33. For the selections from chapters 366 ('The Mahdi's Helpers') and 367 (Ibn 'Arabî's *Mi'râj*), see our more extensive commentary and analysis in "Ibn 'Arabî's 'Esotericism': The Problem of Spiritual Authority," *Studia Islamica,* LXXI (1990), pp. 37-64; and "The Spiritual Ascension: Ibn 'Arabî and the Mi'râj," in *Journal of the American Oriental Society,* 107 (1987), pp. 629-52, and 108 (1988), pp. 63-77.

34. This is the number of "divine Names" specifically enumerated in several famous hadith and reflected in the normal numbers of Islamic prayer beads; the possible connections of specific Names with each of the "Poles" discussed here are not explicit and have not yet been elucidated.

35. Ibn 'Arabî's approach here is unique to him and not found in earlier classical Sufi discussions of the spiritual *maqâmât.*

36. Readers of the Austin translation should also try to consult the missing translation of the Introductory section of the same work ("Excerpts from the Epistle on the Spirit of Holiness *(Risâlah Rûh al-Quds),*" translated by R. Boase and F. Sahnoun) in *Muhyiddîn Ibn 'Arabî: A Commemorative Volume,* edited by S. Hirtenstein and M. Tiernan (Shaftesbury, Element, 1993), which contains seventeen other important translations and critical studies. Austin's book is still available, through the Ibn 'Arabi Society, in the reprinted edition by Beshara Publishers, 1988.

37. Still available in the later version published by the University of California Press, 1984, under the new title: *Sufism and Taoism: A Comparative Study of Key Philosophic Concepts.*

38. Because both works are so highly allusive, personal, poetic, and so deeply rooted in very personal readings of difficult passages from Ibn 'Arabî, the Qur'an and many other Islamic classics, they should certainly be read in the original if at all possible.

39. In English, the paperback edition of Corbin's *Creative Imagination* is now republished under the title *"Alone With the Alone"* (Princeton, Princeton University Press, 1998; with a new preface by H. Bloom).

Divine Names and Theophanies
William C. Chittick

1. *Futûhât*, I 118-21 (Yahya 2, pp. 219-233).

2. Ibn al-'Arabî devotes the fourteenth section of Chapter 198 of the *Futûhât* to the Name the "Last" (*al-âkhir*) and its relationship to the creation of the Dust or "Dust Substance" (*al-jawhar al-habâ'î*), which has no entity in existence and is only made manifest by the forms which take shape within it. It is identical with what the philosophers call hylé (*hayûlâ*) and Ibn al-'Arabî himself sometimes refers to it as the Phoenix (*'anqâ*), *"since one knows about it by hearsay and has a conception of it, but it has no existence in entity and it is not truly known except through the striking of similitudes"* (II 432.3). Ibn al-'Arabî also calls it the "Dark Substance" (*al-jawhar al-muzlam*, II 150.4, 282.20, 648.1) and the *"Substance of the Hylé"* (III 420.35). Cf. II 130.28, 150.24, 656.16, 675.33; III 187.21, 420.35.

3. As indicated in the introduction to this section, Ibn al-'Arabî often employs the term "divine realities" as a synonym for Divine Names, though the term "reality" is commonly used in a broader sense. The "Names" usually refer to the "Most Beautiful Names" revealed in the Qur'an and the Hadith, while "divine realities" may refer to all sorts of things that we know about God on the basis of the Qur'an and the Hadith, very often without a specific Name having been revealed in the context. In this sense the expression divine reality is employed more or less synonymously with "divine root" (*asl ilâhî*) and "divine basis" (*mustanad ilâhî*). For a few examples, cf. *Fut.* II 665.23, 666.6, 668.7; III 28.16, 44.25, 61.22, 61.35, 62.15, 93.17, 94.25.

4. The term *ta'alluh*, meaning "being like unto Allah," has precedents in al-Ghazâlî (e.g., *al-Maqsad al-asnâ*, ed. F.A. Shehadi, Beirut, Dar el-Machreq, 1971, p. 65), Abû Tâlib al-Makkî (*Qût al-qulûb*, Cairo: Mustafâ al-Bâbî al-Halabî, 1961, I, p. 177), and no doubt in Avicenna and other philosophers, since it plays an important role in later philosophy (Mullâ Sadrâ is still today known in traditional circles as al-Hakîm al-Muta'allih). It is not one of Ibn al-'Arabî's commonly employed terms. He much prefers *al-takhalluq bi akhlâq Allâh* or *bi asmâ' Allâh* ("assuming the character traits of God" or "assuming the traits of God's Names"). For another example of the word *ta'alluh*, see *Fut.* II 187.17-18.

5. That everything in the universe is subjected to mankind is the message of several Qur'anic verses, such as 14:32-33, 16:12, 22:65, 31:20. Ibn al-'Arabî employs the term "vassal of God" when conceiving of "Allah" not as the Name of the Divine Essence as such, which is "Independent of the worlds," but as the Name of the level of divinity (*martabat al-ulûhiyya*), to which the world is related by means of the

Divine Names. In this context "Allah" is a correlative *(idâfî)* term, demanding the duality "God"/"vassal of God," just like the Name "Lord" *(rabb)* which demands the existence of the "vassal" *(marbûb).* Cf. *Fut.* II 128.15, 226.23, 244.22, 257.29, 360.7, 591.27, 603.16; III 65.23, 73.5.

6. The "two groups"—the inhabitants of the Garden and of the Fire—correspond to the *"Companions of the Right Hand"* and the *"Companions of the Left Hand"* mentioned in Qur'an 56:27ff. They are often discussed in terms of the "two handfuls" *(al-qabdatân),* to which allusion is made in Qur'an 39:67: *"The whole earth is His handful on the Day of Resurrection, and the heavens shall be rolled up in His right hand."* According to Ibn al-'Arabî, the two handfuls correspond to *"the world of felicity and the world of wretchedness"* (*Fut.* III 75.14). Ibn al-'Arabî sometimes alludes to the hadith, *"God created Adam and struck him on his right side with His right hand; his seed came out on the right hand white like silver and on the left hand black like coals. God said, 'These are in the Garden and it is no concern of Mine* [lâ ubâlî]; *these are in the Fire, and it is no concern of Mine"* (Hakîm Tirmidhî, *Nawâdir al-usûl;* cited in Sa'îd al-Dîn Farghânî, *Mashâriq al-darârî,* ed. S. J. Ashtiyânî, Tehran: Imperial Iranian Academy of Philosophy, 1357/1978, p. 632; cf. a similar hadith but without the expression *lâ ubâlî* in *Muwatta,'* Tirmidhî, and Abû Dâwûd: Graham, *Divine Word,* pp. 161–62). Cf. *Fut.* I 37.30, 123.32; II 86.28, 435.24; III 76.25, 106.28, 485.15.

7. *Tajallî,* one of Ibn al-'Arabî's most important technical terms, derives from the root *j.l.w.* meaning "to be clear, to reveal, to disclose." The word *jalwa* signifies the "unveiling of a bride" on her wedding night. God's *"theophany"* is His Self-unveiling to the servant (and indeed it is often used synonymously with the term *kashf,* "unveiling"). Ibn al-'Arabî cites the definition of theophany given by the Sufis as, *"The lights of the Unseen that are unveiled to hearts"* (*Fut.* II 132.8, 485.20; *Istilâhât* 9). In his own writings he uses the term in a much broader sense, since he often takes it as a synonym for *zuhûr,* i.e., the "manifestation" of Being (which of course is also called "Light") as an objective, "external" phenomenon, not necessarily to the vision of the knower. One reason that theophany or the Self-revelation of God is more elevated in the next world is that death has removed the veil, so the servant's *"sight today is piercing"* (Qur'an 50:22). For a few examples of discussions of *tajallî,* see II 105.6, 193.33, 303–5, 466.23, 473.6, 485 (*bâb* 206), 548.9, 550.12, 557.21, 558.31, 575.17, 597.6, 606.30, 637.11, 657.19, 666–68; III 56.19, 101.23, 117.1.

8. In Ibn al-'Arabî's understanding, *"new creation"* (cf. Qur'an 50:15) refers to the constant renewal of God's creative act at every instant and the continual transformation of created things that takes place as a result. Cf. T. Izutsu, "The Concept of Perpetual Creation in Islamic Mysticism and Zen Buddhism," in Seyyed Hossein Nasr (ed.), *Melanges offerts à Henry Corbin,* Tehran: McGill Institute of Islamic Studies, 1977, pp. 115–48. Cf. *Fut.* II 46.5, 208.30, 372.20, 384.34, 432.12, 471.32, 500.1, 554.19, 639.12, 653.15; III 127.12. A concept closely related to new creation is that of the Divine Boundlessness *(al-ittisâ'* or *al-tawassu' al-ilâhî), "which demands that nothing be repeated in existence"* (I 266.8; cf. II 185.27, 205.32, 302.18, 432.12, 500.1, 657.14; III 127.23).

9. On the two hands or "handfuls," see note 6 above.

10. Attributes, it must be remembered, are in Ibn al-'Arabî's vocabulary practically identical with "Names" *(asmâ').* Attributes of meanings are contrasted with

attributes of self *(nafsiyya)* or essence *(dhâtiyya);* theoretically at least they can be removed while the self or essence remains *(Fut.* I 271.21, 284.34). By Attributes of Perfection Ibn al-'Arabî has the Divine Perfection *(al-kamâl al-ilâhiyya)* in view, not the perfection of the Essence, which can only be described in negative terms (see the following footnote). He cites as examples of Attributes of Perfection Speech, Sight, Hearing (II 383.7), Knowledge, Life, Power, Severity *(al-qâhir)*, and Awareness *(al-khabîr;* I 284.30). These attributes fit into the category of Attributes of Acts or Similarity, which are contrasted with the Attributes of Incomparability (cf. Chapter 558, note 78).

11. Ibn al-'Arabî frequently quotes these two verses to allude to one of the Qur'anic bases for, in the first case, the doctrine of God's Incomparability *(tanzîh)* and, in the second, that of the unknowability of the Divine Essence. He summarizes the relationship between these two teachings when he says, *"The way of declaring God's Incomparability relates only to the Essence [not to the Names]. God said, 'Nothing is like Him' because of the Perfection of the Essence and 'but He is the All-Hearing, the All-Seeing'* [Qur'an 42:11] *because of the Perfection of the Divinity [i.e., the level to which the Names refer]" (Fut.* II 589.2). For a few representative discussions of verse 42:11, see *Fut.* II 84.13, 439.23, 516.32, 589.2; for verse 3:27, see 1126.17, 271.7; II 230.16, 319.18; III 81.30, 233.21; IV 203.35.

12. The reference is to the hadith, *"Meditate upon all things, but do not meditate upon the Essence of God,"* cited in five different versions in al-Suyûtî, *al-Jâmi' al-saghîr* (in al-Munâwî, *Fayd al-qadîr,* Beirut: Dâr al-ma'rifa, 1972, III, pp. 262–63).

13. Ibn al-'Arabî's most detailed discussion of the Universal Reality as such occurs in *Inshâ'* 17ff. He refers to it in *Fut.* III 199.12 in the context of the four objects of knowledge; cf. also *Azal* 9, *Fut.* II 103.29. He identifies it with the Reality of Realities *(haqîqat al-haqâ'iq)* in II 432.16, 433.14, and IV 311.26. He also identifies it with the Dust *(al-habâ',* II 431.32ff.) and Hylé *(hayûlâ,* II 432.8) and less explicitly with the Cloud *(al-'amâ').* Cf. Hakîm, *Mu'jam* 345–47.

14. This is one of the more common terms by which Ibn al-'Arabî refers to the Universal Reality. By his own account he has borrowed it from the writings of 'Abd al-Salâm Abu'l-Hakam ibn Barrajân (d. 536/1141), who in turn derived it from Qur'an 15:85 *(Fut.* III 77.25; II 60.12, 104.6). Sahl al-Tustarî (d. 283/896) refers to the same thing as Justice *(al-'adl; Fut.* II 60.11; III 77.27, 150.7). It is identical with the Cloud *(al-'amâ';* II 283.11, 310.25, 331.24, 391.34), the Breath of the All-Merciful (II 391.34), and the Perfect Man (II 396.6). Or again: *"The Divine Pen… is the First Intellect… the Muhammadan Reality, the Truth through which creation takes place, Justice,… and the Universal Holy Spirit* [al-rûh al-qudsî al-kull]*"* (III 444.245).

15. *Inshâ',* pp. 16ff.

16. Ibn al-'Arabî provides a different list of the four objects of knowledge, with little elaboration, in *Fut.* III 199.12. Three correspond exactly to this list: man, the macrocosm, and the Reality of Realities. But the fourth is given, without any explanation, as *"the Perfect [Man] who possesses the [ontological] level"* (al-kâmil sâhib al-martaba).

17. Bukhârî gives this hadith in the forms, *"God was, and nothing was before Him* [qablah]*"* and *"God was, and nothing was other than He* [ghayrah]*"* (Tawhîd 22; Bad' al-khalq 1). Ibn al-'Arabî often cites the hadith in the present form, e.g., I 5.2, 31.22, 41.25, 61.18, 104.31, 156.35; II 56.3, 561.13. The sentence

that was "incorporated into" the saying, *"And He is now as He was,"* is attributed to al-Junayd (cf. al-Qayṣarī, *al-Tawḥîd wa'l-nubuwwa wa'l-walâya*, ed. S. J. Ashtiyânî, Mashhad: Châpkhâna-yi Dânishgâh, 1357/1978, p. 13; Jâmî, *Naqd al-nuṣûṣ,* ed. W. C. Chittick, Tehran: Imperial Iranian Academy of Philosophy, 1977, p. 67). Ibn al-'Arabî points out that the Prophet could not have said it (*Fut.* II 561.13, 692.24; cf. Jâmî, *Naqd al-nuṣûṣ,* p. 93.19).

18. I.e., the Prophet's cousin and son-in-law, the fourth caliph of Islam and first Imam of the Shi'ites (d. 40/661). His mention of the Dust is also referred to in *Fut.* II 432.3.

19. Al-Tustarî is referred to by Ibn al-'Arabî probably more often than any other Sufi except Abû Yazîd al-Basṭâmî. On some of his specific contributions, see G. Boewering, *The Mystical Vision of Existence in Classical Islam: The Qur'ânic Hermeneutics of the Sufi Sahl at-Tustarî (d. 283/896)*, Berlin: de Gruyter, 1979. For a few references to him in the *Futûḥât*, see II 12.1, 20.19, 40.17, 45.12, 60.11, 93.27, 102.12, 104.7, 171.21, 318.31, 355.14, 365.19, 479.27, 543.4, 551.5, 662.11; III 41.8, 77.26, 86.22, 150.7, 395.23; IV 249.13, 376.18.

20. Verification *(taḥqîq)* is Ibn al-'Arabî's designation for those Sufis who have reached the highest stages of visionary understanding, such as Abû Yazîd and himself (cf. *bâb* 165 [II 267], II 39.33, 318.31, 388.13; *al-Isfâr* 7); he identifies the Verifiers with the Blameworthy (*al-malâmiyya; Mawâqi,* 29). People of Unveiling and Finding *(ahl al-kashf wa'l-wujûd)* is a more general designation, employed rather often (e.g., *Fut.* II 186.14, 190.31, 234.5, 254.7, 467.23, 504.4, 523.11), for those who receive their knowledge not through rational processes but through inspiration and "tasting" *(dhawq)*. Note that *wujûd* is usually translated as Being or existence, but in this expression another side of the term's meaning becomes apparent, one that is not completely obscured in the Arabic when existence or Being is under discussion. The implication is that what exist finds itself, i.e., is aware and conscious of itself by the very fact of existence, and this follows naturally from the fact that the Divine Being is the sheer Light of Consciousness (cf. *bâb* 237, II 537).

21. I.e., the philosophers, as opposed to the People of Unveiling and Finding just mentioned.

22. Uthman Yahya records an interesting variant reading of this last sentence. The *Futûḥât* had two redactions, one finished in 629 and the second in 636. The autograph of the second redaction is being used as the basis for Yahya's new edition of the text. A copy of the first redaction exists in a manuscript made within forty years of Ibn al-'Arabî's death on the basis of the original. The text of this manuscript based on the first redaction reads as follows: *"'Alî ibn Abî Tâlib—God be well pleased with him!—the leader of the world and the inmost mystery of all the prophets* [imâm al-'âlam wa sirr al-anbiyâ' ajma'în]." Yahya points to the Shi'ite inclination of this variant reading; there is an obvious possibility that the passage does not in fact follow the first redaction exactly.

23. For a few passages concerning the Divine Knowledge as the origin of the world, see *Fut.* I 90.23; II 326.26, 385.9, 390.35, 399.31, 421.24, 508.6; III 48.5.

24. Ibn al-'Arabî alludes to the etymological sense of the word *jinn*. Qur'an commentators often refer to the word *jinn* as including the angels; for example, al-Baydâwî writes of Qur'an 6:100, *"It is said that here jinn means the angels... God*

called them jinn because they are 'hidden' [ijtinân] *from sight."* More commonly, and again following the tradition, Ibn al-'Arabî distinguishes between the jinn, created from fire, and the angels, created from light; or between "fiery spirits" *(arwâh nâriyya)* and "light spirits" *(arwâh nûriyya)*. He sees the jinn proper as created under the influence of the Divine Name "Subtle" *(al-latîf)*, which *"bestows upon them their hiddenness"* (II 467.4). He suggests that the above Qur'anic verse can also be interpreted in another sense: *"It may refer to man alone in respect of the fact that he possesses manifest and nonmanifest dimensions* [zâhir wa bâtin]*"* (III 301.10). For a few discussions of the jinn in the *Futûhât* see Chapter 9 (I 131-34), I 273.28; II 106.8, 195.24, 466-468, 470.18; III 3.20, 48.24, 142.9, 253.23, 367.10.

25. That everything in the world is "alive," whether it is normally referred to as animate or inanimate, is a recurring theme in Ibn al-'Arabî's writings. All things partake of life because it is the first of the four fundamental divine attributes that bring the world into existence *(Fut.* I 293.8; II 406.5, 430.14; III 430.25). In other terms, *"Life is the sphere of the Mercy 'which surrounds all things'* [Qur'an 7:156]*; the attribution of Life to the Divine Essence is a precondition for every quality attributed to God, such as Knowledge, Will, Power, Speech, Hearing, Sight, and Perception... So [Life] is the Mercy of the Essence that surrounds all the Names"* (*Fut.* II 107.26). On the fact that *"Everything other than God is alive"* (III 65.30), see, for example, II 393.23; III 38.7, 65-68, 154.19, 324.20; IV 289.29.

26. In at least three of these instances Ibn al-'Arabî has a specific hadith in mind, as he makes clear in III 258.21, where he quotes them in some detail. *1. I know a stone in Mecca which used to greet me. 2.* The Prophet was given a poisoned shoulder of a lamb by a Jewish woman, as reported in Bukhârî (Maghâzî 41, Hiba 28) and other sources. At least one version has, *"This [shoulder] tells [ikhbâr] me that it is poisoned"* (Dârimî, *Muqaddima* 6). *3.* The stump of the palm tree—sometimes called the *"moaning pillar"*—is referred to in several of the standard collections. The Prophet used to use it as a pulpit, but then a platform was built for him. When he started to mount the new pulpit, the stump was heard to moan *(hanîn)* by all present. Then the Prophet *"stroked it with his hand until it became quiet"* (Ibn Mâja, Iqâma 199; Dârimî, *Muqaddima* 6; etc.; cf. *Concordance* I, p. 520, under *hann*).

27. The text of this hadith is found in a number of slightly different versions; Ibn Mâja, Adhân 5; Nasâ'î, Adhân 14; Abû Dâwûd, Salât 31.

28. The blessed in the Garden are referred to by this attribute in Qur'an 15:46, 34:37, 41:40, 44:55. Ibn al-'Arabî most likely has in mind Qur'an 27:89: *"On that day they will be secure from terror,"* since he defines the Secure as *"those who are 'not grieved by the Greatest Terror'"* (Qur'an 21:103; *Fut.* II 415.10). Elsewhere he tells us that these are the greatest of the saints (II 81.12), envied even by the prophets, who grieve for their communities, though not for themselves (cf. II 83.2, 510.21).

29. Abû Muhammad 'Abd al-'Azîm ibn Abû Bakr al-Qurashî al-Mahdawî (d. 6211 1224), a disciple of Abû Madyân, played an important role in the life of Ibn al-'Arabî, who wrote *Rûh al-quds* for him (see Austin, *Sufis of Andalusia,* p. 17) and dedicated to him the *Futûhât* (19.14-10.25; cf. 198.31; II 601.34).

30. The Throne, mentioned in twenty-two Qur'anic verses, is the seat of the

All-Merciful (Qur'an 20:5). According to a hadith, upon it are written the words, *"My Mercy precedes My Wrath."* In Ibn al-'Arabî's cosmology, it marks the outermost limit of the "visible" world; above it lies pure Mercy, while below it is the created domain within which Mercy is mixed with Wrath. The Footstool *"encompasses the heavens and the earth"* (Qur'an 2:154) and is usually identified with the sphere of the fixed stars. The "two feet" of the All-Merciful mark the division of Wrath and Mercy into two different attributes. The Inhabited House (Qur'an 52:4) is said to exist in the seventh sphere directly above the Ka'ba and to be visited by 70,000 angels each day.

31. The first group of relations corresponds to nine of the ten Aristotelian categories (leaving aside substance). For a few other discussions of the categories, see *Fut.* II 211.32, 429.18, 435.9, 481.10; III 10.34ff., 279.32ff.

32. Cf. Chodkiewicz, *Le Sceau des saints,* Chapter 2 et passim.

33. *Fut.* II 104-105.

34. Ibn al-'Arabî's use here of the term "crowning" can be clarified by reference to another passage: *"The visionary Influx* (al-wârid) *informed me... that the allocation of the basmala [the formula, 'In the name of God, the All-Merciful, the All-Compassionate'] to the beginning of each chapter of the Qur'an is the crowning of the chapter's edict by the Divine Mercy, for Mercy embraces everything within the chapter; the basmala is God's mark* ['alâma] *upon each chapter, like the sultan's mark upon his edicts"* (*Fut.* III 100.32).

35. This famous hadith is found in both Bukhârî (Istî'dhân 1) and Muslim (Janna 27).

36. The Divine Perfection is contrasted with the Perfection of the Essence *(al-kamâl al-dhâtî).* The latter pertains to the Essence's Incomparability *(tanzîh)* and Independence *(ghinâ),* while the former refers to the actualization of the perfections pertaining to each of the Divine Names through the existence of the world. *"The Divine Perfection is actualized... through the manifestation of the properties of the Divine Names"* (*Fut.* II 588.30). The full manifestation of the properties of the Names demands the existence of both the corporeal world (made up of composite things) and the spiritual world (made up of noncomposite things); this full manifestation in turn is alluded to in the Qur'anic verse quoted (57:3). Cf. Chapter 6, note 11.

37. The "letter" *(harf)* of a thing is its manifest dimension, the "meaning" *(ma'nâ)* its non-manifest dimension. In short, *"The whole world is a letter which has come to express a meaning. Its meaning is God... so the meaning never ceases to be connected to the letter. God says, 'He is with you wherever you are'"* (Qur'an 57:4) (*Fut.* III 148.10). On the Perfect Man as embracing the four names First, Last, Manifest, and Nonmanifest, see also II 446.21, 468.20, 479.26; *Naqsh* 2.

38. Disengagement is the situation of meanings *(ma'ânî)* known directly by the intellect *('aql),* without the aid of sense perception, thought, or imagination. Most people, in knowing things, perceive them in a "material" form, whether this matter or "substratum"—be corporeal, as in the things perceived by the senses, or imaginal, as with the things perceived by the mind. Knowledge of disengaged meanings, that is, the realities of things as they are in themselves without a locus of manifestation *(mazhar)* in the corporeal or imaginal worlds, is achieved only by the greatest saints. The nature of this disengagement is partially clarified by a

passage in which Ibn al-'Arabî explains the nature of the vision of God achieved by the common people *(al-'âmma)*. *"The share of the common people in gazing* (nazar) *upon Him is imaginal. They are not able to disengage themselves from substrata in whatever meanings they enjoy, whether in this world, in the* barzakh, *or in the next world. Rather, few of the men of knowledge are able to conceive of complete disengagement from substrata. That is why most of the Sharî'a has come according to the understanding of the common people, though it contains allusions for the elect"* (Fut. II 86.6). In order to have knowledge of disengaged meanings, a person must himself be free of the veils of sensory perception and imagination, though this of course does not prevent him from perceiving these veils and discerning their proper place. This station is achieved by the Perfect Men.

39. "Knowledge of the Names" refers to Qur'an 2:31: *"He taught him [Adam] the Names, all of them."* Ibn al-'Arabî invariably understands "Adam" to refer to man as such (cf. *Naqsh* 1), in keeping with certain Qur'anic verses (e.g., 7:11). On this knowledge, cf. *Fut.* I 216.12; II 68.5, 71.22, 88.15, 487.21, 489.28; III 74.1; *Tanazzulât* 144. The All-Comprehensive Words *(jawâmi' al-kalim)* are referred to in the Prophet's saying, *"I was preferred over the [other] prophets through six things: I was given the All-Comprehensive Words..."* (Muslim, Masâjid 6–8; cf. Tirmidhî, Siyar 5). According to Ibn al-'Arabî, the Prophet alludes through this saying to the fact that he possesses the station of unlimited knowledge referred to in the Qur'anic verse just cited. Cf. *Fut.* II 72.3, 88.16; III 142.6.

40. Reference to Qur'an 2:33. Ibn al-'Arabî explains that Adam's special characteristic among the prophets was *"his knowledge of the Divine Names, a knowledge which was hidden from the angels; so they did not glorify God by them until they learned them from Adam"* (Fut. II 52.7; cf. II 355.23; III 278.1).

41. Man's superiority related to his *all-comprehensiveness (jam'iyya)*, i.e., the fact that he is the locus of theophany for all the Names. Though the angels are made of light and hence are superior in ontological degree, they reflect only some of the Names. *"The angels are higher* [a'lâ] *in plane, but man is more all-comprehensive in plane... So man possesses the excellence of all-comprehensiveness. Hence God made him the teacher of the angels and had them prostrate themselves before him"* (Fut. II 202.5; cf. II 355.32).

42. *Fut.* II 110-11.

43. Reference to the hadith of the veils quoted in the third paragraph of the answer.

44. In other contexts Ibn al-'Arabî will often read this Qur'anic verse as *"Everything is perishing except its face,"* a reading supported by the grammatical principle that a pronoun refers back to the closest noun. The unperishing "face" or "essence" of a thing is its reality, for "realities do not change" *(al-haqâ'iq lâ tatabaddal)*, much less perish. Cf. *Fut.* II 100.9, 99.16, 313.15; III 255.22, 420.8. A third interpretation would have *face* refer to the human visage (II 100.3).

45. Ibn al-'Arabî frequently stresses the point that the Names are relations *(nisab)* or attributions *(idâfât)* and not ontological entities *(a'yân wujûdiyya)* i.e., things different in their existence from God Himself. He often points out that his position on the nature of the attributes differs from that of the Ash'arites, who

held that the attributes were extraneous to the Essence, yet eternally existent. Cf. I 42.19, 163.8; III 441.17; IV 294.11.

46. These two kinds of Names, one of which negates attributes from the Essence and the other of which affirms them, are known as the Names of the Acts (or of Similarity) and the Names of Incomparability. See the translation of Chapter 558, note 78.

47. This hadith is not found in this form in the collections indexed in the *Concordance;* the closest hadith to it reads, *"God does not sleep, nor would it be seemly for Him to sleep;... His veil is light; were it to be removed, the Glories of His Face would burn away every creature whose eyes looked upon Him"* (Muslim, Îmân 293; Ibn Mâja, Muqaddima 13). References to the present text of the hadith in the *Futûhât* include II 80.34, 460. 7, 488.10, 542.3, 554.9; III 216.18, 289.32.

48. *Fut.* II 114.

49. The hadith is found in Muslim, Imân 147.

50. God's "loving the world" may simply be an allusion to the love implied by His Mercy, which *"embraces all things"* (Qur'an 7:156); more likely it points to the famous *hadith* which is, as Ibn al-'Arabî puts it, *"sound* [sahîh] *on the basis of unveiling* [kashf], *though not established* [ghayr thâbit] *through transmission* [naql]" (*Fut.* II 399.28): *"I was a Hidden Treasure and I loved to be known, so I created the creatures that I might be known."* (On the principles of Ibn al-'Arabî's hadith scholarship which allow him to rely on unveiling, cf. *Fut.* I 150.19.)

51. Being belongs to God alone; the existence of the things is borrowed if not illusory. *"The possible thing is called 'existent' metaphorically* [majâz], *not truly* [haqîqa]" (*Fut.* II 99.35). Hence, *"There is no existent but God"* (lâ mawjuda illâ Allâh), as Ibn al-'Arabî explains below (cf. *Fut.* II 216.3). Ibn al-'Arabî often cites the statement, *"There is nothing in existence except God"* (mâ fi'l-wujûd illâ Allâh) as a principle accepted by all Verifiers (*Fut.* I 279.6; II 54.16, 148.17, 160.4, 516.33; III 68.12, 80.14, 373.26).

52. Ibn al-'Arabî's position on awe and intimacy needs more clarification than he provides here. In his *Kitâb al-jalâl wa'l-jamâl* (printed in *Rasâ'il*) he points out that most Sufis relate awe to Majesty and intimacy to Beauty. He accepts that there is a certain truth in this, but he holds that in fact the situation is much more subtle: *"The Majesty of God is a meaning that returns from Him to Him and prevents us from knowing Him. But Beauty is a meaning that returns from Him to us and gives us what knowledge we have of Him... Beauty has two things within us: awe and intimacy. That is because Beauty has an elevation* ['uluw] *and an approach* [dunuw]. *We call the elevation the 'Majesty of Beauty.' Concerning it the knowers speak. It is this Majesty of Beauty that reveals itself to them in theophany, but they imagine that they are speaking about the first Majesty which we mentioned. From the human side, this Majesty of Beauty is connected to intimacy, while the Beauty which is approach is connected to awe. When the Majesty of Beauty reveals itself to us in theophany, we feel intimate. Were this not so, we would be destroyed, for Majesty and awe, because of their overpowering authority, leave nothing. Hence [God] counters that Majesty [of Beauty] from Him with an intimacy on our part, so that in contemplation we may be in equilibrium* [i'tidâl] *and be able to understand what we see and not be dazzled.*

But when Beauty reveals itself to us in theophany—and Beauty is God's cheerful expansiveness [mubâsata] *toward us, while Majesty is His Exaltation* ['izza] *beyond us—we counter the expansiveness* [bast] *of His Beauty toward us with awe, for expansiveness along with expansiveness would lead to ill manners* [sû' al-adab]*, and ill manners in the Presence is a cause of expulsion and distance"* (pp. 3-4).

53. This is one of Ibn al-'Arabî's basic arguments to reject the Ash'arite position that the Attributes are extraneous to the Essence. Cf. the translation of Chapter 558, note 90.

54. God's knowledge of all things is often referred to in the Qur'an, whether explicitly (2:282,4:176,5:96,6:101, et al.) or implicitly (e.g., *"Not a leaf falls, but He knows it,"* 6:59).

55. *Al-Tâ'ifa,* i.e., the Sufis.

56. An "Incident" is a true vision that may be seen in sleep, in the "annihilation" *(fanâ')* of normal consciousness brought about by a spiritual state *(hâl),* or in wakefulness. Incidents are considered to be the "beginnings of divine revelation" *(awâ'il al-wahy al-ilâhî),* no doubt in reference to the hadith, *"A true dream is one-forty-sixth part of prophecy"* (al-Bukhârî, Ta'bîr 2, 4, 10, 26; Muslim, Ru'yâ 6-9), and the report of the Prophet's wife 'A'isha, *"The first thing of revelation to appear to the Messenger of God was [visionary] dreams; he never saw a dream without it coming true like the splitting of the dawn"* (Bukhârî, Bad' al-wahy 3, Ta'bîr 1; Muslim, Imân 252).

57. The hadith is not found in the *Concordance.* Al-Ghazâlî cites it in *Ihyâ' 'ulûm al-dîn* I. 1.2. (Cairo: al-Matba'at al-'Amirat al-Sharafiyya, 1326, I, p. 15).

58. *Fut.* II 426-27.

59. On nature and its contrast with light, cf. the translation of Chapter 195, note 69.

60. The three kinds of forms correspond to the three created worlds (cf. the translation of Chapter 311, 42.5ff.). "Spiritual" is not a completely satisfactory translation for *ma'nawî,* since "spirit" *(rûh)* and "meaning" *(ma'nâ)* are not always synonymous. Nevertheless, the contrast between *hiss* (sensory perception) and *ma'nâ* (meaning) is employed synonymously with that between *jism* (corporeal body) and *rûh* (spirit).

61. Allusion to Qur'an 82:7: *"Oh Man! What has deceived thee as to thy generous Lord, who created thee and shaped thee and balanced thee and composed thee after what form He would?"*

62. The four means of *shaping* are mentioned in various Qur'anic verses and hadiths: 1. *"Our only word, when We desire a thing, is to say to it 'Be!', and it is"* (Qur'an 16:40). 2. A number of Qur'anic verses allude to God's one hand (e.g., *"Blessed is He in whose hand is the Kingdom, and He is powerful over everything"* [67:1]), but the reference is more likely to a *hadîth* that Ibn al-'Arabî often quotes: *"He created the Garden of Eden with His hand, He wrote the Torah with His hand, and He planted the tree of Tubâ [in the Garden] with His hand"* (*"He wrote the Torah with His hand"* is found in Abû Dâwûd, Sunna 16; Ibn Mâja, Muqaddima 10; Ahmad 2, 268, 392, 448, 464; *"God created the Garden of Eden and planted its trees with His hand"* is found in Suyûtî, *al-Jâmi' al-saghîr* [Munâwî, *Fayd al-qadîr,* Beirut: Dâr al-ma'rifa, 1391/1972, III,

p. 444]). 3. "Two hands" refers to the creation of Adam as mentioned in Qur'an 38:75: *"Oh Iblis, what prevented thee from prostrating thyself before him whom I created with My two hands?"* 4. The plural *hands* refers to Qur'an 36:71: *"Have they not seen how We have created for them from what Our hands wrought cattle that they Own?"* (cf. *Fut.* III 294.25).

63. The world stands upon quaternity because it derives from four fundamental divine attributes, variously listed as Life, Knowledge, Will, and Power; or Knowledge, Will, Power, and Speech; or First, Last, Manifest, and Nonmanifest. These are reflected throughout the cosmos in various other quaternities. Cf. *Fut.* I 260, 293.8; II 162.18, 270.9, 369.20, 406.7, 422.9, 430.14, 667.32; III 198.8, 201.4, 430.25, 550.7.

64. The Breath of the All-Merciful is Being as the Manifest, within which all the nonexistent entities exercise their properties and effects, just as letters and words exercise their effects in our own breath when we speak. The present chapter (198; cf. especially pp. 394-96) is based upon this symbolism. Each of the twenty-eight letters of the Arabic alphabet corresponds to a Divine Name; just as the letters come together to produce words, so the Names come together to produce existent things. Cf. II 123.26, 181.13, 352.2; III 95.19, 420.3, 452.30.

65. On the role of preparedness in determining the forms of things, cf. the translation of Chapter 140, note 42.

66. I.e., formed by the combination of the four elements: fire, air, water, and earth.

67. The four pillars are also known as the four natures *(tabâ'i')*: hot, cold, wet, and dry, since they are the qualities inherent in nature, i.e., the whole "sensory" world, both imaginal and corporeal existence. In contrast the "elemental" *('unsurî)* level refers only to the corporeal world.

68. The two faculties of the soul, practical and cognitive, are well known in philosophical writings (cf. Fut. I 260.18). For Ibn al-'Arabî they originate in the relationship between the Universal Soul (the Guarded Tablet, *al-lawh al-mahfûz*) and the Universal Intellect (the Supreme Pen, *al-qalam al-'alâ*), a relationship which allows the Soul to receive from the Intellect and transfer what it receives to the lower levels of existence. Cf. I 139.35; II 282.26; 439.8, 675.15; III 28.32.

69. Reference to the oft-quoted hadith not found in the *Concordance, "The first thing created by God is the Intellect"* (cf. Hakîm, *Mu'jam* 1260).

70. The fact that God created Adam with "two hands" is critical to his being made in God's form (*Fut.* I 263.17). *"God attributed Adam to the two hands to honor* (tashrîf) *him... He employed the dual form of 'hands' only in the case of the creation of Adam, who is the Perfect Man"* (III 294.24, 295.6). The two hands allude to the fact that in creating man God turned His attentiveness *(tawajjuh)* toward him in respect of both Incomparability and Similarity. *"So the station of the perfect servant lies between these two relationships; he faces each of them in his essence"* (II 4.10, 26). Cf. II 468.10, 641.23.

71. Concerning this Qur'anic verse, see Chapter 131, note 30.

72. On the "new creation," see Chapter Six, note 8.

73. *Fut.* II 473-74.

74. The divine instruction may come by means of the prophets or the unveiling given to the saints, though of course the latter can never override the former.

For a few examples of the usage of this common expression, cf. *Fut.* II 234.3, 566.4, 601.13, 613.26, 625.30, 636.27, 677.28, 688.26; III 39.22, 132.11, 133.9.

75. Ibn al-'Arabî frequently quotes this verse in connection with the never-ending and never-repeating theophanies through which the servant gains knowledge of God. Cf. *Fut.* II 77.26, 82.6, 218.28, 499.31; III 198.32, 224.32.

76. *Fut.* IV 196-198.

77. "Presence" in Ibn al-'Arabî's vocabulary is often synonymous with world *('âlam)* and sometimes with level *(martaba)*. It is normally connected with a particular attribute or kind of existence. Thus the "Presence of Imagination" is the world or level of existence where imagination dominates, *"for the Presences exercise their effects over those who dwell within them* [al-nâzil fîhâ]" *(Fut.* II 472.30). In the case of Divine Attributes, a Presence is the domain where the given Attribute manifests itself or "makes its presence felt." The Divine Presence is the domain where the Name Allah exercises its effects, i.e., the whole of Being and existence, from the Essence down to the world. *"There is nothing in existence except the Divine Presence, which is His Essence, His Attributes, and His Acts"* (II 114.14; cf. II 173.33, 383.33). In another context Ibn al-'Arabî writes, *"The Divine Presence consists of three levels: an Outward* [zâhir], *an Inward* [bâtin], *and an Intermediary* [wasat]; *the last, through which the Outward becomes distinguished and separated from the Inward, is the Barzakh..., the Perfect Man, whom God made an isthmus between God and the world. He becomes manifest through the Divine Names, and he is God; he becomes manifest through the reality of possible existence, and he is creation"* (II 391.20; cf. IV 282.27 and the translation of Chapter 372, 451.9).

78. Ibn al-'Arabî speaks of these two contrasting categories of Attributes or Names in many passages (e.g., *Fut.* II 257.24, 579.14, 619.15, 641.7). He also employs other terms when making the same distinction; thus Incomparability is often employed synonymously with "negation" *(salb)* of Names from God and is connected with the fact that God is "Independent of the worlds." Attributes of the Acts are also called Attributes of Similarity *(tashbîh)* and are connected to the "affirmation" *(thubût* or *ithbât)* of Names. Attributes of Incomparability refer to the Essence as It is in Itself, while Attributes of Acts allude to the relationships that the Essence assumes with creation (cf. II 110.30, translated in Chapter 73, Question 115). The basic difference between the two kinds of Attributes is explained as follows: *"The Names which seek* [talab] *Incomparability are the Names sought by the Essence in Itself, while the Names which seek Similarity are the Names sought by the Essence because it is a God. The Names of Incomparability are those such as the Independent, the Unique* [al-ahad], *and those which He alone possesses; the Names of Similarity are those such as the Compassionate, the Forgiving, and every Name by which the servant may truly be qualified in respect of being a locus of manifestation, not in respect of his Own entity"* (II 57.30). The Names of Incomparability are also contrasted with *"the Divine Names which call for* [istid'â'] *engendered existence, such as the Author, the Provider, and the King"* (II 573.7; on the Names that denote engendered existence *[asmâ' al-kawn* or *al-asmâ' al-kawniyya]*, cf. II 350.24, 548.9, 557.4; *al-Isfâr,* p. 10). The contrast between Incomparability and Similarity is closely connected with that between what the intellect *('aql)* can grasp about God and what

revelation tells us. Thus, *"Intellect provides half the knowledge of God, i.e., Incomparability and the negation of many properties from Him, while the Lawgiver brings the affirmation of what the intellect with its proofs has negated from Him"* (II 307.20; cf. the translation of Chapter 372, 450.26, and note 92 below; also II 404.14, 407.5, 502.22).

79. Here the problem has to do with what Names may and may not properly be attributed to God, a discussion that is continued below. The general rule is that Names are "conditional" *(tawqîfî)* upon having been revealed (see note 82, below). But is it proper to call God the "Plotter" if the Name itself has not come in this nominal form, but only in verbal form? Ibn al-'Arabî makes the point more explicitly in *Fut.* IV 319.5.

80. Ibn al-'Arabî seems to be passing beyond a grammatical discussion here by looking at the literal meaning of the word *damîr* ("pronoun"), i.e., innermost, secret, hidden. A pronoun is a word used to point to a hidden meaning. In the verse in question, the pronoun is not mentioned but understood.

81. Ibn al-'Arabî often makes this point (cf. the translation of Chapter 470,101.34). For example: *"In this verse God is named by every name that belongs to anything toward which there is poverty in the respect in which there is poverty"* (*Fut.* II 601.11; cf. IV 321.9). This discussion is closely connected to the nature of phenomena or secondary causes *(asbâb)*, which, since they are veils which God has set up for a purpose, need to be observed. Though certain imperfect saints may ignore the phenomena by performing miracles, the Blameworthy *(al-malâmiyya)*, who are the highest of the saints, always follow the outward situation demanded by the phenomena. *"They put phenomena in their places and know the wisdom in them. You might think that they are the ones who had created all things because of the way they affirm phenomena and urge others to do so. They are poor toward all things, since for them each thing is named 'Allah'... They know that there is no poverty except toward Allah, the Independent... In reality they are only poor toward Him in whose hand is the fulfillment of their needs, i.e., Allah, for in this verse He is named by everything toward which there is need"* (III 35.10). Cf. the translation of Chapter 141, note 48; II 262 *(bâb 162)*, 469.4.

82. Cf. *Fut.* II 232.28: *"His Names, in respect of being ascribed to Him, are conditional upon having come from Him. Hence He is not named except by Names He has given Himself, even if it is known that He is denoted by the name. So conditionality in ascription is to be preferred; and He has done this, all of it, only to teach the creatures courtesy toward Him."*

83. On God's decreeing that all things worship *('ibâda)* Him, which results in the fact that worship is intrinsic to all, cf. Chapter 470, note 160. On the radical poverty of all things toward God, a point to which Ibn al-'Arabî returns below, cf. Chapter 131, note 31.

84. As becomes clear from 196.35ff., below, here Ibn al-'Arabî is discussing the fact that the Name Allah comprehends all Names of the Acts.

85. Elsewhere Ibn al-'Arabî explains that it is impossible for this Name itself to be called upon—except by the Perfect Man—since the state of the caller will always delimit it and turn it into one of the specific Names under its sway. For example, *"When the seeker who is in need of provision says, 'Oh Allah, provide*

for me!', *while Allah is also the Preventer* [al-mâni'], *he does not seek through his state anything but the Name' Provider'* [al-razzâq]. *So in meaning he has only said, 'Oh Provider, provide for me!'* "(II 462.9; cf. II 541.5; III 317.28).

86. When a distinction is drawn between creature and originated thing, the second is something made by God without any preexisting matter, while the first is made from something already originated. In general spiritual beings are originated, corporeal beings created from the elements. The relevant Divine Name is *al-badî'*, the Originator. *"Every creature created without a precedent exemplar* ['alâ ghayr mithâl] *is originated"* (*Fut.* II 421.23). *"Through the first creation* [i.e., *of noncomposite things*, basâ'it] *God is the Originator, through the second [i.e., the creation of compound things] the Creator"* (II 422.5; but cf. IV 326.15). The locus of manifestation for the Name Originator is the First Intellect, which Ibn al-'Arabî calls *"the first originated object [existent]"* (awwal maf'ûl [mawjûd] ibdâ'î), in contrast to the Universal Soul, *"the first passively arising object"* (awwal maf'ûl inbi'âthî); cf. II 304.18, 421.30, 427.30, 642.19, 675.8; III 399.29.

87. In other words, there is no plurality in the Essence, even though, from the point of view of the world and vis-à-vis the creatures, the Essence assumes numerous relations known as the Names or Attributes. This is Ibn al-'Arabî's well-known distinction between the Oneness of the Essence and the manyness of the Names; as a result God is the "One Many" (*al-wâhid al-kathîr; Fut.* III 420.15, 451.15). *"God in respect of Himself possesses the Unity of the Unique* [ahadiyyat al-ahad] *and in respect of His Names the Unity of Manyness* [ahadiyyat al-kathra]*"* (III 465.3; cf. II 563.15; *Fusûs* 105/*Bezels* 126). In the same way Ibn al-'Arabî speaks of the Unity of the Combined Totality *(ahadiyyat al-majmû')*, i.e., of the Divine Names (III 289.4, 20).

88. Ibn al-'Arabî often, but not always, distinguishes between "descriptions" and "attributes." He defines *na't* as *"that which seeks nonexistent relations* [al-nisab al-'adamiyya], *such as the First,"* contrasting it with *sifa*, which is *"that which seeks an ontological meaning* [ma'nâ wujûdî], *such as the Knowing"* (*Fut.* II 129.3; cf. *Istilâhât* 17). Elsewhere he writes: *"As for the difference between descriptions and Names or Attributes, descriptions are words that do not denote a meaning subsisting in the essence of that which is described* [ma'nâ qâ'im bi-dhât al-man'ût]*...; they are only words that denote the Essence in respect of correlation* [idâfa]—*we also call them 'Names of Correlation'—like the First..."* (*al-Azal* 15; cf. *Fut.* IV 322.9). However, Ibn al-'Arabî often employs *na't* and *sifa* interchangeably; cf. II 212.21-22, 244.30-31.

89. Speculation may be good or bad, depending upon its object; as long as it does not try to exceed what is asked from it in the Qur'an, it is praiseworthy. Cf. Chapter 372, note 132.

90. This opinion relates to one of the well-known Ash'arite positions (cf. Wolfson, *Philosophy of the Kalam*, p. 214). Ibn al-'Arabî employs the same argument in rejecting it in I 284.19; cf. the translation of Chapter 73, Question 118, fourth paragraph.

91. This is the "Kullabite" formula of the theologians. Cf. chapter 470, note 172.

92. On bewilderment and its causes, cf. I 270 *(bâb* 50), II 307.21, 607.23, 661.13. One of these causes is the intellect's inability to understand those Qur'anic verses that allude to God's Similarity *(tashbîh)* with the crea-

tures (cf. II 128.23, 242.32, 306.11, 319.26, 389.10, 404.9, 502.22, 514.35; III 58.7, 453.11; also Chittick, "Death and the World of Imagination: Ibn al-'Arabî's Eschatology," *Muslim World*, LXXVII [1988], 51–82). The error of the People of Intellect is to want to interpret *(ta'wîl)* the verses that suggest Similarity; *"Sound intellects, which recognize His Majesty, are bewildered; but the People of Interpretation are not bewildered, nor did they hit the mark when they plunged into interpretation"* (II 407.4; cf. I 95.17; II 183.16).

At the End of Time
James W. Morris

1. III 327.10–340.12; the contents of the untranslated passages are summarized in the body of the translation (between square brackets) or indicated in footnotes. The title in Ibn 'Arabî's original "Table of Contents" *(fihrist:* O.Y. ed., I, 107) adds that "this is from the Muhammadan Presence"—i.e., pertaining to the universal Source of all Revelation (the *haqîqa muhammadîya*), which encompasses the spiritual "realities" of all the other prophets and their revelations; see the detailed illustration of this in the *Fusûs al-Hikam*. The special universal significance of this "Muhammadan" stage is further illuminated in the following chapter 367 (see the translation and commentary in this anthology), which contains the key autobiographical account of Ibn 'Arabî's own spiritual Ascension *(mi'râj)* leading to his culminating realization of the "Muhammadan Station" and of the inner spiritual meaning of the universal noetic *"Qur'ân."*

2. *Wuzarâ'* (sing. *wazîr*): the term is more often translated as "minister," but that implies (at least in English) a sort of subordination incompatible with Ibn 'Arabî's insistence that *"the wuzarâ' are the guides* [al-hudât] *and He is the 'guided one'* [al-Mahdî]*"* (III 329.27–28). Instead, the relationship described at the beginning of this chapter often seems to reflect the type of polity in which the ruler was seen as enforcing or applying policies prescribed by this "vizier." On a more profound level, which Ibn 'Arabî brings out only gradually in the course of the middle section (II 1–9 below), all of the accomplished saints may be seen as at least partial "representatives" or "helpers" of the Mahdi (or "Imam": see notes 10, 15–16, 19, 68) insofar as they realize these (and other) essential spiritual functions.

3. In this chapter, as in much of Ibn 'Arabî's work, it would be quite misleading to translate this term (or the related expression *al-shar':* see notes 76 and 105 below) simply as religious or revealed "Law" without some further explanation or qualification. The *sharî'a*, as Ibn 'Arabî uses the term here, is distinguished from what we ordinarily conceive of as "law" by (a) its breadth of reference to *all* the divine norms or precepts *(ahkâm)* for human behavior, but especially those having to do with divine worship *('ibâda)* and the infinite variety of man's inner, spiritual or psychic "actions", which are often without any immediately visible, outward manifestations (which is why one can speak, for example, of the "Sharia" of Jesus); (b) its unconcern (or at least lack of apparent specification) concerning the majority of the worldly matters which are ordinarily (and necessarily) covered by civil laws and/or social customs; and (c) the intrinsic distance between the eternal Reality and divine Source of the Sharia (which is the constant focus of Ibn 'Arabî's

concern) and the multitude of its various historical, popularly accepted images or applications. (This latter contrast is closely paralleled in his treatment of such Qur'anic expressions as "the Pure Religion" and "the Religion of God," at notes 8 and 99 below.) Ibn 'Arabî's understanding of these questions is further clarified in C. Chodkiewicz's translations of chapters 88, 318, 344 and 437 of the *Futûhât* in *Les Illuminations de La Mecque,* Sindbad, Paris, 1988. Now Ibn 'Arabî's understanding, on each of these points, differs substantially from the typical perspective of the later historical disciplines of Islamic jurisprudence *(fiqh, usûl al-fiqh,* etc.), and much of the central part of this chapter (section II, 1-9) is particularly devoted to bringing out the differences between the conceptions of the Sufis ("People of Unveiling", etc.) and the jurists of his day *(fuqahâ' al-zamân).* However his approach to questions of *fiqh* in other connections is frequently more irenic: for a more balanced and comprehensive discussion of his treatment of Islamic law, see the excellent summary by M. Chodkiewicz, "Ibn 'Arabî, la lettre et la loi," pp. 27-40 in *Actes du colloques 'Mystique, culture et société,'* ed. M. Meslin, Paris, 1983. (A number of the references below to related legal discussions in other chapters of the *Futûhât* are drawn from that survey.)

4. See our much more detailed discussion of all these questions, with reference both to chapter 367 and to many other related sections of the *Futûhât,* in our article "Ibn 'Arabî's 'Esotericism':The Problem of Spiritual Authority", pp. 37-74. in *Studia Islamica,* LXIX (1989).

5. Here we have included only the following brief passages dealing with this subject, which are essential for understanding the rest of this chapter: 111,327.16-17, 26-32; 328.11-18; 329.26-28; 331.7-12. In fact, most of this long opening section (III, 327.10-331.33, or more than a third of the entire chapter) is devoted to the quotation of hadith and related eschatological material concerning the Mahdi and the Dajjâl—traditional materials which would give the casual reader no reason to suspect the controversial subjects that are to follow (in section II below). (For further discussion of the structure and rhetorical methods and intentions underlying this sort of construction, see our article on "Ibn 'Arabî's 'Esotericism'..." cited in note 4 above.)

6. This description and the many additional characteristics given in the passage omitted here are taken literally from the numerous hadith concerning the Mahdi (see Wensinck, *Concordance,* s.v., and article *"al-Mahdî"* by W. Madelung in *EI²,* V, pp. 1230-38). Most relevant to the following discussion is the fact that the hadith selected by Ibn 'Arabî all emphasize the Mahdi's close resemblance to the Prophet especially in his intrinsic character and nature *(khuluq),* so that *"he walks in the footsteps of the Messenger of God, and makes no mistake, and he is guided by an unseen angel"*—a description that Ibn 'Arabî mentions repeatedly in the course of this chapter as proof of the Mahdi's divine "protection from error" *('isma).* Clearly Ibn 'Arabî sees Muhammad as the exemplary illustration of all the characteristics (both of the Mahdi *and* of his Helpers) discussed here—a point that takes on added importance in light of the brief allusion (at notes 16-17 below) to Ibn 'Arabî's own unique complementary role as the "Seal of Muhammadan Sainthood."

7. The *jizya*—literally, "compensation" (for remaining non-Muslim)—required of each individual from the peoples of the protected religions under the various systems of Islamic law; see the long article *"Djizya"* in *EI²,* pp. 559ff.

8. For the full significance of Ibn ʿArabî's use of the Qurʾanic expression "the Pure Religion" *(al-Dîn al-khâlis)*, see the references at note 99 below; sections II-7 and II-9 are an extended commentary on the situation to which he briefly alludes here. "Schools" here translates the Arabic *madhâhib;* Ibn ʿArabî sometimes applies this term more broadly to all the "ways" or individual forms of religious belief and/or practice, but here, judging from what follows (especially sections II-7 and II-9 below), he clearly seems to be referring more specifically to the widely accepted "schools of law" (Hanafi, Maliki, etc.) in Islam.

9. *Muqallidat al-ʿulamâʾ ahl al-ijtihâd:* the *ʿulamâʾ* in this case clearly refer to the jurists following the respective founders (the "imams" al-Malik, al-Shâfiʿî, etc.) of the established Islamic legal schools, all of which, for Ibn ʿArabî, were originally grounded in the effort of independent legal judgment *(ijtihâd)* of the early Muslim jurists, based on their use of personal opinion *(raʾy)* or rational analogy and inference *(qiyâs)* concerning the supposed grounds of the particular divine commandments or prescriptions *(hukm / ahkâm)*. In several of the following sections, Ibn ʿArabî goes on to contrast their approach (whether or not they still admit the possibility of *ijtihâd*) with the immediate—and necessarily individual and specific—divine inspiration characterizing the judgments of the Mahdi, the Prophet and the *awliyâʾ*. The roots of his criticism of the *ʿulamâʾ* and their *ijtihâd* (in this legalist sense) are brought out in much greater detail in sections II-7 and -9 below. Ibn ʿArabî's own very different conception of the individual spiritual obligation of *ijtihâd* (and his contrasting sharp criticisms of any claims to an obligation of *taqlîd* on the part of others) are explained in much greater detail, along with their bases in the Qurʾan and hadith, in our article cited at note 4 above.

10. The long intervening passage (to III, p. 328.11) continues with some of the traditional hadith materials concerning the battles of the Mahdi and the descent of Jesus at the end of time, concluding with Ibn ʿArabî's own enigmatic statement that *"[the Mahdi's] age has already come to you, and his time overshadows you."* Rather than reflecting any particular Messianic hopes or assumptions, this aside seems to foreshadow Ibn ʿArabî's subsequent allusions to the perennial manifestation of the Mahdi's spiritual functions through the accomplished saints *(awliyâʾ)* and the "Imam" "or "Imam of the Age"—terms which Ibn ʿArabî actually employs much more frequently than *"al-Mahdî"* throughout the long middle section (II 1-9) of this chapter.

11. The latter part of this phrase (rhyming in the original) apparently alludes to the Qurʾanic mention (Qurʾan 27:16-17) of Solomon's power over the armies of the jinn and his inspired knowledge of the "language of the birds" *(mantiq al-tayr)*—Solomon being another prototype of this divinely inspired earthly ruler. (Ibn ʿArabî himself constantly reiterates—referring both to Qurʾanic allusions and to his own mystical experience—that *all* created beings, even minerals or letters, for example, are "alive" and "speaking"). On the metaphysical plane, at least, this description of the *Mahdi* seems to correspond to certain of Ibn ʿArabî's remarks concerning the lofty station of the "Imam of the Left" in the spiritual hierarchy, the "sword of the Pole," who is responsible for the order and maintenance of this world: see Chodkiewicz, *Sceau,* chapter VI, and Hakim, *Muʿjam,* pp. 109-110. (See also notes 14, 15 and 19 below).

12. The nature of this "victorious support" (*nasr*, a term combining the notions of divine assistance and the "victory" resulting from that support), as Ibn 'Arabî understands it, is explained in his long discussion of the spiritual virtue of *sidq* (truthfulness and inner sincerity of intention) in the immediately following section (III, 238.18-239.25), summarized here. See also chapter 152 of the *Futûhât* (R 246ff.), where *nasr* is treated as one of the distinctive characteristics of *walâya* (i.e., the saints' inner "proximity" to God) and of their spiritual "authority" *(wilâya)* in general. Throughout this section regarding the conjunction of faith, true inner sincerity, and divine support (as in this chapter more generally), Ibn 'Arabî clearly has in mind the paradigmatic example of the Prophet and his Companions.

13. The description of this *hâfiz* cannot but recall Ibn 'Arabî's repeated insistence on his own spiritual realization—which he apparently viewed as unique in his own time—of the rare condition of "pure servanthood" *('abd mahd khalis)* or absolute "spiritual sincerity" *(ikhlâs)*, without any trace of inner opposition to the divine Lordship. See his revealing autobiographical remarks about this in chapters 311 (III, 26-27), 367 (III, 350; section IV-I in this translation), and 29 (O.Y. ed., III 228-29) of the *Futûhât,* along with additional references in Hakim, *Mu'jam,* pp. 765-78.

14. *Hijjîr:* i.e., their constantly repeated formula of divine invocation *(dhikr)*, or simply their spiritually representative "motto" from the Qur'an. See Ibn 'Arabî's detailed discussions of the *"hijjîrs"*—which are all symbolically significant verses from the Qur'an—of the seven *abdâl*, in chapter 15 of the *Futûhât* (O.Yahya edition, II, 381-84), and especially of along series of different spiritual "Poles" *(aqtâb),* in chapters 464-556 (Cairo ed., IV, 88-195; cf. *infra,* W. Chittick's translation of chapter 470). In addition, there also is an apparent pun here on another possible reading of the same Arabic written form as "midday sun" *(hajir).*

15. *Al-Imâm al-Mahdî:* in the rest of this chapter Ibn 'Arabî more often refers to this figure simply as "the Imam" (i.e., the "guide" or leader) or "the Imam of the Age" (see note 19), without any specific reference to the "Mahdi"; in doing so he seems to be alluding—as likewise in the poem opening the chapter, and in the following reference to the "Seal of Muhammadan Sainthood" (note 16)—to the broader spiritual reality or function symbolized by the Mahdi as the "Greatest Imam" *(al-Imâm al-Akbar)* or rather as a particular manifestation or "deputy" *(nâ'ib)* of the Pole *(Qutb)*: as such, the term subsumes, among other things, the various spiritual virtues of the *awliyâ'* and the "people of unveiling" described throughout this chapter. For a more detailed account of the Shaykh's complex understanding of the "Imamate" in this broader spiritual sense, see the references in Hakim, *Mu'jam,* pp. 101-114 and 1103-7 (especially pp. 104-5 and 111), and Chodkiewicz, *Sceau,* chapters VI-VII.

16. For a detailed exposition of Ibn 'Arabî's self-conception of his unique role as Seal of Muhammadan Sainthood, see the discussions and extensive references in Chodkiewicz, *Sceau,* chapters VII-IX, as well as the related entries in Hakim, *Mu'jam,* pp. 373-383. (For the many relevant senses of the key term *hukm,* usually translated here as "judgment," see note 97 below.)

17. See also Ibn 'Arabî's further remarks on the special role of the Qur'an in his spiritual life in section II-7 below and note 64. Here, as throughout the Shaykh's writings, the expression *"Qur'ân"* refers not simply to the sacred Book

revealed through Muhammad, but more broadly to its underlying spiritual Reality, which for Ibn 'Arabî is ultimately inseparable from the universal Logos or "Muhammadan Reality" and "Perfect Man": see the references in Hakim, *Mu'jam,* pp. 903-9. More specifically, he often stresses the etymological root sense of *"al-Qur'ân"* (in implicit contrast to the parallel Qur'anic expression *al-Furqân,* the "Division" or "Separation") as a reference to the comprehensive, universal aspect of the divine Reality, which for him is also symbolically expressed in the divine Name "God" *(Allâh).* This distinction underlies his repeated insistence in the following paragraphs (see note 20 below) on his own superlative knowledge of *"Allâh"* in particular—i.e., the comprehensive divine Reality—rather than of any of the specific divine Names and their manifestations. (See the further discussions of these key distinctions below in W. Chittick's translation from chapter 558.)

18. After briefly alluding to the Prophet's doubts concerning the exact number of years of the Mahdi's reign ("five, seven, or nine years", according to a hadith included in the *Musnad* of Ahmad b. Hanbal, III, p. 21; see note 22 below), and the corresponding uncertainty concerning the exact number of the Mahdi's Helpers, Ibn 'Arabî returns to a lengthy quotation (III 329.31-331.6) of the *hadîth* and traditional accounts concerning the Mahdi's encounters with the Antichrist *(al-Dajjâl)*: see the summary of these materials in the corresponding article in *EI[1]* (A. J. Wensinck) and *EI[2]* (A. Abel).

19. *Imâm al-Waqt:* i.e., the "Pole" *(Qutb)* or "Lord of the Age," etc.: for the different meanings of this term (and at least eight common synonyms in Ibn 'Arabî's technical vocabulary), see Hakim, *Mu'jam,* pp. 678-83, plus the entries for the related terms. For Ibn 'Arabî's conception of the role of the Pole (and his Imams) in the spiritual hierarchy, in both its temporal and universal dimensions, see the extensive references in Chodkiewicz, *Sceau,* chapter VI. In the rest of this chapter (e.g., section II-6, at note 68) he frequently uses this same expression ("Imam of the Age") in an apparently more general reference to other figures fulfilling some of the "Mahdi's" broader spiritual functions in every historical period.

20. The Arabic expression here (literally, "a single foot") more clearly implies the alternative between two possible kinds of spiritual knowledge—either of God (i.e., the universal, comprehensive divine reality: *"Allah"*) or of particular divine Names and their manifestations in the events of this world—that underlies Ibn 'Arabî's discussion here.

21. III, 331.34-338.2; the short passages not translated are identified within the summaries or notes below.

22. See the earlier reference to this hadith at note 18 above; Ibn 'Arabî assumes that the number of Helpers agrees with the number of years of the Mahdi's mission, and mentions (III 331.33) the case of a young Sufi friend who was informed in an inspired vision that the number of the Mahdi's *Wuzarâ'* would be nine—a figure corresponding to the number of their distinctive spiritual qualities described in the rest of the chapter.

23. Or "calling" or "requesting": the Arabic root *d-'-w,* translated here by forms of "pray," refers not to the obligatory, ritual divine service *(salât),* but to the individual's personal prayers to God, often—as is clearly the case here—with the added sense of a specific call or request for some particular divine action or response. (We

have also kept the subject indefinite, as in the original Arabic, since this condition ultimately applies not only to the Mahdi or his Helpers, but to each *walî* participating in this spiritual state, as Ibn 'Arabî states explicitly at note 29 below.)

24. Ibn 'Arabî's expression here apparently refers to his characteristic understanding that each being's inner strivings or petitions to God (i.e., "prayer" in the broadest possible sense, whether or not consciously and appropriately formulated) necessarily are directed toward one or another specific aspects of the overall divine Reality, expressed in Qur'anic terms by the many divine Names ("Lord," "King," etc.), that constitute the ontological "lords" of that individual.

25. *Ilhâh,* a term that implies not only urgency and insistence, but also a sort of specific, determined pleading, close to an open demand. Ibn 'Arabî goes on to explain that this sort of attitude—evidently inappropriate in man's ordinary relationship with God—is apparently permitted the Mahdi as part of the proof of his special, quasi-prophetic function.

26. I.e., to realize this otherwise "impossible" request as one of the unique miracles *(mu'jizât)* performed by the prophetic messengers that constitute part of the decisive divine "Argument" or "Proof" *(hujja)* of their special mission.

27. Ibn 'Arabî is alluding here more broadly to his *own* status as the preeminent "follower of Muhammad" (see references at note 16-17 above), and by extension to the similar position of all the (fully accomplished) "Muhammadan saints," which he brings out explicitly at the end of this section and in the rest of this chapter (especially II-7 and 9 below). For the deeper grounds of this special status of the saints in relation to the "heritage" of Muhammad (which ultimately encompasses the realities of all the other prophets and messengers), see the extended references in Chodkiewicz, *Sceau,* chapters IV-V and Hakim, *Mu'jam,* pp. 1191-1201 (entries on *irth/wârith*).

28. This hadith was quoted in full among the many traditions concerning the characteristics of the Mahdi cited at the beginning of this chapter (see note 6 above), and Ibn 'Arabî repeats this phrase whenever the question of *'isma* (see following note) arises in the following sections (especially II-7 and -9 below).

29. See the excellent, more complete discussion of Ibn 'Arabî's understanding of *'isma*—which is far more profound and universal, in its metaphysical and spiritual dimensions, than the more familiar treatments of this subject in kalam theology (where it is primarily limited to discussion of the prophets and Imams)—in Hakim, *Mu'jam,* pp. 806-10. See also Sections II-7 (note 78) and II-9 below, as well as the more detailed discussion of this typical contrast between the saints (as the true *'ulamâ'*) and the *fuqahâ'* in the article cited at note 4 above.

30. *Rijâl al-ghayb:* this Sufi expression refers to saints of high spiritual rank (especially the *abdâl*) or other spiritual beings (angels, etc.) who may receive a divine mission to become visible or take on human form in another place. As an illustration of this phenomenon, see Ibn 'Arabî's own firsthand account of two personal experiences with the such "mysterious strangers," including an unnamed Iranian Sufi master, at the end of this same chapter (summarized in section III, notes 119-21 below).

31. Ibn 'Arabî frequently interprets in this light the many symbols mentioned in the visions of the Prophet (e.g., during his *Mi'râj,* as explained in chapter 367 [III, 340-54], section II of our translation here); one of his favorite illustrations of the phenomena referred to here is the Prophet's recognition of the "milk" offered

him by an angel (according to a famous hadith) as a symbol of spiritual knowledge. Chapter 311 of the *Futûhât* (III, 41-44; "On the Station of the 'Arisings by Special Designation' *[nawâshi' ikhtisâsiya]* from the Unseen") is entirely devoted to these phenomena of "manifestations" or "projections" — both by Sufi saints and by angels, etc. — in various sensible and imaginal forms. Ibn 'Arabî gives a number of fascinating anecdotes concerning such incidents, analyzes their metaphysical underpinnings (in the "Presence" of Imagination, *khayâl*) and discusses the special unerring ability of the Prophet to perceive the spiritual realities *(ma'ânî)* underlying such phenomena. (See the partial translation by W. Chittick elsewhere in this anthology).

32. Ibn 'Arabî's technical vocabulary for describing the many facets of divine "communication" and its human "reception," which combines a profound concern for the subtleties of Qur'anic expression with close attention to the diverse phenomena of spiritual experience and their complex metaphysical foundations, is so extraordinarily rich that any English equivalents of the key terms can only be very approximate. Here the divine "address" *(al-khitâb al-ilâhî)* or "discourse" is the divine "Speech" *(kalâm/hadîth)* specifically as it is directed toward (and received by) a particular person. Its "delivery" or transmission *(ilqâ':* literally, "projection") into the heart (or hearing or any other senses) of the person thus addressed may take any of the forms described below — since ultimately (for Ibn 'Arabî, but relying on many passages of the Qur'an) all Being is nothing but divine "Speech," an insight that is amplified in the immediately following section (II-3, notes 40-41 below). For an excellent presentation of these and related technical terms in their broader context in the Shaykh's writings (as well as a helpful reminder of the complexities of their actual Qur'anic usage), see Hakim, *Mu'jam,* pp. 400-5 *(al-Khitâb al-Ilâhî)* and 1182-91 *(al-Wahy al-Ilâhî).*

33. Ibn 'Arabî understands and employs this key expression (and related forms of the same root) to convey an extremely wide range of meanings, which — as shown by S. al-Hakim in the long study (pp. 1182-91) cited in the preceding note — closely reflect the broader dimensions and subtleties of Qur'anic usage. In particular, readers familiar with the usual discussions of *wahy* (as the uniquely prophetic form of "revelation") in Islamic theological and philosophical literature (as well as in more apologetically oriented Sufi texts) should take note of the very different parameters and intentions of Ibn 'Arabî's complex usage of this term here and elsewhere in his writings. The critical problem of the relation of the *wahy* of each prophet to that of the saints who are his true "inheritors" (see notes 16 and 27) is clarified in Chapter 14 (On "the Secrets of the Prophets among the Saints... "), O.Y. II 357-62 (Cairo ed., I 149-52).

34. *'Alâ jihat al-hadîth:* here the emphasis implied by this term is on both the (relative) *novelty* of information conveyed and the fact that it is perceived as a message coming from *outside* the person to whom it is delivered — not so much on the usual meaning of verbal "speaking," since this inspiration is perceived by the *heart* and not the sense of hearing (again, see detailed explanation in chapter 14, O.Y. II 357-60). Here and in the other examples described in this section Ibn 'Arabî wants to emphasize the specific kind of divine "address" or inspiration in which there is a conscious awareness of this particular message as something clearly "received" or "projected" into the person's awareness from a higher, divine

source, not as the product or expression of his personal thinking *(nazar)* or previous knowledge. This fundamental aspect of genuine "inspiration" is also brought out in the continuation of the Qur'anic verse opening this section: *"And likewise We inspired in you a spirit from Our Command. You did not know what was the Book nor the Faith..."* (Qur'an 42:52). The decisive importance of the *Heart* (*qalb:* the locus of all spiritual perception; see Hakim, *Mu'jam,* pp. 916-21) as the instrument of this direct inspiration (following the Qur'anic usage of *wahy:* see references at notes 32 and 33), and thus of its immediate spiritual apprehension without any sensible "veil," becomes clearer only in contrast to the immediately following discussion of the auditory and other "veiled" forms of the divine Speech addressed to particular individuals.

35. The "necessary sciences" or forms of knowledge *('ulûm darûrîya)*, used here in the accepted sense of that term in Islamic philosophy and theology, are the abstract universal premises (prior to sense-perception) of all thought (including logic, mathematics, etc.), which therefore underlie all communication and ordinary, non-revealed knowledge; they are innately shared by all human beings and cannot be doubted or questioned, although because of their universality they are not always (or even usually) consciously formulated. For Ibn 'Arabî's own distinctive conception of the "necessary" forms of knowledge, in the broader context of his spiritual epistemology, see chapter 19 (O.Y. ed. III, 78-87).

36. Ibn 'Arabî goes on to reiterate that although our awareness of various forms of knowledge within ourselves may often strike us as a new discovery, it does not ordinarily share the other essential characteristics of this particular form of divine inspiration—i.e., it is not perceived by the heart as a divine "speech" "delivered" to us from a higher source *outside* ourselves.

37. *'Ayn tajallî al-Haqq:* i.e., the theophany or Self-manifestation of the ultimate divine Reality or absolutely Real *(al-Haqq)*. This ambiguous status of all phenomena, which can be either "veils" or "theophanies" depending on the inner state of the person experiencing them, is one of the central themes of all of Ibn 'Arabî's writing: it is frequently expressed, for example, in his typical ontological (and etymological) understanding of *kufr, kafara,* etc.—usually translated as "unbelief"— as "covering up" or "veiling" the infinite Signs of God's presence. It is also strikingly illustrated in his famous remarks concerning the differences in men's "vision" of Paradise, e.g., at the end of the chapter on Ismail, I 94; 109-10 in Austin tr.) in the *Fusûs:* "...*for the matter is one, but in the [same] theophany there is an opposition between the two of them [i.e., the awareness of the man of faith and that of the unbeliever].*" For further references, see Hakim, *Mu'jam,* pp. 265-69 ("theophany," etc.) and 313-18 ("veil," etc.).

38. This "particular," individual modality of the divine Speech *(Kalâm Allâh)* here is illustrated by Ibn 'Arabî with the citation of three Qur'anic verses (9:6, 19:52, 27:8) among those where God is referred to as speaking directly and openly to particular individuals (especially to Moses, *"Kalîm Allâh"*). Again (as at notes 32-36 above) he is stressing the essential phenomenological distinction between this kind of specific, individual divine "address" and the more universal manifestations of the divine Speech. (See the detailed references in Hakim, *Mu'jam,* at notes 32 and 33 above.)

39. It is important to note that Ibn 'Arabî clearly sees *all* of these forms of revelation or inspiration as applying to the case of the Prophet and the Mahdi's

"Helpers," and by extension to all those saints or inspired "knowers" who share in this particular spiritual stage *(manzil)*, and that he is not using these distinctions to justify a particular theological "ranking" of prophets (or of prophets and saints). Instead, this concluding allusion points the discerning reader toward the more essential problem of developing his own awareness and understanding of that "divine address" (in all its dimensions) that is "delivered" personally to him. See again the more detailed treatment of these questions in Chapter 14 of the *Futûhât*, O.Y. ed. II, 357-62 (Cairo ed. I, 150).

40. Perhaps the most pertinent illustration in Ibn 'Arabî's own writing of this sort of "translation" *(tarjama)* of a divine inspiration—in this case received from the hand of the Prophet—into human language is his famous book *Fusûs al-Hikam,* where, in his Prologue, he explicitly sets forth his claim (or wish) to be the Prophet's faithful "translator" *(mutarjim).* Note that this form of divine inspiration is clearly differentiated here from the *direct* angelic "dictation" of the actual words of the revealed Book described in the immediately preceding passage, which evidently constitutes one of the unique attributes of the Qur'an. Ultimately, for Ibn 'Arabî, *every* form of knowledge is based on divine "inspirations" and individual "theophanies," although most often those relying on their own reasoning and inquiry *(nazar)* are unaware of this or take it for granted: see, e.g., *Futûhât,* chapter 19, O.Y. ed. III, 81-82.

41. *Mutarjim:* though the phrase may sound strange in English (and even in the original Arabic), since we would more naturally expect to see the world referred to as a "translation" of the divine Speech, it expresses in a simple formula the very essence of Ibn 'Arabî's central insight into the theophanic, continually recreated nature of all Being and the transcendent, paradoxical unity of the "subject" and "object" of that Whole as it unfolds in the realized vision of the "people of unveiling" *(ahl al-kashf)*, the Heart of the "Perfect Man."

42. "Holders of authority" translates *ûlû' al-'amr,* an allusion to the famous Qur'anic command (4:59) *"… Obey God and obey the Messenger and the holders of authority among you…,"* which has been the source of endless controversy over who are actually the true "authorities" of the Community since the time of the Prophet. However in this section Ibn 'Arabî uses the term as a relatively uncontroversial reference to the various types of judges required to apply the provisions of Islamic law. The "ranks" here, as explained in an untranslated part of this passage, refer to three basic fields of jurisdiction of the religious Law (offenses or disputes involving physical harm, honor or property), and not to specific governmental or administrative posts.

43. *'Ulamâ' al-rusûm:* here this term (used more broadly in the previous section) refers to the formal "knowledge" of the external "traces" of the Prophetic heritage typical of the mass of legal scholars *(fuqahâ')* popularly known as the "learned" *('ulamâ').* The roots of Ibn 'Arabî's radically differing point of view— which at first seems to contradict his own discussion here of individuals whose formal legal "knowledge" is overcome by their passions—are explained more openly throughout sections II-7 and II-9 below. It should be stressed that this term, for Ibn 'Arabî, is primarily used in a "descriptive" and not necessarily pejorative sense, since many of the saints and Sufis (including, for example, the pious judge described in section II-5 below) were outwardly also notable representatives of

this category of *'ulamâ'*. See his discussion of the complementary functions of *"those who preserve (the outward literal) forms of the divine judgment"* as expressed by the Prophet *(hafazat al-ahkâm)* and *"those who preserve (the Prophet's spiritual) states and secrets" (hafazat al-ahwâl wa-l-asrâr)* in Chapter 14, O.Y. ed. II, 361-62 (Cairo, I 151), and the more detailed discussions and references in our article cited at note 4 above.

44. A quotation from the classical hadith account of the characteristics of the Mahdi given at the opening of this chapter (section I, at note 6 above).

45. I.e., Ibn 'Arabî is not specifically pointing to some outwardly "reformable" defect in the teaching and transmission of the Law in his time, nor to the fraudulent pretensions or moral defects of particular individuals (although that latter subject does come up in section II-7 below). Rather he is primarily alluding here (and more clearly in the following sections) to the fundamental—and in our present circumstances, humanly inescapable—problem that the just, appropriate application and interpretation of the traditional sources concerning the divine commands and their historical application by the Prophet usually require a far deeper understanding of both their ultimate contexts and intentions and the relevant factors in each particular case than can be expected of any but the rarest individuals, those whose every action is divinely inspired and protected from error *(ma'sûm:* see the discussion at note 29 above). As he remarks more openly in section II-7 below, those truly qualified "authorities" (the true *wulât*) in any age, whether or not they outwardly rule, are none other than the divinely guided "saints"—i.e., the *awliyâ'* (a term drawn from the same Arabic root as the words translated as "authority" in these passages, and having explicit connotations of spiritual authority *[wilâya]* that are not readily conveyed by the term "saint" in Western languages).

46. I.e., what Ibn 'Arabî calls their "passion" *(shahwa)*, referring to all the various ways in which their personal emotions may run contrary to their knowledge of the legally correct judgment (see the illustrations in the following section). The person exhibiting this moral capacity of rational self-control is called "judicious" *('âqil)*, an expression which Ibn 'Arabî derives from the root sense of "binding" or "hindering" (one's personal emotions, in this case); see the application of this term to the prophets in particular at note 53 below.

47. This Qur'anic verse and the equally famous "divine saying" *(hadîth qudsî)* quoted here *("My Mercy has preceded My Anger")* are of course among the key leitmotifs of Ibn 'Arabî's thought: see references in Hakim, *Mu'jam,* pp. 521-29 and many other citations in this anthology. The brief passages not translated here are simply elaborations and reminders of this fundamental principle that *"God's Anger [eventually] ends for those with whom He is angry* [Qur'an 1:7, etc.], *while God's Mercy is never ending."* (For the sake of consistency, we have followed the customary translation of the Qur'anic term *ghadab* as "anger," although that rendering implies all sorts of anthropomorphic associations considerably removed from the deeper meaning of that expression in the thought of Ibn 'Arabî—and probably in the Qur'an itself. Similarly, the English word "love," especially given its connotations in the Bible—probably comes much closer than "mercy" or "compassion" to expressing the full range of realities implied in Ibn 'Arabî's notion of *rahma.)*

48. *Hudûd Allâh,* a Qur'anic concept which originally includes both the divine "statutes" and prescriptions *(ahkâm:* see note 97)—which can of course be

understood in a more spiritual and universal as well as a more exoteric and legalistic sense—and the earthly punishments and penalties applied for offenses against them in the various historical systems of Islamic Law. (The same term *[al-ḥadd]* is translated as "penalty" when used in that explicitly legal context in the following paragraph.)

49. I.e., to the one who has realized within himself the fundamental justice of the divine Command and has carried out the process of inner repentance and recourse to God's Mercy that has spiritually "purified" him and enabled him to avoid the further consequences of his sin (in this world or the next). Ibn 'Arabî goes on to make clear that his point here actually applies to the inner spiritual situation of *every* individual with regard to the infinite range of the divine "commands" or "limits" more generally understood (see preceding note), not just those infractions that happen to involve "criminal" actions and the external forms of the law.

50. *Al-ḥâkim:* although translated throughout as "judge" (in the more familiar legal sense), this term can also be understood in an extended (and more exact) sense as anyone who seeks to ascertain and apply the divine "judgment" or "commandment" *(ḥukm)* appropriate to a given action or situation—a grave and almost impossible responsibility if viewed from the broader spiritual perspective that Ibn 'Arabî gradually unfolds here and in the following sections. See also note 97 below for the multiple meanings of *ḥukm* ("judgment," "command," etc.) and its verbal forms throughout this chapter.

51. Ibn 'Arabî's conception of the unique qualifications of the accomplished saints *(awliyâ')* in this regard is developed in greater detail in sections 7 and 9 below; but at the very end of this chapter (section III, notes 122-25 below) he places severe restrictions on the situations in which they should even attempt to argue with others on the basis of their revealed insights—i.e., only when they actually receive a divine *order* to do so. These and many other essential qualifications involved in Ibn 'Arabî's understanding of the "spiritual authority" *(wilâya)* of the saints are discussed in much greater detail in our article "Ibn 'Arabî's 'Esotericism': the Problem of Spiritual Authority," cited at note 4 above. A revealing illustration of the complex responsibilities involved in the position of human, worldly judgeship is Ibn 'Arabî's remark at this point (III 334.13) that *"In my opinion none of the questions concerning the religiously prescribed legal judgments is more difficult than* zinâ' *[i.e., adultery and other forbidden sexual relations] in particular; even if the punishment is carried out, after that there still remain other claims [against those responsible] on the part of the persons injured."*

52. An allusion to the many Qur'anic verses insisting that *"the Messenger is only responsible for the clear communication [balâgh]"* (Qur'an 24:54; 29:18, etc.) of God's Word, not for the particular reactions of his listeners—which are discussed in the many other verses alluded to here stressing God's role (and their individual responsibilities) in those reactions. The related and practically crucial question of the limited degree to which the inspired saint should attempt to convince others (by argument) of the insights he has realized at this stage is discussed in the final section translated from this chapter (notes 122-23 below).

53. *A'qal al-nâss* (which could also be "the most intelligent of men"), translated here in accordance with Ibn 'Arabî's earlier discussion (note 46 above) of the

'âqil, in this ethical and juridical context, as the person whose (spiritual) knowledge is in full control of his passions. Clearly the degree of that virtue ideally required here—to the extent of refraining from judging others (even inwardly), based on a full recognition of the inner necessity of their actions—could be expected only of the prophets and the most accomplished saints. For Ibn 'Arabî's understanding of the "prophets" *(anbiyâ')* in general as a group far larger than the small number of "messengers" specifically charged with communicating a specific legislation (i.e., a *rasûl* or *shâri'*)—and his related understanding of the saints *(awliyâ')* as the *anbiyâ'* of the Muslim Community—see the many references in Chodkiewicz, *Sceau,* chapter III; Hakim, *Mu'jam,* pp. 1058-53; and chapter 14 of the *Futûhât,* O.Y. II pp. 356ff.

54. The "sublime knowledge" referred to here appears to be the divine inspiration of the appropriate "judgment" *(hukm)* that, as Ibn 'Arabî goes on to explain (in section 7 below), is shared with the prophets by the "people of unveiling" or *awliyâ';* but it may also refer more specifically here to the prophet's awareness of the inner states of those whom God has made insensitive to the prophetic message, as discussed in the immediately preceding paragraphs. As noted above (note 45) the term used for "having authority" here *(wâlî)* is etymologically very close to the Arabic expression usually translated as "saint" *(walî),* no doubt alluding to Ibn 'Arabî's understanding of the truly inspired "authorities" developed more openly in sections 7 and 9 below.

55. The notion of *rizq,* for Ibn 'Arabî (closely following the Qur'an), ultimately extends to all the physical and metaphysical forms of divine "sustenance" or "nourishment" by which the world and its creatures are given life and being: see the discussion of his usage of this and related terms in Hakim, *Mu'jam,* pp. 531-34. Thus—as in his initial enumeration of the qualities of the Helpers earlier in this chapter—he commonly distinguishes between the spiritual or noetic *(ma'nawîya/ma'qûla)* forms of this sustenance, which are discussed at the beginning of this section, and the material blessings that are discussed in the second half (6-b below).

56. Here Ibn 'Arabî is emphasizing the considerable limits on the realm directly "subject" to the temporal functions of the Mahdi. The Arabic term *nufus* (translated here as "souls") refers specifically in this context only to that very limited aspect of the individual's "soul" which controls his physical body in this "mortal human" *(basharî)* world, not to the infinitely wider dimensions of the "spirit" *(rûh)* which ultimately constitutes man as *insân.*

57. Or simply "themselves" *(anfusihim)*. This final qualification alludes to the insistence throughout Islamic tradition (including the schools of law) on the existence of both disbelieving and believing individuals among the jinn, the latter being followers of one or another of the human prophetic Messengers: see the references to Ibn 'Arabî's discussions of the "jinn"—a term he uses elsewhere in several other, different senses—in Hakim, *Mu'jam,* pp. 279-81.

58. I.e., the spiritual beings who were created from 'light," just as the jinn (according to Islamic tradition) were created from the physical element of "fire."

59. This group of angels *(al-sâ'ihûn),* who *"travel around the roads (turuq) seeking out the people of* dhikr,*"* are mentioned in a long hadith—cited in the *Sahîh* of both Bukhârî and Muslim, as well as in the *Musnad* of Ahmad ibn Hanbal—that Ibn 'Arabî included as number 84 in his personal collection of

hadîth qudsî, the *Mishkât al-Anwâr* (p. 110 in the French translation, with facing Arabic text, by M. Vâlsan, *La Niche des Lumières*, Paris, 1983). The passages included in quotation marks here are an approximate quotation from that hadith. These "travelers" are mentioned again at the end of this chapter in a strange story concerning the "men of the Unseen" *(rijâl al-ghayb:* see note 30 above), summarized at note 120 below.

60. I.e., as he explains later in this sentence, the *dhâkirûn* (who "recall" its true spiritual reality: see note 17 above), not necessarily all those who are merely reciting the words *(tâlin)*. The reference here to "sessions" *(majâlis)* of *dhikr* seems to imply specifically Sufi gatherings; this is clearly the case within his reference to these "travelers" in the anecdote summarized at the end of this chapter (note 120 below). For Ibn 'Arabî's own personal preference, in that practical spiritual context, for *dhikr* of the Qur'an as opposed to the other (primarily musical) forms of *dhikr* popular in Sufi circles, see chapter 182 of the *Futûhât*, "Concerning Knowledge of the Station of *Samâ'* and Its Secrets," II, 366-68.

61. *Ayât:* i.e., the verses of the Qur'an.

62. We have not been able to locate any further biographical details concerning this particular group of disciples and Ibn 'Arabî's role as shaykh during this period, or the reasons for their "loss."

63. *Bathth al-'ilm:* the term implies the unfolding or opening up of what was concealed—apparently in reference to Ibn 'Arabî's increasing literary production (and his provision of many of his works with an *ijâza 'âmma*, a "general permission" for their reading and propagation), pedagogical activities which may have coincided with his growing realization of his unique personal role as "Seal of the Muhammadan Saints" (see note 16 above).

64. See Ibn 'Arabî's earlier statement (section I, at note 17) that *"he [i.e., as the 'Seal of Muhammadan Sainthood'] and the Qur'ân are brothers,"* along with the references there concerning his distinctive personal understanding of what is meant by that term *("al-Qur'ân")*. Ibn 'Arabî's decisive personal realization of the inner Reality of the *Qur'ân* and the comprehensive spiritual "Station of Muhammad" is described in detail in his *Kitâb al-Isrâ' (Rasâ'il Ibn 'Arabî*, ed. Hyderabad, 1948, I, no. 13, pp. 1-2), written in Fez in 594, i.e., roughly the period alluded to here. See the translation and commentary of a key passage from the *K. al-Isrâ'* in our two-part article on "The Spiritual Ascension: Ibn 'Arabî and the Mi'râj" in the *Journal of the American Oriental Society*, vol. 108, no. 1 (1988), pp. 74-77. The same experiential realization is more briefly described as the culminating stage of his own spiritual Ascension in chapter 367 of the *Futûhât* (III 340-54), section IV-I in the translation here.

65. The usage of the first person *plural* here—unlike the case with the preceding sentences, where it may be only a polite form of "I"—appears to be a clear allusion to Ibn 'Arabî's self-conception of his particular role, within the Muslim Community, as the "Seal of the Muhammadan saints" (see note 16 above) responsible for the ongoing spiritual guidance of the entire Community. Likewise, just as the Seal reflects the total Reality of Muhammad (who at that cosmic level *is* the *"Qur'ân,"* for Ibn 'Arabî), so the expression *"I was given the keys of Its understanding"* echoes a fundamental hadith of the Prophet cited repeatedly throughout the Shaykh's writings: *"I was given the totality of the [divine] Words"* (jawâmi' al-kilam).

66. The "intermediaries" *(wasâ'it)*, in this immediate context (and judging from the earlier analysis of the divine "discourse", in section II-2 above), appear to be all the "veils" of the particular "forms" (whether angelic or human prophetic messengers, or perhaps the infinite variety of theophanies in general), through which the divine "inspiration" is more often perceived. (But elsewhere in the *Futûhât* Ibn 'Arabî applies this term more specifically to all the learned transmitters of the external forms and traces of the prophetic heritage; see chapter 14, O. Y. II, 358: "... *the intermediaries—I mean the* fuqahâ' *and the* 'ulamâ' al-rusûm.*")

67. An important reminder—underlying Ibn 'Arabî's understanding of the proper relations between the "guardians of the [divine] commandments" and the "guardians of the [spiritual] states" (see note 43 above)—of the fundamental fact that mere access to the external forms of a prophet's speech and activity, no matter how perfect and exact, is not the decisive (or sufficient) factor in understanding their meaning and intentions. See the further extensive discussions of this question in the article cited at note 4 above.

68. *Imâm al-Waqt:* i.e., the "Pole" *(qutb)* or "Lord of the Age," etc.: see note 19. It is significant that instead of referring to the "Mahdi" here, Ibn 'Arabî uses this ambiguous expression three times (and other forms of "Imam" four additional times) in the space of this relatively short section (III 335.2-17), clearly implying that this responsibility for the just apportionment of the world's material goods is in some sense a perennial spiritual function. The potential political sensitivity of this expression in his own historical context is suggested by the fate of several prominent Andalusian and Maghrebi Sufis (see note 81 below) who were at least accused of claiming the "Imamate" in a more overtly political sense. Ibn 'Arabî does not otherwise suggest that this sort of divine inspiration is different in kind from that discussed in the preceding and following sections, where he is clearly referring to the *awliyâ'* more generally. He thereby seems to imply that the proper, fully adequate approach to this world's material goods—at least from a comprehensive, spiritual point of view—ultimately requires the same kind of inspired guidance, even if once again that can only be practically realized by a few rare individuals.

69. *Baqîyat Allâh:* a reference to the verse 11:86, *"What God has left is better for you all, if you are among the faithful...."* Much of this section stresses the extreme relativity of our judgments concerning the individual "possession" *(mulk)* of what is actually God's and for which we are at best only temporary stewards or custodians in this world.

70. *Tadâkhul al-'umûr:* i.e., the interweaving of the spiritual and noetic *(ma'nawî)* realities and intentions that pervade all things, especially as they are manifested in the events and actions involving particular individuals. Ibn 'Arabî alludes here only briefly to this vast theme—or rather, integral perspective on the nature of all reality—that can be illustrated in virtually every area of his thought: see, e.g., the references to *nikâh ma'nawî* in Hakim, *Mu'jam,* pp. 1069-71. Although his discussions of this notion elsewhere often concern its more abstract metaphysical dimensions (e.g., the various noetic and spiritual principles involved in his schemas of cosmology and cosmogony), here it is focused on the concrete, practical recognition of those spiritual realities underlying the specific "judgments" rendered by the Mahdi (and the *awliyâ'* who possess the same inspired

insight), a recognition made possible by their infallible "penetrating vision" (the spiritual quality discussed at II-1 above). This point was already clearly illustrated in Ibn 'Arabî's earlier discussion of the difficulties of realizing and applying the divine norms while simultaneously taking into account their mundane and ultimate spiritual dimensions (section II-5 above).

71. *Al-sanâ'i' al-'amalîya wa-l-'ilmîya:* this formula—which appears to have been adopted (directly or indirectly) from the *Rasâ'il* of the Ikhwân al-Safâ'—apparently includes all human creative activities in this world, including the all-encompassing role of the divinely inspired ruler, symbolized here by the Mahdi/Imam.

72. *Al-'âqil:* i.e., the person whose reason and knowledge restrain the demands of his passions, as explained at notes 46 and 53 above.

73. See Ibn 'Arabî's discussion of the various modalities of this delivery or "projection" *(ilqâ')* of the divine Speech "addressed" to the prophets and saints in sections II-2 and 3 (notes 32-40) above.

74. *Nikâh ma'nawî:* i.e., of the divine Source and its human receptacle, and more broadly, of all the spiritual, noetic realities and principles manifested in each "material" event: see the references to this vast theme in note 70.

75. "Textual indications": *nusûs,* a term which evidently refers in this context to the outward, literal form of the scriptures and hadith collections—or rather to the specific divine "stipulations" which they are usually understood to contain. The roots of Ibn 'Arabî's fundamental criticism of the common practice of *qiyâs* (legal inference based on "analogy" or "analogical reasoning")—as opposed to the infallible divine inspiration characterizing the Mahdi and saints having reached this spiritual station—are detailed in section II-9 (notes 97-107) below. The key issues of the conditions for a true understanding of the original intentions and meaning of hadith—which are the *sine qua non* of any truly "living" transmission of knowledge—raised in the rest of this section and in II-9 below are beautifully summarized in the conclusion of chapter 29 (I 198; O.Y. ed. III 240-42), concerning the true *"Ahl al-Bayt."*

76. *Al-shar' al-haqîqî al-muhammadî:* the key term *shar'*—which we have generally left in transliterated form in the following pages—is ordinarily understood simply as the religious "law" (the *Sharî'a*) or what was "prescribed" by the Prophet (and ultimately by God) as guidance for human action. Here Ibn 'Arabî, as is often his practice, alludes to the original meaning of that Arabic root as the "opening" or establishment of the authentic "path to water" (i.e., the water of Life)—a sense which does not necessarily contradict the popular usage, but does set it in a larger, potentially transforming perspective. (See also note 107 below, and especially the references at notes 3 and 4 above on the related term *Sharî'a*.)

77. *Al-nusûs,* as at note 75 above; Ibn 'Arabî again (as at note 45 above) stresses that he is not questioning the validity and necessity of the traditionally transmitted forms of earlier revelation as such, but rather the spirit and methods that are frequently applied (by no means only in "legal" situations) to rediscover and realize their more profound truth and actual perennial intentions.

78. Ibn 'Arabî's conception of *'isma,* divinely assured "immunity from error" (in one's spiritual judgment and perception), as an essential concomitant of the

divine inspiration of the saints as well as of the prophetic Messengers was already developed in section II-I above (see references at note 29). The Mahdi's inspired condition of *'isma*—in contrast with the very fallible *ra'y* and *qiyâs* of the ordinary jurists—is again repeatedly emphasized in section II-9 below.

79. *Al-faqîr al-sâdiq:* although the term *faqîr* (literally, one who is "poor" in relation to God, i.e., the perfect "servant") has often been a vague (and sometimes pejorative) popular synonym for "Sufi" in the broadest sense, here it is used quite specifically to indicate the rare spiritual state of pure openness and receptivity allowing the saint who is inwardly "sincere" to receive the inspiration transmitted originally to the prophet Messenger he faithfully "follows" (see the essential references at note 27 above). A clearer sense of the deep-rooted psychic obstacles to this state may be gathered from Ibn 'Arabî's enumeration of the inner motives of those "learned in the outward forms [of religion]" in the following paragraph. For the "Helpers' "(and saints') related condition of *sidq*—*"truth-telling"* in the rare spiritual sense of absolute inner "sincerity" regarding one's inner relation to God—and its "divinely supported" consequences *(nasr)*, see the opening section at note 12 above.

80. *Ashâb 'ilm al-rusûm:* see the further discussions of these *'ulamâ' al-rusûm* in sections II-3, II-4 (note 43) and II-9 below.

81. The term could refer simply to Muslims in general, but more commonly in Ibn 'Arabî and other Sufi writers (following indications in the Qur'an and hadith) it refers quite specifically to the accomplished *awliyâ'* and prophets. The impassioned tone of this passage—combined with what we know of the martyrdom or persecution of many prominent Andalusian and Maghrebi Sufis of the time (Ibn Qasî, Ibn Barrajân and Ibn al-'Arîf)—strongly suggest that the latter sense is indeed intended here. The cases of these famous saints who were intimately involved with certain political events of their time (and some of whom may well have claimed the role of "Imam" in a more openly political sense), also indicate that Ibn 'Arabî's discussions of divine governance in this chapter are probably not purely academic: see the historical references concerning the three above-mentioned Andalusian Sufis in the corresponding articles (by A. Faure) in the *EI²*, vol. III.

82. Although they may well outwardly succeed, Ibn 'Arabî implies, with regard to the things they prize in this world. The full Qur'anic verses alluded to in this sentence are especially important in understanding the critique of the *fuqahâ'* that follows: *"And do not say, regarding what your tongues describe* [as divinely forbidden or commanded] *the lie* [that] *'This is licit, and that is illicit', so that you make up lies against God. Surely those who make up lies against God do not prosper"* (the last phrase is repeated at verse 10:69). Ibn 'Arabî may also be alluding to verses 6:20-21, with their implicit contrast of the two approaches in question here: *"Those to whom we have brought the Book recognize it as they recognize their own sons, [but] those who have lost their souls do not have faith. And who does more wrong than whoever makes up a lie about God and calls His Signs a lie? Surely those who do wrong shall not prosper."* Again, see the full discussion of these critiques in the article cited at note 4 above.

83. "Recollection" or remembrance (of God): the continuous invocation (whether silent or virtually inaudible) of certain prayer formulae or divine Names throughout the day's activities, often with the accompaniment of the *tasbîh*

(prayer beads), a practice frequently—though by no means exclusively—associated with adherence to a particular Sufi order; see the allusions in note 60 above. Ibn 'Arabî's criticism of this group's hypocritical pretense of Sufism already foreshadows the following Qur'anic allusion (to verses 3:77-78, in note 84).

84. Again the full Qur'anic passage (3:77-78) is directly applicable to this psycho-spiritual "type" in a sense which clearly brings out Ibn 'Arabî's understanding of the immediate "contemporary" dimensions of the "Last Day": *"Surely those who buy a thing of little value with God's covenant and their faith, those people have no share in the next world, and God does not speak to them nor does He look at them on the Day of the Rising, and He does not purify them [or "cause them to increase"], and theirs is an excruciating torment. And there is a group of them who twist the Book with their tongues, so that you might consider that [what they say] is from the Book, although it is not from the Book. And they say that [what they say] is from God, although it is not from God— and they say lies against God while they know* [what they are doing]." See the following note for the full hadith to which Ibn 'Arabî alludes at the beginning of this sentence.

85. The phrases in quotes here and in the sentence preceding the previous note are taken from the following saying of the Prophet recorded by Tirmidhî (from Abû Hurayra) and selected by Ibn 'Arabî in his personal collection of *hadîth qudsî*, the *Mishkât al-Anwâr* (no. 35; pp. 64-65 in the translation by M. Vâlsan): *"At the end of time men will appear who will dupe the world with [the pretense of] religion: they will dress up for the people in the skins of gentle sheep and their tongues will be sweeter than honey, but their hearts are the hearts of wolves. God will say: 'Are they completely deluded about Me, or do they openly dare [to affront] Me?! I swear by Myself that I shall surely send those men a trial (or torment:* fitna) *that will leave even the calmest of them completely dismayed.'"*

86. The last phrase, evoking the Qur'anic references to the fate of the "wrong-doers" *(mujrimûn)*, is an allusion to Ibn 'Arabî's assumption that the people of Gehenna nonetheless do take a certain pleasure in precisely those things which—in distracting them from God—ultimately help constitute their punishment; see, for example, the famous verse at the end of the chapter on Ismail in the *Fusûs al-Hikam* (I, 94; *Bezels*, pp. 109-10), and the longer discussions in the eschatological section of this anthology.

87. The vast extent of these bloody internecine conflicts between these and other legal and theological schools serving as rallying points for a wide variety of ethnic and social loyalties—and fueling civil wars, riots and repeated massacres which over more than a century effectively destroyed, even before the Mongol conquests, important parts of the major Persian cities of Nishapur, Rayy and Isfahan—are surveyed in W. Madelung's (too modestly titled) article "The Spread of Mâturîdism and the Turks," pp. 109-69 in his *Religious Schools and Sects in Medieval Islam* (London, 1985); Madelung also traces the spread of these violent "legal" conflicts to the Ayyubid realms where Ibn 'Arabî spent much of the latter part of his life. The particularly dramatic role of this Hanafî-Shâfi'î conflict (frequently cited by al-Ghazâlî) in the century-long self-destruction of Nishapur—strikingly similar to that of modern-day Beirut—is detailed in R. Bulliet's *The Patricians of Nishabur* (Cambridge, 1972).

88. I.e., the "imams" or founders of their particular legal schools (Shâfi'î, Mâlik, etc.), as already at note 9 above. In the long chapter 69 of the *Futûhât* on ritual prayer (I 386-546), Ibn 'Arabî, stressing the diversity of the evidence of hadith on particular details of religious practice, repeatedly criticizes the *fuqahâ'* of his day for hypocritically and arrogantly denying *ijtihâd* while simultaneously insisting that everyone else follow their own legal school. See, e.g., his ironic remark at I 494: *"So the first [person] to deny them on the Day of Resurrection will be their [own] Imam!"* For Ibn 'Arabî, in contrast (at I 392), the perennial obligation of *ijtihâd* for *all* believers (with the necessary qualifications to interpret the Qur'an and hadith) follows from the divine injunction: *"And strive* (jâhidû) *for God with the striving due to Him. He picked you out and did not place any constriction* (haraj) *upon you in Religion..."* (Qur'an 22:73).

89. I.e., the state of "pure servanthood" *('ubûdîya)* characterizing Ibn 'Arabî's typical conception of spiritual superiority of the *afrâd* (also termed *al-malâmîya,* the "people of blame," etc.)—whose spiritual rank is often "invisible" to the outside world and whose lives frequently exhibit this same characteristic of extraordinary devotion to their "ordinary" responsibilities—as embodying the very summit of the spiritual path. The repeated references in this chapter to Khadir (one of the archetypal representatives of the *afrâd,* for Ibn 'Arabî) point in the same direction. See the references from other chapters of the *Futûhât* to this "ultimate stage of *walâya,"* which is one of the recurrent themes of his religious thought, in Chodkiewicz, *Sceau,* chapter VII (pp. 133-143).

90. Ibn 'Arabî emphasizes the broader metaphysical significance of this story, that God becomes manifest (whether or not we are aware of it) in the form of man's desire, virtually every time he deals with the figure of Moses: see, e.g., the end of the chapter on Moses (no. 25) in the *Fusûs al-Hikam* (Affifi ed., I 212-13), the beginning of the concluding chapter on Muhammad, and especially Ibn 'Arabî's own encounter with Moses during his autobiographical spiritual Ascension in chapter 367 of the *Futûhât* (III 439-40), section IV-G of our translation and commentary here.

91. Ibn 'Arabî illustrates this point (concerning the "external Imams," those with a visible, public role in this world) with a brief story about the extreme conscientiousness of 'Umar ibn 'Abd al-'Azîz in regard to his public responsibilities.

92. Here Ibn 'Arabî mentions Khadir's "original", genealogical name (going back to Noah), as given by Islamic tradition: see the article *"al-Khadir"* by Wensinck, summarizing the historical sources, in *EI²,* vol. IV. The story of Khadir's discovery of the fountain of Life is apparently taken from the popular literature of the "Tales of the Prophets" *(qisas al-anbiyâ'),* rather than from the hadith. For the broader role of Khadir in Ibn 'Arabî's thought (building on an extensive pre-existing body of Sufi tradition), see his description of his personal encounters with Khadir on three separate occasions in chapter 25 (I 186-88; O.Y. ed., III 180-85); the numerous references in Chodkiewicz, *Sceau,* Index s.v.; and the chapter focusing more specifically on Khadir's initiatic function in H. Corbin, *L'imagination créatrice...,* pp. 43-54.

93. Here Ibn 'Arabî interrupts this story with a long aside (III 336.32-337.5) describing his first personal encounter with Khadir, in the person of a stranger (during his youth in Seville) *"who taught me to surrender to the spiritual masters and not to dispute with them [even when they are wrong]";* it was Ibn

'Arabî's master at the time (one Abû al-'Abbâs al-'Uraybî) who subsequently identified that mysterious individual as being Khadir. This anecdote itself (summarized in H. Corbin, *L'imagination créatrice...*, p. 51) is translated in the biographical study at the beginning of Asin Palacios' *L'Islam christianisé* (French translation, Paris, 1983), p. 36. Another longer version of the same story—along with descriptions of Ibn 'Arabî's subsequent meetings with Khadir—is given in chapter 25 (I, 186-188; O.Y. ed. III, pp. 180-182), where it is also implied that the subject of this dispute was the identity or name of the Mahdi (and that Khadir confirmed the validity of Ibn 'Arabî's own vision in that regard). For "water" as one of Ibn 'Arabî's primary symbols—based on passages in the Qur'an and several key hadith—for the "throne of divine Life" flowing through all things, see chapter 317 (III 65-66) and further extensive references in Hakim, *Mu'jam,* pp. 1071-77.

94. It is not entirely clear whether the pronoun here refers to the "Imams" discussed earlier in the chapter; to *"those who have faith in God and the Last Day"* (from the immediately preceding Qur'anic verse [58:22] not translated here); or—what is most probable, and could include the previous two categories—to the accomplished saints *(awliyâ')* in general. This description again seems to allude to Ibn 'Arabî's conception of the *afrâd* or *malâmîya,* the largely unrecognized "true servants of God" who represent the highest stage of sainthood (see references at note 89 above).

95. *Sha'n* suggests an activity or occupation as well as a general state or condition. For Ibn 'Arabî, this verse is usually taken in reference to the universal process of "theophany" *(tajalliyât)* through which the world (i.e., the "other-than-God") is continuously re-created and made manifest: see the references in Hakim, *Mu'jam,* pp. 639-43 *("al-sha'n al-'ilâhî").*

96. See section II-1 (at notes 23-29) above on the special efficacy of the Mahdi's prayers, corresponding to his quasi-prophetic function.

97. *Nâzila,* usually translated here as "event," could equally be translated, in this legal context, as "case"—i.e., in the broad sense of a unique "event" subject to a particular judgment, not necessarily as a generalizable legal type or precedent *(qâdîya,* also translated as "case" below). As in earlier sections, *hukm* is usually translated here as "judgment" (and its verbal forms accordingly), although the actual meaning tends to vary in emphasis, according to the context, between the following: (a) the timeless divine "commandment" or "standard"; (b) the particular inner aspect of the "case" or circumstance to which that standard actually applies; (c) the human religio-legal "statute", "rule" or precept (supposedly corresponding to the first two meanings); (d) the actual act of applying these standards to particular circumstances (whether or not in an explicitly legal context); and (e) the resulting "verdict" or conclusion. In other, earlier contexts (corresponding partially to meanings "d" or "e" here), *hukm* has instead been translated as "influence."

98. *Mubâh:* i.e., what is "permitted" in the sense of what is neither explicitly illicit *(haram)* nor positively prescribed by the divine Law *(shar'/sharî'a:* see notes 3, 4, 76 and 107). The usual translation of this term as "indifferent," while appropriate for its traditional legal usage as a category in Islamic law, fails to convey the positive and much wider "ontological" perception Ibn 'Arabî is pointing to here. Historically speaking—and this is the ground of Ibn 'Arabî's vehement

protests in this chapter (see notes 8, 9, 80-87 and the rest of this section) and in many other places—virtually all the schools of Islamic law (both Sunni and Shiite) used some schema of "analogies" (in the sense described here) to set up complex systems of graded categories of "preference" or "prohibition" (or "purity" and "impurity") extending, at least in theory, to virtually every imaginable human action. The extremely limited meaning of *"mubâh"* in that legalistic context—where it at best implies a "neutral" value and implicitly a rather dubious religious status in relation to the extensive "positive" categories—is therefore substantially different from what Ibn 'Arabî actually intends by that term here. For his own distinctively positive and more comprehensive usage, see notes 104-7 below and especially the translated selections at the beginning of section III below, as well as the more complete discussion and references in our article cited at note 4 above.

99. *Dîn Allâh:* this is only one of several related Qur'anic expressions—e.g., *al-Dîn* and *al-Dîn al-Khâlis* (Qur'an 39:3), "the Pure Religion," both used in a similar sense in the opening sentences of this chapter (note 8 above)—referring to the eternal, divine Reality that is the Source of the prophets' message, in contrast to the many religions of men. In a certain sense, all of Ibn 'Arabî's works constitute a sort of extended commentary on this distinction: see the extensive references and careful analysis of these key terms in Hakim, *Mu'jam,* pp. 475-83, and especially Ibn 'Arabî's moving description of his own decisive realization of this fundamental insight in the following chapter 367 (III 350; section IV-1 of our translation here) and in his *K. al-Isrâ'* (see the translation and commentary in our article cited at note 64 above).

100. The technical terms here are taken from the traditional discipline of *usûl al-fiqh* ("principles of jurisprudence": see the articles *usûl* in *SEI* and *fiqh* in *EI²*) which, from the third century (A.H.) onward, gradually elaborated the theoretical rationales underlying the practice of the earlier Islamic jurists *(fuqahâ')*. In the practice of *qiyâs*—upon which most of the influential historical forms of Islamic law were largely dependent—the hypothetical "reason" *('illa)* seen as underlying a particular commandment or decision *(hukm)* derived from the Qur'an or more commonly from the many reported actions and sayings of the Prophet, was "extracted" or "deduced" from that particular precedent and then "extended" to a wider range of supposedly analogous cases. Ibn 'Arabî's personal criticisms of *qiyâs,* here and elsewhere, specifically presuppose the continued *presence* of the Prophet (i.e., of His spiritual Reality) as realized among the accomplished Sufis (the *ahl al-kashf* or "People of Unveiling"), as he explained in section II-7 above (III, 335). As stressed by M. Chodkiewicz (*"Ibn 'Arabî, la lettre et la loi,"* pp. 29-30, Ibn 'Arabî—while rejecting *qiyâs* (and *taqlîd,* for reasons detailed at II 165) for *himself*—does not necessarily reject the usage of *qiyâs* by those who do not fulfill these (admittedly rather rare) conditions; thus his position should not be confused with the universal (if problematic) condemnation of *qiyâs* typical of the Zâhirî legal school.

101. The Qur'anic passage (Qur'an 80:1-10) alluded to here is a particularly striking illustration of Ibn 'Arabî's argument that man—at least in his ordinary, "uninspired" state—should not pretend to decipher the essential "reasons" underlying God's specifically stated commands and prohibitions, much less attempt to

extend those principles beyond their *explicitly* prescribed areas of application. In these verses the Prophet is reproached for having distractedly turned away a poor blind man who came asking about faith while he was talking with an important notable—i.e., for judging on the basis of outward appearances—and reminded that *"perhaps [the blind man] will grow in purity or come to remember [God]..."*

102. The full verse is again assumed in this powerful allusion: *"Or do they have partners who prescribe as law for them concerning Religion that about which God is unaware [or 'does not permit']."* This paragraph therefore explains in detail the basic principles underlying Ibn 'Arabî's remarks (in section II-7 and at the very beginning of this chapter) concerning the hatred of the *fuqahâ'* for the Mahdi, as well as his impassioned assertions (at notes 82-84 and 98 above) that in fact even the most well-meaning of them unconsciously "make up lies about God."

103. I.e., *qiyâs*, in the legalistic sense—and above all with reference to its intrinsic suppositions about the very nature of religion—described in the preceding paragraphs. For the Mahdi's refusal to act on the basis of both *qiyâs* and even explicit scriptural stipulations *(nass)*, where he has not been directly inspired by God, see also section 11-7 (at notes 75-78 above).

104. Hence the more profound justification of Ibn 'Arabî's earlier insistence (at note 98 above) that all that is not most explicitly commanded or forbidden is "permitted" *(mubâh)*, in an unrestricted, essentially positive sense very different from its usage in the legal categories of the *fuqahâ'*. This is brought out more powerfully in the further allusions at the end of this chapter (translations at the beginning of section III, notes 110-118) to the saints' theophanic perception of the religiously unrestricted—indeed intrinsically "paradisiac" and "marvelous"—nature of everything in the world not bound by the rare explicit divine indications to the contrary.

105. This hadith is mentioned by both Bukhârî (*I'tisâm*, 2) and Muslim (*Hajj*, 411). As Ibn 'Arabî explains in his brief chapter 262 "On the Inner Knowledge of the Sharia" (II 561-62), the Sharia includes both *"the precepts* [ahkâm] *God prescribed of His own accord* [ibtidâ'an]*"* and *"what was prescribed at the request of the community,"* so that *"if they had not requested it, then that [precept or commandment] would not have been sent down."* The Prophet's saying was therefore intended to avoid the unnecessary proliferation of this latter category of religious prescriptions and the resulting burden of obligation on His community. Elsewhere (II 162-6; chapter 88 "On the Inner Knowledge of the Secrets of the Principles of the Precepts of the *Shar'* "), Ibn 'Arabî points out the parallel between this hadith and the following Qur'anic injunction: *"O those who have faith, do not ask about things which, if they were revealed to you, would harm you. And if you ask about them when the* Qur'ân *is being sent down, they will be revealed to you... For a people before you did ask [such] things, and after that they began to disbelieve in them."* (Qur'an 5:101-2) In the same section (II 165) he explains in detail his conviction *"that the Lawgiver only wanted to reduce [the burden of religious prescriptions] of this Community."* See also following note.

106. *Hukm al-asl:* In Chapter 88 (II 165; see preceding note), Ibn 'Arabî clearly states that this primordial state of affairs is *"that there is no* taklîf *[i.e., divinely*

imposed religious obligation] and that God created for us the totality of everything on earth... " In other words, as far as the Sharia is concerned, everything God has not expressly forbidden or made obligatory is implicitly permitted *(mubâh)* for man's delight in His creation—as Ibn 'Arabî had already indicated at notes 98 and 104 above. The grammatical subject of these sentences could also be the Prophet, but appears more likely to be the Mahdi, judging from the context of the following sentences.

107. *Al-shar' al-muhammadî:* see the longer discussion of this eternal reality underlying the actions and prescriptions of each of the prophets *(anbiyâ')* at note 76 and in the opening description of the Mahdi (at note 9 above). The few phrases omitted here (337.28-30) simply reiterate what was said at the beginning of this section concerning the Mahdi's inspired foreknowledge of what will happen to his subjects.

108. Ibn 'Arabî does not even mention the Mahdi's "Helpers" here, or how this statement is to be reconciled with his earlier remarks (see notes 2 and 15) concerning their essential collective role in providing the Mahdi's "'right guidance" with regard to these matters. The few untranslated lines of this concluding section (337.31-338.2) stress points already mentioned repeatedly in this chapter: the inner identity of the Mahdi with the spirit of Muhammad, from whom he "inherits" his spiritual knowledge through divine inspiration, and his special status as a "perfect follower" of Muhammad, likewise divinely protected from error *(ma'sûm)* in all his judgments.

109. III 338.3-340.12. The complete list here includes some fifty-four kinds of spiritual knowledge, and the descriptions translated in this section make up items 8-10, 23 and 24 in that enumeration.

110. "Burden of anguish": *haraj,* referring here to the inner state of constraint, oppression, anxiety, distress, etc. that usually accompanies and underlies (whether consciously or not) much of our everyday psychic and outward activity. In connection with the subject of this chapter and the special divine inspiration characterizing the Mahdi (or his "Helpers"), a number of Qur'anic verses stress that there is *"no haraj for you in Religion" (al-Dîn;* see Qur'an 22:78, etc.) or in the *"Book sent down"* from God (Qur'an 7:2), and that this state of inner distress is a sign of those *"wandering astray,"* while it is removed from these whom God *"guides rightly"* and who inwardly surrender to Him (Qur'an 6:125).

111. This phrase could also be translated as "to kill his *nafs*" (i.e., in Sufi psychology, the "carnal self," *al-nafs al-ammâra,* directly responsible for this sense of oppression and anxiety), in the hope of eliminating this torment.

112. See, among others, the longer discussions of this immediate experience of Paradise (by the Prophet and other saints) as a reality already *present* in this world in our translations from chapters 302 and 351 (III 12-13) in the following section on Ibn 'Arabî's understanding of eschatology.

113. *Adab,* the proper respect or "principles of conduct" regarding God in every aspect of one's spiritual life, whose expression, as Ibn 'Arabî indicates here, obviously varies greatly according to one's inner state or "rank." For example one of the later "kinds of knowledge" in this section (the 25th in the list, p. 339.23-25; not translated here) concerns the kind of *adab* the person in this (very high) station should follow with God in order to avoid "taking for granted" the gift of true faith he is enjoying.

114. An allusion to the central, recurrent theme in Ibn 'Arabî of the beatific "divine vision" of the true Knowers (*'urafâ', muhaqqiqûn*, etc.) who fully experience the theophanic nature of all Being and therefore realize that they are seeing, in a sense, with "God's" eye, i.e., the "eye of the Heart." See all the translations in the eschatology section here. The next phrase in this sentence is a reminder that the regard of such individuals is not always, or even primarily, turned toward the visible world.

115. Or "good" or "virtuous" actions: the Arabic root *hasan* (translated with forms of "beautiful" throughout this paragraph) covers much the same semantic range as the Greek *kalos*. (Likewise the term translated as "ugly" could also be understood as "vile" or "displeasing" in a more strictly moral sense.) This final phrase—as so often in Ibn 'Arabî—could equally be understood with God as the subject: *"...for He comes to meet [the true seer], by His very Essence, with beautiful Actions."*

116. Here, as so often, Ibn 'Arabî (following al-Ghazâlî), adapts for his own Sufi purposes a formula of the *mutakallimûn* which, as he was well aware, derives from an intellectual context having little to do directly with the profound spiritual "unveiling" he is pointing to here.

117. The latter phrase no doubt alludes to the fact that the verbal root translated here as "ugly" *(q-b-h)* appears only once in the entire Qur'an (at 28:42, applied to the fate of Pharaoh and his army on the Day of Resurrection). The fundamental object of Ibn 'Arabî's remarks here and in the following section—as in his earlier criticisms of those jurists who *"make up lies about God"* (at notes 82, 84 and 99, etc., above)—is the way the endless (and for the most part unconscious) likes, dislikes and particular "judgments" of each individual soul tend to obscure man's primordial, innate perception of the intrinsic perfection and beauty of God's creation.

118. *Kharq al-'âda:* this expression (again borrowed from *kalam* and used in a radically different, quite concrete spiritual context) is used throughout this section as a sort of pun corresponding to two very different conceptions of the divine "habit" or "custom" *('âda)*. Ordinarily this term refers to the unenlightened perception of the usual course of affairs in the world, which the "people of habits" *(ashâb al-'awâ'id)* heedlessly take for granted: hence the usual understanding of *kharq al-'âda* as some exceptional "miracle," "prodigy" or "supernatural" event departing from that unconscious norm. But the true Knowers—those who, as in the preceding paragraph, actually "see things as they really are"—are profoundly aware of the genuinely "miraculous" re-creation of the world at every instant, of the "marvelous," never-repeated theophany of Being in all Its infinite self-manifestations.

119. *Rijâl al-ghayb:* the ability to see these mysterious spiritual beings even when they do not wish to be seen was earlier described as one of the basic signs of the "penetrating (spiritual) vision" characterizing this particular mystical state in section II-1 (note 30) above.

120. Here (III 339.21) Ibn 'Arabî also mentions that he is writing down this story in the year 635 (i.e., only three years before his death and shortly before the completion of this final recension of the *Futûhât*); lacking a critical edition of this section, we do not know how much of this present chapter may have been added to the first version.

121. See the earlier discussion of this special group of angels who seek out

the gatherings of those who are remembering or invoking God (or the Qur'an) at section II-6, notes 59-60 above.

122. Given Ibn 'Arabî's repeated claims, throughout the main body of this chapter, for the superior insight and spiritual authority of the accomplished saints—as opposed to the so-called *'ulamâ'*—as the only fully qualified "interpreters" (see section II-3, notes 40-41) of the truly divine Law and as the genuine "heirs" of the larger body of religious tradition, this section provides some extremely important guidelines for determining the degree to which the *walî* should directly attempt to communicate his "revealed" spiritual inspirations beyond himself and those who voluntarily seek out his guidance. It also underlines another essential difference separating the lawgiving "messenger" *(rasûl/shâri')* ordered to fulfill a universal mission from the rest of the "prophets" *(anbiyâ')*, including the *awliyâ'*. Perhaps even more important in this context are what these criteria imply about the even more limited spiritual utility of any sort of "disputing" about religion for those who would not pretend to have reached this rare and lofty station.

123. I.e., the "saints" *(awliyâ')* or accomplished Sufis, such as those having realized this high spiritual station. Again there is a typical ambiguity in the expression *(intamâ ilâ)* translated here as "depend on," which can also mean, especially in everyday speech, "belong to" in the sense of joining or adhering to a particular group; Ibn 'Arabî used the same verb in that sense earlier in this chapter to allude to the followers of the different "schools" of Islamic law and *kalam* (and their founders). Here he clearly implies that there is no point in even raising this question with regard to such groups, since arguing or "disputing" *(jidâl)*—along with the underlying aim of converting others or otherwise imposing their own opinions—is inherent in their very methods and presuppositions. For the same reasons, the key expression "one who has truly surrendered to God" *(muslim)* would of course be understood rather differently by those groups.

124. This is a literal translation of the Qur'anic expression, which colloquially means simply "in a friendly or polite manner"—i.e., not, for example, using the methods followed by (among others) the supporters of the juridical and theological schools involved in the bloody sectarian disputes Ibn 'Arabî alludes to at note 87 above.

125. I.e., he is really trying to establish his own self-righteousness and satisfy the cravings of his own *nafs* rather than actually carrying out the divine Will (as expressed in their current state of unreceptiveness). This section echoes Ibn 'Arabî's earlier remarks (see section II-5 and notes 50-52 for the Qur'anic background) stressing the essential distinction between the general prophetic task of "communicating" the divine Message and the even more difficult responsibility of acting as a divinely-appointed "judge" *(hâkim)*.

Lesser and Greater Resurrection
James W. Morris

1. In this regard, there is no real substitute for close reading of the relevant passages of the Qur'an, with careful attention to the context of each verse, despite the unavoidable impoverishment of its richly evocative (and often enigmatic) eschatological vocabulary in even the best translations, because of the lack of any similar range of equivalents in Western languages. In comparison, the problem for hadith is far greater, given the relative lack of adequately annotated and commented translations even of the Six Books (the earliest comprehensive collections of hadith). This is especially true since the deeper meaning of hadith—as one finds repeatedly in Ibn 'Arabî's own interpretations—often lies precisely in nuances and details of Arabic expression, along with allusions to the Qur'an and other hadith, that are seldom evident in a paraphrase or uncommented translation. Perhaps the most accessible and useful translations of hadith for a general reader in this particular context—although they represent only a small fraction of the relevant hadith sources—are the representative *hadîth qudsî* ("divine sayings" transmitted by the Prophet, largely focused on eschatological matters) translated and commented in Graham, *Word,* pp. 113-224; and the translation by M. Vâlsan (*La Niche des Lumières,* Paris, 1983) of Ibn 'Arabî's *Mishkât al-Anwâr,* his personal collection of 101 *hadîth qudsî,* including several sayings that are especially important for his eschatological thought. (Both translations are accompanied by the Arabic texts.) Other secondary sources and relevant translations are discussed in a number of notes below (see especially note 14). In general, most of the available secondary literature on Islamic eschatology (including related articles in the EI^2 and *SEI*) can easily mislead nonspecialist readers who lack access to or close acquaintance with the original sources, since they cannot readily distinguish between the actual scriptural data and the particular interpretive or narrative schemas within which they are usually discussed. A notable, if somewhat superficial, exception is the study by S. El-Saleh, *La vie future selon le Coran,* Paris, Vrin, 1971; pp. 109-21 are devoted to the explicitly eschatological chapters of the *Futûhât.*

2. Without entering into the details, it is noteworthy in this regard that the key expression *al-âkhira* (the "other world" or "next world") alone appears 115 times in the Qur'an, exactly the same number as its correlate, *al-dunyâ,* "this world." (See the prophet Idrîs' comment concerning the inner meaning of these two terms during his encounter with Ibn 'Arabî in chapter 367 of the *Futûhât,* quoted at note 23 below.) The significant linkage of true faith (or hope) in "God *and* the Last Day" *(al-yawm al-âkhir)* likewise recurs more than 20 times in the Qur'an.

3. The best available summary account, for the general reader, is W. Chittick's article on "Eschatology" in *Islamic Spirituality I,* ed. S. H. Nasr (volume XIX of *World Spirituality: An Encyclopedic History of the Religious Quest,* New York, Crossroad, 1987), which concentrates on the mystical and philosophic interpretations (e.g., the especially influential theories of al-Ghazâlî and Avicenna) and clearly brings out Ibn 'Arabî's decisive influence on most subsequent Islamic eschatological thought. Gerhard Böwering's study of the Qur'anic interpretations of the early Sufi Sahl al-Tustarî (d. 283 / 896), *The Mystical Vision of Existence in Classical Islam,* is an accessible and much more detailed illustration

of one particular line of Sufi understanding that apparently had some bearing on Ibn 'Arabî's eschatological thinking.

4. *Rasâ'il,* I, no.12, pp. 2-3; see Yahya, *R. G.,* no. 33. This treatise, which is remarkable for its relatively straightforward and concise presentation of practically crucial spiritual questions, has been translated by M. Asin Palacios (abridged and without any annotation), in *El islam cristianizado,* Madrid, 1931, pp. 433-49 (French translation, *L'Islam christianisé,* Paris, 1982, pp. 321-33); by R. T. Harris, *Journey,* pp. 25-64 (complete and relatively unannotated, but with helpful excerpts from the commentary [based on the *Futûhât*] by the famous Sufi 'Abd al-Karîm Jîlî, pp. 69-103); and in Chodkiewicz, *Sceau,* chapter X (slightly abridged, but with by far the most helpful and complete commentary and annotation).

5. The term *mawtin* is described here (*Rasâ'il,* I, no.12, p. 2) as *"an expression for the locus of the moments of the [forms of perception and experience] that come to be in it" (mahall awqât al-wurrâd...).* This definition assumes Ibn 'Arabî's typical understanding that all human experience—in *any* of these realms of being—is in fact constituted by the "arrival" (*wârid,* i.e., from God), at each atomic moment or "instant" *(waqt),* of constantly renewed theophanic manifestations of the divine Names. See the detailed explanation of these technical terms and further references in Hakim, *Mu'jam,* pp. 1202-7 *(wârid)* and 1225-27 *(waqt).* While Ibn 'Arabî goes on to say that "we are now in" the *mawtin* of this world *(al-dunyâ),* this clearly refers only to his *physical* location then, since his writings are full of discussions of his (and many other prophets' and saints') direct spiritual perceptions and experiences, even in this life, of all the other planes of being—most notably in the selections translated below and in all his accounts of the Mi'raj; see also our translation and commentary on chapter 367 elsewhere in this anthology.

6. I.e., of the primordial Covenant, *mîthâq,* mentioned at Qur'an 7:172, by which all the descendants of Adam acknowledged God as their Lord—a conception which plays a key role in virtually all Sufi discussions of man's spiritual origin and destiny. See the representative interpretations of this crucial metaphysical episode, from the *Futûhât,* at II 247; III 465; IV 55, 349, etc.

7. The complex eschatological role of this *barzakh* and its ontological and epistemological underpinnings in Ibn 'Arabî's understanding of the "imaginal" plane of being and experience *(khayâl)* are discussed in detail in chapter 63 (I 304-7; O.Y., IV, 416-25); the full translation and commentary of this chapter will be included in our planned book on Ibn 'Arabî's eschatology (note 12 below). These and dozens of other references to the *barzakh* (in an eschatological context) throughout the *Futûhât* are discussed in the article by W. Chittick, "Death and the World of Imagination: Ibn al-'Arabî's Eschatology," *Muslim World* LXVII (1987), who also refers to the broader treatment of the role of *khayâl* in Ibn 'Arabî's religious and philosophic thought in the classic studies by H. Corbin and T. Izutsu. The "greater death" here refers to the physical fate shared by all men, while the "lesser death"—an expression based on indications in the Qur'an (e.g., at 39:42) and hadith discussed in notes 18 and 19 below—refers both to the experience of sleep and dreams (i.e., man's "imaginal" life in general) and more specifically to that initiatic "death" and "lesser Resurrection" which is the main subject of the translated selections II and III (from chapters 351 and 369 of the *Futûhât*) below.

8. These verses and the many other allusions in the Qur'an and hadith to the events and sites of the "Day of Resurrection" *(yawm al-qiyâma)* are discussed, according to the sequence and imagery followed by the more popular narrative accounts (see note 14 below), in chapter 64 of the *Futûhât* (I 307-317; O.Y. ed., IV, 426-79); this chapter will also be part of our planned book on Ibn 'Arabî's eschatology (note 12 below). As indicated in the latter part of this Introduction (and in the notes to several of the readings translated below), Ibn 'Arabî's more profound and complex personal understanding of those scriptural symbols, however, is in fact scattered throughout the *Futûhât*.

9. Ibn 'Arabî's initial discussion of the scriptural indications concerning the reality of Gehenna and the levels of "the Fire" *(al-nâr)* is included in chapters 61-62 of the *Futûhât* (I 297-304; O.Y. ed., IV, pp. 366-89 and 390-405); the comparable, but far more complex discussion of the levels and types of "Gardens" (of Paradise) is included in chapter 65 (I 317-22; O.Y. ed., V, 59-89), which also includes the preliminary discussion of the "Dune" of beatific Vision (following note). As with the two preceding "realms," Ibn 'Arabî's initial discussions there must be supplemented by hundreds of other, often more personally revealing allusions scattered throughout the *Futûhât;* these chapters and the related discussions will likewise be included in our planned book-length treatment of this subject (note 12 below).

10. See the detailed references (including the main hadith sources) and discussions of Ibn 'Arabî's conception of this universal "eschatological" reality—which in fact underlies his most central and best-known metaphysical theses—in the introduction and notes to the translations of selections V and VI (from chapter 73 of the *Futûhât*) below. As indicated there, Ibn 'Arabî's discussions of this topic elsewhere (e.g., in chapter 371) make it clear that this divine vision *(ru'ya)* is partially shared even by the "people of the Fire."

11. E.g., in the context of his partially autobiographical account of his own spiritual Ascension in chapter 367 (section IV of our translation in this anthology), or in his discussion of the Mahdi and his "Helpers" in chapter 366 (also included in this anthology). For some of the likely explanations for this typical procedure of "esoteric" writing in the *Futûhât*, see the references and discussions at notes 13, 21 and 25 below.

12. As indicated in the preceding notes, we are preparing such a book-length study of these and other as yet untranslated eschatological sections of the *Futûhât*. In the meanwhile, readers may consult the excellent article of W. Chittick (focusing more particularly on the *barzakh*) and related studies cited at note 7 above.

13. These important passages from the *muqaddima* (O.Y. ed., I, pp. 138ff.) are discussed briefly at the beginning of our article on "Ibn 'Arabî's Esotericism: The Problem of Spiritual Authority," in *Studia Islamica*, vol. LXIX, 1989, and in Part II-A of our article "Ibn 'Arabî and His Interpreters," in the *Journal of the American Oriental Society*, vol. 106, 1986, no. 4, pp. 742-44. A more complete study of the *muqaddima* (including partial translation and commentary) is now available in our *How to Study the Futûhât: Ibn 'Arabî's own Advice*, pp. 73-89 in *Muhyiddîn Ibn 'Arabî: 750th Anniversary Commemoration Volume* (ed. S. Hirtenstein, Shaftesbury, Element Books, 1993). The fundamental characteristics of this highest level of spiritual knowledge, as described in that section, are that: *1.* it is attained

only by grace and inspiration (not through reflective thinking, *nazar*); 2. that "the person who knows it *knows all the forms of knowledge" (al-'ulûm kullahâ)*; and 3., that any attempt to "reveal" or publicly express this spiritual understanding—as indicated by several hadith and sayings of the Prophet's closest companions—would surely lead to that person's being silenced or put to death (i.e., for "heresy"). However, some possibilities of what this might imply, in the eschatological context, can be gathered from the more open writings of other Sufis whose works are less affected by such considerations: see, e.g., the discussion of the eschatological theses of the later Persian Sufi 'Azîz al-Nasafî, in the *JAOS* article cited immediately above, pp. 745-51, and the related discussion of these issues at the end of this Introduction, at notes 21 and 25 below.

14. Probably the most accessible introduction to these popular conceptions, based on five "popular manuals" of sermonizing or theological literature from medieval Islam and focusing on "their influence on the popular masses" (p. viii), can be found in the opening chapters of *The Islamic Understanding of Death and Resurrection,* by J.I. Smith and Y.Y. Haddad, New York, 1981; that work also includes an extensive bibliography of both classical Islamic and modern secondary sources focusing almost exclusively on the same type of popular homiletic materials. As indicated above, notes 1 and 3, this type of popular medieval literature, like its modern "Bible-story" equivalents, is usually marked by the (often only implicit) imposition of its own highly reductive interpretive structures (in this case usually theological or moralizing in nature) and frequently by the addition of all sorts of literary and rhetorical devices and striking legendary materials. One highly self-conscious literary example of this sermonizing eschatological genre is al-Ghazâlî's *K. al-Durrat al-Fâkhira,* available in translations by L. Gautier *(la Perle Précieuse,* Leipzig, 1877, with notes and edition of the Arabic text) and by J.I. Smith *(The Precious Pearl,* Missoula, Montana, 1979). The more profound and historically influential spiritual dimensions of Ghazali's personal eschatological understanding are developed in his Sufi writings, briefly discussed in the article by Wm. Chittick cited at n. 3 above, and in the notes and commentary to our study of Sadr al-Dîn Shîrâzî's *K. al-Hikmat al-'Arshîya (The Wisdom of the Throne: an Introduction to the Philosophy of Mulla Sadra,* Princeton, 1981).

15. See the excellent summary treatment of this fundamental topic (with regard to many aspects of Shaykh's thought) in M. Chodkiewicz's article *"Ibn 'Arabî: la lettre et la loi,"* pp. 27-40 in *(Actes du colloque) Mystique, Culture et Société,* ed. M. Meslin, Paris, 1983, and the further illustrations of this perspective discussed in our article "Ibn 'Arabî's Esotericism: The Problem of Spiritual Authority," cited at note 13 above.

16. Compare the bibliography and popular Islamic sources mentioned in note 14 above. Ibn 'Arabî's own distinctive personal approach to the question of the "authenticity" of the canonical hadith collections (and the related problem of his selective choice of hadith to interpret) are discussed in our article in *Studia Islamica* mentioned in note 13. See also the very similar contextual use of hadith (and concomitant implicit exclusion of popular legendary elements) illustrated in detail in his treatments of the Prophet's Mi'râj in chapter 367 of the *Futûhât* (translated in this anthology) and in his other Mi'râj narratives discussed in our

Introduction and notes to that translation.

17. One typical illustration of this is Ibn 'Arabî's delicate treatment of Moses' theophanic vision—and corresponding mystical "death"—during their encounter described in chapter 367 (section IV-G of our translation in this anthology).

18. In addition to the translated selections from the *Futûhât* concerning this "Lesser Resurrection" (especially II and III below), see also chapter 106 (II 187-88; cf. I 258 and IV 352) on the "four deaths" (used in a technical Sufi sense to refer to different stages of the mortification of the *nafs* or carnal soul); chapter 360 (III, 288) on the "voluntary death" (with important indications from the Qur'an and hadith); and further references in Hakim, *Mu'jam*, pp. 1028-33. Ibn 'Arabî sometimes uses the expression "lesser death" *(al-mawt al-asghar)* to refer to sleep (as at IV 99, following Qur'an 39:42), and sometimes to refer to the entry into the *barzakh* or spiritual world prior to physical death (as at IV 424). (For the inner connection between sleep—or rather dreams—and the *barzakh,* see the references at note 7 above.)

19. The famous hadith in question—all frequently cited in this connection in earlier and later Sufi literature—include the following Prophetic sayings mentioned in the selections translated below: *"Whoever dies has already begun his resurrection"* (cited at notes 56 and 70, selections III and IV below); *"Not one of you will see his Lord until he dies"* (at notes 43 and 58, selections II and III); *"death is before the meeting [with God]"* (note 43); and *"Between my grave and my pulpit is one of the meadows of the Garden..."* (note 34). Among the other equally famous hadith—not all found in the canonical collections—frequently cited by Ibn 'Arabî and other Sufis in this same connection are the following: *"Die before you die!"; "People* [al-nâs] *are sleeping; when they die they wake up"* (also sometimes attributed to 'Alî ibn Abî Tâlib); *"This world is a dream, and people are passing over and crossing through it";* and the Prophet's statement that this world *"is the dream of a sleeper,"* and the distance between it and the next world *"is the blink of an eye."* See the references (from Ghazâlî, Rûmî, etc.) collected in B. Furûzânfar's *Ahadîth-i Mathnawî,* Tehran, 1334/1955, pp. 81, 116, 141, etc., and compare the similar use of these hadith throughout the eschatological sections of Sadra, *Wisdom.*

20. The eschatological dimensions of this subject are developed in the greatest detail in the long chapter 371 of the *Futûhât* (III 416-48), but they are also treated to a considerable extent in chapters 61-62 (on Gehenna or Hell, in its close relation with the physical universe) and chapter 63 (on the ontological dimensions of the *barzakh* or intermediate, "imaginal" world), discussed at notes 7 and 9 above. These connections with his eschatology are also mentioned in the notes to some of the selections translated below. (For Ibn 'Arabî's cosmology more generally, see Nyberg, op. cit., and the representative chapters from the *Futûhât* included in this anthology.)

21. It should be stressed that these diverse points of view regarding Qur'anic eschatology and the problems to which they give rise can also be found throughout earlier and later Sufi literature: see, e.g., further historical references in the encyclopedia article by W. Chittick (at note 3 above); the extended philosophic discussion of these problems (with constant reference to Ibn 'Arabî and his commentators) throughout Mulla Sadra's eschatology (*Wisdom,* note 14 above, with reference to the longer discussions in Sadra's *K. al-Asfâr al-Arba'a);* and the contrast of Ibn

'Arabî's eschatological conceptions (and their written expression) with those of two important later Iranian Sufis, Nasafi and Kâshânî, in Part II of our *JAOS* article cited at note 13 above.

22. In addition to the references in chapter 369 below to the "Greater Resurrection" *(al-qiyâmat al-kubrâ)*, note the following related expressions in the selections translated here: the "General Gathering" *(al-hashr al-'âmm,* chapter 351 after note 47); the "Supreme Gathering" *(al-hashr al-a'zam,* chapter 369 at note 59); the "Greater Hour" *(al-sâ'at al-kubrâ,* chapter 73, question 62, at note 71, with especially important clarifications); the "Greater Visit" *(al-zawr al-a'zam,* chapter 73, question 59, at note 80 below); and the "Greater Reviewing" *(al-'ard al-akbar,* in chapter 367, section IV-B of our translation here, again with important explanations). The elaboration and clarification of this distinction is one of the primary subjects of the latter part of Sadra, *Wisdom* (note 14 above), which can largely be read as an extended commentary on Ibn 'Arabî's eschatological interpretations; see also the discussion of the similar eschatological interpretations of another of Ibn 'Arabî's later Iranian commentators, Sayyid Haydar Amulî, in the article of Wm. Chittick cited at note 3 above (with a helpful diagram summarizing the distinctions in question).

23. Chapter 367 (III 348). See also the closely related discussion of the Greater Hour" translated in selection IV (chapter 73, question 62, at noun 71) below: It "is related to the (individual) 'Hours' of the breaths *as the year is related to the totality of its days....*" Earlier in chapter 367 (section IV-B of the translation here), Adam likewise speaks to Ibn 'Arabî from a position "outside" or beyond time; from that perspective, as he points out, the "Greater Reviewing" (on the Last Day) "has already come to an end."

24. In addition to the references in the three preceding notes, see the following discussions of "time" *(zamân)* in the *Futûhât:* chapter 12 (I 143-47; O.Y., II 342-45), on the cycles of esoteric and exoteric time; chapter 59 (I 290-92; O.Y., IV, 330-40) on the time of the cosmos; chapter 390 (III 546-50) on the inner meaning of time; and further references in Hakim, *Mu'jam,* pp. 1253-54 (entry for "Day," *yawm*). Again, it should perhaps be emphasized that these shifting perspectives and meanings of "time" closely correspond to certain typical grammatical and linguistic features of Qur'anic expression which are largely invisible in most available translations: cf. Sadra, *Wisdom,* pp. 120-21, 129, 175, 179, 204-5, etc.

25. See the references cited at note 13 above.

26. See the whole of selection III (from chapter 369, III, 388-90) below as well as, the contrast between the divine "vision" *(ru'ya)* of the true spiritual "Knowers" and that of the (exoteric) *'ulamâ'* and their followers in the two concluding selections from chapter 73 (questions 69 and 71, R 85-86).

27. Ibn 'Arabî cites a great many Qur'anic verses (e.g., 82:8; 32:7-9; 23:12-14; 75:38; 87:2) expressing this same conception of the "two-stage" creation of the individual's spirit and physical body. This is why, as he goes on to explain here (III, 12.20ff.), a given individual of our material species *(bashar,* in Qur'anic terms) may actually have the (spiritual) form of a donkey, dog, pig, lion, etc., while only certain of them are (spiritually) a *"truly human being* [insân], *which is the most perfect of the spirits and attributes."* The apparent divine injustice implied by this conception, *if* it is viewed from a limited literalist perspective, points to some

of the deeper dimensions of Ibn 'Arabî's understanding of man's "return" about which he is (in comparison with some other Sufi writers) relatively reluctant to speak more openly.

28. III 13.20-22. The hadith mentioned here, Ibn 'Arabî adds, is one of those *"considered sound by the people of unveiling,"* even if the science of hadith transmission *('ilm al-naql)* has cast doubt on the reliability of those who are supposed to have reported it. See his discussion of the special ability of the saints and "people of unveiling" to realize the spiritual authenticity or falsity of certain hadith, by way of direct inspiration (even to the point of recognizing the person who originated a spurious report), in chapter 29 of the *Futûhât* (O.Y. ed., III, 240-41) and in his *K. al-Fanâ' fî al-Mushâhada (Rasâ'il,* vol. L no. 1), p. 4 (translation by M. Vâlsan, *Le livre de l'extinction dans la contemplation,* Paris, 1984, pp. 32-33).

29. III, pp. 10.23-13.27 (translation, III 12.26-13.23). The title— *"Concerning Inner Knowledge of the Stage of the Passing Away of the Higher World and the' Finding'* [or 'Being,' *wujûd*] *of the Lower World..."*—concludes that this knowledge is "from the Presence *(hadara)* of Muhammad, Moses and Jesus." The fact that this is the *only* stage among chapters 270-383 in this *fasl al-manâzil* (which are usually connected with the reality of only one of these prophets) to be qualified at once by *all three* of these spiritual presences may indicate the particular universality and wider importance of the issues discussed here.

30. This is an apparent allusion to the eschatological views of Avicenna (Ibn Sînâ), which were further developed in later eschatological writings by (or attributed *to)* al-Ghazâlî—who is probably the "fellow" Sufi alluded to here—and found their fullest expression in the strongly Neoplatonic philosophy of Suhrawardî. Ibn 'Arabî mentions Ghazâlî's influential theory that *"the plane of the other world is originated from the soul"* in chapter 64 of the *Futûhât,* 1,312 (O.Y. ed., IV, 455). See the detailed discussions of these somewhat ambiguous theories of Avicenna in the study by Jean Michot, *La destinée de l'homme selon Avicenne: Le retour à Dieu (ma'âd) et l'imagination,* Louvain-la-Neuve, Peeters,1987.

31. *'Alam al-dunyâ:* here this term (as opposed to *al-âkhira*) is evidently understood in an exceptionally broad or "temporal" sense that includes the intermediate spiritual world *(barzakh)* and all the phenomena preceding the universal Resurrection *(qiyâma)* and final Judgment. Clearly the "group" *(tâ'ifa)* mentioned here is a reference to Ibn 'Arabî's own position developed in his discussion of the intermediate spiritual realm *(barzakh)* and the Qur'anic symbol of the "Trumpet" in chapters 63-64 of the *Futûhât.*

32. *Al-Sûr:* Ibn 'Arabî's identification of this "Trumpet" (or "forms") mentioned in the Qur'an (23:101; 39:68) with the Presence of the *barzakh* (23:l00) or imaginal world *(khayâl),* along with his interpretation of the hadith concerning it and the angel Isrâfil (cf. Wensinck, *Concordance,* V, 372), are developed in great detail in chapter 63 of the *Futûhât* (O.Y. ed., IV, 414-22). The following sentence alludes to his discussion in chapter 64 (O.Y. ed., IV, 455-57) of the "bodily resurrection" of those spiritual forms in terms of the symbolism of Isrâfil's "blowing" on this Horn. Both these passages from the *Futûhât* are elaborately interpreted in Sadra, *Wisdom,* pp. 184ff. (corresponding to *Asfâr,* IX, pp. 244-77).

33. Ibn 'Arabî's interpretations of the complex descriptions of Gehenna in the Qur'an and *hadîth* are summarized in chapter 61 (O.Y. ed., pp. 366-89), although

other allusions to that reality are scattered throughout the *Futûhât.*

34. For the canonical sources of this saying and a number of closely related hadith frequently cited in Sufi discussions of eschatological questions, see Wensinck, *Concordance,* R 319 (and related discussions in Sadra, *Wisdom,* pp. 128,176-79).

35. The reference is to an incident described in several hadith (including Bukhârî, *bad' al-khalq,* 6) about the Prophet's nocturnal Ascension (*isrâ'/mi'râj*), just hefore Muhammad reaches the heavenly Temple, in which it is Gabriel who explains to the Prophet that these rivers are "in the Garden." Ibn 'Arabî quotes this hadith from Muslim (*îmân,* 264) at the beginning of his chapter 367 on the Mi'râj (III, 341.35-342.5), where he is the one who states that the Nile and Euphrates will be in the Garden "after the Resurrection" and who identifies these rivers with the four mentioned at Qur'an 47:15; see our translation, section IV-I. For Ibn 'Arabî's usual symbolic interpretation of these four rivers as different types of "divinely granted knowledge" or spiritual wisdom, see the extended references in ch. 367 (note to section IV-I of our translation) and Hakim, *Mu'jam,* pp. 1071-77, as well as the contrasting interpretation in the context of the spiritual ascent described in chapter 161, where they are taken to signify the Qur'an, Torah, Psalms and Gospels.

36. For the exceedingly complex Qur'an and hadith sources underlying Ibn 'Arabî's allusions to man's spiritual "veiling" and resulting "blindness," see the detailed references in the notes to our translation of chapter 367, section IV-G (the encounter with Moses and the discussion of his theophanic vision), along with the passages concerning the spiritual vision *(ru'ya)* of the saints and common people in the final two selections (V and VI) translated from chapter 73 below.

37. According to the lexical entries in *Lisân al-'Arab* and *Tâj al-'Arûs,* Muhassir is a valley of Mecca located near Muzdalifa, between Mina and 'Arafat, and mentioned in several hadith. Although the name occurs as a geographical reference in certain hadith, we have not been able to locate a hadith explicitly referring to its "infernal" character. But see the following similar allusion (reference courtesy of Prof. D. Gril), from Azraqî's *Akhbâr Makka* (ed. Wustenfeld), II 93, citing al-Fakîkî: *"Muhassir is the place in which it is considered religiously preferable [presumably on the basis of the Prophet's example] for the pilgrim to hurry..."* and *"...the people of Mecca call it 'the valley of Hell.'"* (The latter epithet is also cited in the *Tâj al-'Arûs.*) A number of other hadith referring to different "sites" of Hell (especially the springs of Barhût in Hadramawt) are discussed in Sadra, *Wisdom,* pp. 221-22 (and more elaborately in his *K. al-Mabda' wa al-Ma'âd,* ed. J. Ashtiyani, pp. 474-84 and *Asfâr,* IX, pp. 322-28). Ibn 'Arabî, in his long chapter on the pilgrimage (ch. 72, I 718), mentions a similar tradition concerning the "infernal" character of a spot near 'Arafat favored by Iblîs.

38. Ibn 'Arabî describes a personal experience with such a person of "scrupulous piety" *(ahl al-wara')* in chapter 61 (O.Y. ed., pp. 381-83). The point of these stories is that the "illicit" character of the food in question has to do with the (outwardly unknowable) way it was ultimately acquired (i.e., through theft, corruption, abuse of power, etc.), and not with the type of food itself.

39. This whole passage can he seen as another allusion to the famous *hadîth al-nawâfil,* a "divine saying" which is probably one of the most frequently cited hadith both in Ibn 'Arabî and among Sufi authors more generally: *"... My servant*

continues to draw near to Me through the supererogatory works [of devotion] until I love him. Then when I love him I am his hearing with which he hears, and his sight with which he sees..." This saying is recorded by Bukhârî (*riqâq,* 38), and Ibn 'Arabî included it in his personal collection of *hadîth qudsî,* the *Mishkât al-Anwâr* (no. 91; *Niche,* pp. 118-121); see the full text and translation and additional references in Graham, *Word,* pp. 173-74. Ibn 'Arabî's numerous discussions of this *hadîth* in the *Futûhât* are almost always intended (e.g., in chapter 317, III, 67-68) to bring out his "ontological" understanding of it as an allusion to the individual realization of what is in fact an underlying universal condition: see also I 203, 406; II 65, 124, 126, 298, 326, 381, 487, 502, 513, 559, 563, 614; III 63,143, 189, 298; and IV 20, 24, 30, 312, 321, 449; and *Fusûs al-Hikam,* I 81.

40. See especially the references at note 19 above.

41. Chapter 351 ("Concerning Inner Knowledge of the Stage of the Sharing of the Souls and Spirits in the [Divine] Attributes..."), ninth subsection *(wasl);* III 223.8-10, 18-33.

42. The many versions of this hadith are included in virtually all the canonical collections: see Muslim *(dhikr,* 14, 16-18); Bukhârî *(riqâq,* 41); and the citations from Tirmidhî, Nisâ'î, Ibn Mâjja, Dârimi, and Ahmad Ibn Hanbal in Wensinck, *Concordance,* VI 140.

43. Referring to the famous hadith *"Not one of you will see His Lord until He dies,"* recorded by Muslim *(fitan,* 95) and Tirmidhî *(fitan,* 56); see additional references to Ibn 'Arabî's discussions of this hadith (and the related subject of the beatific vision, *ru'ya*) in the following selection (chapter 369), note 58. The same idea is conveyed in another hadith recorded several times by Ahmad Ibn Hanbal (VI 44, 55, 207, 232): *"Death is before the meeting with God"* (cf. Wensinck, *Concordance,* VI 140). (See also note 19 above.)

44. *'Ayn hayâtinâ:* this expression, which could also be understood more literally simply as "in the midst of our life," apparently alludes in this context to the symbolic "fountain of life" mentioned, e.g., in the stories of al-Khadir, Dhû-l-Qarnayn, etc. Sufis usually understood that symbol as referring to the mystic's reawakened awareness of the divine "Life" pervading all things (even the most "inanimate"): see following note.

45. This phrase echoes the famous Qur'anic verse 17:44 (as well as many other verses expressing the same idea): *"...there is not a thing that does not glorify Him with praise—and yet you do not understand their glorification...."* For Ibn 'Arabî, such scriptural references all refer to the universal reality of "Life" (and corresponding modes of "praise") pervading all things, a reality which is directly perceived by the true "Knowers" *('ârifûn).* See especially the excellent discussion of this universal "Life" which extends "to every atom"—and which is carefully distinguished from the more familiar "life" limited to the "spirits" (of men, angels and jinn)—in chapter 317 (III 66-67); there Ibn 'Arabî likewise stresses that this is always the case, but that only the spiritual "unveiler" *(mukâshif)* is able to see it already in this world. See also further references in Hakim, *Mu'jam,* pp. 363-69. The same realization is also expressed, for Ibn 'Arabî, in the famous *hadîth al-nawâfil* discussed at note 39 above, and is closely related to the Knowers' enlightened perception of the "ever-renewed creation" of all

things at every instant, discussed at note 47 below.

46. See the discussion of the stages of "certainty" *(yaqîn)* flowing from this spiritual awakening throughout the following selection from chapter 369 (especially at notes 62-63 below).

47. *Ma'a al-anfâs:* this is one of Ibn 'Arabî's most common expressions for the knowers' immediate awareness of the "ever-renewed creation" *(khalq jadîd/tajaddud al-khalq)* of all manifest being—including the realms of the "next world" as much as this world—at every instant. See the famous description in the chapter on Shu'ayb in the *Fusûs al-Hikam* (I 124-126; *Bezels,* pp. 153-55) and the following discussions in the *Futûhât:* II 46, 208, 372, 432, 471, 500, 554, 639, 653; III 127, along with further references in Hakim, *Mu'jam,* pp. 429-33.

48. This description of the "inversion" of man's *bâtin* and *zâhir* in the "realm of the other world" *(al-nash'at al-ukhrâwîya)*, here and in the following paragraph, is further elaborated in Ibn 'Arabî's chapter 65 on the Gardens and Stages of Paradise (O.Y. ed., V 86-88). There he again insists (at V 67-68) that he has personally "tasted" or experienced this realm of being, in an apparent reference to the "imaginal" realm of *khayâl* (discussed at greater length in chapter 63 on the *barzakh*). (This would also explain his enigmatic concluding statement here that *"when we have undergone our transformation, nothing will have been added to the way we were."*)

49. Ibn 'Arabî's contrast here between the individual "lesser Resurrection" of the knowers and saints already in this world and the universal "Greater resurrection" (following men's physical death) likewise corresponds to the (only apparent) "repetition" in the following two verses (102:3-4): *"Surely you will know; then again, surely you will know."*

50. Chapter 369, *"Concerning Inner Knowledge of the Station of the Keys of the Treasuries of Divine Bounty,"* section *(wasl)* 13 (translation, III 388.33-389.9, 13-16; 389.34-390.5). The long section 11 of this chapter (III 385.27-387.26) is also devoted to important clarifications of the relation between the ontological, "macrocosmic" Fire *(al-Nâr)* of Gehenna and the psychic, microcosmic "Fires" tormenting the sinners, supplementing the earlier summary exposition of these problems in chapters 61, 62 and 64.

51. This is an allusion to a famous prayer of the Prophet frequently cited in Sufi literature: *"O my God, show me things as they really are."* See references in B. Furûzânfar, *Ahadîth-i Mathnawî,* Tehran, 1347, p. 45; we have not succeeded in finding this hadith in the canonical collections.

52. The Qur'anic phrase *'alâ bayyina* (cf. Qur'an 6:57, 47:14, etc.) is frequently used by Ibn 'Arabî as a sort of shorthand reference to the special conditions of divine guidance and inspiration realized by the accomplished saints *(awliyâ, muhaqqiqûn,* etc.). Within this anthology see, for example, sections II-1 through II-3 in our translation from chapter 367; further references to this key concept are given in Hakim, *Mu'jam,* pp. 229-30. The Qur'anic term *basîra* is used here (and throughout the *Futûhât*) in much the same manner.

53. *Mashî'a:* for a careful explanation of Ibn 'Arabî's important theological and philosophic distinction between the divine *Irâda* and *Mashî'a,* with extensive references to the *Futûhât,* see Hakim, *Mu'jam,* pp. 633-39.

54. Albeit of a very different sort: this is an allusion to Ibn 'Arabî's controver-

sial suggestion—best known from the allusions at the end of chapter 7 in the *Fusûs al-Hikam (fass Ismâ'îl:* L 94; *Bezels,* 110)—that even for the "people of Gehenna who remain there eternally" (i.e., who are not ultimately redeemed through the intercession of their prophets), their "torment" *('adhâb)* will eventually be made "sweet" *('idhâb).* For the development of similar conceptions in the *Futûhât,* see the more detailed explanations in chapter 371 (III 435-36), as well as I 656; III 673; and IV 248, 408. For the ongoing controversy surrounding these remarks—almost always taken out of context—in later Islamic thought, see Sadra, *Wisdom,* pp. 235-41 (corresponding to *Asfâr,* IX, 346-62). Ibn 'Arabî usually treats such questions in the broader context of the preeminence of the all-encompassing Attribute of divine "Mercy" or Compassion, *rahma,* which is one of the keystones of his religious thought: see, e.g., the exposition of this point of view with regard to the punishments of Hell (and its scriptural sources) that is given by Adam during Ibn 'Arabî's account of his own spiritual Ascension in chapter 367 (section IV-B of our translation here), as well as the brief allusion at the end of selection V from chapter 73 (note 105 below).

55. This whole passage involves a complex interplay between allusions to the Qur'anic passages concerning the "presence of death" (Qur'an 4:18, etc.) and the literal meaning of the words *uhtudira* or *ihtidâr,* which would ordinarily be translated simply as "dying" or "death." Ibn 'Arabî's essential point, which he goes on to make more clearly in the following section, is that the true reality of "death," the "lesser Resurrection," is the profound theophanic awareness of God's spiritual Presence at once "within" oneself and pervading all being (i.e., the "perpetually renewed creation" discussed in the preceding selection from chapter 351, at note 47).

56. See the references to this and other related hadith and their interpretation by Ibn 'Arabî (following many earlier Sufis), summarized in our Introduction to these eschatological selections, note 19 above.

57. *Ahl al-ru'ya:* the term applies at once to the accomplished saints *(muhaqqiqûn, 'ârifûn,* etc.) and to those who enjoy the full beatific vision in the other world, as described in selections V and VI (from chapter 73) below, since for Ibn 'Arabî the revelatory experiences of the former (as described here and in many other passages of all his writings) are clearly understood as the prefiguration of the heatific vision *(ru'yat Allâh)* described in many different hadith. (In a more purely eschatological context, Ibn 'Arabî's longest description of that vision at the *kathîb al-ru'ya* is to be found in chapter 65 [O.Y, V, 59-891] on "Inner Knowledge of the Garden.") See especially the crucial discussions of this initiatic "death" and concomitant theophanic vision in Ibn 'Arabî's discussions with Moses during his own spiritual Ascension in chapter 367 (III 349-50; section IV-G of our translation here, with extensive references), and further important treatments of this subject in chapter 302 (III 12-13); chapter 351 (III 223); chapter 369 (III 388-99); and particularly chapter 371 (III 442-43).

58. This well-known hadith is recorded by both Muslim *(fitan,* 95) and Tirmidhî *(fitan,* 56); see the many related hadith discussed in the introduction, note 19 above. In the discussion with Moses during Ibn 'Arabî's own Mi'râj in chapter 367 (see preceding note), Moses explicitly points out that the Prophet was referring to the initiatic or spiritual "death" *(sa'aqa:* see references at that point in our translation) which

is itself the divine vision and man's true "awakening" and "return."

59. The following discussion of the *Ba'th* and *Hashr* (mentioned in the Qur'an) as aspects of the universal "Greater Resurrection" follows the relatively exoteric, popular account given in the corresponding section of chapter 64 (O.Y. ed., IV 466-80).

60. In Ibn 'Arabî's autobiographical account of his own realization of this culminating experience later in chapter 367 (III 350; section IV-I of our translation), he sums up this insight—and at the same time, its metaphysical presuppositions—in the following dense formula: *"Then I saw all [the divine Names] returning to One Subject* [musammâ wâhid] *and One Essence* [or ' Eye': 'ayn wâhida], *so that that Subject was what I witnessed* [mashhûdî] *and that Essence [Eye, Source, etc.] was my Being."* The same decisive experience is described in even greater detail in the corresponding section of his *K. al-Isrâ'* (*Rasâ'il,* pp. 12-14); see the translation and commentary in the concluding section of our article "The Spiritual Ascension: Ibn 'Arabî and the Mi'râj," in the *Journal of the American Oriental Society,* vol. 108, 1988, pp. 74-77. In all of the passages mentioned above, Ibn 'Arabî is careful to stress that this crucial experience of *fanâ'* or "immersion" in God, and the corresponding "divine vision," should not be considered the final or ultimate stage of spiritual realization. For him, that ultimate stage of perfection, as indicated in the rest of this passage, necessarily requires a final process of integrative "return" to the world that finally allows the Knower to perceive all things "as they really are," in the enlightened awareness of their direct relation with God; see note 62 below.

61. For detailed references and an extensive discussion of Ibn 'Arabî's distinctive understanding of this famous Sufi saying and controversial hadith (not included in the canonical collections), see M. Chodkiewicz's Introduction to his translation of A. Balyânî's *Epître sur l'Unicité Absolue* (a work often misattributed to Ibn 'Arabî), pp. 27-30; for some representative discussions in the *Futûhât,* see I 112, 328, 331, 347, 353; II 40, 298, 472, 508; III 44, 73, 101, 289, 301, 536; IV 245, etc.

62. As indicated in note 60 above, this highest stage of spiritual perfection is the special distinction of "those who return" *(al-râji'ûn)*—including the prophets and the highest rank of saints, the *malâmîya:* see the discussion of the increased knowledge of God's Self-manifestation *(tajalliyât)* in the world that accrues to the *râji'ûn,* in chapter 19 (O.Y. ed., III, 84), and the many references and related discussions in Chodkiewicz, *Sceau* (index, s.vv.). In Ibn 'Arabî's account of his own spiritual Ascension in chapter 367 (III 349; section IV-F of our translation), this point is repeatedly emphasized by the prophet Aaron, who strongly criticizes those mystics who would conclude from their experience of *fanâ'*—in itself real and necessary, he insists—that the rest of the world is merely an "illusion": *"They were lacking in the knowledge of the way things are to the extent of what they missed* [in their *fanâ'* in God], *since the world was nonexistent for them. For the whole world is precisely the Self-manifestation of the Truly Real* [tajalli al-Haqq], *for whoever really knows Him."*

63. In addition to the Qur'anic (and earlier Sufi) background of these distinctions mentioned in our introduction to this section, see Ibn 'Arabî's definitions of these three expressions in his *K. al-Istilâhât* (definitions 56-58; English translation by R.T. Harris, *Journal of the Muhyiddîn ibn 'Arabî Society* III, pp. 35-36); they are

also found in the corresponding section of the *Futûhât* (II 132.27-29), chapter 73, question 153 (II, 128-134), which contains the same material as the *K. al-Istilâhât*, but in reverse order. See also chapter 269 (II 570) and the extensive references in Hakim, *Mu'jam*, pp. 1243-52.

64. As mentioned in the introduction to this section, the familiar image of the "pearl" (*al-jawhar:* literally, "gem" or "essential substance") of the angelic soul and its Source in the divine "spirit" *(rûh)* is combined here with a subtle interpretation of verse 25:53, understood in this case as a reference to the unique "comprehensiveness" of the Perfect Man, whose form alone encompasses the full reality of being—the spiritual and material realms, and the *barzakh* (the imaginal world) that lies between them: *"And He it is who mixed the two seas; this one sweet, fresh; and this one salty, bitter. And He put between them a* barzakh *and a restricting barrier."* The allusion no doubt also extends to the occurrence of the same two terms in verse 35:12, which immediately follows an account of man's physical creation: *"And the two seas are not alike: this one is sweet, fresh, pleasing to drink; and this one is salty, bitter. But you eat from both of them... and extract from them ornaments which you wear... "*—especially since the term "ornaments," in Ibn 'Arabi's usage, often refers to the different kinds of spiritual knowledge.

65. The original text of Tirmidhî's questions, along with the replies from the *Futûhât* and Ibn 'Arabî's much shorter responses in his book *al-Jawâb al-Mustaqîm* (cf. alternative titles, etc. in O.Y., *R.G.*, I, no.177; contrary to what is indicated there, this work is entirely distinct from the much longer answers in the *Futûhât*), is available in O. Yahya's edition of Tirmidhî's *K. Khatm al-Awliyâ'* (Beirut, 1965), pp. 142-346 (chapter 4). (There are small differences in the order and wording of questions in the two works.) See also W. Chittick's translations of questions 108, 115 and 118, dealing with metaphysical and cosmological questions, elsewhere in this anthology and the translation of Tirmidhî's work, with extensive introduction, by O. Yahya (based on his previously unpublished thesis). Tirmidhî's important influence on the conception of the relations between prophecy *(nubuwwa/risâla)* and spiritual sanctity or divine "proximity" *(walâya)* throughout subsequent Sufism, including the works of Ibn 'Arabî, is traced in detail in Chodkiewicz, *Sceau*, chapter 2 (with extensive references); the same work also summarizes and clarifies much of the important opening section of chapter 73 (II 1-39), which is perhaps Ibn 'Arabî's most comprehensive discussion of the spiritual "types," functions, and relations among the saints. See also the most complete bio-bibliographical study, B. Radkte's *al-Hakîm at-Tirmidhî: Ein islamischer Theosoph des 3./9. Jahrundert*, Freiburg, 1980.

66. See notes 22-24 (in the introduction), 47 (chapter 351) and 59 (chapter 369) above and the references at notes 69-71 in this selection below.

67. II 82.16-32; the exact text of Tirmidhî's question, along with the shorter reply of Ibn 'Arabî in his *al-Jawâb al-Mustaqîm*, is to be found in Tirmidhî's *K. Khatm al-Awliyâ'* (ed. O.Y.), pp. 229-30.

68. This Arabic verb (itself a common Qur'anic term) actually combines meanings of "speeding" and "striving" or "intending"—all of them relevant to Ibn 'Arabî's understanding here—that are difficult to convey in a single English expression. The etymological link he proposes between the two terms here is simply a literary

device in this particular case, since their Arabic roots are actually not the same.

69. "Breaths" in this paragraph, as often in Ibn 'Arabî, refers to the timeless instants of the perpetually renewed creation of all manifest being *(khalq jadîd,* etc.); see the references in the second selection above (chapter 351) note 47, and Hakim, *Mu'jam,* pp. 429-31, as well as the references concerning his conception of "time" *(zamân,* etc.) in note 24 above.

70. See the references to this famous hadith (and related Prophetic sayings) in the preceding selection from chapter 369 (at note 56 above). Here it is similarly understood as a reference to each individual's "lesser Resurrection" *(al-qiyâmat al-sughrâ)* in the intermediate, imaginal world, "preceding" the final and universal "greater Resurrection" (corresponding to the "greater Hour" discussed in the following sentence here).

71. As already noted in the introduction to this selection, there is a clear parallel between Ibn 'Arabî's notions here and his more frequently expressed distinction between the "greater" and "lesser" Resurrections outlined in the passages translated in the preceding selection (from chapter 369). However here he rather strongly suggests that the actual relation between the spiritual realities indicated by these pairs of symbols may not be a "temporal" or sequential one, but should rather be understood as the integral, intrinsic relationship between individual "aspects" constituting a larger—indeed universal and all-encompassing—whole. Cf. Adam's similar reference to the "Greater Reviewing" *(al-'ard al-akbar)* in Ibn 'Arabî's encounter with him during his spiritual Ascension in chapter 367 (III 345; section IV-B of our translation here), and further discussions of Ibn 'Arabî's conception of time at notes 22-24, 47 and 59 above.

72. The "peopling" or "habitation" *('amâra)* of the "Abodes" of Paradise and Gehenna because, as Ibn 'Arabî—closely following indications in the Qur'an and hadith—explains at length elsewhere in the *Futûhât* (e.g., in chapter 367, III 345; chapter 371, III 421; and chapter 61 on Gehenna, O.Y. ed., IV 366-89), their creation and the existence of those metaphysical realities is in fact an integral aspect of the primordial creation of the universe.

73. See the important discussion of the "eye of [spiritual] Imagination" *('ayn al-khayâl)* and its essential differences from the "eye of the [ordinary] senses" *('ayn al-hiss)* in chapter 63 on the *barzakh* (1,304-07; O.Y. ed., IV, 406-25), along with further references in Hakim, *Mu'jam,* pp. 447-43, and in the article by W. Chittick ("Ibn 'Arabî's Eschatology: Death and the World of Imagination") cited in the introduction above (note 7).

74. Apparently recounted by the famous early Sufi master Dhû al-Nûn al-Misrî (d. circa 246/861), as Ibn 'Arabî explains at the end of this section (note 76 below).

75. *Wâqi'a:* defined in Ibn 'Arabî's *K. Istilâhât al-Sûfîya (Rasâ'il,* 29), p. 12, as *"whatever comes into the heart from that [i.e., the spiritual] world in whatever way, whether by direct address [khitâb] or symbolic image [mithâl]."* See the related discussion in question 118 of chapter 73 (II 114.14-28) of the knowledge of the prophets and saints from "beyond the stage of the intellect" *(warâ' tawr al-'aql),* which extends to rationally "impossible" things that are nonetheless made known to them by visionary *wâqi'ât,* and especially the explanation of the metaphysical basis of such occurrences (and the dramatic illustration in the story of Awhad al-Dîn

Kirmânî's master) in the passages translated here from chapter 311 (III 41-44).

76. For Dhû al-Nûn, one of the most famous and most influential early Sufi shaykhs, see *EI²*, II, 242. Although we have not been able to locate another reference to this story or these "six topics" in the classical Sufi texts concerning Dhû al-Nûn, the terms Ibn 'Arabî uses to refer to him here strongly imply (although not with absolute certainty) that this story of Jawharî formed part of some larger writing or discussion of his. A manuscript of a detailed work by Ibn 'Arabî entitled *al-Kawkab al-Durrî fî Manâqib Dhî al-Nûn al-Misrî* (not mentioned in O. Yahya's *R.G.*, but cited in other authentic writings of the Shaykh and mentioned by later Sufi authors) has been discovered in Istanbul by Prof. R. Deladrière, who plans a critical edition and fully annotated translation; see his French translation: *La vie merveilleuse de Dhû-l-Nûn l' Egyptien* by Ibn 'Arabî, Paris, 1988, Sindbad.

77. Although the divine Name *al-Qawî* appears in ten Qur'anic verses, the aim of this particular allusion (Qur'an 22:74) is apparent from its larger context: *"They do not appraise God as He should rightfully be appraised: surely God is the Omnipotent, the Almighty."*

78. "These powers" here clearly refers to the distinctive spiritual powers and perceptions of the prophets and saints (the *awliyâ'*, those "close" to God), which—for Ibn 'Arabî—are bound up with their profound awareness of the all-encompassing metaphysical reality of "Imagination" *(khayâl)*. In chapter 34 (O.Y. ed., III 316-17), Ibn 'Arabî insists that *"the connections [between our knowledge and things perceived] is only a matter of custom ('âda)... [since] God has other servants for whom he has broken this custom in regard to their perception of the forms of knowledge."* After citing the preeminent example of the Prophet's perfect inspired knowledge and the general problem of *firâsa*, he goes on to mention in detail other saints who received their spiritual insights through the "senses" of smell, sight, taste, etc.

79. For Ibn 'Arabî's discussions of the Prophet's Mi'râj—the particular "events" of which he often cites in illustration of the power of *khayâl*—see the opening parts of chapter 367 (III 340-42; section II of our translation here).

80. In fact, question 59 (II, 80-81), concerning the spiritual understanding of the *awliyâ'* (in terms of God's "veils" of Light described in certain other hadith) on the Day of the "Greater Visit" (*al-zawr al-a'zam*: cf. notes 22-24; 59, and 70-71 above), already evokes most of the principles developed in these questions, but in a form too dense and technically complex to be translated here. For the corresponding passages concerning the "Day of the Visit" and beatific vision in their larger eschatological context, see chapter 65 (O.Y. ed.,V 75-78) and chapter 371 (III 442-43). The latter passage is especially important in bringing out explicitly the wider metaphysical and cosmological assumptions underlying Ibn 'Arabî's discussion here. A number of other relevant hadith concerning man's "vision" of God (*nazar* or *ru'ya*) or spiritual "unveiling" (*kashf*) in the next world are also included in Ibn 'Arabî's personal collection of *hadîth qudsî* ("divine sayings"), the *Mishkât al-Anwâr* (numbers 18, 66, 100, 101; *Niche,* pp. 40-41; 92-93; 132-41).

81. This particular hadith is recorded in essentially the same version by Tirmidhî (*sifat al-janna*, 15, 25; *birr,* 54) and Ibn Mâjja (*zuhd,* 39)—from which the quotations are taken here—as well as by Dârimî (*riqâq,* 116) and in a number of places by Ahmad ibn Hanbal (see full references in Wensinck, *Concordance,* V, 542-43). It

is important to distinguish this extremely long hadith, which only touches on the question of the "Market of Paradise," from another much shorter, but highly enigmatic hadith transmitted by 'Alî (recorded in Muslim, *janna*, 13; Tirmidhî, *sifat al-janna*, 26; etc.) which Ibn 'Arabî often alludes to in support of his conception of man's varying "forms" in the Gardens in the other world: *"In the Garden there is a Market [sûq] in which there is no buying or selling except for the forms of men and women: so whenever a man desires a form, he enters into it."* (This particular description of this "Market" is *entirely different* from the account included in the longer hadith of the "Dune" summarized in the introduction here.) For Ibn 'Arabî's interpretations of this particular shorter hadith in the *Futûhât*, see, e.g., I 131, 142, 149; II 183, 312, 628, etc.

82. I.e., *yawm al-Jum'a*, or Friday; but the reference is essentially to the fact that all the people of Paradise, whatever their rank, are brought together on this "Day." The vague phrase *fî miqdâr* underlines the very different nature of whatever "time" is appropriate in this context.

83. Reading *danî'* (with the version in our copy of Ibn Mâjja), i.e., of base or defective moral character, and not *danî* (as in our copy of Tirmidhî)—although the written form would ordinarily be the same—which brings out the real contrast with *adnâhum*. This seems to be the interpretation of Ibn 'Arabî, who insists especially in chapter 371 (III 442) that all the people of Gehenna likewise have their place at the Dune of Vision on the Day of the Visit, and goes on to give a careful explanation of how this is so.

84. Cf. Ibn 'Arabî's similar insistence, at the end of the passage translated below (note 103), that each person "returning" from the Day of the Visit thinks that he is among the saints and prophets—because he *only* sees God in the form he already expected and held in his belief. The term translated here as "pedestals" *(kursî)* is close in meaning to the "platforms" *(minbar)* in the preceding phrase—the essential idea being that they afford a better "view" of the Divinity: see Ibn 'Arabî's interpretation of these particular symbols in chapter 65 (O.Y. ed., V 75ff.) and chapter 371 (III 442).

85. Here we must omit the remaining two-thirds of this hadith—not immediately relevant to the selection translated below—which Ibn 'Arabî interprets at length in chapters 65 and 371. That part of the hadith describes God's intimate conversation with each individual, in which he discovers that *"it is through My Forgiveness that you have reached your level here."* Then God shows them the "Market of the Garden" with its indescribable angelic "garments," and the people of the Gardens return to their spouses in this "transformed" state—the same "transformation" *(inqilâb/taqallub*: cf. Qur'an 26:227) Ibn 'Arabî discussed at the end of selection II (chapter 351) above.

86. This extremely long hadith also goes on to conclude with the Prophet's answers to several questions concerning the "vision of God". The most pertinent section for Ibn 'Arabî (summarized in the introduction here) is included in his *Mishkât al-Anwâr* (no. 26; *Niche*, pp. 55-57), where he gives the *isnâd* going back to the *Sahîh* of Muslim. The full hadith is also recorded twice by Bukhârî; for full references, see Graham, *Word*, pp. 133-34. For some representative discussions of this hadith in the *Futûhât*, see I 112, 305, 328, 331, 353, 377; II 40, 81, 277, 298, 311, 333, 495, 508, 590, 610; III 25, 44, 48, 73, 101, 289, 301, 315, 485, 536; and IV

245; cf. also the many famous sections of the *Fusûs al-Hikam* concerning the "god created in beliefs," e.g., I 119-24; 178; 182-186; 194-196 (*Bezels*, pp. 148-53; 178; 182-86; 194-96).

87. See especially the discussions of this theme and all the related problems of man's "vision" of God in Ibn 'Arabî's encounter with Moses during his own spiritual Ascension in chapter 367 (III 349-50; section IV-G of our translation here, with extensive references).

88. Translation, III 85.1-22; corresponding to *K. Khatm al-Awliyâ'* (O.Y. ed.), pp. 234-36.

89. This particular group, as Ibn 'Arabî explained earlier (at II 76), refers to certain *"prophets who received a divinely revealed law [only to be applied] with regard to their special case"* (anbiyâ' tashrî' fî khâssatihim) and that of their immediate disciples, as in the case of Isrâ'îl mentioned in the Qur'an (93:3). For more details on this and other essential distinctions—almost all carefully based on the Qur'an and hadith—in Ibn 'Arabî's complex prophetology, see the full discussion and references in Hakim, *Mu'jam*, pp. 1038-53, as well as the discussions throughout Chodkiewicz, *Sceau*.

90. In fact, Ibn 'Arabî at this point in the chapter actually discusses the prophetic and saintly "followers" *(al-anbiyâ'/al-awliyâ' al-atbâ')* as "two divisions" of the same rank *(martaba)*, since both share in the spiritual reality of "absolute prophecy" *(nubuwwa mutlaqa);* again, see the more detailed discussions of his prophetology cited in the preceding note. As for the *awliyâ' al-fatarât,* Ibn 'Arabî says that saints of this latter group belong either with the *awliyâ'* who received their inspiration directly from God (see below), or else with the "people of rational inquiry" *(ahl al-nazar)*, if that sort of speculation was the source of their religious insight. In chapter 65 (O.Y. ed., V 75-76) he states explicitly that the "knowers of God through *nazar*" form a distinct—and relatively highly placed—group at the "Dune of Vision," since with regard to their knowledge (although not their *actions*, which are rewarded in the other, sensual "Gardens") they are "ahead" of the faithful ordinary believers (the *mu'minûn*).

91. The term "revealed to him" translates *yûhâ ilayh;* the term *wahy* often refers more specifically to the direct divine inspiration reserved for the Messengers *(rusul)* among the prophets *(anbiyâ')*, although Ibn 'Arabî—following Qur'anic precedent—frequently uses it more broadly; see the excellent summary (including the complex Qur'anic usage) and cross-references in Hakim, *Mu'jam,* pp. 1182-91, and the more detailed discussions of the modes of divine "inspiration" in section II-2 (with accompanying notes) of our translation here from chapter 366. In Ibn 'Arabî's understanding of the problems of divine inspiration, the saints actually "inherit" their inspirations through the "mediation"—which can be understood in a metaphysical as well as an outward, historical sense—of the spiritual Realities or "heritages" of the prophets; this conception is dramatically illustrated in his accounts of his own realization of the "Muhammadan Station" in the culminating stage of his Ascension in chapter 367 (section IV-I of the translation here). See the further references and explanations of these notions (which also underly the structure of the *Fusûs al-Hikam*) in chapter 366 (sections II-I to II-3 of the translation here), as well as the extensive references in Chodkiewicz, *Sceau,* chapters IV and V, and Hakim,

Mu'jam, pp. 1191-1202 and 400-405. For Ibn 'Arabî's understanding of *taqlîd*, the outward and formal imitation or acceptance of the teachings and instructions of the prophets—and of its abuses by certain groups claiming such spiritual authority—see the discussions in the following selection (VI) and further references in our article "Ibn 'Arabî's 'Esotericism':The Problem of Spiritual Authority," in *Studia Islamica* (full references at note 13 above).

92. *Awliyâ' Allâh:* the combination of these two terms—which occurs only in this place in the Qur'an, referring to those who have reached *"the Supreme Attainment" in "this world and the next,"* and who are *"untouched by fear or grief"*—has a special meaning for Ibn 'Arabî in this context, referring to those rare individuals who are able to receive (or perceive) the realities and inner "beliefs" expressing the whole spectrum of divine Names (summarized in the "comprehensive Name," *ism jâmi', "Allâh"*), an idea he develops more fully in the following paragraphs; see also the translation of chapter 558 (IV, 196-198) in this anthology and Chodkiewicz, *Sceau*, chapters 1-3. The same idea is expressed in the following allusion to the "Yathribi," Muhammadan Station (next note). The "two levels" mentioned here apparently refer to the two sorts of saints *(awliyâ' atbâ'/awliyâ' al-fatarât)* already mentioned above (note 90), although it could possibly also be taken as an allusion to the distinction—discussed in the following paragraph—between saints who receive their spiritual insights from inner "unveiling" *(kashf)* and those who rely on reflection and inquiry *(nazar)*.

93. This last phrase alludes to the advanced spiritual condition of the "knower of *'Allâh'*"(i.e., of the Divinity in all Its knowable aspects) symbolized for Ibn 'Arabî by the Qur'anic reference to the *"people of Yathrib"* in 33:13. See, e.g., *Futûhât*, III 177, 216, 500; IV 28, and further references in Hakim, *Mu'jam*, p. 1244 and Chodkiewicz, *Sceau*, pp. 92ff., as well as the dramatic evocation of Ibn 'Arabî's own realization of this station in chapter 367 (section IV-I of our translation).

94. *Nasab sahîh:* strictly speaking, the *nasab* is the genealogical relationship of kinship or descent; the adjective *sahîh* also conveys the idea of its being complete, perfect, whole and unbroken, as well as rightful and authentic, truly valid—all characteristics that distinguish the relationship of the true *"awliyâ' Allâh"* (cf. preceding notes), as Ibn 'Arabî goes on to describe them here.

95. *Hijâb al-fikr:* this inherent restrictiveness or "limitation" (*'aql*, in its etymological sense) of conceptual thinking, usually leading to a purely "abstract" notion of the divine Reality *(tanzîh)* is a recurrent theme in Ibn 'Arabî's thought, usually with particular reference to the assumptions and procedures of *kalâm* theology. At the same time, it must he stressed that the metaphysical notion of "veil," for Ibn 'Arabî, always reflects an inherent ambiguity between the two simultaneous aspects of "concealment" and "revelation"—since the "veil" is in reality a theophany or Self-manifestation of the divine. The predicament is a universal one, and Ibn 'Arabî, as already noted (note 90 above), does place the "people of *nazar*" in a relatively high position with regard to their *knowledge* of God. (See also Hakim, *Mu'jam*, pp. 313-18, and the related discussion of all these questions in Ibn 'Arabî's encounter with Moses during his own spiritual Ascension in chapter 367, section IV-G of our translation.)

96. *Sharâ'i'*, the plural of *Sharî'a*; the revelation of those "prescriptions"—at

once legal, moral, ethical and spiritual—is a function restricted to the small group of divine "messengers" *(rusul)* inspired by *wahy*. See the chapters translated here (pp. 185-238) on the essential reality of the Sharia, and Ibn 'Arabî's development of the basic differences between his conception of the Sharia and that of the *fuqahâ'* throughout the translation of chapter 366, supplemented by the discussions in our article "Ibn 'Arabî's 'Esotericism': The Problem of Spiritual Authority" (full references at note 13 above).

97. *Al-rijâl:* here, as often with Ibn 'Arabî and other Sufi authors, this term of praise refers not to a particular sex but to a select group of truly realized human beings *(insân)*, the spiritually accomplished individuals he goes on to describe in this section, roughly corresponding to those he calls the "elect" *(al-khâssa)*; see the detailed discussions at the beginning of this same chapter (II 1-38) and further references in Hakim, *Mu'jam*, pp. 515-21. Among his more explicit statements in this regard, from chapter 73 alone, are the following: *"… and everything we mention concerning those men [i.e., the* awtâd, *or highest representatives of the spiritual hierarchy] is about the 'spiritual men'* (al-rijâl), *so they may also be women"* (II 7.7); *"…likewise in each group of the saints we have mentioned there are men and women"* (II 26.6); *"and there is no attribute which the [spiritual] men have but that women also share in it"* (II 35.1). See also Chodkiewicz, *Sceau*, pp. 126-27.

98. *Maqâla:* often translated as "doctrine," but literally "what is said" (concerning the issue in question). In this context, the expression must not be taken in too rigid or narrow a sense, since Ibn 'Arabî referring here—as whenever he deals with questions of "belief"—primarily to the (often only partially conscious) inner beliefs and spiritual orientations of absolutely every individual, not simply to the intellectually elaborated theses or religious teachings propounded by official "theologians."

99. The Qur'anic allusion here refers to the entire verse: *"And the East and the West are God's: Wherever you may turn, there is the face of God—surely God* (Allâh) *is the All-encompassing, the All-knowing"* (Qur'an 2:115); equally important given Ibn 'Arabî's concern for the interrelations of the divine Names, is the fact that the Name "All-encompassing" *(wasî')* in the Qur'an almost always occurs in conjunction with the Name "All-knowing" *('alîm)* as a description of *"Allâh,"* the "all-inclusive Name" *(al-ism al-jâmi':* see the translation of chapter 558 here). The significance for Ibn 'Arabî, in this context, of this reference to the "Face *(wajh)* of God"—corresponding here to the sound or valid "aspect" *(wajh)* of each profound human belief—is developed in more detail in the rest of this selection.

100. Here and in the following paragraphs forms of "contemplation," "regard," or "looking" are used to translate the verb *nazara*, which in this context—unlike earlier passages where it referred specifically to purely conceptual or rationalistic reflection—combines the meanings of "looking at" and "considering" or "thinking about", etc. (cf. the Greek *theorein*). Like the term *ru'ya* (spiritual "vision"), it must be understood throughout these passages in an extremely broad (i.e., by no means exclusively optical) sense; the two terms *(ru'ya* and *nazar)* are used more or less synonymously in many of the hadith discussed in the introduction above.

101. This formula is clearly an intentional paraphrase of the Qur'anic verse (2:115) discussed at note 99 above, giving its full weight to the absolute university

of that assertion; the same point is made by Moses and Aaron during Ibn 'Arabî's spiritual Ascension in chapter 367 (sections II-F and II-G of the translation here). In his longer discussion of these questions in chapter 371 (III 443), Ibn 'Arabî much more explicitly underlines the deeper metaphysical underpinnings and implications of this spiritual insight:

"...*Now the Truly Real* (al-Haqq) *is the Vision* (basar) *of the world, and He is the Seer* (al-Râ'î) *[in the 'mirror' of all contingent things]...and everything that appears is a sign pointing to the Seer, Who is the Truly Real: so reflect—and know who you [really] are!"* (See also the famous, if more prudent, formulation of the same conceptions in the opening chapter on "Adam" in the *Fusûs al-Hikam*.)

102. This Qur'anic theme of the paradoxical "clarity" or "obviousness" *(wudûh)* of the divine Reality or Truth *(al-Haqq)*, which ordinarily escapes our awareness precisely because of God's "excessive proximity" *(qurb mufrit)* and omnipresence, is a central leitmotif of Ibn 'Arabî's thought, as indeed of Sufi literature more generally. (Cf. the recurrent images in Persian mystical poetry of the invisibility of water for fish or of the air for birds, of "black light," etc.) For a representative treatment of this insight in the *Futûhât,* see the translation of chapter 372 (III 450)—in connection with the famous verses 56:85 and 50:16—as well as II 220 and 615.

103. I.e., the ordinary believer is aware that the saint shares his own belief or perspective on reality—but is unaware that saint likewise realizes the truth underlying other beliefs and points of view. Here this is clearly an allusion to a key point mentioned in both of the important hadith discussed in the introduction to this selection (at notes 81–86 above).

104. Or "finding [of God]": *Ahl al-kashf wa-l-wujûd,* one of Ibn 'Arabî's most common expressions for the true Knowers and *muhaqqiqûn.*

105. See the discussion cf. Ibn 'Arabî's controversial (and often misunderstood) conceptions of the eventual "felicity" (or at least "enjoyment") of those in Gehenna in selection III (chapter 369, at note 54) above. In chapter 371 (III 442), Ibn 'Arabî explains that the people of the Fire actually have two "visions" *(ru'yatayn)* of God: the first one, on the Day of Vision, which is "with a veil"—that itself constitutes their punishment and distance from God's proximity; and the second one, after undergoing their punishment, through whatever "spiritual virtues" *(makârim al-akhlâq)* they have attained in their lives.

106. The details of the situation of this vast majority of mankind who are not "dwellers" in the highest level of Paradise (where the "Dune of [beatific] Vision" is located) and who must therefore "return" to their Gardens of sensual delights (or to their level of Hell) after the "Day of the Visit," are described at length in chapters 65 (O.Y. ed., V 59-89) and 371 (III 442-43), and in a great many other allusions scattered throughout the *Futûhât*—again usually in the form of interpretations of the many Qur'anic verses and hadith on this subject.

107. See the references to this problem in our translation of chapter 366 here and especially the more detailed discussion in our article "Ibn 'Arabî's 'Esotericism': The Problem of Spiritual Authority," in *Studia Islamica* (full references at note 13 above).

108. The bridge between these two essential aspects of Ibn 'Arabî's treatment of *khayâl* (and the *barzakh* or "intermediate world" of being) is brought out with particular clarity in chapter 63 (O. Y. ed., IV 406-25), where Ibn 'Arabî also dis-

cusses (pp. 417-18) two favorite hadith which he constantly cites in regard to the key religious role of this "creative imagination": *"God is in the* qibla *of the person who prays,"* and *"Worship God as though you see him..."* (the famous hadith of Gabriel on *ihsân*). See further references in our introduction to these eschatological selections (especially the article of W. Chittick on "Death and the World of Imagination," cited at note 7 above) and the classic studies of this topic by H. Corbin and T. Izutsu.

109. The translation includes Ibn 'Arabî's whole response (II 86.3-9) to this question, corresponding to Tirmidhî's *K. Khatm al-Awliyâ'*, p. 237, and also the last lines of the following response (II 86.19-20), which summarize his approach to the problem of "vision of God" throughout questions 67-72.

110. The expression *taqlîd* here (as in the previous selection, at n. 91) implies a very different sort of "following"—i.e., a sort of mimicking of outward forms and practices, often passing by the heart of the matter—than the saints' inner realization of the full spiritual reality and intentions in each prophetic "heritage" (note 91 above). Therefore the phrase *"what they have understood"* (fahimû) of that imitation must be intended here in the broad sense of *"however they happen to have interpreted and applied it"* in general, and not in the sense of contrasting a true understanding (*ma'rifa*, in Ibn 'Arabî's terminology) with whatever might have been misunderstood. For related dimensions of Ibn 'Arabî's attitude toward *taqlîd*, especially as understood by the jurists, see our article in *Studia Islamica* cited at note 13 above.

111. "The learned," throughout this selection, translates *al-'ulamâ'*, i.e., the "men of [formal religious] knowledge," usually referring primarily to *fiqh* and *'ilm al-hadîth* (and secondarily to the other religious and linguistic sciences often associated with those two disciplines). This seems to be the case here, since his explanation of the phrase "according to their ranks" in the following sentence would correspond to his usual representation of the procedures of the *muhaddithûn* (i.e., as those faithfully transmitting that formal knowledge without distorting it) and of the *fuqahâ'* and *mutakallimûn* (whose religious "knowledge" is often shaped and distorted by many conscious and unconscious interpretive factors). See the forceful illustration of these points in the translation of chapter 366 here, and related discussions and extensive references in our article on "The Problem of Spiritual Authority" cited above (note 13). Elsewhere—e.g., in interpreting the famous hadith *"the learned are the heirs of the prophets"*—Ibn 'Arabî strongly insists on the rightful role of the saints and Verifiers *(muhaqqiqûn)* as the true "knowers," the *'ulamâ'* in the sense of those who alone truly know God (see the preceding selection and all of our translation of chapter 366 here). However that meaning of the term, which is far closer to the usual meaning of *'ilm* (as divine "Knowledge") in the Qur'an, does not seem to be at issue here, since the saints (in Islam or elsewhere) were not ordinarily known for their claims to the public authority of *taqlîd*.

112. See the probable explanation of this allusion (i.e., to the *muhaddithûn* and *fuqahâ'*) and the references cited in the two preceding notes.

113. *Al-fitar:* here Ibn 'Arabî uses this term in the plural as more or less synonymous with the particular bodily (and psychic) "constitution" *(mizâj)* which is different for each individual. This usage in the plural is quite different from the

more familiar usage of the definite singular expression, *al-fitra,* in a celebrated hadith, to refer to mankind's primordial "spiritual nature," which is identical for all human beings prior to their acculturation.

114. As pointed out in the introduction to selection I (from chapter 302), note 27 above, Ibn 'Arabî—following many Qur'anic indications—is always careful to distinguish between two separate aspects of man's "creation": the "generation" of the physical body, with all the differences that flow from that psycho-physical "constitution" *(mizâj)*, and God's "infusion" of the "spirit" *(rûh)* or angelic soul "mounted" on the body. The difficult question of the interrelations between the spirits and each individual's unique psycho-physical "preparedness" or "predisposition" *(isti'dâd)*, which are alluded to throughout Ibn 'Arabî's works (especially in relation to the apparently "privileged" cases of many of the saints), deserves further detailed study. In particular, it is possible that—as with other Sufi writers—they may not be unconnected with Ibn 'Arabî's more profound understanding of the "eschatological" process of the soul's ongoing purifications and progression.

115. The connection here of the "elect" *(al-khâssa)* with these verses indicative of God's absolute transcendence *(tanzîh)* must be seen in the light of Ibn 'Arabî's constantly repeated insistence—most obviously, in the immediately preceding reading, but also throughout most of the texts in this anthology—that the full human perfection *(kamâl)* realized by the saints and "Perfect Men" necessarily requires the *simultaneous* affirmation and inner realization of *both* God's "likeness" *(tashbîh)* with and transcendence of all manifest being. In general, he is far more sympathetic to the unconscious but spiritually fruitful *tashbîh* of the ordinary believer than to the rationalistic and effectively "agnostic," purely conceptual *tanzîh* which he usually connects with the theological doctrines of the *mutakallimûn* and the approaches of the (unnamed) "philosophers."

116. II, 86.19-21; the final lines of Ibn 'Arabî's response to the following question (no. 72), which are intended to summarize his conception of the general problem of divine "vision" posed in question 59 and throughout questions 67-72.

117. *Sûq al-janna:* see the discussion of this key hadith (or rather "family" of hadith) and full references in the introduction to the preceding selection (V), note 81 above.

Towards Sainthood: States and Stations
William C. Chittick

1. On servanthood, cf. *Fut.* II 92.26, 153.26, 424.16, 451.3, 487.6, 515.35, 561.14, 573.23, 588.7, 603.14, 615.28, 616.7, 627.2, 635.4, 640.33; III 18.30, 32.10, 57.25, 78.21. On worship, cf. the translation of chapter 470, note 160; on poverty, cf. chapter 131, note 31.

2. Cf. W. Chittick, "Ibn al-Arabî and His School," in S. H. Nasr (ed.), *Islamic Spirituality* II (vol. XX *of World Spirituality: An Encyclopedic History of the Religious Quest,* New York: Crossroad, 1991.)

3. *Fut.* II 214-15.

4. God is called "Independent of the worlds" in several Qur'anic passages, but Ibn al-'Arabî probably has in mind the verse, *"Oh people, you are the poor [i.e.,*

needy], and God—He is the Independent, the Praiseworthy" (35:15).

5. Ibn al-'Arabî considers Abû Yazîd (or Bâyazîd) al-Bastâmî (d. 261/874) one of the greatest masters (cf. *Fut.* II 40.17, 318.31, 386.23; III 34.11) and quotes from him probably more than any other Sufi. For other discussions of this saying, see Fut. II 16.31, 263.18, 487.8, 561.15.

6. Elsewhere the word "serve" has been translated "worship," which is closer to the sense of the Arabic, but here "service" is employed to show the linguistic connection with the word "servant."

7. 'Abdallâh ibn 'Abbâs (d. 68/687-88) was a cousin and Companion of the Prophet. Though only thirteen when the latter died, he is the narrator of many hadiths and is considered one of the greatest authorities on jurisprudence and Qur'an commentary.

8. I.e., Ibn al-'Arabî is not claiming to know for certain the reason behind Ibn 'Abbâs's explanation.

9. The He-ness *(huwiyya)* is the Essence, referred to in the Qur'an by the word "He" or "His" *(huwa, hu;* cf. *Fut.* II 128.35, 579.29). The All-Comprehensive Name *(al-ism al-jâmi')* is Allah.

10. That Muhammad will be the lord of men on the Day of Resurrection is mentioned in several hadiths (e.g., Bukhârî, Anbiyâ' 3, Tafsîr Sûra 17,5; Muslim, Îmân 327, 328), but relatively few of these include the phrase "without boasting" (those that do are Tirmidhî, Tafsîr Sûra 17, 18; Ibn Mâja, Zuhd 37; Abmad 1, 281, 295).

11. God is called the Proud and Tyrannical in Qur'an 40:35. That these are divine attributes to which the servant cannot lay claim (except in certain special circumstances) is also pointed out in *Fut.* II 244.32, 276.12, 342.16; III 36.26.

12. These words are addressed to the unbelievers in the Fire, who—in the present interpretation—have attempted to appropriate for themselves these two Divine Names. Mighty is mentioned as a Name of God in several Qur'anic verses, Generous in 27:40, 82:6.

13. The full text of this hadith is, *"Oh God, I seek refuge in Thy Good Pleasure from Thine Anger and in Thy Forgiveness from Thy Punishment, and I seek refuge from Thee in Thee; I am not enumerating Thy praises—Thou art as Thou hast praised Thyself"* (Muslim, Du'â' 222; Abû Dâwûd, Salât 148, Witr 5; Tirmidhî, Da'awât 112; Ibn Mâja, Du'â' 3; Nasâ'î, Tahâra 119, Sahw 89). Ibn al-'Arabî explains his meaning here in another passage: *"When the servant makes the Divine Names manifest in accordance with the divine command* [al-amr al-ilâhî], *he is in the proximity* [qurb] *of God's deputyship* [niyâba]...*But if he should make some of them manifest without a divine command, he is in the distance* [bu'd] *from which refuge is sought in the Prophet's words, 'I seek refuge in Thee from Thee'... 'Pride' and 'Tyranny' are attributes of God. When they appear in the servant, God has appeared in the servant; so he seeks refuge from Him, and there is none greater than He in whom to seek refuge"* (*Fut.* II 561.22).

14. There is no true sharing *(ishtirâk)* of affirmative attributes by God and the creature; only the names of the attributes may be said to be shared. The reason for this is the fundamental Incomparability of the Essence, which means that the reality of every divine attribute is Eternal, while the reality of every created attribute is temporally originated (cf. I 194.11, 271.23, 352.3). Affirmative Names or Attributes denote positive qualities that are attributed to God, such as Life,

Knowledge, Will, Power, Hearing, and Sight. Negative Attributes are those that reflect God's Incomparability *(tanzîh)*, such as the Independent, the Exclusively One *(al-ahad)*, and other Names which belong exclusively to God. Correlative attributes are those which can only be understood in terms of opposites that are also attributed to God on the same level, e.g., the First and the Last, the Manifest and the Nonmanifest (cf. the translation of chapter 558 [IV 197.8]; *Azal* 15). Correlative Names do not seem to be the same as contrapositive Names *(al-asmâ' al-mutaqâbila or asmâ' al-taqâbul)*, such as Life-giver *(al-muhyî)* and Slayer *(al-mumît)* or Exalter *(al-mu'izz)* and Abaser *(al-mudhill)*, which can be understood without reference to their opposites (on contrapositive Names, cf. II 157.21, 251.30, 272.11, 308.1, 335.15, 425.19, 544.7; III 98.23, 137.23, 167.12; in III 109.3 correlation and contraposition are contrasted).

15. Tasting is knowledge gained as a result of spiritual practice and the opening *(fath)* of the door to "theophany" *(tajallî)*. Cf. *Bâb* 248 (II 547); I 31.13; IV 221.2.

16. In *Istilâhât* Ibn al-'Arabî says, *"When a person contemplates himself belonging to his Lord, his station is servitude"* (17). In the parallel section of the *Futûhât* he writes, *"Servitude is the ascription of the servant to Allah, not to himself; if he is ascribed to himself, that is servanthood, not servitude. So servitude is more complete"* (II 128.31). Elsewhere he emphasizes that servanthood is the servant's own attribute, *"and he who contemplates his own servanthood is with that which he contemplates"* (II 519.1) and is therefore far from God. He points out that the servant is first ascribed to God (servitude), and only after that can there be talk of servanthood, which is the servant's ascription to the divine locus of manifestation. Servitude is inherent to the immutable entity, which in its nonexistence accepts the command to come into existence ("Be!"). *"Then the servant is a locus of manifestation, to which it is said, 'Do this!' and 'Do not do that!'; if he disobeys, it is because he is a locus of manifestation, but if he obeys and does not delay, that is in respect of his [immutable] entity"* (II 88.26). In short, servitude has to do with the original state of a person where he belongs totally to God, whereas servanthood demands an admixture of individuality which keeps him far from God. Hence the saint *"returns to his own specific attribute, which is a servitude that does not compete with Lordship. He becomes adorned* [tahallî] *by it and sits in the house of his immutability, not in his existence, gazing upon the manner in which God turns him this way and that"* (II 153.26; cf. II 515.35).

17. Necessity *(wujûb)* is either "through itself" *(bi nafsihi)* as in the case of the Necessary Being, or "through the Other," as in the case of those possible things that have been given existence. In other words, once the possible things come into existence, they are known to have been necessary because God has willed them to exist, and nothing can gainsay His Will. But "before" they are given existence, one judges that they are possible: He may give them existence, or He may not.

18. The Being of God is the Manifest and the Nonmanifest. Through its manifestation, Being appears in all things, but colored by the locus of manifestation, which is determined by the properties of the possible thing *(al-mumkin)*. For references to Ibn al-'Arabî's frequent discussions of *mazhar*, cf. the translation of Chapter 205, note 74.

19. *Lays wara'Allâh marmâ.* This proverbial expression is also quoted in *Fut.* II 42.35.

20. Cf. *Fut.* II 519.4.

21. *Fut.* II 215-16.

22. That is, numbers do not exist as such in the world outside the mind. We can count ten apples, but we cannot find a thing called a "ten." In the same way the entities—all the possible things—can be perceived and understood, but they have no real existence, since Being belongs to God alone. *"The entities are nonexistent within the reality of That which becomes manifest through them"* (II 54.16). Cf. the translation of chapter 140, 226.28ff.

23. Again, the "entities" of the possible things are the immutable objects of God's knowledge. As long as God does not "choose" *(tarjîh)* the side of their existence over their nonexistence, the possible things remain known to God as immutable entities; but once He does choose to bring them into existence, they then become the manifestation or outward form of the entities, which are plural; so the possible things cannot but be plural. All this goes back to the plurality of the Divine Names.

24. The *butayrâ'* is defined as a form of ritual prayer consisting of a single cycle *(rak'a),* or a prayer which is at first intended as two cycles, but is then cut off at one cycle. A hadith forbidding it is found in Ibn Mâja, Iqâma 116.

25. Ibn al-'Arabî seems to be saying that the possible thing possesses no independent existent entity, since its true entity is the Manifest, the One Being through whom it appears. From this point of view, there is no servant/Lord dichotomy; the servant is the Lord, and nothing exists that would allow one to claim an independent "servanthood."

26. This hadith is found in Bukhârî (Tawhîd 12, Shurût 18, Da'awât 69), Muslim (Dhikr 5, 6), Tirmidhî (Da'awât 82), and Ibn Mâja (Du'â 10).

27. Elsewhere Ibn al-'Arabî makes the same point by saying that every existent thing is a Name of God (II 69.32; IV 196.34 [see translation of chapter 558]; *Fusûs* 65/*Bezels* 68); or that there is nothing in existence but God's Essence, Attributes, and Acts (II 54.16; cf. the translation of chapter 73, question 118, third paragraph).

28. This is the "Truth through which creation takes place," an important technical term; cf. chapter 6, note 14.

29. As Ibn al-'Arabî often reminds us, there are not two entities—God and His Name—there is only the Divine Essence, which, viewed in terms of various relationships, is named by many Names. The Name has no existence apart from God's existence, so the Name is God. Cf. the translation of chapter 558.

30. Ibn al-'Arabî quotes few Qur'anic verses as often as this. Cf., for example, *Fut.* II 69.10, 379.6, 438.21, 444.14, 471.3, 553.8; IV 41.1, 213.16; *Fusûs* 185.

31. Ibn al-'Arabî considers "poverty," that is, the possible thing's need for God for both its existence and attributes, to be its fundamental defining characteristic. For him it is the Qur'anic synonym for the philosophical term "possibility" *(imkân).* It is contrasted with the divine Independence, in keeping with several Qur'anic verses, especially 35:15: *"Oh people, you are the poor toward God, and God is the Independent, the Praiseworthy."* Cf. *Fut.* II 57.17, 100.34, 200.32, 262 *(bâb* 162), 454.19, 502.34, 508.13, 561.16, 590.29, 600.32, 639.14, 654.26; III 208.8, 321.8, 372.34.

32. The exact nature of the acts attributed to the servants was endlessly debated by the theologians, with the Ash'arites tending toward a predestinarian interpretation and the Mu'tazilites preferring an approach that guaranteed complete free choice. Ibn al-'Arabî returns to the problem again and again, often alluding in the process to the debates of the theologians. Though in the present passage he seems to be saying that the Ash'arite position is the correct one, he often points to the truth of the Mu'tazilite view; e.g., *"Hence in attributing the acts to the servants the Mu'tazilites spoke the truth in one respect, given a Qur'anic proof [of their position provided by a number of verses]; while in attributing all acts to God their opponents spoke the truth in another respect, given a Qur'anic proof as well as a rational proof"* (*Fut.* I 276-79). On the whole Ibn al-'Arabî maintains that the truth lies somewhere between the two extreme positions (*Fut.* II 517.28; cf. II 513.21, 580.10, 604.11, 630.7, 633.34, 635.27, 641.31; III 211.30). In one passage he declares that the difference of viewpoint will never be resolved, whether in this world or the next, *"since each person has been fixed in his belief by God,"* and God will manifest Himself in the next world in accordance with that belief (II 606.33ff.). He concludes, *"There is no problem related to the knowledge of God within which bewilderment [hayra] is greater and more tremendous than the problem of the acts"* (II 607.23).

33. Allusion is being made here to the famous hadith of supererogatory works (*nawâfil*): *"My servant never ceases gaining proximity to Me through supererogatory works until I love him. Then when I love him, I am his hearing through which he hears, his sight through which he sees, his hand through which he grasps, and his foot through which he walks"* (Bukhârî, Riqâq 38; for other sources and a more complete translation, see W. Graham, *Divine Word and Prophetic Word in Early Islam* [The Hague: Mouton, 1977, p. 173). Ibn al-'Arabî refers to the hadith frequently. Cf., e.g., *Fut.* I 203.9, 406.7; II 65.21, 124.19, 126.4, 298.17, 326.28, 381.8, 487.4, 502.14, 513.22, 559.27, 563.31, 614.6; III 63.30, 67.35, 143.12, 189.8, 298.21; IV 20.23, 24.6, 30.13, 312.20, 321.5; *Fusûs* 81.

34. *Al-Luma'*, p. 373. Cf. *al-Risâlat al-Qushayriyya*, pp. 460-63.

35. *Fut.* II 226-27.

36. God considered in respect of His Essence is Incomparable and "Independent of the worlds," but as soon as we view Him in respect of the fact that He is the Reality that embraces all the Divine Names, we see that in this respect He is not independent of creation, since many of the Names demand correlative terms; "Creator" demands "created," "Lord" demands "vassal", etc. (cf. the translation of Chapter 6, notes 5 and 11). In the first paragraph below, Ibn al-'Arabî explains this property of the Divinity; in the next paragraph he contrasts God considered as the Divinity with God considered as the Essence.

37. The nearest Qur'anic verse to this is, *"If He will, He can put you away, Oh people, and bring others"* (4:132).

38. The Essence is not only "Independent of the worlds," It is also Independent of this independence. Ibn al-'Arabî commonly makes this point in referring to God's Nondelimitation *(itlâq)*: God is not only Nondelimited, He is also not delimited by this Nondelimitation. Hence He can assume any delimitation without thereby becoming limited, as He does when He creates the creatures, i.e., when He reveals Himself in theophany as the existent things. *"If He were to be delimited by His Nondelimitation, He would not be He"* (*Fut.* I 290.7; cf. III 72.22, 162.24).

39. The term "assumption of traits" derives from a saying usually quoted as a *hadîth* in Sufi sources: "Assume the character traits of God" *(takhallaqû bi akhlâq Allâh)*; these traits are normally identified with the Divine Names. Ibn al-'Arabî writes, *"This path [Sufism] is founded upon assuming the traits of the Divine Names" (Fut.* II 42.3); *"Assuming the character traits of God—that is Sufism"* (II 267.11). For other references to *takhalluq*, see *Fut.* I 124.14, 216.15; II 54.10, 93.30, 94.11, 126.9, 128.20, 153.3, 166.3, 232.4. "Realization" is a higher station than "assuming traits," especially because of its close connection if not synonymity with Verification *(tahqîq)*, that path of Sufism which Ibn al-'Arabî identifies as belonging to himself and the greatest masters. Ibn al-'Arabî also speaks of the *"realization of the Names" (Fut.* II 480.25) and declares that the Pole *(qutb)*—the person highest on the spiritual hierarchy—is *"described by all the Names, both through assuming their traits and through realization"* (II 573.19).

40. On the connection between poverty and possibility, cf. the translation of chapter 131, note 31.

41. "Making claims" *(iddi'â)* is something that the servant has no right to do, since he is totally "poor" toward God, while God—Being—is Independent of him and possesses total power, so He can claim what He will. Thus Ibn al-'Arabî defines pride *(kibr)* as *"the claims made by the creatures within the domain of Lordship by saying 'I'"* (II 104.13). He contrasts making claims with "acquitting oneself" *(tabarrî)* of acts by attributing them to God, who is Manifest through the forms of the acts. *"Concerning us and people like us who have acquitted themselves of acts—since the existence of the acts becomes manifest from God—God says,* 'Say: There is no power and no strength except in God, the High, the Tremendous' *[a standard formula found in all the hadith collections], since no one can share acts with Him... So the claimer will be called upon [in the next world] to prove his claims, but not the acquitter"* (II 158.17; cf. II 102.8, 345.10, 528.23; III 36.21). Jealousy *(ghayra)* is God's response to the existence of the "other" *(ghayr);* it demands that nothing belong to the other, neither existence nor attributes, since *"God does not want there to be any connection between His servants and other than He"* (II 351.26). Hence He names Himself by every name when He says, *"You are the poor toward God [and toward no other]"* (Qur'an 35:15), so that no one will have need of the other (II 601.9; cf. the translations of chapter 470, note 164 and chapter 558, note 81).

42. "Preparedness" is an important technical term employed in discussions of how Being becomes delimited in order that it can Manifest Itself through the possible things. In short, Being manifests Itself in Its fullness, but the entities of the possible things receive *(qabûl)* that manifestation only to the degree of their own measures, i.e., preparednesses. Hence Being becomes manifest in different degrees, just as the light of the sun is absorbed or reflected within the things of the world depending upon their different natures. *"God says,* 'The bestowal of Thy Lord is not confined' [Qur'an 17:20], *i.e., God bestows continually, but the loci receive this bestowal in the measure of the realities of their preparednesses. In the same way we say: The sun spreads its rays over all existent things and is not stingy in its light toward anyone. But the loci receive that light in the measure of their preparedness"* (I 287.10). *"Through their preparednesses the loci of manifestation bestow upon That which is Manifest within them the forms within*

which It becomes manifest" (II 378.20). Cf. II 55.5, 151.11, 517.23.

43. In respect of the Essence God is "with all things." His absolute Nondelimitation allows Him to assume all forms, to reveal Himself as all existents. The Essence—Being—is the Single Reality or Self *(al-'ayn al-wâhida)* "*within which shapes becomes distinguished and God's Names become manifest*" (*Fut.* II 216.10; cf. II 305.3, 415.24; III 314.6). Each of these shapes or forms—each possible thing—exists at a particular "level" in relation to all other forms. "*Each form in the world has a level possessed by no other; so the levels are infinite; they are the 'degrees'* [referred to in Qur'an 40:15: *'Exalter of degrees is He'*]; *among them is the exalted and the more exalted*" (II 469.10). The highest of the "levels" is Divinity, the lowest servanthood (III 408.11). God's Incomparability pertains to His Essence, which is beyond all levels, while our understanding of Him pertains to the levels. "*So the Lord demands a vassal, the Powerful an object of power... The loci of manifestation pertain to the level [i.e., to God as the Divinity], not to the Essence. So He is not worshipped except inasmuch as He is God, nor are His Names assumed as traits* [takhalluq]—*and this is identical with worship— except inasmuch as He is God... If the Essence qua Essence made the loci of manifestation manifest, It would be known; were It known, It would be encompassed; were It encompassed, It would be limited; were It limited, It would be circumscribed; were It circumscribed, It would be owned—but God's Essence is greatly exalted above all of this*" (II 597.16).

44. Reference to Qur'an 51:56: "*I did not create the jinn and men except to serve Me.*" Cf. the translation of chapter 130.

45. On the servant's poverty toward phenomenal things, cf. the translation of chapter 141, p. 261.

46. *Fut.* II 227-28.

47. On the poverty that defines the possible thing, cf. the translation of chapter 131, note 31.

48. The term *asbâb* is the plural of *sabab,* meaning cause, normally in the sense of secondary or apparent but nonessential cause. Thus, for example, food is a *sabab* or apparent cause of our continued existence, but God is the true cause, or Causer of causes *(musabbib al-asbâb).* In the Sufi usage of the term *sabab,* especially in the plural, the idea of causation was pushed to the background and the term came to be applied to the things that appear to us in the world. Thus in Ibn al-'Arabî's vocabulary *sabab* is practically synonymous with form *(sûra)* and veil *(hijâb),* both of which conceal and at the same time make manifest the reality of something. Ibn al-'Arabî often points out that the great Sufis never try to get around the phenomena of the world (e.g., by performing miracles), since they know that God has established all things in keeping with His wisdom. Affirming the reality and necessity of the *asbâb* and displaying his own poverty toward them is thus the station of the Perfect Man (*Fut.* II 469.3). Cf. the translation of chapter 558, note 81; II 208.16, 331.15, 414.1, 417.24, 420.1, 428.28, 429.1, 469.8, 471.25, 553.5, 568.11; III 35.10, 72.31, 134.25.

49. This hadith is found in several versions and in most of the standard sources. Those things listed which have a "right" upon people include: Lord *(rabb),* self *(nafs),* wife *(ahl, zawj, zawja),* women *(nisâ'),* guest *(dayf, zawr),* body *(jasad),* eye *('ayn),* and friend *(sadîq).* Cf. *Concordance I,* p. 487 under *inna*

'alayka haqqan. Ibn al-'Arabî often alludes to this hadith since—as can be seen in the present passage—he considers it a definition of the responsibilities of the Perfect Men, who are those who "*'give to each thing its right* [cf. Bukhârî, Sawm 51], *just as* 'God bestows upon each thing its creation'" (Qur'an 20:50). (*Fut.* III 106.18; cf. *Fusûs* 219/*Bezels* 276). For a few references to the hadith see *Fut.* II 532.23, 549.23, 653.4; III 104.1, 106.18, 158.12.

50. Reference to the Proximity of Supererogatory Works. See chapter 131, note 33.

51. This is a hadith (Abû Dâwûd, Adab 91; Tirmidhî, Adab 2, 3; Da'awât 128).

52. The account is found in Mâlik's *al-Muwatta'*, Sifat al-Nabî 28.

53. Specific attentiveness *(tawajjuh khâss)* means that the servant turns to God in respect of a specific Name such as the Nourisher or the Bestower, not in respect of His All-Comprehensive Name, Allah. Hence on the one hand Ibn al-'Arabî states that *"Nothing God gives to His servants comes from the property of the Name Allah, since it is the Name that comprehends all the realities of the Divine Names; for nothing accrues to a determinate person* (shakhs mu'ayyan) *in engendered existence except from a determinate Name"* (*Fut.* II 541.6; cf. II 462.7; III 317.28; the translation of chapter 558, 196.28); on the other hand, pointing out that God calls Muhammad the "servant of Allah" in the Qur'an (72:19), he declares that the *"Pole pertains forever to this All-Comprehensive Name, for he is the servant of Allah"* (II 571.20).

54. Ibn al-'Arabî is referring to the Qur'anic verse, *"You shall have within it [the Garden] whatever your souls desire* [tashtahî] *[a verbal form of* shahwa, *'passion']"* (41:31). He takes this Qur'anic verse as a declaration of the ontological state of the Garden, where "imagination" rules. Whatever a person desires—whatever his "passion" seeks—that is given to him; hence his desire or passion determines his situation.

55. This hadith is found in Muslim (Tawba 9-11) and Tirmidhî (Janna 2, Da'awât 98).

56. *Fut.* II 387-88.

57. C. W. Ernst, *Words of Ecstasy in Sufism*, Albany: SUNY Press, 1985.

58. *Al-Luma'*, pp. 375-76; cf. Ernst, *Words*, p. 12.

59. On the hadith, see chapter 130, note 10.

60. This hadith is found in this form in many early sources, especially Sufi works; in Tirmidhî (Manâqib 1) and Ahmad ibn Hanbal (4, 66; 5, 59 and 369) the text reads, *"... while Adam was between the spirit* [al-rûh] *and the body* [al-jasad]." Ibn al-'Arabî often cites the hadith in its present form (e.g., *Fut.* I 134.35, 143.29, 243.34; III 22.33).

61. *Fut.*, chapter 198 (II 396-478). See the translations of subsections 11 and 46 from this chapter.

62. Cf. the translation of chapter 73, question 108.

63. The Qur'anic passage under discussion reads, *"And He made me blessed wherever I was; and He enjoined on me prayer and alms so long as I remained alive, and likewise cherishing my mother; He did not make me mighty, unprosperous. Safety be upon me, the day I was born, and the day I die, and the day I am raised up alive."*

64. Life is an intrinsic attribute of spirit, *"so every possessor of life lives through his spirit"* (*Fut.* I 168.30; cf. III 65.18; *Fusûs* 138 / *Bezels* 175).

65. Reference to Qur'an 2:154: *"And say not of those slain in God's way, 'They are dead'; rather they are living, but you are unaware."*

66. By "death" Ibn al-'Arabî only means to contrast the situation in the *barzakh* or "grave" with the "life" attributed by the Qur'an in this world and the next world, not to imply that people have no share of life in the *barzakh*.

67. The "Folk *[ahl]* of Allah" or "Folk of the Qur'an" is one of Ibn al-'Arabî's common designations for the highest saints. The terms are taken from the hadith, *"God has two folk among the people. They are folk of the Qur'an, who are the folk of Allah and His elect* (khâssa)" (Ahmad III, 128, 242). Cf. *Fut.* II 30.17, 299.18, 352.27, 372.14, 471.6, 510.10, 522.33, 523.29, 554.21, 569.9; III 103.34, 104.5, 121.3, 161.15.

68. Cf. Ibn al-'Arabî's remarks on *sîmiyâ'*, which would seem to be the specific form of sorcery he has in mind here (chapter 311, note 109).

69. The root meaning of the word nature, *tabî'a*, is to impress, imprint, stamp, or seal; hence nature is that level of existence within which impressions are made. It can be viewed on two levels: *1.* In one sense it may be seen as the underlying stuff of the universe, in which case it is another name for the "Breath of the All-Merciful" (II 420.16, 487.33) or the Cloud *(al-'amâ';* III 420.19). In this respect Nature is luminous, and its lights are present in *"everything other than God"* (II 487.33; cf. II 647.34); *2.* Nature is more often considered as the shadow of the Universal Soul through which sensory (including imaginal) things come into existence (II 236.17, 304.19, 430.3, 647.34, 675.11; III 296.1). The first nature is known as the Greatest Nature *(al-tabî'at al-'uzmâ)*, while the second is its "daughter" (III 420.21, 34). Nature in the second respect is receptive and passive with no active role to play in the world; it is the mother *(umm)* of all things (I 138.29; II 354.25, 430.35; III 125.6; IV 150.15). Activity comes from the side of the spirit, which is light, while nature, the spirit's opposite, is darkness. Ibn al-'Arabî writes that the human spirit which governs the body *"has a face turned toward sheer light, which is its father, and a face turned toward nature, which is sheer darkness and its mother. So the rational soul is intermediate* [wasat] *between light and darkness... It is like a* barzakh *between light and darkness, giving to each its due. When one of the two sides dominates over it, it belongs to the dominating side"* (II 239.24). *"For the most part the soul remains in the control of its [natural] constitution* [mizâj]. *Few are the people whose souls rule over their natures and constitutions"* (III 138.32). Finally, by using the synonymous term *tab'* in this passage instead of *tabî'a*, Ibn al-'Arabî calls to mind the Qur'anic usage of the word, where it means "to seal" in the negative sense of shutting and closing. Hence the verse, *"God seals the hearts of the unbelievers"* (7:101; cf. 4:155, 9:93, 16:108, etc.; *Fut.* II 342.19).

70. *Fut.* II 484-85.

71. Here God's realities *(haqâ'iq al-haqq)* can be considered synonymous with the Divine Realities *(al-haqâ'iq al-ilâhiyya)*, which Ibn al-'Arabî identifies with the Divine Names *(Fut.* II 395.2; cf. II 299.30, 665.23). The point seems to be that through revelation God manifests His Names, which are said to be *tawqîfî*, i.e., our knowledge of them is "conditional" upon the revelation (cf. chapter 558, note 82); at the same time, the existence of the entities—the things manifest in the world—display His Names to us, though strictly speaking we do not know the Names except through revelation.

72. I.e., chapter 198. In the passage to which Ibn al-'Arabî is referring, he does not seem to be saying this. The relevant sentence reads as follows: *"In the Divine Oaths* [al-aqsâm al-ilâhiyya] *the Breath of the All-Merciful reaches the furthest extent of its manifestation. In God's Oath the men of knowledge see Him acknowledging the tremendousness* [ta'zîm] *of that by which He swears, since there can be no oath unless a thing possess a certain level* (martaba) *in tremendousness. Hence through His Oath, God acknowledges the tremendousness of the whole world, whether its existent or nonexistent parts"* (II 477.12). In other passages, however, Ibn al-'Arabî does make the point. For example: *"The reason God swears by things is that He wants the creatures to acknowledge their tremendousness, lest they neglect some of the things that denote God* [al-dâlla 'ala Allâh], *whether that denoter be felicitous or wretched, nonexistent or existent, or anything else. This is so even though God's aim* [al-qasd al-ilâhî] *in the Oath is Himself, not the things. Rather, His aim is the two together"* (II 673.1). On the subject of Divine Oaths see also *Risâlat al-qasam al-ilâhî bi'l-ism al-rabbânî* (*Rasâ'il* 9).

73. Reference to such Qur'anic verses as, *"His command, when He desires a thing, is to say to it 'Be!' and it is"* (36:82).

74. Ibn al-'Arabî makes use of the concept of *mazhar* to explain the nature of the existence of the entities in many passages (cf. the translation of Chapter 130); he considers it *"a path which we alone have brought forward in [explaining] existence"* (*Fut.* II 520.22). In short the locus of manifestation is the particular form within which God as the Manifest reveals Himself in a given situation. Both the existence and the properties of the locus belong to the Manifest, yet, since God is appearing under a specific guise, it still makes sense to speak of this or that locus as distinct from God Himself. *"That which is qualified by existence is not the entity of the possible thing; it is only the Manifest within the entity of the possible thing; hence the possible thing is called a 'locus of manifestation' for the Being of God"* (II 99.26). See the translation of chapter 130. Cf. II 90.4, 93.35, 95.20, 96.33, 99.34, 100.27, 103.30, 116.26, 122.15, 160.1, 353.9, 444.16, 500.31, 513.25, 514.32, 517.22.

75. Allusion to a hadith describing what is to be said during the movements of the canonical prayer. Ibn al-'Arabî quotes the relevant sentence as, *"God says upon the tongue of His servant, 'God hears him who praises Him'"* (*Fut.* 1454.27). In Muslim (Salât 62, 63) and Nasâ'î Tatbîq 23, 101; (Sahw 44), the sentence reads, *"God says upon the tongue of His Prophet..."*

76. That all things in the world "speak," each in its own manner, is stated in such Qur'anic verses as, *"There is nothing that does not glorify His praise, but you do not understand their glorification"* (17:44). Ibn al-'Arabî often discusses this fact, e.g., *Fut.* II 77.16, 457.12, 489.12, 510.1, 537.7, 625.14, 628 (*bâb* 285); III 38.5, 65.30, 151.16, 158.2, 393.25. This topic is closely connected to the life intrinsic to all things; cf. chapter 6, p. 82 and note 14.

77. *Fut.* II 516-17.

78. Part of a definition found in Sarrâj, *Luma'* 339.

79. Daqqâq (d. 405/1015) was an important early Sufi and the teacher and father-in-law of the famous Qushayrî (d. 465/1072-73), who often quotes from him—as in the case of this definition (p. 254)—in his *Risâla* (ed. 'A. Mahmûd and Muhammad ibn al-Sharîf, Cairo, 1972). Cf. *Encyclopaedia Iranica*, I, 255-57.

80. Al-Qushayrî provides a similar definition, from which the present one may he derived (*Risâla* 255).

81. Cf. al-Qushayrî, *Risâla* 257.

82. Quoted from ibid., p. 257.

83. This may be derived from ibid., p. 258.

84. We read *fard* for *fart,* following ibid., p. 259, and Sarrâj, *Luma'* 340.

85. On the fact that attributing existence to oneself entails unjustified claims, cf. chapter 140, note 41.

86. The principle that God has foreordained all meanings contained in a Qur'anic verse forms an important basis for Ibn al-'Arabî's Qur'anic interpretations. *"Every sense supported by every verse in God's Word—whether this be the Qur'an, the Torah, the Psalms, the Gospel, or [other] scripture [sahîfa]—in the mind of him who knows the language is meant by God in respect of that exegete, since God's Knowledge comprehends all senses..."* (*Fut.* III 19.21; cf. II 567.14, 581.5). Concerning 42:11, the verse cited here, cf. chapter 6, note 11.

87. We resort to this awkwardism to remind the reader that in this and similar passages Ibn al-'Arabî is employing a single term, *wujûd,* while we are employing two, "Being" or "existence" (since we would like to maintain the distinction between the two terms in English and French). But in Ibn al-'Arabî's terminology, the term *wujûd* embraces both Being and existence, and in many passages, such as the present, arguments can be made for translating the term either way. It should also be remembered that the term *wujûd* conveys in addition the ideas of "finding" and "self-consciousness," which are perhaps closer to the root meaning of the word. The only thing that truly "finds itself" is God, whether in Himself—at the level of "Being" or the Essence—or in the "others," which make up the level of the existence of the world.

88. That relations are not "entities" *(a'yân)* is a fundamental theme of Ibn al-'Arabî's metaphysics. Thus the Divine Names, the most basic of concepts for understanding Ibn al-'Arabî's teachings, can only be conceived of as relationships between God and the creatures; there is no Creator without creatures, no Powerful without objects of power, and even the Name Allah demands its Own vassal *(ma'lûh).* To conceive of the Names as entities—as did some of the proponents of Kalâm (II 619.7)—is to fall into polytheism. Moreover, there is in the last analysis nothing in existence but the Names of God, since they are infinite, each creature denoting a particular relationship with God. Hence there are no entities in existence, only relations; and since relations are "things pertaining to nonexistence" *(umûr 'adamiyya),* what exists, is God alone, while what becomes manifest is colored by the properties of the nonexistent things. Moreover, since the things that appear in the world, as things, are only relationships, the universe is nothing but a collection of relationships or *barzakhs* ("isthmuses") among things. *"There is nothing in existence but* barzakhs, *since existence is put in order by things between things, just like the present moment* [zamân al-hâl]...*So engendered existence* [al-kawn] *has no edges* [taraf]... *Every part of it is a* barzakh *between two other parts"* (III 156.27). On the Names as relations and the importance of relationships in general, cf. II 278.17, 516.34, 671.5, 673.6, 684.12; III 289.5, 397.4, 441.17, 452.12.

89. One such clear proof is translated in chapter 131, 216.3. Cf. the deeper

analysis in the translation of chapter 205, which shows that "acquisition" of existence is in fact impossible.

90. On the importance of number, cf. the translation of chapter 131; on preparedness, cf. chapter 140, note 42.

91. Allusion to Qur'an 4:164.

92. The reference is to a long *hadîth qudsî* found in Muslim (Salât 38, 40). Ibn al-'Arabî often refers to it, e.g., I 229.35; II 110.30, 167.27; IV 140.28; *Fusûs* 222/*Bezels* 279.

93. Allusion to a hadith found in Muslim (Salât 62, 63) and Nasâ'î (Tatbîq 23,101; Sahw 44).

94. Reference to the views of the Ash'arites and Mu'tazilites respectively. Cf. the translation of chapter 131, note 32.

95. By "synopsis of this book" Ibn al-'Arabî apparently means chapter 559 of the *Futûhât* (IV 326-444), which alludes in some of the most enigmatic passages of the whole work to the "mysteries and realities" of each individual chapter. However, there is no apparent reference there (IV 375.3) to this saying or its speaker.

96. *Fut.* III 41-44.

97. Cf. III 45.11-46.3.

98. In saying this Ibn al-'Arabî is explicitly identifying himself as a Perfect Man. Cf. the introduction to chapters 130 and 131.

99. 'Utbat al-Ghulâm ibn Abân was a "follower" *(tâbi'î)* and ascetic from Basra around the beginning of the 2nd/8th century. He is said to have been martyred in a war with the Byzantines. For various anecdotes about his piety and character (excluding that related here), see Abû Nu'aym al-Isfahân," *Hilyat al-awliyâ'*, ten volumes, Cairo: Matba'at al-Sa'âda, 1971-79, VI, pp. 226-38. Ibn al-'Arabî refers to the same anecdote in *Fut.* III 124.27.

100. The word "plane" *(nash'a)* derives from the same root as "arisings" and might be translated more literally as "place of arising."

101. That God brought the world into existence without any precedent exemplar or model (i.e., creation *ex nihilo*) is mentioned employing this term *mithâl* in Shi'ite hadiths from both the Prophet and various Imams and became an axiom for Islamic theology. Cf. W. Chittick, *A Shi'ite Anthology*, Albany: SUNY Press, 1981, pp. 25, 33.

102. This clause is part of a long hadith found in Bukhârî (Îmân 15, Adhân 129, Tawhîd 24, Riqâq 52), Muslim (Îmân 299, 302, 304-06), and other sources; it refers to those whom God takes out of hellfire because of their faith—and despite their bad works—and then places in the Water of Life.

103. Here reference is made to a series of hadiths and a Qur'anic verse: *1*. The Prophet was given a glass of milk in a dream; when asked about the interpretation, he replied, "Knowledge" (Bukhârî, 'Ilm 22, Ta'bîr 15; Muslim, Fadâ'il al-sahâba 16; Dârimî, Ru'yâ 13). *2*. "Perseverance in religion" is given in several sources as the Prophet's interpretation of a "cord" seen in a dream (Bukhârî, Ta'bîr 26; Muslim, Ru'yâ 6; Abû Dâwûd, Adab 88; Ibn Mâja, Ru'yâ 10; Dârimî, Ru'yâ 13). *3*. "Pillar" (*'amûd* in the hadiths rather than *'amad* as here) refers to a dream of 'Abdallâh ibn Salâm; the Prophet explained that it alluded to his Islam and showed that he would enter Paradise (Bukhârî, Ta'bîr 23; Manâqib al-ansâr 19; Muslim, Fadâ'il al-sahâba, 148, 150). *4*. "Handle" occurs in the same hadith as "pillar" but is

also interpreted to mean Islam in the sources cited here; Ibn al-'Arabî may be referring to another version of this hadith or to a totally different saying not recorded in the *Concordance*. 5. Dihya al-Kalbî was a Companion of the Prophet considered to be the most beautiful man of the time. According to a hadith (Ahmad ibn Hanbal 2, 107) Gabriel sometimes appeared to the Prophet in Dihya's form. 6. The nomad in whose form Gabriel appeared (though he is called simply "man" *[rajul])* is mentioned in the famous Hadith of Gabriel, in which the Prophet defines *islâm, îmân,* and *ihsân* (Bukhârî, Tafsîr Sûra 31, 2; Îmân 37; Muslim, Îmân 1; Abû Dâwûd, Sunna 16; Tirmidhî, Îmân 4; Ibn Mâja, Muqaddima 9). 7. Gabriel's appearance to Mary is referred to in the Qur'anic verse, *"We sent unto her Our Spirit, which imaginalized itself to her as a man without fault"* (19:17).

104. The Unseen World is a totality, filling every dimension of existence intrinsically invisible to us, so no "space" or "vacuum" is left to be filled; the visible world is a similar totality.

105. On the vastness of imagination, cf. I 306.17; II 311.3, 312.4; III 290.8.

106. Though at the beginning of this section Ibn al-'Arabî calls the World of Imagination intermediary between the Unseen and the visible, in relation to the visible world it is considered Unseen (just as, in relation to disengaged meanings, it must be considered visible). The World of Imagination in question is that of "discontiguous imagination" *(khayâl munfasil)*, independent of our minds, not the "contiguous" *(muttasil)* kind that we produce through our minds. Cf. W. Chittick, "Death and the World of Imagination: Ibn al-'Arabî's Eschatology," *Muslim World,* LXXVIII (1988), 51–82.

107. Abû 'Abdallâh Qadîb al-Bân of Mosul (d. 570/1174) is referred to elsewhere by Ibn al-'Arabî as possessing this ability or the ability to say "Be!" thereby bringing things into existence *(Fut.* I 259.34; II 65.30, 333.33, 632.7). See Nabhânî, *Jâmi' karâmât al-awliyâ',* Beirut, n.d., pp. 390–95.

108. Ibn al-'Arabî relates a shorter version of this anecdote in *Fut.* I 127.25, specifying that its source is Awhad al-Dîn Hâmid ibn Abi'l-Fakhr Kirmânî (d. 635/1238). The other account adds little to the present version, only that Awhad al-Dîn was at the time a "young man" *(shâb)* and that the "guide of the road" *(sâhib al-sabîl)* was also the "commander" *(amîr)*. On Awhad al-Dîn, cf. B. M. Weischer and P. L. Wilson, *Heart's Witness,* Tehran: Imperial Iranian Academy of Philosophy, 1978; B. Furûzânfar, ed., *Manâqib-i Awhad al-Dîn Hâmid ibn Abi'l-Fakhr Kirmânî,* Tehran: Bungâh-i Tarjama wa Nashr-i Kitâb, 1347/1968.

109. *Sîmiyâ',* derived from the Greek *sêmeia,* is one of the occult sciences and given various rather vague definitions in different reference works. In his translation of Ibn Khaldûn's *Muqaddima,* F. Rosenthal renders the term as "letter magic" (Princeton: Princeton University Press, 1967, III p. 171). It is a science through which the practitioner is able to make it seem that extraordinary or miraculous events *(mukhâlif al-'âda)* are taking place. Ibn al-'Arabî derives the word from Arabic *sima,* meaning sign, a word whose sense is not very different from the Greek *sêmeia.* He writes, *"In other words, it is the science of the signs which are produced by reactions stemming from combining letters and compounding names and words. Some people are given all of this through the mere [pronunciation of the phrase], 'In the Name of God'"* (Fut. II 135.29). He cites as an example of *sîmiyâ'* the magic of Pharaoh's sorcerers (II 135.28), who were able to *"put a spell upon the people's*

eyes" (Qur'an 7:116) and *"make [Moses] imagine, by their sorcery, that their ropes and staffs were sliding"* (Qur'an 20:66). Ibn al-'Arabî also states that the jinn give to certain people *"the science of the properties of plants, stones, names, and letters— this is the science of* sîmiyâ' "(I 274.2). Cf. II 274.15; III 288.9.

110. *Qalfatîrât* is, through metathesis, identical with *falaqtîrât* (a form found in *Fut.* II 371.31, though perhaps through a scribal error) and the Greek *phylaktêrion*, English "phylactery," a leather case for carrying passages of scripture or relics. The sense in which Ibn al-'Arabî understands the word is not clear. In another passage he writes, *"Miraculous acts* [kharq al-'âdât] *are of many kinds.... They may occur on the basis of certain known, natural contrivances* [hiyal tabî'iyya ma'lûma], *like* qalfatîrât" *(Fut.* II 371.31; cf. II 274.33).

111. In a number of passages Ibn al-'Arabî refers to the fact that his first encounter with the Unseen World took place at the hand of Jesus, though apparently he does not give any details of this meeting. *"Jesus is our first shaykh, at whose hands we returned* [raja'nâ]; *he has tremendous solicitude* ['inâya] *toward us"* (*Fut.* III 341.21). *"I repented* [tubtu] *at the hands of Jesus"* (IV 77.30). *"Our return* [rujû'] *to this path took place through a dream-vision* [mubashshira] *at the hand of Jesus, Moses, and Muhammad"* (IV 172.13). *"Jesus looked upon us when we entered into this path in which we are today"* (I 155.26). Moreover, Ibn al-'Arabî's first shaykh in the way of Sufism was Abu'l-'Abbâs 'Uryabî (III 539.26), who was an *"'Îsawî," or a saint with a special connection with Jesus* (I 223.21); to him it was said, *"You are Jesus, son of Mary"* (II 365.19).

112. The hadith is found in many sources, e.g., Bukhârî, Sawm 20, 49, 50, Hudûd 42, I'tisâm 5, Tamannâ 9 (cf. *Concordance* III 547.59).

113. In his long chapter 178 on the station of love *(Fut.* II 320–62) Ibn al-'Arabî tells many anecdotes about lovers, including the present one (II 346.19)

114. That a person can become manifest in Paradise in any form he wishes is often discussed by Ibn al-'Arabî, especially in connection with the hadith of the *"Market of the Garden"* (Tirmidhî, Janna 15; Ahmad 1, 156; cf. Dârimî, Riqâq 116; Muslim, Janna 13). See *Fut.* I 131.3, 142.3, 149.12; II 183.21, 312.26, 628.3.

115. "Opening," an important technical term, is closely related to the title of the *Futûhât* itself.

116. Dominion *(malakût)*, a Qur'anic term, is used by Ibn al-'Arabî as a synonym for the World of the Unseen (cf. *Fut.* II 129.16; *Istilâhât* 16).

117. The narrator of this hadith is 'Umar, the second caliph.

118. For sources of this hadith, see above, note 99, no. 6.

119. By common people *(al-'âmma)*, Ibn al-'Arabî does not mean non-Sufis, but rather the great majority of the Sufis, excluding only those like himself who have attained to the highest degrees of realization.

120. The term, which alludes to the symbolism of letters, is used to refer to the correspondence between microcosm and macrocosm on the one hand, and God and man on the other. Thus *"I saw [in this station] the science of the contraposition* [taqâbul] *of the two transcriptions and that man is in himself the book* [kitâb] *of his Lord"* (III 352.17). *"Man is the all-comprehensive word* [al-kalimat al-jâmi'a] *and the transcription of the world"* (I 136.30). The Perfect Man is *"a transcription of the world, letter by letter"* (II 615.34) and *"a transcription of the Divine Presence"* (II 383.33). Cf. I 216.30.

121. In using this term Ibn al-'Arabî is alluding to the "hadith of transmutation" referred to in the last paragraph of this section.

122. As Ibn al-'Arabî is well aware, the term *tashabbuh* or "gaining similarity [with God]" is taken over from the Muslim philosophers. *"As for the Sufis, they speak of assuming the traits of the Names* [al-takhalluq bi'l-asmâ'];*the expressions are different, but the meaning is the same"* (II 126.8; cf. II 93.30, 385.13, 483.28; III 44.22, 86.7, 125.22, 126.16; cf. al-Jurjân," *al-Ta'rîfât*, the definition of philosophy *(falsafa)*: *"Gaining similarity to God to the extent of human capacity, as was commanded by the Prophet: 'Assume the character traits of Allah.'"* Since Ibn al-'Arabî accords a high place to *takhalluq* and even considers it the definition of Sufism (cf. chapter 140, note 39), he may appear to be contradicting himself in the present passage. In fact he is emphasizing one side of the situation while speaking only indirectly, in the next few lines, of the other side; the servant does manifest the traits of his Master, but "he does not know that from himself," since he knows that everything he manifests belongs to God. In other passages Ibn al-'Arabî makes the contrasting points of view clearer. For example, he discusses two sayings from Abû Yazîd al-Bistâmî, in one of which God says to him, *"Approach Me through that which I do not have, abasement* [dhilla] *and poverty* [iftiqâr],*"* while the other quotes God as saying, *"Abandon yourself and come."* The first saying refers to proximity *(qurb)* through servanthood, the second to proximity through assuming the Divine Names (II 561.15). The first corresponds to the profession of Incomparability, the second to the profession of Similarity. Both are necessary for perfection.

123. Often cited as a hadith by Sufis, this saying has been attributed by the hadith specialists to the Sufi Yahyâ ibn Mu'âdh al-Râzî (d. 258/871). Cf. Massignon, *Essai*, p. 127; Chodkiewicz, *Epître*, pp. 27ff.; Hakîm, *Mu'jam*, p. 1261. For a few references to it by Ibn al-'Arabî, see II 243.3, 298.30, 472.35, 500.16, 508.11; III 44.27, 80.24, 101.18.

124. Îmân 302. For a few other references to this hadith in the *Futûhât*, see I 305.14; II 81.14, 277.28, 311.26, 333.34, 495.28, 590.6, 610.1, 620.32; III 25.1, 44.21, 48.10, 315.20, 485.6.

125. *Fut.* III 449-51.

126. Îmân 147.

127. By employing the word *abda'* Ibn al-'Arabî shows that he is alluding here to the saying of Imam Muhammad al-Ghazâlî, *"There is nothing in possible existence more wondrous than what is,"* words which sparked a long debate among Muslim thinkers (see E. L. Ormsby, *Theodicy in Islamic Thought: The Dispute over Al-Ghazâlî's "Best of All Possible Worlds,"* Princeton: Princeton University Press, 1984). Ibn al-'Arabî often refers to the saying, sometimes mentioning Ghazâlî. Cf. *Fut.* I 4.33, 259.35; II 96.13, 103.34, 244.23, 345.22, 395.25; III 11.15, 110.4, 166.19, 449.9; IV 101.11; *Inshâ'* 18; *al-Masâ'il (Rasâ'il*, no. 22) 27.

128. This verse is one of the most oft-quoted in Ibn al-'Arabî's works. Cf,.e.g., *Fut.* II 68.18, 217.27, 244.24, 267.33, 299.22, 464.13, 489.20, 654.20, 672.1; III 163.21, 449.10; *Bezels* (where the verse is consistently mistranslated), pp. 68, 106--07, 149, 166, 168, 276.

129. E.g., *Fut.* II 326.27.

130. On the connection between the theophany of the Divine Beauty and awe, cf. the translation of chapter 73, question 118, note 52.

131. Allusion to Qur'an 41:53: *"We shall show them Our signs in the horizons [the outside world] and in themselves, until it is clear to them that this is the truth."*

132. The Qur'an urges the faithful to "gaze" upon the earth and God's creatures in order to gain knowledge and awareness; e.g., *"Gaze upon what is in the heavens and the earth!—but neither signs nor warnings avail a people who have no faith"* (10:101). The word is often employed to refer to the activity of rational thinkers, especially with the adjective *'aqlî*, and in this sense Ibn al-'Arabî usually looks upon it in a negative light (e.g., *Fut.* II 252.5, 298.1, 556.35, 644.19). But he also acknowledges that the Law commands us to employ our "rational gaze" in such verses as Qur'an 7:185 *(Fut.* II 163.6, 230.27).

133. Allusion to a whole series of Qur'anic verses. Here we can cite one example for each attribute mentioned: *"He makes clear the signs to the people; haply they will remember"* (2:221). *"Even so We distinguish the signs for a people who reflect"* (10:24). *"Even so God brings the dead to life and He shows you His signs, that haply you may show intelligence"* (2:73). *"Surely in that are signs for a people who have faith"* (6:99). *"We have distinguished the signs for a people who know"* (6:97). *"Surely in that are signs for a people who can hear"* (10:67). *"In the earth are signs for those having sure faith, and in yourselves; why, do you not see?"* (51:21). *"Surely in that are signs for men with understanding"* (20:54). *"Surely in the creation of the heavens and the earth and in the alternation of night and day there are signs for men possessed of minds"* (3:190).

134. Reference to Qur'an 51:56. *"I created jinn and men only to worship [or 'serve'] Me,"* and Ibn 'Abbâs's explanation of "worship" as knowledge. Cf. chapter 130.

135. Cf. chapter 470, introduction and note 159.

136. Reference to such Qur'anic verses as *"To God prostrate themselves all who are in the heavens and the earth"* (13:15) and *"There is nothing that does not glorify His praise"* (17:44).

137. The station of bewilderment achieved by the great knowers reflects their knowledge of the properties of the All-Comprehensive Name "Allah," which is the coincidence of opposites *(jam' al-diddayn).* Cf. the selection from chapter 558. Ibn al-'Arabî often expresses this vision through commenting on Qur'an 8:17, *"You did not throw when you threw, but God threw"* (cf. chapter 131, note 30). For the expression *huwa lâ huwa,* cf. *Fut.* II 379.8, 444.14, 501.4.

138. Ibn al-'Arabî often employs this term in connection with the fact that all things are ranked in degrees. It derives from the Qur'anic *tafdîl,* which translators have rendered as "prefer," "made to excel," "favor"; e.g., *"Do not covet that whereby God has preferred one of you in bounty over another"* (4:32); *"And God has preferred some of you over others in provision"* (16:71). In one passage, after citing several Qur'anic verses employing the term, Ibn al-'Arabî quotes 13:4, *"Some of them [palm trees] We have preferred for eating over others."* He comments: *"This is true even though they have been 'watered with one water'* (13:4). *There is no verse more precise in showing relative preference in existence than this, since He says, 'watered with one water.' Hence diversity in flavor becomes manifest from the One by something being preferred over something else"* (*Fut.* II 416.11). The relevance to the present discussion is brought out clearly by the following

passage: *"God sent down the world in keeping with [various] levels [of existence, marâtib] so that the levels might be fully inhabited* [ta'mîr]. *If there were no relative preference in the world, some of the levels would be ineffectual* [mu'attal] *and uninhabited. But there is nothing ineffectual in existence; on the contrary, all of it is inhabited. Hence every level must have inhabitants whose properties are in keeping with their level. Therefore God prefers some parts of the world over others. The root of all this in the divine things* [ilâhiyyât] *is the Divine Names. How can the compass* [ihâta] *of the Knower* [al-'âlim]—*compare to that of the Willing* [al-murîd], *or that of the Willing to that of the Powerful* [al-qâdir]*? For the Knower is distinguished from the Willing and the Willing from the Powerful by the level of that with which relationship is established* [muta'allaq]. *Thus the Knower is more general in compass; hence it is greater than and preferred over the Willing and the Powerful by means of something not possessed by the Willing and the Powerful in respect of their being the Willing and the Powerful. For God knows Himself without being qualified by Power over Himself or by Willing His own Being; for Will by its very reality relates only to that which is nonexistent, while God is Existent. And Power by its nature relates only to a possible thing* [mumkin] *or to something that is necessary by means of something else* [wâjib bi'l-ghayr]. *But God is the Necessary Being in Himself From here then relative preference becomes manifest within the world, because of the relative preference of the levels. Hence there must be relative preference among those that inhabit the levels"* (*Fut.* II 527.11) For more discussions of *tafâdul,* cf. II 61.8, 68.17, 281.20, 429.13, 469.12, 568.16, 580.19, 588.13, 603.25, 637.9; III 53.32, 96.6, 99.9, 121.9, 157.34, 452.33, 510.7; IV 10.1, 135.15.

139. Reference to Qur'an 55:29, *"Every day He is upon some task,"* one of Ibn al-'Arabî's favorite verses, often cited in connection with the world's constant transformation, the "new creation" at each instant. God's "tasks" are all the creatures and everything they do. *"Every state in the world is identical with a divine task"* (*Fut.* II 77.26). Cf. II 82.6, 102.31, 208.30, 218.28; III 198.32, 224.32; *Ayyâm al-sha'n* (*Rasâ'il,* no. 5).

140. *Bi'l-'umûm wa'l-khusûs.* In other words, some of the Names have a wider and more "general" scope than others. Thus, for example, the Knower is wider in scope than the Willing or the Powerful; the Merciful is more general in its connection *(ta'alluq)* to the world than the Wrathful. Cf. *Fut.* II 469.19: *mâ hiya 'alayhi al-asmâ'u al-ilâhiyyatu min 'umûm al-ta'alluq wa khusûsihi;* also the usage of the terms "general" *('âmm)* and "more general" *(a'amm)* in II 34.2, 248.1, 527.14; IV 228.14.

141. I.e., God is so near to us that we do not perceive Him, just as we do not see our own eyes. Cf. *Fut.* II 220.3, 615.19.

142. In order to explain the analogy of the falling wall, Ibn al-'Arabî turns to an interpretation of part of the story of Moses and Khadir in the Qur'an (18:78, 83), where the two of them built up a wall beneath which was hidden a treasure—though Moses was not aware of the secret—in order that the treasure would remain hidden and eventually become the property of two orphans who were its rightful owners. Khadir manifests God's Jealousy because he keeps the mysteries of divine knowledge hidden. Cf. chapter 470, note 162.

143. The singular of *amthâl,* i.e., *mathal,* is sometimes used synonymously with

mithâl, which in turn is employed technically as the synonym of *khayâl*. Although Ibn al-'Arabî himself most commonly uses the term *khayâl* to refer to the World of Imagination, many of his followers prefer *mithâl*, a term which he often employs, either as such or in various derivative or related forms like *tamthîl* and *tamaththul*, which are taken from Qur'anic usage (the appearance of Gabriel to Mary by means of *tamaththul*, 19:17) and many hadiths (especially the saying, *"The Garden was imaginalized* [muththilat] *for me in the width of this wall"* [cf. Bukhârî, Adhân 91]). Cf. *Fut.* I 307.19; II 105.27, 128.34, 151.35, 152.5, 210.34, 275.14, 292.7, 337.23, 390.3, 475.34, 495.28, 514.17, 596.24, 650.1; III 37.12, 62.23, 113.34, 136.33, 290.18.

144. The Muslim philosophers define *wahm* as one of the three faculties, along with sense perception and imagination, that is shared with the animals and perceives particular things, thus contrasting it with intellect, which perceives universals. Through it a person gains cognizance of things that cannot be perceived through the senses or imagination, such as enmity, sincerity, and aggressiveness; from it arise hope and fear in relation to sensory things. It is often difficult to discern between *wahm* and *khayâl*, and Ibn al-'Arabî tends to use the two terms interchangeably. As Izutsu has pointed out, *wahm*—which he translates as imagination—is the faculty that perceives Similarity *(tashbîh)*; it is contrasted with intellect *('aql)*, which perceives Incomparability *(tanzîh;* cf. *Sufism and Taoism,* chapter 4, especially p. 64). Cf. Ibn al-'Arabî's long discussion in *Fut.* III 364.27.

145. The theme of the contrast and complementarity between the two points of view represented by Similarity and Incomparability is central to Ibn al-'Arabî's metaphysics. The view of the knowers and Verifiers—the Perfect Men—brings together both positions, as pointed out below. Cf. the translation of chapter 558, note 77; *Fusûs/Bezels*, chapter 3; Izutsu, chapter 4; *Fut.* I 290.4; II 3.28, 57.30, 116.7, 307.26, 439.24, 483.33, 541.33, 573.7; III 106.20, 132.11, 160.31, 161.20, 177.2; IV 132.30.

146. This term may refer to God or the Prophet or both at once, depending on the context.

147. Reference to a hadith that Ibn al-'Arabî often quotes, *"God is in the* qibla *of him who prays the canonical prayer."* He also quotes similar sayings, e.g., *"When the servant prays, he turns his face toward his Lord"* (which is cited in Dârimî [Salât 22] as, *"When one of you turns his face toward the* qibla, *he is turning his face toward his Lord"*). Cf. *Fut.* I 225.24, 306.8, 385.16; IV 321.16.

148. Reference to the hadith often quoted in Sufi texts, *"My heavens and My earth do not encompass Me, but the heart of My faithful servant does encompass Me"* (cf. al-Ghazâlî, *Ihyâ' 'ulûm al-dîn* III. 1.7 [Cairo, 1326/1908, III, p. 12]; *Fut.* II 603.12; III 128.26). Ibn al-'Arabî sometimes discusses the great scope of the heart in connection with the saying of Abû Yazîd: *"Were the Throne and everything it contains placed 100,000,000 times in a corner of the knower's heart, he would not notice them"* (*Fut.* II 361.6; *Fusûs* 120/*Bezels* 148).

149. Allusion to the hadith of supererogatory works: *"... When I love him, I am his hearing through which he hears... "* Cf. chapter 131, note 33.

150. That is, the imaginal faculty does not function in those who employ the intellect, unless they should be among the Perfect Men; it is clear from what has just been said that this faculty does function in those who profess Similarity. The "Men"

312 • MECCAN REVELATIONS

(al-rijâl) is one of Ibn al-'Arabî's common designations for the highest saints.

151. Reference to the famous hadith quoted in note 148.

152. *Al-Muhît*, the Circumference or "He who surrounds," is a Divine Name mentioned several times in the Qur'an.

153. Allusion to Qur'an 39:67: *"The whole earth will be His handful on the Day of Resurrection, and the heavens will be rolled up in His right hand."*

154. In Ibn al-'Arabî's cosmology, the Void is the "place of the world" *(makân al-'âlam,* II 310.24), an imaginary extension *(imtidâd mutawahham)* filled with the Universal Body *(al-jism al-kull)*, which embraces everything in corporeal existence, from the Throne to the earth (II 433.27; cf. 1291.7; II 395.9, 396.32, 433.27, 436.28, 676.7, 677.14; III 119.30, 253.13, 420.6, 506.8; *'Uqla* 57).

155. On this expression, cf. chapter 558, note 87.

156. *Fut.* IV 100-02.

157. Cf. e.g., chapter 270 (II 571-74).

158. Reference to two Qur'anic verses: *"He gave each thing its creation"* (20:50, on which see chapter 372, note 127) and that quoted in the title of the present chapter.

159. Reference to Qur'an 17:23 quoted at the beginning of the paragraph below. There is a play on words, since the Arabic for "fulfill" is the same as that for "decree" in the verse.

160. Ibn al-'Arabî often quotes this verse to prove that people worship none but Allah, no matter whom or what they think they are worshipping. Theologians and jurists read the verse as a "prescriptive command" *(amr taklîfî)*, telling people what they ought to do, but Ibn al-'Arabî reads it as an "engendering command" *(amr wujûdî)*, which brings the universe into being in worship *(Fut.* III 117.7; hence he distinguishes between inherent or fundamental worship *('ibâda dhâtiyya* or *asliyya)* and derivative worship *('ibâda far'iyya)*; cf. II 153.33, 308.30, 328.8, 409.4, 588.33, 591.19). On the verse cf. I 328.15, 450.31, 589.17; II 248.10, 591.7, 661.25. See also the translation of chapter 558, note 83.

161. Allusion to al-Ghazâlî's famous statement, *"There is nothing in possible existence more wondrous than what is."* Cf. chapter 372, note 127.

162. A well-known *hadîth qudsî* found in Muslim and other sources. See Graham, *Divine Word,* pp. 182-85. Cf. *Fut.* I 229.35; II 100.30, 167.27, 517.19; IV 140.28; *Fusûs* 222-23/*Bezels* 279-80.

163. The command to *"take God as a Guardian"* comes most explicitly in Qur'an 73:9. Cf. *Fut.* IV 100.19: *"God delegates [us]* (tafwîd) *in His words, 'Expend of that in which He has made you vicegerents' [57:7]; we delegate [Him], since He commanded us to take Him Guardian in that in which He made us vicegerents."*

164. For Ibn al-'Arabî as for other Sufis God's Jealousy *(ghayra)* is closely connected to the ambiguous status of the "others" *(ghayr)*, i.e., the created things. *"The station of jealousy entails a bewilderment that is difficult to pass beyond… It calls for the affirmation of others, but in reality there are no others except for the entities of the possible things in respect of their immutability* (thubût), *not in respect of their existence" (Fut.* II 10.11). On the one hand, *"The Divine Jealousy requires that none be qualified by existence except God,*

given the claims [da'wâ] *that existence demands; hence in this view it is known that attributing existence to the possible thing is impossible, since Jealousy is a limit that prevents it"* (II 226.29). On the other hand, *"Jealousy is a Divine Attribute that demands the 'other'* [ghayr], *which is why it is called* ghayra;... *The 'Powerful Divinity' demands the 'vassal of divinity'* [al-ma'lûh] *and the 'object of Power'* [al-maqdûr], *i.e., the other. So that thing whose existence God demands must exist"* (II 244.21). Cf. II 500 (*bâb* 213), 554.8, 582.11; III 18.14, 102.10, 117.7.

165. On this verse, often cited by Ibn al-'Arabî to point to God's Incomparability, cf. chapter 140.

166. The reference is to the trench built to defend Medina in the year 5/627. A version of the hadith is recorded in Nasâ'î, Jihâd 42. The relevant section of the historian Wâqidî's account, which seems to be somewhat closer to the version referred to here, has been translated as follows: *"By the light of the first I saw the castles of the Yemen; by the light of the second I saw the castles of Syria; by the light of the third I saw the white palace of Kisra at Madâ'in. Through the first hath God opened unto me the Yemen; through the second hath He opened unto me Syria and the West; and through the third the East"* (M. Lings, *Muhammad*, New York: Inner Traditions, 1983, p. 218).

167. *Lâm al-'illa*, a particle employed at the beginning of verbs to indicate the cause of something. In the present context Ibn al-'Arabî has in mind the Qur'anic verse in the title, where this *lâm* is translated "to": *"I have not created jinn and mankind except to worship Me."*

168. On this interpretation of the word *jinn* see chapter 6, note 24.

169. On this verse and its connection to *asbâb*, cf. chapter 558, note 81.

170. This is the often cited hadith of supererogatory works. Cf. chapter 131, note 33.

171. On this important concept, see chapter 372, note 138.

172. Reference to the well-known "Kullabite" formula of the theologians: "They [the Divine Attributes] are neither He nor other than He" (*mâ hiya huwa wa lâ hiya ghayruhû*). Cf. H. A. Wolfson, *The Philosophy of the Kalam*, Cambridge: Harvard University Press, 1976, pp. 206ff. On Ibn al-'Arabî's view of the formula, cf. the translation of chapter 558, p. 197.22.

173. Reference to Qur'an 3:181: *"God has heard the saying of those who said, 'Surely God is poor, and we are rich.' We shall write down what they have said... and We shall say, 'Taste the chastisement of the burning.'"*

Ibn 'Arabî's Spiritual Ascension
James W. Morris

1. In this Introduction we have usually employed the expression *Mi'râj* ("Ascension") most commonly used in Islamic languages, although Ibn 'Arabî himself prefers to follow the Qur'an (for reasons detailed in the following note) in referring instead to the *isrâ'* of the Prophet and the saints. In most of the hadith accounts of this Ascension the revelations alluded to in the Qur'anic verses 53:1–18 play an integral (even decisive) role, and they are understood in that

context by Ibn 'Arabî in all of his Mi'râj narratives. Ibn 'Arabî's own distinctive use of the canonical hadith materials is outlined in n. 8 below and followed in detail in the notes to the translation. For further references, see the general indications (from a historicist perspective) and bibliography in the articles *"Isrâ'"* (B. Schreike) and *"Mi'râj"* (J. Horovitz) in the *SEI* and *EI¹;* the full range of hadith and legendary materials studied in the opening chapters of M. Asin Palacios' *La Escatologia musulmana en la Divina Comedia* (Madrid, 1919) (abridged English translation—eliminating many references to the Arabic sources—as *Islam and the Divine Comedy,* London, 1926; repr. 1968); and G. Widengren, *The Ascension of the Apostle and the Heavenly Book,* Uppsala, 1950. See also the striking pictorial representations of many stages of the Mi'râj—incorporating, however, a wide range of legendary or popular materials not used by Ibn 'Arabî—by the 15th-century Timurid school of Herat in *"The Miraculous Journey of Mahomet"/Mirâj Nâmeh* (London/Paris, 1977).

2. There are a number of shades of meaning in the Qur'anic expression *asrâ* (at 17:1 and in the related hadith) that help explain Ibn 'Arabî's preference for that term: in addition to its being used to describe a complete spiritual journey involving both "ascent" and *"return" (rujû')*—a fundamental dimension he emphasizes especially in the *R. al-Anwâr*—the term refers more specifically to a *"nocturnal voyage,"* with all the implications of a "hidden," profoundly inner spiritual transformation that are so decisive for the "journeys" of the saints described in all these narratives. Finally, the verbal form clearly insists on *God* as the (ultimate) Agent and Source of this movement, pointing to the key factors of divine grace and individual "predisposition" that are also central to Ibn 'Arabî's consideration of this journey (whether for the Prophet or the saints), especially in the autobiographical context of the *K. al-Isrâ'*. (None of this is implied by the much broader and less specific Qur'anic usage of *mi'râj*—in the plural—at 43:33 and 70:3).

3. While acknowledging the uniquely "physical" nature of the Prophet's Mi'râj (in section II below), Ibn 'Arabî stresses the primary importance of the spiritual *isrâ'ât*—even for Muhammad—in the proportions implied by the Prophet's "thirty-three" other, purely spiritual journeys mentioned at the end of that section (note 46 below). The crucial importance of the notion of the saints' participation in the prophetic "heritage" *(wirâtha)* is assumed throughout all of these Mi'râj narratives: for Ibn 'Arabî, its ultimate verification (and perhaps even its source) is to be found in the revelation of the "Muhammadan Station" in section IV-I and in the corresponding passage from the *K. al-Isrâ'* (pp. 12-14: see the translation and commentary in our article on "The Spiritual Ascension: Ibn 'Arabî and the Mi'râj", cited at note 13 below). For further references to this key notion in Ibn 'Arabî's religious thought, see Chodkiewicz, *Sceau,* chapter 5; and Hakim, *Mu'jam,* pp. 1191-1201.

4. A fundamental point that is openly stressed here in the reminder of Yahya (John the Baptist, at the beginning of IV-F, the sphere of Aaron) that *"each person has a path* [tarîq] *that no one else but he travels,"* which *"... comes to be through the traveling itself."* The more specifically personal, "autobiographical" dimensions of Ibn 'Arabî's Mi'râj accounts are most evident in the *K. al-Isrâ'* (see the important passage translated in our *JAOS* article cited at note 13 below) and in the conclud-

ing section (IV-I) of this chapter from the *Futûhât*.

5. This is brought out more fully in the cross-references in the notes to this translation. In particular, it is clear that the spiritual phenomena underlying this particular schema provided by the Miʿrâj are not essentially different from the realities Ibn ʿArabî discusses elsewhere in terms of other traditional Sufi categories, such as the metaphor of the spiritual "journeys in God" *(asfâr)* or the complex distinctions of "stations" *(maqâmât)*, "stages" *(manâzil)*, etc. employed throughout the *Futûhât* itself: see, for example, his revealing remarks concerning Ansârî's classic *Manâzil al-Sâʾirîn* and his own *Manâhij al-Irtiqâʾ* near the end of the Ascension outlined in chapter 167 (II 280; *Alchimie,* pp. 112-13).

6. In addition to Ibn ʿArabî's own explicitly metaphysical language, that perspective is more dramatically represented in chapter 367 of the *Futûhât* (translated below) by the spirits of the different prophets, especially Adam, Idrîs and Aaron—all of whom tend to speak here, as is often the case with God in the Qurʾan, from a transcendent divine or "supra-temporal" perspective.

7. Hence the central importance of the celebrated divine saying *(hadîth qudsî)* with which he concludes the opening section (at note 37): *"My earth does not encompass Me, nor does My heaven, but the heart of My servant, the man of true faith, does encompass Me."* He returns to stress the fundamental position of the Heart, in a more autobiographical and experiential context, in section IV-H (notes 168-72) below. For further references to this fundamental concept in Ibn ʿArabî's thought, see Hakim, *Muʿjam,* pp. 916-21, and the famous chapter on the "Wisdom of the Heart" (Shuʿayb) in the *Fusûs al-Hikam,* I 119-26; *Bezels,* pp. 145-57.

8. These works provide a perfect illustration of Ibn ʿArabî's typical (and highly complex) approach to hadith. (See our more general discussion of this topic in our article on "Ibn ʿArabî's 'Esotericism': The Problem of Spiritual Authority," in *Studia Islamica* LXIX, 1989.) He scrupulously and literally follows the sayings and deeds of the Prophet as recounted in the canonical collections—in this chapter (367), relying especially on the *Sahîh* of Muslim (who devotes a special section [*îmân,* 254-94] to the events connected with the Miʿrâj) and to a slightly lesser extent, on the *Sahîh* of Bukhârî—and most often develops his own spiritual interpretations from close attention to the slightest literal details of those narratives (thereby implicitly excluding the vast body of non-hadith legends that had become popularly associated with these events). Rather than focusing on the external differences or apparent contradictions among various hadith (which are quite apparent, for example, concerning the number or order of stages in the Ascension), Ibn ʿArabî typically—one might say "ecumenically"—concentrates on conveying the spiritual meaning and intentions implicit in *each* Prophetic saying, pointing to a level of understanding unifying what might otherwise be seen as differing or conflicting expressions. (This approach mirrors his more general attitude to the various Islamic sects and schools of law, and ultimately to the observable diversity of human religions and beliefs.)

9. Fortunately, these elements are much less important here than in chapter 167 (see below), which assumes a far more detailed acquaintance with alchemy, Ptolemaic-Aristotelean astronomy, a wide body of traditional astrological lore concerning the particular influences of the stars, and additional "esoteric sciences." In

any case, it is important to note that virtually all those matters—which Ibn 'Arabî treats there as inherently knowable by man's natural observation and "reasoning" *(nazar)*—primarily concern the symbolic framework for the Mi'râj narrative, and not its universal spiritual "content," which is usually expressed in much more immediately accessible form in this chapter (367).

10. Allusions in both of these areas are clarified in the footnotes as they are mentioned, usually by cross-references to related passages in the *Futûhât, Fusûs* and other writings. We should add that other prophets not explicitly mentioned in the hadith and these narratives concerning the Mi'râj are elsewhere frequently associated by Ibn 'Arabî with particular heavenly spheres: see, for example, Noah's connection with the sphere of the sun, mentioned at the end of chapter 3 of the *Fusûs* (in reference to a longer account in Ibn 'Arabî's *K. al-Tanazzulât al-Mawsilîya*).

11. There are also a number of other, shorter or less complete treatments of the Mi'râj theme in Ibn 'Arabî's extant writings, some of which are cited in notes below. The longest (and most accessible) is the passage on the Ascension of the Prophet—understood as the cosmic "Muhammadan Reality" or "Perfect Man"—in the possibly apocryphal *Shajarat al-Kawn* (R.G., no. 666), now available in translations by A. Jeffery, "Ibn 'Arabî's *Shajarat al-Kawn*," in *Studia Islamica,* vol. X, pp. 43-78, and vol. XI, pp. 113-60 (Mi'râj section at pp. 145-60); and by M. Gloton, *L'Arbre du Mcnde,* Paris, 1982 (Mi'râj section pp. 93-106). Although the French translation does give more useful references to the Qur'an and hadith background of this passage, neither version provides sufficient annotation to make intelligible most of this treatise's extremely complex metaphysical, theological and cosmological allusions, whose density is comparable to that of the *K. al-Isrâ'*. Unlike the treatments of the Mi'râj discussed below, the protagonist of this Ascension (in *Shajarat al-Kawn*) is the Prophet himself—although often described in metaphysical terms clearly applicable to the "Perfect Man" in general—and Ibn 'Arabî does not bother to mention here the various intermediate stages of his celestial encounters with the earlier prophets which are so prominent in the other accounts (and in the original hadith). Instead he here assumes, as throughout the *Shajarat al-Kawn*, the universal presence of this cosmic "Muhammadan Reality," and takes a relatively few elements from the Mi'râj narratives (especially those of the divine Throne and the Prophet's different "steeds") as symbols for celebrating that central metaphysical theme.

12. See *R.G.,* no. 313; this entry mentions several alternative titles and an extant commentary by Ibn 'Arabî's close disciple Isma'îl b. Sawdakîn, which is extremely useful in deciphering this difficult work. References here are to the text given in the *Rasâ'il,* I, no. 13, pp. 1-92. The date and place of composition are mentioned in the author's own colophon (p. 92). The article by Joanna Wronecka, *"Le kitâb al-isrâ' ilâ maqâm al-asrâ' d'Ibn 'Arabî,"* pp. 15-27 in *Annales Islamologiques,* Cairo, vol. XX, 1984, contains only brief first impressions of this book and the translations of a number of section headings (plus several verses from the concluding *munâjât*), while announcing the author's plans to begin a dissertation on this subject at the University of Warsaw.

13. See especially our translation and commentary of a crucial autobiographical passage (pp. 13-14)—perfectly complementing the culminating stage of Ibn

'Arabî's spiritual ascension here (section IV-I below)—in "The Spiritual Ascension: Ibn 'Arabî and the Mi'râj," *Journal of the American Oriental Society,* vol. 108, 1988, no.1, pp. 74-77. The *K. al-Isrâ'* as a whole conveys a mood of excitement and immediacy that must reflect the relative proximity of some decisive (and perhaps not yet fully assimilated) personal spiritual inspiration. More specifically, the *K. al-Isrâ'* does not yet seem to distinguish with complete clarity between what Ibn 'Arabî later calls the *"maqâm muhammadî"* (the spiritual "station of Muhammad")—or that supreme part of it uniquely reserved for himself as the "Seal of Muhammadan Saints"—and what he then calls the "station of Proximity [to God]" *(maqâm al-qurba)* attained more generally by the highest rank of the saints, the *afrâd* or *malâmîya*. In the *K. al-Isrâ',* he frequently alludes to his own attainment of a lofty "Muhammadan station," but still employing terms—as continued to be the case with many later Sufis—that also suggest he is speaking of a spiritual rank ultimately accessible to other Muslim saints as well. For a careful discussion and extensive references concerning the broader context of this important question for our understanding of Ibn 'Arabî's own spiritual autobiography, see Chodkiewicz, *Sceau,* chapter IX, as well as the famous opening passage of the *Futûhât* recounting Ibn 'Arabî's subsequent experience (or complete recognition) of his "investiture" as the "Seal of the Muhammadan Saints": this event is described in the *Khutbat al-Kitâb* (I, pp. 2ff.; O.Y. ed., I 43-55), and is also accessible in a French translation by M. Vâlsan, *Etudes traditionnelles,* Paris, 1953, pp. 300-11.

14. *Bayn al-marmûz wa-l-mafhûm (Rasâ'il* I, no.13, p. 3): most of this labyrinth of symbols and allusions to the Qur'an and hadith (usually through only a single word or brief phrase) could potentially be elucidated by extensive reference to the *Futûhât* and other works. However, such a commentary would often require page-long notes of explanation for virtually every other word—an approach which could not hope to convey the poetic, immediately expressive emotional quality which is the essential trait of this work.

15. The autobiographical nature of the *K. al-Isrâ'* is not even thinly disguised. At p. 66, Ibn 'Arabî explains his continued reference to himself as a *"sâlik"* in terms of his desire to emphasize the fact that *"even now [i.e., after reaching the highest spiritual station] I am still voyaging"*—in other words, as evidence that he is not claiming "union" in the sense of some absolute mutual identity with God.

16. For the date and place of composition, see *R.G.,* no.33; the long list of manuscripts there may likewise reflect the relatively accessible character of this short work. Page references are to the Arabic text in the *Rasâ'il* I, no.12, pp. 1-19. To facilitate reference by non-Arabists, citations of this text in the notes below also mention the relevant sections from both of the following French and English translations. The complete English translation by R.T. Harris, *Journey to the Lord of Power* (London/New York, 1981), although without any annotation, does have the advantage of being accompanied by long and useful selections from Jîlî's commentary, which itself consists largely of citations (mostly unidentified in the translation) from related sections of the *Futûhât*. The concluding chapter of Chodkiewicz, *Sceau,* pp. 181-221, consists of a translation of most of the *R. al-Anwâr* accompanied by an extensive set of explanations and complementary developments drawn from many of Ibn 'Arabî's writings, including more particularly selections from the two Mi'râj-narratives (chapters 167 and 367 of the

Futûhât) discussed below. The first European translation of this text, by M. Asin Palacios, in *El Islam Cristianizado* (Madrid, 1931), was neither complete nor annotated. Asin's work is now also available in French translation, *L'Islam christianisé* (Paris, 1982), with the translation of *R. al-Anwâr* on pp. 321-32.

17. "The Treatise of Lights, Concerning the Secrets Bestowed on the Person in Spiritual Retreat *[sâhib khalwa]*." (Other titles are mentioned in *R.G.*, no. 33.) For the Sufi practice of spiritual retreat more generally, see the references in the article *"khalwa"* (by H. Landolt) in *EI²*. Chapters 78-79 of the *Futûhât* (II, 150-52), on the stations of *khalwa* and *tark al-khalwa*, involve a more metaphysical approach to the subject; see also the French translations of those chapters by M. Vâlsan, in *Etudes traditionnelles,* Paris, 1969, pp. 77-86.

18. These cosmological features are all most elaborately developed in chapter 167 of the *Futûhât* (described below). In particular, the *R. al-Anwâr* does not contain any of those personal encounters with the prophets symbolically associated with each sphere (or with each planet's respective "spiritual entity" *[rûhânîya]*, such as Mercury, Mars, Venus, etc.) that make up the major part of the Mi'râj-narrative in both chapters of the *Futûhât*, as well as in the corresponding section of the *K. al-Isrâ'*.

19. The extensive commentary by M. Chodkiewicz (*Sceau*, chapter X) provides important references to many other works of Ibn 'Arabî (especially sections of the *Futûhât*) further illustrating both of these key themes. (The latter point, in particular, is also stressed in a number of important sections of chapter 367 translated below.)

20. II 270-84; also available in French translation by S. Ruspoli, *L'alchimie du bonheur parfait,* Paris, 1981. An earlier partial French translation of this chapter, without notes or commentary, was also published by G. Anawati, in the *Revue de l'Institut Dominicain d'Études orientales du Caire, Mélanges* 6 (1959-61), pp. 353-86.

21. The best general survey of this difficult subject (although by no means complete) probably still remains the introduction (pp. 29-159) of H.S. Nyberg's *Kleinere Schriften des Ibn al-'Arabî*, based largely on Ibn 'Arabî's *K. Inshâ' al-Dawâ'ir.* Within the *Futûhât*, one of the most comprehensive treatments can be found in chapter 360 (III, 416-448), while the same themes are also developed in the earlier chapters 4-12 (I 98-149). A much briefer and more accessible account can also be found in the translation and introduction, by D. Gril, of Ibn 'Arabî's short *R. al-Ittihâd al-Kawnî (R. G.,* no. 317), entitled *Le Livre de l'Arbre et des Quatre Oiseaux,* Paris, 1984. See also the related cosmological chapters from the *Futûhât* translated by William Chittick in this anthology. This cosmological perspective accounts, in particular, for the many additional "levels" or "sites" marking the final phases of this Ascension in chapter 167—especially the third, purely "noetic" *(ma'nawî)* stage (II, 282-84; *Alchimie,* pp. 130-41)—which are not explicitly mentioned in the hadith concerning the *isrâ'.* These distinctions correspond to the initial, most abstract stages of Ibn 'Arabî's cosmological system, and in fact he even stresses there that the "rationalist" thinker accompanying the saint also participates to a considerable extent in the awareness of the universal metaphysical-cosmological principles perceived at that stage. In terms of their *spiritual* content, therefore, these stages do not constitute a "higher" or more "advanced" station than the cul-

minating revelation described in the final section of chapter 367 (IV-I below).

22. *Sâhib nazar*: the insights of this allegorical character (or psycho-spiritual "type") reflect features of several different "rational sciences" of Ibn 'Arabî's day, including *kalâm* (especially for its "negative theology" or *tanzîh* concerning the highest insights into the divine nature), the popular mixture of astrology (concerning, e.g., the particular influences and qualities of various planets) and Aristotelean-Ptolemaic astronomy, and even more "esoteric" sciences of the time, such as alchemy. (However, it should be stressed that the alchemical vocabulary used in this particular chapter is not at all mysterious; it is used here in a clearly spiritual, symbolic sense whose meanings—corresponding to familiar Sufi technical terminology—are copiously illustrated and explained elsewhere in Ibn 'Arabî's work.)

23. Such cross-references in the notes are concentrated on other chapters of the *Futûhât* and corresponding sections of the *Fusûs al-Hikam*, especially given the relatively greater accessibility of translations and commentaries of the latter.

24. Although all of section IV, the greater part of this chapter, is narrated in the "first person," that is often clearly a literary device in those cases where the prophets are explaining what readers can readily recognize as Ibn 'Arabî's own characteristic insights and perceptions. However, section IV-I clearly summarizes his own direct personal experiences of what were evidently—judging by his ensuing account of what was "seen" there—some of the most important stages on his own spiritual path.

25. Which, as he reminds us at the beginning of Section IV, closely parallels his earlier autobiographical descriptions of the same personal spiritual itinerary in the *Kitâb al-Isrâ'*; see our translation and commentary of a key corresponding passage from that work in the article cited at note 13 above.

26. III, pp. 340-54; sections omitted from our translation are clearly indicated in the accompanying notes or summarized (within brackets) in the body of the text. The enigmatic title of this chapter is partially illuminated by a brief passage near the end (III, 351.21-22), where this mysterious "fifth *tawakkul*" is again briefly mentioned as one of the distinctive forms of spiritual knowledge Ibn 'Arabî saw in his culminating vision of the "Muhammadan Station": "...*And I saw in it the knowledge of the person who acts deliberately and [at the same time] relies on God, and this is the fifth* tawakkul, *and it is [expressed in] God's saying in Sûra 73:'[... There is no god but Him,] so take Him as your Trustee (wakîl)!'"* (73:9). Elsewhere (chapter 198, II, p. 420, 36th *tawhîd*), Ibn 'Arabî explains this same Qur'anic verse as a reference to man's inherent ontological status as a pure "servant," with no possessions of his own, a description resembling the inner state of "pure servanthood" Ibn 'Arabî also realized in his culminating revelation (IV-I below). Similarly, a key phrase in this description, "to act deliberately" *(itta'ada)*, is applied in Ibn 'Arabî's cautionary advice earlier in chapter 367 (at note 143 below; III 349.13) to those Sufis who would mistakenly take the ecstatic state of "annihilation in God" *(fanâ'*, implying a heedlessness of the external world) to be the end and goal of the spiritual Path. All of these hints seem to point to this highest form of "trust in God" as reflecting an advanced inner state of spiritual insight in which the saint's absolute reliance on God—an attitude that in lower stages of *tawakkul* is usually conceived of as implying a sort of ascetic disdain and unconcern

for the "secondary causes" *(asbâb)* or things of this world—is now seen as simultaneously "affirming the secondary causes" (a phrase from opening poem of this chapter, at III 340.15), which are finally perceived in their true metaphysical status, as necessary and intrinsic manifestations of the ever-present divine Reality. This form of *tawakkul* would thus closely correspond to Ibn 'Arabî's characteristic emphasis on the superiority of the state of "enlightened abiding" in the world *(baqâ')* characterizing those saints who—like the Prophet—have "returned" (the *râji'ûn*) from the station of divine Proximity while retaining the ongoing realization of that insight in the world. The term *tawakkul*, "trust" or "inner confidence" in God, occurs many times in the Qur'an and gradually became a key term in Sufi spiritual psychology; see, for example, chapter 118 of the *Futûhât* (II 199-201), on the *maqâm al-tawakkul*, where Ibn 'Arabî mentions at the end that *"the levels of tawakkul, for the true Knowers, are 487..."* Near the beginning of the *R. al-Anwâr* (Chodkiewicz, *Sceau*, p. 189; *Journey*, p. 30) he also discusses *tawakkul* as the last of the preparatory stages before the spiritual Mi'râj, marked by four distinctive "charismatic powers" *(karâmât)*.

27. This famous Qur'anic verse, with its paradoxical "double negations" (corresponding to the *shahâda*) of God's "resemblance" to created things, is usually treated by Ibn 'Arabî as a classic reference to the mystery of the simultaneous immanence *(tashbîh)* and transcendence *(tanzîh)* of the Divine Reality reflected in the Perfect Man which is the central intuition of all his work. Often he even interprets the expression *"His Likeness"* in this verse as a direct reference to the Perfect Man, alluding to Adam's creation (according to a famous hadith) "in the image of the Merciful": see the famous discussions of this verse in the chapters on Noah (chapter 3) and Hûd (chapter 10) in the *Fusûs al-Hikam,* and further references in the *Futûhât* I 62, 97, 111, 220; II, 129, 510, 516-17, 541, 563; III 109, 165, 266, 282, 340, 412, 492; IV 135, 141, 306, 311, 431. In addition to the ambiguity of the expression *kamithlihi* (which can also be read simply as "like Him"—i.e., like *God*), Ibn 'Arabî likewise stresses the apparently paradoxical contrast between the absolute insistence on divine transcendence at the beginning of this verse and the apparent anthropomorphism of its conclusion. Thus, according to either reading, the absolute universality of the divine Presence implied by this verse includes all the particular, "restricted" modalities of the divine "descent" *(nuzûl)* and Self-manifestation indicated in the following verses and hadith—each of which is likewise the subject of numerous discussions throughout the *Futûhât*.

28. For Ibn 'Arabî, this verse is simply a direct implication of the broader truth implied in the opening verse: this inner correspondence between the different manifestations of God and the Perfect Man *(al-Insân al-Kâmil)*, at all the levels of being (or "worlds"), is assumed throughout the rest of this chapter. More generally, the reality of the divine "compresence" *(ma'îya,* "witness") with all things expressed in this verse, is discussed in many parts of the *Futûhât*, including a number of the shorter metaphysical or cosmological excerpts included in this anthology.

29. A reference to a famous "divine saying" *(hadîth qudsî)* which Ibn 'Arabî included in his own collection of such hadith, the *Mishkât al-Anwâr* (no. 56 [cited from the *Sahîh* of Muslim]; *Niche*, pp. 86-87): *"Our Lord descends every night to the heaven of this world when the last third of the night remains, and then He says: 'I am the King! Whoever calls on Me, I answer him. Whoever asks [some-*

thing] of Me, I give to him. Whoever requests My forgiveness, I forgive him.'" (This hadith is recorded, with a number of minor variations, by Muslim, Mâlik, Bukhârî, Tirmidhî, Ibn Mâja, and Ahmad b. Hanbal: see detailed references and variants in Graham, *Divine Word and Prophetic Word in Early Islam,* Paris/the Hague, 1977, [subsequently abbreviated as *"Word"*], pp. 177-78.)As Ibn 'Arabî explains in detail in the latter part of chapter 34 of the *Futûhât* (O.Y. ed., III 320-32), the "night," in this hadith, *"is the place of the descent in time of God and His Attribute"* (of Mercy), and this "last third of the night"—which, Ibn 'Arabî insists, lasts *forever*—is none other than the Perfect Man (the first two "thirds" being "the heavens and the earth," man's "two parents"). The following verses and hadith (at notes 30-32 here) are interpreted in chapter 34 as references to different ontological degrees or "moments" of that universal divine Self-manifestation.

30. There are seven Qur'anic verses referring to God's being "mounted *(istawâ')* on the Throne", often following "the creation of the heavens and the earth" (i.e., what lies "beneath" or constitutes the Throne in its cosmological sense). For Ibn 'Arabî's understanding of these verses, see the extensive references to the *Futûhât* in Hakim, *Mu'jam,* pp. 791-803 (on the many meanings of the divine "Throne," *'arsh*) and pp. 622-29 (on *istiwâ'*). For Ibn 'Arabî, however, an even more fundamental meaning of the "Throne" is "the Heart of the man of true faith" (which is "the Throne of the Merciful", according to a famous hadith), i.e., the Perfect Man (see Hakim, *Mu'jam,* pp. 916-21, on the *qalb*). The inner connection between these two senses is brought out explicitly in the famous *hadîth qudsî* discussed at note 7 above and quoted at note 37 below, and is a basic assumption throughout sections III and IV below, since the "Heart" is precisely the "theater" of the entire journey: that point is made most forcefully in sections IV-G and IV-I below. Elsewhere (e.g., in chapter 34, O.Y. ed., III 320ff.), Ibn 'Arabî frequently stresses the particular importance of the Qur'anic specification (at 5:20) that it is "the Merciful" *(al-Rahmân),* the Source of all being, Who is "mounted" or "seated" there.

31. A reference to the following hadith, concerning the Prophet's response to the question "Where was our Lord before He created the creation?": *"He was in a Cloud* ['amâ'], *without air above it and without air below it, and He created His Throne upon the Water."* (This famous hadith is found in the collections of Ibn Mâja, Tirmidhî and Ahmad b. Hanbal.) Our translation here reflects Ibn 'Arabî's interpretation in chapter 34 of the *Futûhât* (O.Y. ed., III 323ff.), where he also stresses the fact that this particular ontological reality concerns the divine Name "Lord" *(rabb)*—and not "the Merciful" (see note 30). For the broader meaning of the term *'amâ'* ("the Cloud") in Ibn 'Arabî, see the references in Hakim, *Mu'jam,* pp. 820-26 and in the *Futûhât* II 310, as well as its treatment in the penultimate stage of the cosmological *mi'râj* in chapter 167 *(Alchimie,* pp. 138-40).

32. This phrase is contained (with minor variations) in a number of other Qur'anic verses (3:5; 10:61; 14:38; 22:70) all insisting on God's intimate acquaintance with all things: see, for example, *"Our Lord, surely You know what we say openly and what we hide: not a thing upon the earth and in heaven is hidden from God"* (Qur'an 14:38); or even more appropriately, *"He is God in the heavens and upon the earth; he knows your secret* [sirr] *and what you proclaim, and He knows what you gain"* (Qur'an 6:3).

33. Ibn 'Arabî's understanding of the divine "nearness" (see the related notion of

"withness," *ma'îya*, at note 28 above) expressed in this Qur'anic phrase is intimately bound up with the reality of "perpetual creation" *(khalq jadîd)* expressed in the rest of the verse and its immediate context: *"… yet they are in confusion about the [ever] renewed creation; but surely We created man* [al-insân] *and We know what his soul insinuates to him and We are closer to man than his jugular vein"* (Qur'an 50:15-16). As indicated in the Introduction, for Ibn 'Arabî the spiritual "station of Proximity" *(maqâm al-qurba),* in which one actually realizes the full extent of this intimate relation with God, is the ultimate goal of the Ascension of the saints outlined in this chapter: that relation is outlined schematically, in the theological language of *'ilm al-kalâm,* in section III and discussed in more experiential terms in the final two parts of section IV. (See the extensive references in Hakim, *Mu'jam,* pp. 936-40 and Chodkiewicz, *Sceau,* index s.v. *[maqâm al-qurba].*)

34. While Ibn 'Arabî is alluding in particular to the "reason" for the Prophet's Ascension described at Qur'an 17:1 (see following note), the same phrase (with only minor variations in the pronouns) is addressed to mankind more generally in a number of other Qur'anic verses (27:93; 31:31, etc.). Of these, certainly the most important and best known is the verse 41:53—to such an extent that it is clearly assumed whenever Ibn 'Arabî mentions the divine "Signs" *(âyât): "We shall cause them to see Our Signs on the horizons and in their souls, so that it becomes clear to them that He is the Truly Real* [al-Haqq]—*or is your Lord not enough, for surely He is witnessing every thing! What, are they in doubt about meeting their Lord? Does He not surely encompass all things?"* Especially important, for Ibn 'Arabî as for so many other Islamic thinkers, is the insistence in this verse on the coincidence of the Signs "on the horizons," i.e., in the external world (but note also Muhammad's decisive revelation at the *"Loftiest Horizon,"* Qur'an 53:7) and those "in the souls," in the totality of awareness of the "Perfect Man" *(al-insân al-kâmil).* Secondly, Ibn 'Arabî always emphasizes the *causative,* active meaning of the verb form *'Arâ* as to *make* someone see," not just "to show": for him, God's "Signs" are *already* there, in the totality of our experience, but usually "unseen" *(ghâba)*—i.e., not perceived as such. Thus the whole purpose of the spiritual journey is simply to open our (spiritual) eyes to the reality of "things" as Signs, or as Ibn 'Arabî goes on to explain immediately below (and in more detail in section III), to recognize the divine Names "in *our* states." All this is implicit in the famous prayer of the Prophet likewise assumed throughout this chapter: *"Oh my God, cause us to see things as they really are!"*

35. The *masjid al-harâm* ("Sacred Place of Worship") was a common name for the sanctuary of the Ka'ba at Mecca, but there is some disagreement in the hadith surrounding the identification of the *masjid al-aqsâ:* it was sometimes, especially in later traditions, identified with the site of the Temple at Jerusalem *(al-bayt al-maqdis,* "the sacred House") where Muhammad stops to pray before his heavenly ascension according to several hadith accounts (including that followed by Ibn 'Arabî below); but the earlier traditions agree that it refers to the "furthest point" *(al-darâh)* or goal of the Mi'râj (i.e., where Muhammad received the culminating revelation described in Sûra 53), and is therefore more or less identical with the "Inhabited House" or heavenly Temple of Abraham *(al-bayt al-ma'mûr),* the symbol of the Heart discussed in section IV-H (notes 168-72) below. Ibn 'Arabî implicitly seems to follow the latter interpretation. See also the articles from the *SEI/EI[1]* cited in note

1 above. Throughout this chapter (and in the *K. al-Isrâ'*, etc.) Ibn 'Arabî generally uses the Qur'anic expression *isrâ'* to refer to the Prophet's ascension and its spiritual analogues—possibly because the term *mi'râj* might appear limited only to the "ascending" portion, whereas Ibn 'Arabî always is at pains (as in sections III and IV-F below, and at the end of his *R. al-Anwâr*) to emphasize the critical importance of the "descending" phase of return *(rujû')*, which distinguishes the highest rank of the saints (and of course the prophets). We have consistently translated *isrâ'* and its related verbal forms here as "journey," but it must be kept in mind that the Arabic term refers specifically to a *nocturnal* journey: for Ibn 'Arabî, especially, this nuance no doubt corresponds to the fact that the spiritual *isrâ'*, at least, is an inner, "secret" process largely hidden from outward observation, especially in those saints (the *afrâd* or *malâmîya*) who have followed it through to the end. In the *K. al-Isfâr 'an Natâ'ij al-Asfâr* (*Rasâ'il*, II, no.24), pp. 17-21, Ibn 'Arabî offers an elaborate interpretation of this same Qur'anic verse (17:1) focusing—as is typically the case in his reading of the Qur'an—on the complex inner significance of the grammatical and lexical details of its particular Arabic expressions, such as the apparent duplication of "at night" *(laylan)* and *'asrâ* (meaning "to cause to journey at night"), etc. Our translation cannot convey most of those nuances or alternative meanings.

36. Here, as so often with Ibn 'Arabî (see especially section III below), the pronouns are rather ambiguous; in this case the intended meaning is clarified by the following untranslated lines (III 340.25-30) which cite several other hadith and Qur'anic passages where God shows some of "His" creations to certain prophetic messengers in order to teach them a particular lesson. Here Ibn 'Arabî implicitly contrasts this *spiritual* journey of the saints (and ultimately of all men) through their inner "states"—i.e., the "Signs in your souls" of verse 41:53 (see notes 34 and 72)—with the physical (or possibly "imaginal") journey through *places* which, as he explains below (end of section II), was the exclusive privilege of the Prophet on this single occasion.

37. An allusion to the celebrated *hadîth qudsî* already mentioned at note 7 above: *"My earth does not encompass Me, nor does My heaven, but the heart of My servant, the man of true faith, does encompass Me."* This famous divine saying (not found in the canonical collections, but favored by many Sufi authors) is cited repeatedly by Ibn 'Arabî, who takes it as a classical reference to the role of the "Heart" (of the "Perfect Man," as realized by the accomplished saints) as the complete mirror of the divine *tajalliyât*. See the references at notes 30 and 33 above, and all of section IV-H (notes 167-73) below.

38. Although Ibn 'Arabî does not identify his hadith sources in this section or explicitly distinguish his "quotations" (or paraphrases) from his own more personal comments and explanations, the particular *hadîth al-isrâ'* (III 340.30) which he follows for the basic order of events and encounters up to the "Lotus-Tree of the Limit"—both here and in the other Mi'râj narratives discussed in the introduction—is the first one given in the corresponding section of Muslim's *Sahîh* (*îmân*, 259, from Anas b. Mâlik). Here and in his other Mi'râj narratives he adds many additional details (e.g., the four mystical "rivers" flowing from the Tree of Life, the sound of the divine "Pens," the milk and other drinks offered the Prophet) which are taken for the most part from the following related traditions in Muslim (*îmân*, 260-294)—although most of these hadith are also to be found in the other canonical collections

with minor variations in the order and description of the events. Here, for example (at III 341.12-14), Ibn 'Arabî explicitly mentions the fact (i.e., as an exception) when he refers to a particular hadith taken from Bukhârî. Relevant details concerning these particular hadith and Ibn 'Arabî's interpretation of them underlying individual events or locations during the Mi'râj are discussed in the notes to the corresponding parts of section IV below.

39. *Ithbât al-asbâb:* i.e., the affirmation of all the "realities" or phenomena other than God (the ultimate and Primary Cause). This assertion of the reality and importance of all phenomenal existence as perceived from the highest and most comprehensive spiritual perspective—a central leitmotif of Ibn 'Arabî's thought, and an attitude by no means shared by all Sufis—was already stressed in the title and opening line of the poem beginning this chapter, where he stresses that the true, ultimate state of *"tawakkul* (absolute trust and reliance on God) affirms the secondary causes." See the discussion of this point, in connection with the mysterious "fifth *tawakkul"* mentioned in the title of this chapter, at note 26 above.

40. The existence of those two groups on either side of Adam is mentioned in the second long Mi'râj hadith (from Abû Dharr) given by Muslim (*îmân,* 264); however, that hadith does not mention Muhammad's seeing *himself* there, so that this aspect may possibly be Ibn 'Arabî's own addition.

41. For the simultaneous presence of each soul—even if we are usually unaware of the fact—in its own Garden (or Hell) already during *"this* life", see the illustrative passages in this anthology (eschatology section) taken from chapter 302 (III 12-13) and chapter 73, question 62 (II 82). More generally, this experience of the simultaneous presence of one's essential individual reality (*'ayn:* translated as "precisely himself" in this passage) in different planes of being is only one illustration of Ibn 'Arabî's universal perception of the reality of all manifest being as theophanies (*tajalliyât, mazâhir,* etc.) of the "Realities" or Names within the divine Essence and of the "eternal individual entities" (*a'yân thâbita*) in the divine Knowledge—a conception for which he frequently uses this image of mirrors and reflections. See the famous metaphysical development of this image in the first two chapters of the *Fusûs al-Hikam;* in the *Futûhât* I 163 and IV 2; and further references in Hakim, *Mu'jam,* pp. 499-505, as well as the striking set of diagrammatic representations of these "mirrors" of God and man provided by Haydar Amulî in the introduction to his vast commentary on the *Fusûs al-Hikam, Nass al-Nusûs ("Le texte des textes"),* ed. H. Corbin and O. Yahya, Tehran/Paris, 1975, plates 3-30.

42. The special role of Jesus in the beginning of Ibn 'Arabî's own spiritual path is alluded to repeatedly in the *Futûhât:"He was looking after us when we entered upon this Path we are following today"* (I 15.26); *"I returned [to God:* tubtu] *at the hands of Jesus"* (IV 77.30); *"Our return to this path was through good tidings* [mubashshira] *at the hand of Jesus, Moses and Muhammad"* (IV 172.13); and *"we found that station [of immediate spiritual 'feeding'] within ourselves and had the immediate experience* [dhawq] *of it at the beginning of our journeying, with the spiritual reality* [rûhânîya] *of Jesus"* (III 43.20-21). This may be connected with Ibn 'Arabî's mention that his own first Sufi shaykh, Abû al 'Abbâs 'Uraybî, was distinguished by his special spiritual relationship with Jesus (*'îsawî*): see references in the *Futûhât* at I 223; II 365; and III 539. In addition to the chapters of the *Futûhât* (chapters 20, 35-36, 195, etc.) and the *Fusûs* (chapter 15)

specifically devoted to Jesus, see more particularly the sections concerning Ibn 'Arabî's conception of Jesus' perennial spiritual function as the "Seal of *Universal* Sainthood," mirroring the Shaykh's own role as "the Seal of Muhammadan Sainthood." Those references are summarized in Chodkiewicz, *Sceau,* chapters V-IX.

43. This succinct phrase, whose implications Ibn 'Arabî expands in thousands of words here and in his other treatments of the Mi'râj, is all that is actually stated by the various hadith in regard to this ultimate stage of the Ascension; here they clearly echo the Qur'anic verse 53:10 *(awhâ...mâ awhâ)* concerning Muhammad's vision of one of *"the Greatest Signs"* at 53:18. "Revealed" here translates *wahy,* the highest form of divine "inspiration" distinguishing the prophetic messengers *(rusul).*

44. For Ibn 'Arabî's complementary treatment of this decisive question of man's "vision" *(ru'ya)* or contemplation of God—as differing only "qualitatively," but not in its "form," from the contents of his innermost "beliefs"—in an *eschatological* perspective, see the illustrative passage in this anthology from chapter 73, questions 67 and 71 (II 85-86).

45. It is not clear how Ibn 'Arabî means for the reader to reconcile this insistence (repeated at the beginning of section III below) on the "bodily" nature of this particular journey of the Prophet with his earlier statement in this chapter (at III 340.34) that *"Burâq is a mount from the* barzakh" (i.e., from the intermediate, imaginal world), as well his own frequent interpretation of the Prophet's visions as taking place on that plane of being. However, for Ibn 'Arabî, the events and perceptions taking place in the *barzakh* are also "bodily" and "sensible" in a certain respect. See also, in this regard, Ibn 'Arabî's pointed advice to his fellow spiritual voyagers (in section III below) not to mention the "way" in which one travels— which is likely to lead to controversy—but only what one has actually *seen,* which in itself remains beyond dispute.

46. We have not been able to locate a hadith source for this assertion. In any case, the relative proportions this implies do suggest the primary importance of the *spiritual* journey of each soul, which is the essential subject of the rest of this chapter (and of Ibn 'Arabî's other major treatments of the Mi'râj theme).

47. III 342.34-345.25; passages omitted from the translation are indicated and summarized as they occur.

48. *Isrâ'ât rûhânîya barzakhîya:* in the rest of this chapter the forms of *asrâ (isrâ',* etc.) are translated simply as "journey," without the adjective "nocturnal," which would be misleading (if taken literally) in English. As already noted above (note 35) Ibn 'Arabî's own usage in this context refers to the inward, "invisible" nature of these spiritual voyages (i.e., from the perspective of an external observer), not to the time they may occur.

49. I. e., the saints: for the central importance of Ibn 'Arabî's conception of the saints as "heirs" of the different prophets (and all of them ultimately as heirs of the "Muhammadan Reality," whose heritage encompasses all the earlier prophets), see Hakim, *Mu'jam,* pp. 1191-1201, Chodkiewicz, *Sceau,* chapters III and V, and of course the massive illustration of this theme throughout the *Fusûs al-Hikam.*

50. This phrase has two possible meanings: if it refers to the purely spiritual or noetic *(ma'nawî)* phases of the mystical journey symbolically surpassing even

the outermost celestial sphere, then this would roughly correspond to Ibn 'Arabî's enumeration of the forms of knowledge gained in his culminating vision, at the end of this chapter (IV-I), a stage which is described in more detail in Chapter 167 of the *Futûhât (Alchimie,* pp. 131-41) and in the *Kitâb al-Isrâ' (Rasâ'il* I, no.13, pp. 45ff.). Or if—as appears more likely here—it refers to what is spiritually "above" the *physical* spheres and planets (and therefore the intellectual sciences that can be deduced from their observation, as outlined in chapter 167), then Ibn 'Arabî is pointing to the entire "autobiographical" spiritual narrative in the *K. al-Isrâ'* and the rest of this chapter (section IV below).

51. *Kitâb al-Isrâ':* see the discussion of the autobiographical nature of this work in the introduction to this chapter (notes 12-15), the key passage describing Ibn 'Arabî's own culminating revelation translated in our *JAOS* article cited at note 13 above, and further cross-references at each stage of section IV below. This paragraph is followed by a short poem (III 343.6-17), not translated here, recapitulating the "order of the journey," i.e., the various symbolic stages (seven heavens, Lotus-tree of the Limit, divine Throne, etc.) found in virtually all of Ibn 'Arabî's versions of the Ascension.

52. "Modalities of their journey" *(masrâhum)* could also refer to their "point of departure," the "place" or "time" of the journey, the particular "route," etc. See section IV-F below, where Yahyâ (John the Baptist) explains to Ibn 'Arabî that each journey is different and "each traveler creates his own path." Elsewhere Ibn 'Arabî, often following earlier Sufi writers, offers a variety of typologies for the soul's spiritual voyage: e.g., the fivefold division of *sulûk* in chapter 189 (II 380-82); the classical "four journeys" *(asfâr);* or the more elaborate division into dozens of "stations," "stages," "meeting-places," etc., underlying the chapter divisions of the *Futûhât* as a whole. The key distinctions in such cases differ according to the particular focus and intentions of each section, and such categories therefore do not necessarily overlap in a systematic fashion. (Thus, for example, the three essential aspects of the saints' voyage "in God" described in this section seem to be treated as *separate* journeys in other contexts.)

53. *Hall tarkîbihim:* i.e., the process of "dissolution" or "disassembly" into its constituent elements (organic, mental, psychic and spiritual) of the original "composition" *(tarkîb)* constituting the psycho-social "self" *(dhât)* in the broadest sens—as opposed to the *sirr* (note 55), the "innermost reality" or "secret" that is the true essence of each individual. The terms "dissolving" *(tahlîl)* and "reintegration" *(tarkîb)* are drawn from a larger body of alchemical vocabulary which Ibn 'Arabî uses in this spiritual sense throughout the *Futûhât,* most notably in chapter 167 (see introduction above), on the "Alchemy of Happiness."

54. The term "world" *('âlam)* refers here to the different "levels of being" or ontological "planes" *(nash'ât, hadarât,* etc.) of divine manifestation; the "simple" ones being the purely noetic *('aqlî)* or spiritual Realities, while most phenomena are a "composite" *(murakkab)* involving some degree of materiality or manifest form in either the physical or intermediate, imaginal worlds.

55. Or "personal face" *(al-wajh al-khâss):* this key technical term of Ibn 'Arabî designates each creature's unique and unchanging inner "existentiating" relationship with God, prior to whatever knowledge or other transformations that may be acquired through its actions and "mediated" relationships in the course of life. (See

the extensive references from the *Futûhât* in Hakim, *Mu'jam,* pp. 1139-42.) The paradoxical relationship (of simultaneous identity and non-identity) between this "divine Mystery" or "secret" *(al-sirr al-ilâhî)* and the voyager's own innermost reality *(sirr)* is brought out more openly in the culminating stages of Ibn 'Arabî's own *mi'râj* recounted in section IV-I and in his description (from the *K. al-Isrâ'*) of a similar culminating experience of "unveiling" translated in our article cited at note 13 above.

56. *Hijâb al-sitr:* the "veil" *(sitr)* in this case seems to refer not to a further particular obstacle, but rather to all the forms of attachment and implicit idolatry *(shirk)* "dissolved" in the course of the traveler's ascension, which together blocked him from the realizing his inner relation to God (the "divine Mystery," *sirr,* mentioned in the preceding note). For further discussion of these central concepts in Ibn 'Arabî's thought, see Hakim, *Mu'jam,* pp. 561-662 *("sitr")* and 313-318 *("hijâb").*

57. *Huwa lâ huwa:* literally, "He [and] not-He"—a formula whose meaning is clarified in the following lines (summarized here). For Ibn 'Arabî, the term "servant" *('abd)* frequently has the special technical meaning—closely corresponding to its usage in certain Qur'anic passages—of those rare individuals among the saints (and prophets) who have fully realized their inner relation to their Creator, to the Reality encompassing all the divine Names, and who are therefore not unconsciously subject to the "lordship" of any other creatures. See especially the references to his decisive discovery of his own true nature as "pure servant" *('abd mahd)* at the culmination of his own spiritual ascension, in section IV-I (note 198) below, and the detailed discussion and further references in Hakim, *Mu'jam,* pp. 765-78.

58. Or "in him" (i.e., in the servant). The ambiguity is again probably intentional: as Ibn 'Arabî goes on to explain, this voyage is "in God" (i.e., consciously, not simply "ontologically"), but it is also "in the servant" insofar as he can only know the divine Names in their manifestation within himself, in his own states and experience. The description of this second stage of the spiritual journey of the saints resumes at III 344.4.

59. The classic summary of this inner "correspondence" of man, God and creation in Ibn 'Arabî (and including many of the hadith and Qur'anic verses he commonly cites to illustrate it), is to be found in the opening chapter (on Adam) of the *Fusûs al-Hikam* (I 48-58; *Bezels,* pp. 50-59); for readers without Arabic the version of T. Burckhardt *(La Sagesse des prophètes,* Paris, 1955), because of its helpful annotation, is probably still the most understandable translation of this extremely complex section.

60. Or "within *Him*": the pronoun here—in an essential ambiguity to be found throughout Ibn 'Arabî's writings—could equally be read as referring to God *(al-Haqq)* as well as to the "servant," given the profound connection (although not simple identity) between the two that becomes apparent at this advanced stage of spiritual realization (see notes 55, 58-59). "God," throughout this paragraph, translates *al-Haqq* ("the Truth"), i.e., the ultimate or absolute divine Reality encompassing—and at the same time transcending—all the particular "Names" through which It becomes known and manifest. The mention of man's being created "according to the form" *('alâ sûra)* or "in the image" of God is an allusion to the well-known hadith (with

evident Biblical parellels):"God created Adam in His image..." (The hadith is recorded by Bukhârî, Muslim and Ahmad b. Hanbal; see also Graham, *Word,* pp. 151-52.)

61. An allusion to the famous Qur'anic verse 7:180: *"For God's are the most beautiful Names, so call Him by them; and leave those who go astray with regard to His Names..."* Here Ibn 'Arabî evidently refers to the natural human tendency to become attached to the Names of divine Beauty *(jamâl)* while failing to come to terms with the manifestations of what the Sufis traditionally called the Names of divine "Majesty" or "Severity" *(jalâl).* At the very end of this chapter (III, 354.15-16), Ibn 'Arabî mentions that this insight into the ultimate Unity of the divine Reality "named" *(ahadîyat al-musammâ)* by each of the divine Names, constitutes one of the many kinds of knowledge he realized in the culminating stage of his own spiritual ascension. There (as also, e.g., in the *Fusûs,* chapters 4 and 21) he acknowledges the earlier development of this thesis in a work by the famous Andalusian Sufi Ibn Qasî (d. 546/1151), *Khal' al-Na'layn.* For Ibn 'Arabî's own long commentary on that work, see *R.G.* no.681 (II, pp. 463-64). The inner spiritual "verification" of that reality is one of the key features of the culminating realization described in section IV-I and in the corresponding passage from the *K. al-Isrâ'* translated and commented in our *JAOS* article cited at note 13 above.

62. "Colorings" translates *talwînât,* a traditional Sufi expression for all the constantly changing psychic states and conditions of every individual, equivalent to the incessant inner "transformations" *(taqallubât)* of the soul discussed in the following paragraph (note 65). As Ibn 'Arabî indicates here, the manifestations of the divine Names ultimately constitute all our experience aud reality. Hopefully this theological terminology, unfamiliar as it may be for most modern readers, will not obscure the universality of his metaphysical perspective.

63. An allusion to the famous Qur'anic verse 55:29: *"... Every Day He is [occupied] in an affair."* Ibn 'Arabî typically takes the term *sha'n* ("affair," "concern," etc.) in this verse to refer to the infinite particular aspects of the divine "Activity" at each instant in time: see, e.g., *Futûhât* II 77, 82, 218, 499; III 198, 224; and the further references in Hakim, *Mu'jam,* pp. 639-42.

64. The translation here omits a brief poem (III 344.8-11) illustrating this central theme of Ibn 'Arabî's thought and foreshadowing his own inner realization of this truth in the culminating vision described in section IV-I below.

65. "Transformations" *(taqallubât)—a* meaning which, for Ibn 'Arabî, underlies the Arabic term for the Heart *(qalb),* since these constantly renewed transformations of being ultimately constitute all our experience: see his classic exposition of this realization in the *Fusûs,* chapter 12 (on Shu'ayb and "the Wisdom of the Heart"), and further references in Hakim, *Mu'jam,* pp. 916-21. His mention here of the "states of the world" is an important reminder that these "transformations" and the divine activity of "ever-renewed creation" encompass *all* the forms of experience and perception—not just what we ordinarily consider "inner" or "spiritual" phenomena—and all the forms of manifest being. For the multiple meanings of the complex term *walî* (translated as "saint" here), see note 79 below.

66. This opening phrase could likewise be translated so as to "invert" this relationship (although that meaning is also implied, in any case, in the second half of the sentence): *"And that transformation is what is brought about in us by the essence of those Names."* In either case, this sentence aptly summarizes the rela-

tion of inherent "reciprocity" between God and the creatures (or the Names and their manifestations) which underlies Ibn 'Arabî's frequent and apparently paradoxical statements that God (and the Names) "need man" (in order to be manifest and known), or that the caused thing "causes its Cause."

67. The translation is uncertain. We have again omitted some further illustrations (III 344.20-24) of this metaphysical relationship between certain divine Names and their manifestations in our experience.

68. See note 53 and the accompanying text above for the meaning of the "self" *(dhât)* in question here and the preliminary process of its "dissolving" *(tahlîl)* into the various components of its "composite nature" *(tarkîb)* in each level ("world") of being. For further details on Ibn 'Arabî's understanding of this key category of *al-râji'ûn*—"those who have returned" to complete the full process of enlightenment by reintegrating all the descending levels of being in their true, divine context and reality—see chapter 45 of the *Futûhât* (I 250-53) [also available in the French translation by M. Vâlsan, *Etudes traditionnelles*, no. 307, 1953, pp. 120-39] and the detailed references in Chodkiewicz, *Sceau*, chapter VII.

69. That is, he is now fully aware of the divine Ground and the Names underlying each of those "things" in the world (or in his "self") which he had originally seen as a reality independent of God, and which had been temporarily "veiled" from his attention during the spiritual ascension; or in other words, he has become profoundly aware of *all* things as God's "Signs" (as indicated in Ibn 'Arabî's allusions to the famous Qur'anic verse 41:53, at notes 34 and 72).

70. This paragraph, opening with a phrase from the *hadîth al-isrâ'* (section II above), alludes to Ibn 'Arabî's reminder earlier in this chapter (III 342.27-33) of the sceptical, even hostile reaction of many Meccans to the Prophet's insistence on the physical, bodily nature of his nocturnal journey. (Those events are vividly recounted in Ibn Ishâq's *Sîra:* see pp. 182-84 in *The Life of Muhammad*, trans. A. Guillaume, Oxford, 1955.) It is also another allusion to Ibn 'Arabî's understanding (see notes 2 and 35 above) of the "hidden," spiritual character of this voyage of realization for the saints. In the *R. al-Anwâr* (*Rasâ'il*, p. 17; *Journey*, p. 59), Ibn 'Arabî explains that the fact that Muhammad—unlike, for example, Moses after his return from Mount Sinai—showed no outward signs of his Ascension and revelatory encounter with God is an indication of his superior spiritual state of "perfect realization," corresponding to the equivalent "invisibility" of the *afrâd* and *malâmîya* among the saints "who return," the *râji'ûn*.

71. The first phrase is clearly an allusion to the following verse (Qur'an 49:11): "*Oh you who have true faith, do not [let] a group make fun of a group who may well be better than them...*"; the second probably refers to the well-known words (from 59:2): "*... so draw a lesson, you who have [true] vision*"—the latter group (*'ûlû 'al-absâr*), for Ibn 'Arabî, clearly being the saints or people of true spiritual vision.

72. The continuation of this famous verse—underlining its universal metaphysical (or eschatological) dimension—is also assumed here: "*... until it becomes clear to them that He is the Truly Real [al-Haqq]—or is your Lord not enough, that He is Witness of every thing? Are they still in doubt about meeting their Lord? Is He not surrounding every thing?*" (See also the earlier allusions to this verse in section I above, at notes 34 and 36.)

73. *Al-'âlam:* literally, "(the people of) the world"; "(spiritual) journey" here, as

throughout this section, translates *isrâ'*, the term applied in the Qur'an to the Prophet's "nocturnal journey" (see note 35 above).

74. The Qur'an applies the same formula to man's usual lack of spiritual awareness in a number of different contexts (especially with regard to the eschatological realities), but this particular verse (Qur'an 23:56) seems to be most relevant here: *"We hurry to them with the good things, but no, they do not notice!"*

75. "Innermost being" (*sirr;* see note 55 above). "Inspired" here translates the verb *alhama*, a term that is much broader in meaning than the special divine "revelation" *(wahy)* characterizing the prophetic messengers, since here it evidently extends to the results of thinking *(fikr)* and "rational inquiry" *(nazar bi-l-'aql)*, as well as the fruits of spiritual practice and mystical experience (the "polishing of the soul") which are Ibn 'Arabî's primary focus here (see following note).

76. *Kashfan shuhûdan dhawqan wujûdan:* see the extensive references to Ibn 'Arabî's usage of each of these key terms in Hakim, *Mu'jam*, pp. 971-72 *(kashf)*, 654-67 (*shuhûd* and related forms), and 492-95 *(dhawq)*, as well as his discussions concerning the necessary role of this "direct experience" *(dhawq)* in his encounters with Joseph and Moses in section IV (notes 108 and 145) below.

77. I.e., instead of grasping the inner reality of God's symbols, those that already exist (and which ultimately constitute all reality). "(Ordinary) people" here translates *al-nâs*, a Qur'anic expression with much the same meaning here as *al-'âlam* (note 73) in the preceding sentences—i.e., everyone but the accomplished saints, the "Friends of God" discussed in the following paragraph. The phrase in quotation marks here (and in the various Qur'anic verses discussed below) could also be translated as "making up likenesses (or symbols) *of* God"—and that activity certainly accounts for an important part of Ibn 'Arabî's criticism. However, it gradually emerges from the subsequent discussion that the main focus of his critique here is man's natural (and more universal) tendency not to grasp and assimilate the "likenesses" (or "symbols," *amthâl*) contained in the divine revelation (in all its infinite forms and "Signs"), but rather to impose his own limiting conceptions and standards on God and the world.

78. Or "to (the meaning of) that *verse*": the individual verses of the Qur'an are traditionally referred to as the divine "Signs" *(âyât)* par excellence.

79. Or "those close to God," *awliyâ' Allâh:* the term *walî* (plural *awliyâ'*) has usually been translated here as "saint," but in this case Ibn 'Arabî is more clearly stressing the root sense of their special closeness or proximity to God—a meaning which is also brought out in the Qur'anic verses concerning these rare individuals *"who have no fear and are not sad,"* who have reached *"the ultimate Achievement" (al-fawz al-'azîm)*. (See also the more comprehensive discussion in Chodkiewicz, *Sceau*, chapters I and III.)

80. Although the phrase *"... God knows, but you do not know"* completes the Qur'anic verse (16:74) already quoted in the preceding paragraph, its more illuminating use in the other two verses evidently forms the background for this particular allusion: in Qur'an 3:66 it is applied to those who *"dispute concerning that of which they have no knowledge,"* and in verse 2:216 it follows the reminder that *"Perhaps you abhor something although it is good for you, and perhaps you love something and it is bad for you."*

81. In the remainder of this section (III 340.6-25), Ibn 'Arabî first insists on the

decisive importance of considering every single detail of expression in the revealed divine "likenesses" or symbols (which he illustrates here with reference to the famous Light-verse of the Qur'an, 24:35). This point, in his opinion, was rarely respected by those interpreters (*mutakallimûn*, philosophers, etc.) who relied on their own reasoning *(nazar)* to decipher the meaning of those symbols. He then goes on to stress the decisive differences between such "rationalist" approaches and the methods of the saints, who rely solely on inspired "unveiling" *(kashf)* and direct "witnessing" *(shuhûd)* of the divine intentions in those cases (see note 76 above).

82. III 435.26-35.

83. *Fî asmâ'ihi min asmâ'î:* a dense formula that summarizes Ibn 'Arabî's complex metaphysical understanding of the divine Names in their relation to each individual's experience, as outlined in the immediately preceding section. This relatively abstract formulation is made more explicit in his discussion of the Heart—of the Knower, but ultimately of each individual—as the true Temple or "House of God," in section IV-H (notes 168-72) below, and finds its ultimate confirmation in the revelatory personal experiences described in section IV-I.

84. *Imkânî*, referring to each creature's inner dependency on God (and the particular "lords" constituted by certain divine Names) for its very being and manifestation. In Ibn 'Arabî's description of the culminating revelation of his own universal, "Muhammadan Station" (III 350; section IV-I below), he says that God "took away (his) contingency," so that he could "realize the inner realities of all the divine Names." "Burâq" is the name of the Prophet's mysterious steed described in the hadith accounts of the *Mi'râj* and *Isrâ':* see the translation at note 39 above and Ibn 'Arabî's longer discussion of the "Burâq" of each of the prophetic Messengers in section II at III, 341.2-4 (passage not translated here), as well as the article *"Burâk"* (by R. Paret) in *EI².*

85. This brief passage (III 345.27-35) therefore symbolizes all the relevant dimensions both of the individual's natural "predisposition" *(isti'dâd)* and of his voluntary spiritual "work" that are actually necessary to overcome and escape the animal tendencies and attachments ordinarily flowing from his bodily/psychic nature. The experiential dimensions and practical presuppositions of this task of "purification" or "dissolution" of those attachments *(tahlîl:* see notes 52 and 67 above) are brought out much more explicitly in the longer opening passages of the *R. al-Anwâr* (see notes 16-19 above). In particular, Ibn 'Arabî describes there (Chodkiewicz, *Sceau*, pp. 193-94; *Journey*, pp. 36-39) the voyager's necessary passage through the mineral, vegetal and animal realms before he can begin the properly "human" *(insânî)* stage of this spiritual journey. The indispensable role of these "lower" dimensions of being in man's complete perfection—through which he surpasses even the angels (who lack this experience of the full range of existence)—is underlined in the vivid and partially autobiographical descriptions at the end of the chapter on Elias (no.22) in the *Fusûs al-Hikam* (I 186-87; *Bezels*, p. 185).

86. "Heaven," throughout these sections, translates *samâ',* a term referring both to the various concentric heavenly spheres universally assumed by the astronomical theories of the time (as well as the Qur'an and the hadith accounts of the Ascension) and—more importantly, for Ibn 'Arabî—to the spiritual or noetic realities (i.e., the *rûhânîyât* or *asrâr* of the various prophets named in the hadith) symbolically associated with each of those spheres. This meaning is therefore quite

different from the "gardens" *(jannât)* and other abodes of "Paradise" *(al-janna)* that together constitute what we ordinarily call "heaven" (as opposed to "hell").

87. *Nash'atî al-badanîya: nash'a,* literally "arising" or "appearing [in existence]", is one of Ibn 'Arabî's most common expressions (following the Qur'an 56:62, etc.) for the different "planes" or realms of being. As already mentioned in the Introduction, the purely spiritual (and nonphysical) nature of these "passages" (at least for the saints, unlike the special case of the Prophet; see text at notes 46 and 49 above)—which depend only symbolically on the astronomical theories of Ibn 'Arabî's time—is brought out quite explicitly in the other Mi'raj narrative in chapter 167 of the *Futûhât.* There *(Alchimie,* pp. 57-58), for example, this "departure" from the physical world is explicitly explained as the inner liberation from "domination by the carnal desires" *(hukm al-shahawât).*

88. III 345.1-20; the sections translated in full here correspond to lines 9-20 (omitting part of lines 14-15). While the *R. al-Anwâr* does not refer at all to Adam and his sphere, chapter 167 of the *Futûhât (Alchimie,* pp. 57-63) primarily deals with the cosmological functions of this sphere in the sublunar realm, matters which are also partially accessible to the "rationalist" thinker who accompanies the Prophet's "heir" in that voyage. However Ibn 'Arabî does allude there to fundamental spiritual points which are greatly elaborated in the *K. al-Isrâ'* and later on in this chapter (367): *1.* the fact that "Adam" teaches each person *only* those divine Names (and the spiritual knowledge flowing from them) that can be accepted by that individual's particular constitution or predisposition; and *2.* the fundamental importance of the "particular divine aspect" *(al-wajh al-khâss:* see note 55 above), the divine "mystery" *(sirr)* uniting each creature directly to God, which Ibn 'Arabî calls the "Elixir of the true Knowers" *(Iksîr al-'Ârifîn),* the secret of their inner knowledge of God (and of its particular limits for each individual). Ibn 'Arabî's important account of his revelatory experience at this stage in the *K. al-Isrâ' (Rasâ'il,* pp. 12-14)—which closely corresponds to the culminating section (IV-I) of this chapter 367 in the *Futûhât*—is translated and commented in our article cited at note 13 above.

89. Both of these points are listed among the different kinds of knowledge which Ibn 'Arabî "saw" during the culminating "revelation" described at the end of this chapter; see the translation of those particular points at the end of section IV-I below. (See also the related discussions of these issues and further references in our translated selections from chapters 73, 302, 351 and 369 in the eschatological section of this anthology.)

90. See the corresponding passage of the *hadîth al-isrâ'* in section II (at notes 40-41) above; according to the original hadith (only partially translated here), Muhammad first sees all the descendants of Adam divided among the blessed (literally, "the happy": *su'adâ'*) at his right hand and the "wretched" or "suffering ones" *(ashqiyâ')* on his left.

91. This phrase is quoted from a longer "divine saying," presupposed throughout this section, which Ibn 'Arabî included in his personal collection of *hadîth qudsî,* the *Mishkât al-Anwâr* (no. 24, where it is attributed to Tirmidhî; *Niche,* pp. 50-53). There God—having created Adam and sent him to greet the angels—shows Adam His two closed Hands, saying: "Choose whichever one of them you want," and Adam replies: "I choose the Right Hand of My Lord, although both Hands

of my Lord are right and blessed." "Then He opened (His Hand), and in It were Adam and his descendants..."

92. Ibn 'Arabî alludes here to his controversial conception, developed at length in the *Fusûs* (e.g., at the end of chapter 7 on Ismail) and in the eschatological sections of the *Futûhât*, that it is precisely the exclusive choice of certain limited "enjoyments" (whether bodily or imaginal), varying according to each person's predispositions and inner tendencies, that—by veiling him from the full awareness of God—ultimately constitutes each individual's "dwelling" *(maskan)* among the many levels of Hell. Thus it is only with the lifting of that veil of (spiritual) ignorance that the person becomes fully aware that what he considered "happiness" at the same time is both his suffering and his (potentially purifying) punishment. But Ibn 'Arabî also suggests (*Fusûs* I 94; *Bezels*, p. 110) that even for the "people of Gehenna who remain there eternally" (i.e., who are not ultimately redeemed through the intercession of their prophets), their "torment" *('adhâb)* will ultimately be made "sweet" *('idhâb)*. For the development of similar conceptions in the *Futûhât*, see, e.g., I 656; III 673; IV 248, 408; and further references in the eschatological section of this anthology.

93. *Al-'ard al-akbar:* the "Reviewing" or "Presentation" *('ard)* of souls and their actions mentioned in the Qur'an (11:18; 18:48, etc.) and elaborated in certain hadith was popularly understood as one of the "events" occurring when all souls are gathered together on the "Day" of Resurrection; see Ibn 'Arabî's brief summary of this particular stage of the Resurrection—formulated in relatively exoteric, popular terms—in chapter 64 of the *Futûhât* (I 307-17), on the "stages of the Resurrection" (O. Y. ed., IV, p. 466). Here—following Ibn 'Arabî's usual distinction between the "greater" (universal) and "lesser" (individual) Resurrection (see, e.g., chapter 369 [III 388-90] and Hakim, *Mu'jam*, pp. 945-46)—the "Greater Reviewing" evidently refers to the total, comprehensive process of all human actions and spiritual destinies (or at least those within one cosmic cycle) as viewed from the all-encompassing, metahistorical divine standpoint. That is why it can be perceived here, by the universal "Adam" who stands beyond time, as "already finished." The "lesser Reviewing" would then apparently be the same reality as perceived from the standpoint of an individual soul. The same distinction between the "lesser" (i.e., microcosmic) and "greater" (macrocosmic) "Hour," "Visit," "Gathering," etc., is developed in many of the eschatological readings (from chapters 73, 302, 351, etc.) in this anthology; see especially our general Introduction to those selections.

94. Or "that [His] sanctions be applied" *(iqâmat al-hudûd)*: the Qur'anic conception of the divine *hudûd* has two related senses—both equally important here—that cannot be adequately conveyed by a single English expression: they are both the divine "laws" or "limits" *and* the "sanctions" or "penalties" (primarily corporeal in this world, but in another form in the next) prescribed for their infringement. Although the two senses are apparently separated—for us—by the passage of time and other contingencies, they are in reality inseparable and indeed "simultaneous" from the comprehensive, divine perspective represented by Adam here.

95. *Hukm:* with regard to the divine Names, this term usually refers to their power or authority to become manifest in the various realms of being, and thus, by extension, to all their specific "influences" or "manifestations." (It is therefore translated as "influence" in the rest of this section.)

96. We have left this entire paragraph in quotes—even though much of it is clearly Ibn 'Arabî's own paraphrase, using his typical technical vocabulary—because the Arabic text does not clearly indicate where the direct quotation of Adam's words might end.

97. Or simply "in time" *(bi-l-zamân)*: *Zamân*—in its ordinary, popular usage (see the following note for references to Ibn 'Arabî's more complex personal understanding)—usually refers specifically to the "physical time" marked out by the motions of the cosmos and the heaveuly spheres. Judging from the context here—which apparently refers to the "Greater Resurrection" *(al-qiyâmat al-kubrâ)* encompassing all the souls of the universe—he may be alluding to a sort of cyclical reversion of the whole universe to its Source, therehy marking a cosmic "end of time." However, if the reference here is understood as applying to the "Lesser Resurrection" of each individual soul (see references at note 93), then the final phrase could he translated as *"in* time," with the period of fifty thousand years being that allotted for the perfection and purification (including punishment) of each *particular* soul. See the further discussion of these problems in our Introduction and notes to the eschatological selections in this anthology.

98. For some representative aspects of Ibn 'Arabî's complex understanding of"time" *(zamân)*, see chapter 12 on the cycles of esoteric and exoteric time, I 143-47 (O.Y. ed., II 342-45); chapter 59 on the time of the cosmos, I 290-92 (O.Y. ed., IV 330-40); chapter 390 on the inner meaning of time, III 546-550; and the further references in Hakim, *Mu'jam*, pp. 1253-54 (entry for "Day," *yawm*).

99. The "ignorance" involved in this almost universal attitude—an "ignorance" which, Ibn 'Arabî repeatedly stresses, is profoundly rooted in us and can only be overcome by an inner transformation involving both divine Grace and the spiritual efforts of the individual—is grounded in the implicit assumption that God (or the divine "Mercy," Being, etc.) is manifest only in certain specific phenomena or forms of experience.

100. For a brief but clear explanation of Ibn 'Arabî's central metaphysical conception of the divine Names as "relations" *(nisab)* whose reality only becomes manifest through the being of the created "individual entities" *(a'yân)*, see chapter 222 (R 516-18). See also the many further references in Hakim, *Mu'jam*, pp. 591-618 (on the divine "Names") and 506-13 (on the related concepts of each Name as "lord," *rabb* and *marbûb*).

101. This theme of the universality of the divine "Mercy" as the Source and ground of all Being—and therefore on a very different level from the other divine Names—is developed in more detail (along with most of the other topics of this section) in chapter 21 of the *Fusûs* (concerning Zachariah), and throughout the *Futûhât:* see the extensive references in Hakim, *Mu'jam*, pp. 521-28.

102. 111 346.20-347.20 (summarized here). See also the references to discussions of Jesus in the *Futûhât* (including his key role in Ibn 'Arabî's own entry into the spiritual path) at note 42 above. In the hadith concerning the Mi'râj (section II above), Muhammad encounters Yahyâ only in the *fifth* heaven, along with Aaron; that is where he also reappears later in this chapter (at the beginning of section IV-F). (He explains his special ability to travel through the intervening spheres in an untranslated passage at the end of this section.) Jesus and John are likewise

mentioned together in this second heaven in chapter 167 of the *Futûhât*. However, there is no further discussion of John in that section (*Alchimie*, pp. 63-72), which focuses instead on the miracles of Jesus and the life-giving powers of the divine Spirit more generally. The corresponding section of the *K. al-Isrâ'* (pp. 15-18) does not mention Yahyâ/John at all, but focuses instead on Jesus' role as the "Seal of (universal) Sainthood" and his descent with the Mahdi at the end of time (see explanations in Chodkiewicz, *Sceau,* chapter VII and index s.v.), as those are explained to the "voyager" by Mercury *(al-Kâtib).* That section also evokes (at p. 18) Ibn 'Arabî's own exceptional preparedness for the "Station of Perfection" *(maqâm al-kamâl).*

103. An allusion to Ibn 'Arabî's typical conception of the knowledge and powers of the saints as being "inherited" from the spiritual reality of one or more of the prophets (who are all encompassed by the "Muhammadan Reality"): see the extensive references in Chodkiewicz, *Sceau,* chapters IV and V, and Hakim, *Mu'jam,* pp. 1191-1202. The association between Jesus (and the second heaven) and the power of Life—in the sense both of spiritual knowledge and of physical or "animal" *(hayâwânî)* animation—is equally fundamental in the corresponding passages of chapter 167 and, in extremely allusive form, in the *K. al-Isrâ'* and the *R. al-Anwâr.* A more complete discussion of these questions, bringing out more clearly the primary importance, for Ibn 'Arabî, of the revivifying spiritual *knowledge* brought by the prophets, is to be found in the long chapter on Jesus (15) in the *Fusûs* (I, pp. 138-50; *Bezels,* pp. 174-86) together with chapter 20, on Yahyâ/John the Baptist.

104. The first of these is a famous *hadîth qudsî* (found in Bukhârî, Muslim, Ibn Mâja, Dârimi, and Ahmad b. Hanbal; see the analysis and translation in Graham, *Word,* pp. 202-03) concerning the "sacrifice of death," in the form of a spotted ram, on the Day of Resurrection. The Qur'anic verses explained here include 19:7, referring to the inner significance of Yahyâ's name ("he lives," in Arabic), "... *We did not give the name to anyone before him";* 19:12-15, on the special divine blessings granted him; and 3:39, concerning his spiritual purity or "chastity" *(hasûr:* the subject of an excursus on the unique condition of Mary) and the special condition of "righteousness" *(salâh)* he shares with Jesus and other prophets.

105. A subject to which Ibn 'Arabî alludes on a number of other occasions (e.g., in chapter 390, III 548, where he remarks that "God showed us a likeness of this" in the cases of Mary and Jesus, or Adam and Eve).

106. Chapter 15 (I pp. 138-50; *Bezels,* pp. 174-86): this chapter is almost exactly the same length as the concluding one on Muhammad, and the two are considerably longer than any other chapters of the *Fusûs.* See also the related chapters of the *Futûhât* cited at note 42 above.

107. III 347.20-348.11 (only lines 347.29-31 are fully translated here).

108. This insistence on the indispensable role of personal "direct experience" *(dhawq)* in a fully adequate appreciation of spiritual matters is also one of leitmotifs of Ibn 'Arabî's encounter with Moses (IV-G below).

109. This particular section lacks the references to the metaphysical principles of beauty, harmony and artistic inspiration (traditionally associated with both Joseph and Venus, the planet of this sphere) found in chapter 167 of the *Futûhât* (*Alchimie,* pp. 72-76), and it does not deal at all with the profound questions of

the nature of "Imagination" (both cosmic and human) and Joseph's special powers of spiritual interpretation *(ta'wîl)* that are the focus of the famous chapter 9 of the *Fusûs*. The corresponding section of the *K. al-Isrâ'* (pp. 18-21) also includes a brief dialogue with the allegorical figure of Venus *(al-zahrâ')*.

110. III 348.11-349.2; the sections translated below correspond to 348.14-21 and 348.24-35, with minor omissions. In Islamic tradition, especially in the popular "tales of the prophets" *(qisas al-anbiyâ')*, the figure of the prophet Idrîs, who is mentioned only briefly in the Qur'an (19:57-58 and 21:85-86), is closely associated (and often simply identified) with a number of prophetic or quasi-prophetic figures who are generally distinguished by the traits of supernatural longevity (or at least frequent historical "reappearances" in different forms). These different "facets" of Idrîs include: Enoch and Elias (the Qur'anic *Ilyâs*), each of whom is the subject of a chapter in the *Fusûs* (see notes 114-15 below); the threefold persona of "Hermes," father of many esoteric arts and sciences according to Hellenistic traditions that were widely integrated in Islamic culture; and even the mysterious initiatic figure of al-Khadir. (For the historical background and sources concerning each of these personages, see the respective articles in EI^2, volumes III and IV.)

111. In the corresponding encounter with Idrîs in the *Kitâb al-Isrâ'* (*Rasâ'il*, p. 21), Ibn 'Arabî is likewise greeted as "Master of the Saints" *(sayyid al-awliyâ')*.

112. For Ibn 'Arabî's understanding of Idrîs' position as the heavenly "Pole" *(qutb)* and summit of the perennial spiritual hierarchy—whose two "Imams" at that eternal level are Jesus and Ilyâs—see the references to the *Futûhât* and other works, and the explanations (including the relation of these figures to their successive terrestrial "deputies") in Chodkiewicz, *Sceau*, chapter VI, and in Hakim, *Mu'jam*, pp. 909-15 and 101-14. The *R. al-Anwâr*, at this point in the mystical ascension (see Chodkiewicz, *Sceau*, pp. 201-13; *Journey*, p. 43 at bottom), adds that all the preceding spheres belonged to the realm of the "Imam of the Left Hand," while "this is the place of the Heart," where "you will discover the degrees of the Pole."

113. *Al-kharq:* i.e., more strictly speaking, of any phenomena that appear to "break" the "accustomed order" *('âda)* of events in the world. The term is more general than the probative miracles *(mu'jizât)* performed for the prophetic messengers, and likewise distinct from the "wonders" or "blessings" *(karâmât)* that are among the charismatic powers attributable to the spiritual force or *himma* of certain saints. (See the additional references to these distinctions in Hakim, *Mu'jam*, pp. 961-71).

114. Alluding to the Qur'anic description of Idrîs' miraculous preservation from death (and its traditional elaborations, mentioned in the preceding notes): *"And mention Idrîs in the Book: he was a man of truth* [siddîq], *a prophet* [nabî], *and We raised him up to a lofty place"* (Qur'an 19:56-57). See also Ibn 'Arabî's considerably more detailed discussions of these verses in chapters 4 and 22 of the *Fusûs* (I 75-80 and 181-87; *Bezels*, pp. 82-89 and 230-34).

115. The meaning of this exchange, and of the outward, cosmic symbolism of Idrîs' supreme spiritual rank and function, is brought out in much greater detail in the long chapter 4 of the *Fusûs al-Hikam* concerning "Enoch" (who is there explicitly identified with Idrîs). Chapter 22 of the *Fusûs* likewise concerns "Elias who is Idrîs..." (opening sentence). There Ibn 'Arabî explains that Idrîs "who was a prophet before Noah," was first *raised to a lofty place* (Qur'an 19:57), but was

then sent down again to earth—in the form of the prophet Elias—to experience fully the divine "intimacy" with even the lowest (animal, mineral and vegetal) degrees of creation. The contrast between these two chapters of the *Fusûs* suggests that "Enoch" is associated in particular with the divine transcendence *(tanzîh)* and "Elias" with the equally essential aspect of divine immanence *(tashbîh)*—symbolizing the two indispensable aspects of Idrîs' *comprehensive* perfection in his spiritual function as Pole and his reality as "Heart" of the cosmos.

116. This term is ordinarily understood to refer to the outward "profession of divine Unity" ("there is no god but God...") contained in the *shahâda* (the "word of *tawhîd*" in the following sentence), but Idrîs understands it here in the far more profound sense of the *reality* of divine Unity—at once both transcendent and immanent—which is at the heart of Ibn 'Arabî's conception of the "Unity of Being" (see additional references in the following note). In the larger body of Islamic tradition the prophet Idrîs (like the figure of "Hermes" with whom he was often identified: see note 110 above) was known not for bringing a particular revealed divine Law *(sharî'a)*, but rather for his institution of the whole range of rational or "philosophic" arts and sciences (by no means simply the "hermetic" ones). Thus Ibn 'Arabî goes on to address him (in a sentence not translated here) as "founder of the (arts and sciences) of wisdom" *(wâdi' al-hikam)*.

117. I.e., the *reality* of *tawhîd* which—since it constitutes the very nature of Being and the primordial core of man's nature—is necessarily expressed in all the planes of manifestation and the corresponding degrees of spiritual realization. Ibn 'Arabî often refers (e.g., at I 405) to the Qur'anic statement *"Your Lord has decreed that you worship none but him..."* (Qur'an 17:23), taken as an expression of this universal metaphysical *reality* (as well as a command). See likewise his discussion of the underlying meaning of the traditional formula of *tawhîd* in the profession of faith (the "word" or "saying," *kalima*, of *tawhîd* in this sentence), in chapter 67 of the *Futûhât* (I, 325-29), and especially his subtle treatment of the 36 different Qur'anic expressions of *tawhîd*—in both their ontological and "subjective" spiritual dimensions—in chapter 198, *fasl* 9 (II 405-20; French translation by C.A. Gilis, *Le Coran et la fonction d'Hermês*, Paris, 1984). Further references can be found in Hakim, *Mu'jam*, pp. 1172-80.

118. Or "It": "Truly Real" *(al-Haqq)*, which could also be translated here simply as "the Truth" or "God"—since in this context the "ontological" and "theological" perspectives are virtually inseparable for Ibn 'Arabî. Similarly, "things said" *(maqâlât)* could also be translated here as (theological) "schools" or (religious) "denominations".

119. "Constitution" *(mizâj:* strictly speaking, the mixture of physical "temperaments" distinguishing each person) must be understood very broadly here to include all the factors—spiritual, social, psychic, etc. as well as physical—ultimately helping determine the distinctive outlook and understanding of each individual with regard to every aspect of reality (not just "theological" matters). Idrîs returns to elaborate this point in the latter half of this section.

120. Or "I saw" *(ra'aytu)*, if this is taken as an allusion to Ibn 'Arabî's visionary revelation of the unity of the prophets and their teachings within the "Reality of Muhammad" or the *"Qur'ân"* which he describes in section IV-I below (and in the key passage from the *K. al-Isrâ'* translated in our article cited at note 13 above).

121."Direct relationship" translates *'ill*, a term that can refer either to a blood relationship or to a pact or covenant (as in the Qur'an 9:8-10). In either case, the term here refers to the relation of immediate divine inspiration—in itself implying both "kinship" and covenant—that, for Ibn 'Arabî, distinguishes the spiritual state of the prophets and saints, as opposed to the fallible and often quite divergent results of man's ordinary "reasoning" or "inquiry" *(nazar)*.

122. I.e., such unanimous agreement—unlike the usual and expected state of disagreement among the "people of *nazar*" or individual reasoning (see preceding note)—points to the truth of their conclusion on that particular point. See the excellent summary discussion of the various kinds of inspired knowledge attained by the prophets and saints "beyond the stage of the intellect" *(warâ' tawr al-'aql)* in chapter 73, question 118 (II 114.14-28). There Ibn 'Arabî distinguishes between those realities that are rationally "impossible" (see following paragraph here)—but whose truth is nonetheless revealed by a "visionary incident" *(wâqi'a)*—and the far more extensive domain of knowledge "which cannot be (verbally) expressed" or spoken about, which is the realm of the "sciences of direct experience" *('ulûm al-adhwâq)*.

123. This last phrase is a paraphrase of a well-known *hadîth qudsî* (cited a number of times, with minor variations, by Bukhârî, Muslim, Tirmidhî, Ibn Mâja, Ahmad b. Hanbal, etc.; see Graham, *Word*, pp. 127-30), of which Ibn 'Arabî quotes two versions in his *Mishkât al-Anwâr* (no.13 and 27; *Niche*, pp. 36-37, 56-57): *"I am in accordance with what My servant supposes concerning Me, and I am present with him when he remembers* [root dh-k-r] *Me... "* For the broader metaphysical underpinnings of this saying in Ibn 'Arabî's thought, see the references scattered throughout the *Fusûs al-Hikam*, including his discussion of this hadith in the closing lines of that work (I 226; *Bezels*, pp. 283-84) and his development of the key notion of the "god created in beliefs," in the chapters on Shu'ayb (I 119-24; *Bezels*, pp. 148-53), on Elias/Idrîs (I 182-86; *Bezels*, pp. 230-34), on Zachariah (I 178; *Bezels*, pp. 224-25), and Aaron (I 194-96; *Bezels*, pp. 246-48).

124. This encounter is described in greater detail in chapter 390 of the *Futûhât* (devoted to the inner meaning of "time," *al-zamân*), in a passage (III 459.8-14) which clearly brings out the "visionary," dreamlike character of this particular experience: *"Now God caused me to see, in the way that the sleeper sees (in his dreams)—while I was going around the Ka'ba...."* There this mysterious "ancestor" also reminds Ibn 'Arabî of a hadith of the Prophet stating that "God created 100,000 Adams."

125. I.e., *dunyâ* ("this world") and *âkhira* (the "next world"): their etymology alludes both to the full ontological range of levels of Self-manifestation and to the reality—as Idrîs mentions explicitly later in this discussion—that their "closeness" (or the contrary) is relative to the perspective of each observer, since all are equally present with God.

126. *Ajâl:* this term is used many times in the Qur'an—often in close association with "the Hour" (see note 128 below)—to refer to the ultimate fate of men in general (e.g., in verses 6:2, 60, etc.), of "every community" (*umma*, a term which for Ibn 'Arabî encompasses every type of created being: at Qur'an 7:34; 10:49, etc.), or the motion of the sun and the moon (at Qur'an 31:29, etc.).

127. *Ma'a al-anfâs:* this is one of Ibn 'Arabî's most common expressions for the ever-renewed creation of the whole universe at every instant *(khalq*

jadîd/tajaddud al-khalq), a metaphysical reality which is only directly visible to the true Knowers and accomplished saints, as he explains in a famous section of the chapter on Shu'ayb in the *Fusûs al-Hikam* (I 124-26; *Bezels,* pp. 153-55). For some representative discussions of this recurrent theme in the *Futûhât,* see II 46, 208, 372, 384, 432, 471, 500, 554, 639, 653; III 127; and further references in Hakim, *Mu'jam,* pp. 429-33.

128. There are some 48 Qur'anic references to the "Hour" *(al-sâ'a)* and the many questions surrounding it (e.g., at 33:63; 79:42), as well as a vast body of hadith, especially concerning Its "conditions" or "signs" (*shurût,* a term mentioned in Ibn 'Arabî's following question here). Ibn 'Arabî frequently discusses these matters along lines already followed by many earlier Sufis, so the apparent naiveté of his questioning here is almost certainly a literary device. See especially our translation of his discussion in response to Tirmidhî's question (72) concerning the "Hour" in chapter 73 (II 82), in the eschatological part of this anthology.

129. "People" here translates *al-nâs,* a Qur'anic term which Ibn 'Arabî generally understands (e.g., at note 77 in section III above) as referring more particularly to the condition of "most people" or "ordinary people" (i.e., *al-'âmma*), as opposed to the enlightened state of the saints ("people of God," "true men," "true servants," etc.). On this specific point, see the translation of his remarks concerning the saints' visionary awareness of the *contemporary* presence of the "Hour," in chapter 73 (I 81-82) in the eschatological part of this anthology.

130. (Cf. the related treatment of *dunyâ* and *âkhira* at note 125 above.) "You" throughout this sentence is given in the *plural,* since Idrîs is referring to all of mankind (see "Adam" in Idrîs' previous explanation), and ultimately to the "Perfect Man": see the famous opening chapter on Adam (and the Perfect Man) in the *Fusûs al-Hikam,* as well as the extensive references to "Adam" (in this broader metaphysical sense) in Hakim, *Mu'jam,* pp. 53-60. Idrîs' essential message in this phrase, that man "carries this world *(al-dunyâ)* with him into the next," is among the many kinds of knowledge Ibn 'Arabî says he "saw" in his culminating revelation; that reference is translated at the end of section IV-I below.

131. Or possibly the (divine) "Command" *(al-'amr)*—in which case Ibn 'Arabî (through Idrîs) would be referring to the universal "existentiating Command" manifested in the ever-renewed creation of all beings: see the discussion of the technical meanings of this Qur'anic term in Hakim, *Mu'jam,* pp. 93-101.

132. *Mâ thamma:* i.e., in the manifest world or the world of bodies subject to these perpetual transformations? (The exact reference is unclear.)

133. The two Qur'anic expressions translated here as "what is right" *(sawâb)* and "error" *(khat'a)* originally refer respectively to hitting one's target or "getting it right" and to "missing" it: thus the usage of both terms here implies a focus on the *subject,* the person who is judging rightly or wrongly—not simply on an abstract logical question of the relations of truth and falsehood. In addition, *khat'a* (in its Qur'anic context) has strong overtones of *moral* error—i.e., "sin" or "trespass" (against the divine limits: see note 94)—so that the "ethical" (or religious) and "ontological" dimensions of Ibn 'Arabî's argument here are, as so often, intentionally intermingled.

134. I.e., of God (or the Truth and True Reality, *al-Haqq*) and of each individual creature. As Idrîs goes on to remind us, in reality there can only *be* what really

is (al-wujûd), the True Reality *(al-Haqq)*: in relation to that ontological Principle *(asl)*, "error" is necessarily "relative" and "accidental" *(idâfî)*—i.e., a necessarily subjective and partial perspective which is therefore close to "nonexistence" *('adam)*.

135. The larger context of this verse, however, suggests the extreme rarity of this awareness, as well as the "divine perspective" it assumes: *"On the Day when the Spirit and the angels stand in rows, they do not speak, except for whoever the Merciful permits, and he speaks what is right—that is the True Day* [al-yawm al-haqq]..."

136. In the final lines of this section, Idrîs reiterates some of the more familiar principles of Ibn 'Arabî's thought: that the world is created from the divine attribute of "Bounty" *(jûd)*; that the world and man all "return" to that divine Mercy which "encompasses all things" and gives them being; and that the knower (i.e., the Perfect Man) is even "more prodigious" *(a'zam)* than whatever in the world may be known—a point that was already stressed in section III above (at note 59).

137. III 349.2-15 (the few minor omissions in this translation are indicated in the accompanying notes). It is noteworthy that the topics discussed here are not mentioned at all in Ibn 'Arabî's parallel versions of the mystical Ascension. The brief corresponding sections of the Mi'râj narratives in both the *K. al-Isrâ'* (pp. 23-24) and the *R. al-Anwâr* (see Chodkiewicz, *Sceau*, p. 205; *Journey*, p. 44) allude mainly to the "martial" qualities of anger, discord, etc. traditionally associated with Mars, the planet and "spiritual entity" *(rûhânîya)* of this sphere. The account of this stage in chapter 167 of the *Futûhât (Alchimie*, pp. 78-79) is mainly devoted to Ibn 'Arabî's controversial interpretation of the "faith of Pharaoh" and the universality of the divine Mercy, topics which are discussed in even more detail in the chapters on Aaron and Moses in the *Fusûs al-Hikam* (I 191-213; *Bezels*, pp. 241-66).

138. *Al-wârith al-mukammal*—i.e., the saint who has fully combined the prophetic "inheritances" of *all* the Messengers, which are integrally contained in the "Muhammadan Reality"—still another allusion to Ibn 'Arabî's unique status as the "Seal of Muhammadan Sainthood." (See the similar greeting by Idrîs at the beginning of section IV-E, note 111 above.) For the central notion of the saints as "heirs" of the different prophets (and all ultimately as heirs of the "Muhammadan Reality"), see the references given in note 49 above.

139. I.e., Ibn 'Arabî's question (and implicit criticism) concerns the relative *evaluation* of that spiritual state, not the reality and importance of the experience of *fanâ'* (annihilation in God) itself. See his remarks in the following section (IV-G) on the necessity of *fanâ'* at a certain point on the path, in regard to Moses' initiatic "death" *(sa'aqa)* on Mount Sinai, and his use of a similar Arabic term *(afnâ)* in describing a decisive phase in his own spiritual development in the key passage from the *K. al-Isrâ'* (pp. 13-14) translated in our article cited at note 13 above. More generally, the contrast between the lower, "immature" state of those "Knowers" *('ârifûn)* who deny the reality of this world, and the station of the *wârithûn* (the true "heirs" of the prophets) who are always aware of God's theophanic Presence throughout this world, is a recurrent subject in the *K. al-Isrâ'*.

140. See the longer discussion of the inner meaning of this incident, from a very different standpoint (i.e., Moses' and Aaron's differing awareness of the divine

Mercy) at the beginning of the chapter on Aaron (24) in the *Fusûs* (I 191ff.; *Bezels,* pp. 243ff.).

141. *Kawnuhu:* the term *kawn* usually refers to the engendered, manifest state of being (translated as "existence" here), so the most obvious reference, given the preceding context, is to the external "world" or whole manifest "universe" *(al-'âlam)*. But as so frequently in Ibn 'Arabî, the pronouns in this verse could also be taken, without any ultimate contradiction, to refer either to God *(al-haqq,* the Truly Real) or even to the human "observer"—i.e., man in his ultimate reality as the "Perfect Man," which may well be what is indicated by "the perfect one" *(al-kâmil)* at the end.

142. The concluding, untranslated lines allude to the well-known dangers and illusions involved in taking the ecstatic experience of "extinction" *(fanâ')* of the self in contemplation of God as the ultimate goal and highest stage of the spiritual path, at least in this world. This caution, which is probably connected with the title of this chapter (see notes 26 and 39 above), is amplified and repeated in the following encounter with Moses (section IV-G), and it is also an important theme in the passage from the *K. al-Isrâ'* translated in our article cited at note 13 above. Although the subject of Aaron's remark is a constantly repeated theme in Ibn 'Arabî's writing, it should be stressed that those dangers and the ultimate superiority of the saints' subsequent "enlightened abiding" *(baqâ')* in the world, as exemplified above all in the life of Muhammad, were likewise stressed almost unanimously in earlier Sufi literature and practice. The intensity and centrality of Ibn 'Arabî's insistence on the realization of the nature and importance of this "world" as an essential aspect of human perfection *(kamâl)*—and indeed as the essential grounds of man's superiority to the angels and purely spiritual beings—can best be measured by comparing his writings to the familiar currents of "monistic" mysticism, such as the Sufism of Ibn 'Arabî's Andalusian contemporary, Ibn Sab'în. See, among others, the careful comparison of these two perspectives—which have their parallels in many other mystical traditions—in the translation and study of the *Épître sur l'Unicité Absolue (R. al-Ahadîya)* of Awhad al-Dîn Balyânî (a 13th-century Persian Sufi in the school of Ibn Sab'în) by M. Chodkiewicz, Paris, 1982.

143. III 349.16-350.5 (translated in full with exception of summarized passages at lines 16-20 and 23-25). The corresponding section in chapter 167 *(Alchimie,* pp. 89-97) also deals with "theophanic" nature of the world, but from a very different standpoint. In keeping with the more abstract, cosmological focus of that chapter, Ibn 'Arabî uses the Qur'anic account of the transformations of Moses' staff (Qur'an 20:17-21) to illustrate some of the basic principles of his ontology, especially the relation between the unchanging noetic "realities" *(haqâ'iq)* or "individual entities" *(a'yân)* and the constant transformations of the phenomenal world. In other words, it points to the objective "knowledge" underlying the focus on Moses' immediate *experience* of theophany in this chapter. The traveler's encounter with Moses in the *K. al-Isrâ' (Rasâ'il,* pp. 25-28), on the other hand, is devoted to entirely different subjects: Moses first stresses the differences between the *'ârif* (the "mystic" who publicly parades his spiritual discoveries) and the *wârith* (the Prophetic "heir" or true "Muhammadan," *al-muhammadî*), who "conceals his secrets" and who "sees (God's) Essence in his essence, His Attributes in his (own) attributes, and His Names in his (own) acts"—i.e., whose inner

Ascension corresponds to the particular type of "nocturnal" spiritual voyage *(isrâ')* Ibn 'Arabî described in section III above, that which is outwardly indistinguishable from the life of "ordinary people." In the *K. al-Isrâ'*, Moses goes on to summarize for the "voyager" the remaining stages to be encountered in his journey, with particular emphasis on the importance of the "descent," the *"return"* to life in this world, for the completion and perfection of that voyage.

144. This story is included in the long *hadîth al-isrâ'* (from Muslim: see note 38 above) given by Ibn 'Arabî at the beginning of this chapter (III 342.20-27, an untranslated part of section II); it also appears, with minor variations, in many of the other canonical hadith concerning the Mi'râj. According to this particular version, the prescription of *"fifty* prayers in each day and night" was "part of all that was divinely revealed" (by *wahy*) to the Prophet at the very summit of his Ascension, in his direct encounter with God. During Muhammad's descent back to earth, Moses—relying on his own immediate experience *(dhawq)* with his Community in this same matter—twice persuades the Prophet to return to God and plead for a lessening of this burden, so that the required number is reduced to ten and then five. On the second occasion the Lord says to Muhammad: "They are five and they are fifty: *with Me, the Word is not changed!*" (alluding to the Qur'an at 50:69).

145. Moses goes on to conclude this section by again stressing the decisive role of *dhawq*, the inner "tasting" of spiritual states, in the realizations of the prophets and saints. See Joseph's similar insistence on the indispensable, irreducible character of direct personal experience (as opposed to what can be gained by mental reflection or purely imaginative participation), at note 108 above. "Immediate contact" *(mubâshara:* literally "hands-on" experience) at the end of this sentence has essentially the same meaning as *dhawq*, since both refer to insights realizable only through a unique "spiritual state" *(hâl)*.

146. This interpretation of the Qur'anic verses (28:29ff.)—according to which Moses discovered the burning bush only "accidentally," while seeking fire to warm his family—is amplified in chapter 366 (III 336.16-25), where Ibn 'Arabî takes this incident as a symbol of the rare virtue of disinterested service which characterizes "all the just leaders *(Imams)*." There he also explains that this was exactly how Khadir first discovered the Source of eternal Life, while seeking water for his fellow soldiers.

147. Paraphrasing the following Qur'anic verse: *"God said: 'Oh Moses, surely I have chosen you over the people with My Message and My Word...'"* (Qur'an 7:144).

148. Referring to the Qur'anic verse 7:143, parts of which are quoted or paraphrased throughout the rest of this section: *"And when Moses came to Our appointed time and His Lord spoke to him, he said: 'My Lord, make me see, that I may look at You.' He said: 'You will not see Me, but look at the mountain: if it stays firmly in its place, then you will see Me?' So when His Lord manifested Himself to the mountain, He made it crushed flat, and Moses fell down stunned. Then when he awakened he said: 'I have returned to You, and I am the first of the men of true faith.'"*

149. A paraphrase of a well-known hadith recorded by both Muslim (*K. al-fitan*, no. 95) and Tirmidhî (*fitan*, no. 56); several of the canonical hadith collections

contain specific sections concerning the "vision of God" *(ru'yat Allâh)* in the next life. For Ibn 'Arabî's broader understanding of this question, both in the eschatological context and as prefigured in the divine vision of the prophets and saints—which follows from their initiatic "death" to this world and concomitant "resurrection" in the awareness of their eternal spiritual self—see, among others, the selections from chapter 302 (III 12-13), chapter 351 (III 223), chapter 369 (III 388-99), and chapter 73, questions 62, 67, 71 (II 82, 84, 86) translated in the eschatological section of this anthology.

150. Or "my (initiatic) 'death' *(sa'aqatî)*": in other Qur'anic verses referring to the Resurrection (see following note), the same root is used virtually as an equivalent of "death." Here, however, Ibn 'Arabî is evidently using this term—which in its root sense means literally being "thunderstruck," "struck dead by lightning" or "rendered senseless" by a loud noise—in a more technical sense, referring to the spiritual state of "extinction of the ego *(fanâ')* in the Self-manifestation *(tajallî)* of the divine Lordship." This definition is from his *K. Istilâhât al-Sûfîya* (item no. 131; p. 45 in the English translation by R. T. Harris, *Journal of the Muhyiddîn Ibn 'Arabî Society*, III, 1984); see also the more detailed discussion of his technical usage of this term in Hakim, *Mu'jam*, pp. 695-96.

151. In the untranslated lines (III 349.23-25), Ibn 'Arabî alludes to a saying of the Prophet expressing uncertainty as to whether Moses' mystical "death" or "stunning" *(sa'aqa:* explained in preceding note) exempted him from the similar fate which is promised more generally at the "blowing of the Trumpet" on the Day of Resurrection: *"... then those who are in the heavens and on the earth are thunderstruck* [sa'iqa], *except for whoever God wishes..."* (Qur'an 39:68); *"So leave them until they meet their Day, in which they will be thunderstruck* [yus'aqûn]*"* (Qur'an 52:45). Moses replies that he was indeed rewarded with the anticipatory experience of that "death" (and the concomitant "resurrection") on Mount Sinai. That event, for Ibn 'Arabî, clearly represents a more general stage and type of theophanic experience: Moses is cited as a symbol of this sort of spiritual realization throughout the Shaykh's many works.

152. The verb here *(raja'a)* is different from that in the immediately preceding Qur'anic verse *(tâba:* usually translated as "to repent," but with the root sense of "turning back" [to God]); the equation of these two terms—with its implicit stress on the metaphysical ground of all "repentance"—is to be found throughout Ibn 'Arabî's writings. See, for example, the similar equivalence of these two expressions in Ibn 'Arabî's accounts of the beginnings of his own "conversion" to the spiritual path ("at the hand of Jesus") at note 42 above.

153. Or "those who know *through* God" *(al-'ulamâ' bi-illâh)*, i.e., on the basis of what God teaches them (and not by their own reflection, *nazar)*, as Moses goes on to explain below. For Ibn 'Arabî, this expression usually refers to the very highest group of true spiritual "knowers"—i.e., the prophets and the saints, who alone are knowers of "God" (i.e., of *"Allâh,"* the comprehensive divine reality), and not simply of the "Lord" *(rabb)* manifested by one or more of the particular divine Names.

154. *Wujûb 'aqlî*: i.e., "necessary" according to his own knowledge and the conclusions of the intellect *('aql)* concerning the nature of the world—because, as he goes on to explain below, *all* "vision" is really vision of God, but without the crucial additional element of direct, first-hand experience *(dhawq)* essential to

this realization. This whole exchange therefore clarifies Ibn 'Arabî's earlier assertion (section II, at note 44 above) that Muhammad, at the culminating stage of his Ascension, *"saw* what he had *known* and nothing else; the form of his belief did not change."

155. *Mawtin,* a term that could be translated more literally as "home," "homeland" or even, in its Qur'anic context (9:25) as "(spiritual) battlefield": in Ibn 'Arabî's technical usage, it refers to the various "planes of being" in which man dwells and makes his home, all of which are present for the Perfect Man. In an important passage of the *R. al-Anwâr (Journey,* pp. 27 and 72-77 [commentary of 'Abd al-Karîm Jîlî, mainly quoting the *Futûhât];* Chodkiewicz, *Sceau,* pp. 185-86), the Shaykh explains that although these *mawâtin* are virtually infinite, "they are all derived from six": *1.* the primordial state of man's covenant *(mîthâq)* with God (Qur'an 7:172); *2.* "the (physical) world we are now in"; *3.* the *barzakh* or "intermediate" spiritual world "through which we travel after the lesser *and* greater deaths"; *4.* "the Resurrection on the earth of Awakening" (Qur'an 79:14); *5.* "the Garden and the Fire [of Hell]"; *6.* and the "Dune of Vision [of God]", which is evidently the "dwelling" that became present for Moses on Sinai. See our translation of many passages from the *Futûhât* dealing with the divine "Vision" in the eschatological section of this anthology.

156. Moses' exceptional use of the first person *plural* here and in some of the following sentences—since he otherwise uses the singular in discussing his own personal experiences—seems to refer to *all* the "Knowers of [or through] God" *(al-'ulamâ' bi-Allâh)* mentioned at note 153 above and the text at note 161 below.

157. The full Qur'anic verse apparently alluded to here (Qur'an 83:15) is as follows: *"But no, surely they are veiled from their Lord on that Day!"* The allusion could also extend to the numerous hadith concerning the "raising of veils" and "vision of God," including, among others, certain *hadîth qudsî* recorded in Ibn 'Arabî's *Mishkât al-Anwâr,* such as no.18 (from the *Sahîh* of Muslim) and no. 66 *(Niche,* pp. 41-43, 92-93). The metaphysical concept of "veil," for Ibn 'Arabî, almost always reflects an inherent amhiguity between the two simultaneous aspects of "concealment" and "revelation" (since the "veil" is in reality a theophany or manifestation of the divine): for him, the difference between the two aspects ultimately resides in the *viewer,* not in the "phenomenon" or form itself. In this regard it is noteworthy that among the spiritual realizations flowing from Ibn 'Arabî's culminating revelation enumerated at the end of this chapter is his seeing "that God is what is worshipped in every object of worship, from behind the veil of (each particular) form" (III 303.7; translated at the end of section IV-I below). See also at note 123 above the references (from the *Fusûs al-Hikam*) to the related question of "the god created in beliefs," and further passages cited in Hakim, *Mu'jam,* pp. 313-18 *("hijâb").*

158. *Al-Haqq,* which could equally be translated as "the Truth" or simply "God." This phrase is close in form to the celebrated Sufi saying, sometimes considered a hadith of the Prophet and sometimes attributed to the Imam 'Alî b. Abî Tâlib: "People are sleeping; when they die, they wake up." Like the rest of this section, it also clearly recalls the famous Prophetic injunction to "Die before you die!"

159. See note 155 above on the meaning of *mawtin.* Here Ibn 'Arabî is almost certainly referring to the "dwelling" in Paradise of the "Dune of Vision [of God]"

(kathîb al-ru'ya) mentioned in a famous *hadîth qudsî,* which he discusses at length in chapter 65 (II 317-22) and elsewhere in the *Futûhât*. (See our translations of many of those passages concerning the "Day of the Visit" in the eschatological section of this anthology.)

160. Ibn 'Arabî's favorite scriptural reference to this reality—which for him is also clearly applicable to man's capacity (or incapacity) for "theophanic vision" already in this world—is a famous hadith concerning the testing of mankind with regard to their forms of belief *(ma'bûdât)* on the Day of the Gathering, often known as the "hadith of the transformations."According to this account, God will present Himself to this (Muslim) community "in a form other than what they know, and will say to them:'I am your Lord'"; but the "hypocrites" among them will fail to recognize Him until He appears in the form they already knew (according to their beliefs in this world). The most pertinent section of this hadith is recorded in the *Mishkât al-Anwâr* (no. 26; *Niche,* pp. 55-57), where Ibn 'Arabî gives the *isnâd* from the *Sahîh* of Muslim.The full hadith, which deals with the Prophet's answers to several questions concerning the "vision of God," is also recorded twice by Bukhârî; see further references in Graham, *Word,* pp. 133-34. For some of Ibn 'Arabî's representative discussions of this hadith in the *Futûhât,* see I 112, 305, 328, 331, 353, 377; II 40, 81, 277, 298, 311, 333, 495, 508, 590, 610; III 25, 44, 48, 73, 101, 289, 301, 315, 485, 536; and IV 245. (It is also presupposed in most of the sections of the *Fusûs al-Hikam* concerning the "god created in beliefs" cited in note 123 above.)

161. *Al-kawn:* the term can also refer by extension to "the people of this world"(which appears to be the main reference here), although Ibn 'Arabî may also be referring more broadly to his familiar critiques of exclusive reliance on limited human "reasoning" *(nazar)* about the manifest world. For the "Knowers of (or 'through') God", see notes 153 and 156 above.

162. I.e., what Ibn 'Arabî has just claimed (concerning the "divine control"over his own spiritual progress) is ultimately true for everyone—without in any way removing the need for each individual's best efforts. What Moses goes on to explain about the different capacities of each person for understanding and assimilating the teachings of the prophets and Messengers is only one illustration of this crucial insight.

163.The phrase "by means of us" in this sentence is an allusion to Ibn 'Arabî's assumption that the greatest part of the knowledge of the saints is gained "indirectly," through their spiritual participation in the manifold "heritages" of divine Knowledge received directly by each of the prophets and Messengers. See his careful explanation of this mediating relationship of the prophets and saints in chapter 14 of the *Futûhât* (I 149-152; O.Y,. ed., II 357-62) and the many additional references in Chodkiewicz, *Sceau,* chapters IV and V.

164. Here Ibn 'Arabî intentionally uses a verb *(intasaba)* usually employed to describe someone's "joining" or "belonging to" a particular religious (or legal, political, etc.) school, party or sect.The root sense of the verb—also quite appropriate here—refers to a person's kinship relation of ancestral allegiance and descent, his *nasab*. Thus the final phrase could also be translated as "join Him" or "take your lineage [directly] from Him."

165. Alluding to Qur'an 4:164: *"... and God spoke to Moses with Speech."* For

Ibn 'Arabî's understanding of the possible apprehension of the divine revelation *(wahy)* through "hearing" and any of the other senses, see the beginning of chapter 14 (I 149ff.; O.Y., ed., III, pp. 357ff.), as well as the discussion of the various modalities of prophetic inspiration in our translation of chapter 366, III 332. (See also the related hadith discussed in the following note.)

166. This whole passage is an allusion to the famous *hadîth al-nawâfil* (the "supererogatory acts" of devotion), which is perhaps the "divine saying" most frequently cited both by Ibn 'Arabî and by Sûfi writers more generally: it is recorded in the canonical collection of Bukhârî (*Riqâq*, 38) and included in Ibn 'Arabî's own collection of *hadîth qudsî*, the *Mishkât al-Anwâr* (no. 91; *Niche*, pp. 118-21). (See also the full text and translation and further references in Graham, *Word*, pp. 173-74.) The relevant section (and that most often alluded to by Sufi authors) is as follows: *"...And My servant continues to draw near to Me through the supererogatory works [of devotion] until I love him. Then when I love him I am his hearing with which he hears, and his sight with which he sees, and his hand with which he grasps, and his foot with which he walks. And if he asks Me [for something], I surely give [it] to him; and if he seeks My aid, surely I help him..."* For some of Ibn 'Arabî's discussions of this hadith in the *Futûhât*, which usually bring out his understanding of it as alluding to the individual realization of an underlying universal condition, see I 203, 406; II 65, 124, 126, 298, 326, 381, 487, 502, 513, 559, 563, 614; III 63, 67, 143, 189, 298; and IV 20, 24, 30, 312, 321, 449.

167. III 350.5-20 (only lines 18-20 are translated in full here).

168. In the corresponding part of chapter 167 (*Alchimie*, pp. 97-107), Abraham advises the "follower" (of Muhammad) to "make your heart like this House, by being present with God *(al-Haqq)* at every moment". Ibn 'Arabî's understanding of the nature of the Heart as a mirror of the Truly Real in all of its states is emphasized in that chapter by his use of the famous Sufi parable—almost certainly borrowed here (but without acknowledgement) from Ghazâlî's *Mîzân al-'Amal*, and most famous in the form of the tale of the "Greek and Chinese artists" at the beginning of Rumi's *Masnavî—of* the royal "contest" between a marvelous artist (whose painting is the world) and a sage whose polished "mirror" (the soul of true Knower) reflects both that painting and the "artists" and "king" (i.e., the metaphysical world and each individual's "particular relation" to God) as well. The lengthy corresponding section of the *K. al-Isrâ'* (pp. 28-34) is far too rich and complex to be summarized here. There, after evoking the highest stages of the nocturnal journey of Muhammad and the true Knowers (pp. 29-30), Ibn 'Arabî makes the entry into this celestial "House" dependent on attainment of the highest spiritual station, the "Station of Yathrib" (see Qur'an 32:13 and *Futûhât*, III 177, 216, 500, etc.) or the "Station of no Station," in which the Heart is perfectly open to every form of theophany, in a state of selfless "bewilderment" *(hayra)*. See chapter 50 on the "men of *hayra*" (I 270-72) and the further extensive references in Hakim, *Mu'jam*, pp. 1245 *(Yathribî)* and 357-63 *(hayra)*. Since for Ibn 'Arabî this is precisely the "Muhammadan Station" (discussed here in section IV-I below), the rest of this passage in the *K. al-Isrâ'* (pp. 30-31) alternates between the voyager's own moving poetic descriptions of that decisive spiritual realization—whose attainment is assumed throughout that work—and Abraham's praises of Muhammad and reminders of the many forms of superiority of those who have

been granted that supreme attainment. These comparisons of other prophets or saints with Muhammad (for example at p. 33) could also highlight the essential contrast between the conditions of those who must "work" their way gradually toward spiritual perfection, drawn by divine love *(mahabba),* and the much rarer state of those who—like Ibn 'Arabî himself—benefit from the unique grace of divine "preference" *(îthâr),* who are suddenly "pulled" *(majdhûb)* by God into the highest stages of realization.

169. *Al-Bayt al-ma'mûr:* the "inhabitants" of this mysterious celestial site—often identified with the "Furthest Place of Worship" *(al-masjid al-aqsâ)* mentioned in the Qur'an as the culmination of the Prophet's nocturnal voyage (Qur'an 17:1), although the indications in the hadith themselves are very limited—are apparently the angels mentioned in the various hadith (see following note). Its location "with Abraham," mentioned in several hadith outlining the *Mi'râj* (including the *hadîth al-isrâ'* from Muslim cited here by Ibn 'Arabî, at III 341.29-34),seems connected with his role as builder of the Ka'ba, the earthly Temple *(al-bayt).* For Ibn 'Arabî's identification—following earlier Sufis—of this heavenly "House" (and several others mentioned in the Qur'an) with the Heart (of the Knower, and ultimately of the Perfect Man), see chapter 6 of *Futûhât* (I 120) and the further references in Hakim, *Mu'jam,* pp. 222-28. The hadith on this subject (see Wensinck, *Concordance,* IV pp. 353-54) are for the most part the same ones concerning the Mi'râj in general discussed at note 38 above.

170. The hadith of Anas b. Mâlik (Muslim, *Imân,* 259/*bâb al-isrâ',* 1) followed by Ibn 'Arabî in section II (note 38) at the beginning of this chapter (III 341.29-34) states that: *"70,000 angels enter It each day, and they do not return there";* the other hadith concerning this subject in Muslim *(Imân,* 264) differs only slightly, while the corresponding hadith in Bukhârî *(bad' al-khalq,* 6, also from Anas, with slightly different *isnâd),* has Gabriel add that the 70,000 angels "*pray* there every day" and that "*when* they leave they do not return." Here—where the meaning of this House as the "Heart" is his primary concern—Ibn 'Arabî clearly implies a connection between these "70,000 angels" and the "70,000 veils" mentioned in another famous hadith (see following notes), where both numbers can be seen as symbols of the infinite, *never-repeated* divine theophanies, whether they are considered in the world or in their "reflections" in the Heart of the Perfect Man. In his earlier discussion of the Mi'râj hadith (III 341; an untranslated part of section II), however, he interprets the saying cosmologically: the angels' *"entry is through the door of the rising of the stars, and [their] departure is through the door of the setting of the stars."* (This latter interpretation is also apparently assumed in his remarks at this point in chapter 167 of the *Futûhât.*)

171. (As usual, *al-Haqq* and the corresponding pronouns could also be translated as "the Truth," "It," etc.) This translation assumes the inner connection between God and the Heart *(qalb)* that is expressed for Ibn 'Arabî in the famous *hadîth qudsî*—in this case, one not recorded in the canonical collections—to which he alludes throughout his writings: *"My earth and My heaven do not encompass Me, but the heart of My servant, the man of true faith, does encompass Me";* see his citation of this saying in a key opening passage of this chapter, at note 37 above. Concerning Ibn 'Arabî's conception of the "Heart" more generally, see the key chapter on the "Wisdom of the Heart" *(Shu'ayb)* in

the *Fusûs al-Hikam* (I 119-26; *Bezels,* pp. 147-55) and the extensive references in Hakim, *Mu'jam,* pp. 916-21. For the Shaykh, following a number of Qur'anic indications, the phrase "My servant"—i.e., the "servant" *('abd)* of the divine "I"—is understood as a reference to the very highest spiritual state, in which the saint perfectly mirrors the divine Will: see note 198 below on Ibn 'Arabî's own self-realization as a "pure servant" and Hakim, *Mu'jam,* pp. 773-76.

172. The rest of this paragraph partially cites a celebrated hadith (one of the main subjects of Ghazâlî's famous *Mishkât al-Anwâr;* see the excellent translation by R. Deladrière, *Le Tabernacle des Lumières,* Paris, 1981), usually given according to the version recorded in Ibn Mâja, I 44: *"God has seventy [or 700, or 70,000] veils of light and darkness: if He were to remove them, the radiant splendors of His Face would burn up whoever was reached by His Gaze."* (Muslim, *îmân,* 291 cites a similar hadith which mentions simply a "veil of Light," without any specific number.) Ibn 'Arabî interprets this hadith in greater detail in chapter 426 (IV 38-39), focusing on the question of how "light" can be a "veil"; chapter 73, question 115 (II 110), on the meaning of "God's Face"; and in his *K. al-Tajalliyât* (ed. O. Yahyâ, Beirut, 1967), VI, 728. Other discussions, usually mentioning the different versions of this hadith, can be found in the *Futûhât* at II 80, 460, 488, 542, 554; III 212, 216, 289; and I 72. Here, by choosing to mention the number 70,000— although the canonical hadith, as just noted, include several possible numbers (or none at all), Ibn 'Arabî clearly implies an intimate connection with the "angels" of the "Inhabited House" mentioned at the beginning of this section (see preceding notes), so that both the 70,000 "veils" and "angels" are understood as symbolizing the infinite range of theophanies *(tajalliyât)*. For Ibn 'Arabî's typical understanding of the divine "veils" as an expression for those theophanies (in this and many other contexts), see the references in Hakim, *Mu'jam,* pp. 313-18.

173. Literally, "the world of creation" *('âlam al-khalq)*: i.e., the realm of existence constituted by those "veils" or the divine Self-manifestation in all created being—as opposed to the primordial, "internal" Self-Manifestation or noetic differentiation of the Names and Realities within the divine Essence, the *fayd al-aqdas* and the "world of the Command," *'âlam al-amr* (which is the site of the final, purely noetic stages of the Ascension described in chapter 167).

174. III 350.20-32 (translated in full). As explained in the Introduction, this brief section summarizes an experience (or series of realizations) that is elaborated at much greater length in the other Mi'râj narratives. (See especially the key passage from the *K. al-Isrâ',* pp. 13-14, translated in our article cited at note 13 above.) Although Ibn 'Arabî's recounting of the Prophet's Ascension early in the chapter (section II, at III 341.3-342.20) goes on at this point to mention a number of additional details and "stages" drawn from a variety of hadith, his association here in the autobiographical portion of this chapter between the "Lotus of the Limit" (see following note) and the final, culminating revelations—expressed in several hadith by the formula: "God inspired *(awhâ)* in me what He inspired" (alluding to the Qur'anic verse 53:10)—exactly corresponds to the first hadith on the *isrâ'* given by Muslim (*Imân,* 259) and coincides with the other hadith elaborating on the symbolic allusions to Muhammad's vision in that sûra *(al-Najm),* whose opening verses are usually considered to recount the culminating stages of the Prophet's Ascension.

175. This *sidrat al-muntahâ* (where Muhammad *"saw Him in another descent"*) is part of a longer Qur'anic description (53:2-18) of two extraordinary occasions of revelation *(wahy)*—in the form of direct *vision* (Qur'an 53:10-13 and 17-18) by the "heart" *(fu'âd:* Qur'an 53:11) which are integrated into the hadith of the *mi'râj/isrâ'* quoted earlier (in section II, see notes 8 and 38), but whose details are also the subject of many separate hadith. (See for example, the separate section on the *sidra* in Muslim, *îmân,* 280ff.) While some of these hadith attempt to explain this vision as being of Gabriel's true angelic form (as opposed to his usual manifestation in human guise), Ibn 'Arabî's understanding here and in the *K. al-Isrâ'* clearly relies on those hadith which stress that *1.* this vision was in the Prophet's *Heart (qalb or fu'âd* [see Qur'an 53:11], as in the hadith of Ibn 'Abbâs at Muslim, *îmân,* 285-86); and *2.* that it was of the *"Lord"*; *3.* in a form of *"Light"* (or "veils of Light": see the famous hadith just cited at note 172), as at Muslim, *îmân,* 292-95. This latter hadith, in which Muhammad is asked how he saw his Lord (at verse 53) and responds that he saw God "as Light," is discussed in more detail in chapter 426 (IV, 38-39). In his earlier elaboration of the hadith descriptions of the *sidra* at this point (341.33-343.8) Ibn 'Arabî, in addition to stressing the ineffable Light surrounding it ("no one among God's creatures would be able to describe its beauty," says one hadith [Muslim, *îmân,* 259]) and discussing the particular points described here (see following notes), also adds a cosmological explanation of the word "limit", paraphrasing a hadith (Muslim, *îmân,* 280): *"It is the end of what descends to it from above and the end of what ascends to it from below."* (In chapter 167, the Lotus-tree is therefore presented as the threshold of the lowest gardens of Paradise.)

176. The branches and fruit of this cosmic tree are described in several of the hadith of the *mi'râj* drawn on in Ibn 'Arabî's earlier account (section II). Given that he interprets this tree below as the "form of Man" (i.e., the Perfect Man)—and therefore a symbolic "Tree of the World"—its "lowest *(dunyâ)* and highest branches" would refer to the totality of existence, encompassing every realm of being. See note 178 below and the translations of Ibn 'Arabî's own cosmological treatise, the "Tree of Existence" *(Shajarat al-Kawn)* mentioned in note 11 above; the same cosmological symbolism is developed in more detail in his *R. al-Ittihâd al-Kawnî,* translated by D. Gril as *Le Livre de l'Arbre et des Quatre Oiseaux,* Paris, 1984.

177. *Arwâh al-'âmilûn:* this feature (referring to *all* men's actions, not just to their good deeds or to the souls in Paradise) is also implied in certain hadith and mentioned explicitly in Ibn 'Arabî's synthesis of those materials in section II above (see references in preceding notes); it may be connected with the mention in the same Qur'anic passage (53:15) that *"with It is the Garden of Refuge"* (i.e., one of the Gardens of Paradise), or it could be interpreted as referring to the intermediate world *(barzakh,* which is also a *muntahâ* or "limit" between the sensible and spiritual realms) more generally. In cosmological terms—e.g., in his discussion in chapter 167 of the *Futûhât*—Ibn 'Arabî takes this "limit" to constitute the boundary between Paradise (located in the sphere above it) and Gehenna (constituted by all the lower spheres of the material world).

178. *'Alâ nash'at al-insân:* i.e., comprising all the same planes of being *(nash'a)* contained within the Perfect Man, both spiritual and bodily or material.

The metaphysical and spiritual equivalencies that this implies, especially the essential correspondence between the Perfect Man and the Reality of Muhammad, are elaborated in Ibn 'Arabî's own *Shajarat al-Kawn* ("The Tree of Existence"; Yahya, *R.G.,* no. 666), also available in the English and French translations by A. Jeffery and M. Gloton discussed at note 11 above; see also the additional cosmological references cited at note 21.

179. Earlier in this chapter (section II, at III 341.35-342.5) Ibn 'Arabî mentions the following hadith description (taken from Muslim, *îmân,* 264) where these rivers precede the "Inhabited House"; there is a parallel version, in same order as here, in Bukhârî, *bad' al-khalq,* 6: *"He saw four rivers flowing forth from its roots, two outward rivers and two inner [spiritual] ones* [bâtinân]... ", and Gabriel points out that *"the two inner ones are in the Garden [of Paradise], while the two external ones are the Nile and Euphrates."* Ibn 'Arabî then goes on to explain that the two "outer" ones also become rivers of Paradise after the Resurrection, thereby constituting the *four* rivers (of milk, honey, water and wine) promised to the blessed in parts of the Qur'an and hadith. (For Ibn 'Arabî's interpretations of those and related symbols, primarily as different kinds *or* modalities of spiritual wisdom, see Hakim, *Mu'jam,* pp. 1071-77). In the corresponding section of chapter 167 *(Alchimie,* pp. 109-11), however, he interprets these symbols more freely as referring to a single great River (understood as the *Qur'ân,* in the universal sense of the Reality of Muhammad and the *Umm al-Kitâb)*—i.e., the River of Life—and three smaller rivers (the Torah, Psalms and Gospels) emerging from It, along with the smaller streams of the other revealed Books *(suhuf)* mentioned in the Qur'an.

180. *Marâtib 'ulûm al-wahb:* this is the title of a separate extant treatise (also known under many other names) described in the *R.G.,* no. 423 (II, pp. 366-367). According to Osman Yahya (in the same entry), the end of this treatise mentions that it is also included in the *Futûhât,* and its contents correspond to the following sections: I 157-72 (chapters 16-21), III 501-5 (chapter 380) and IV 37-38 (chapter 425).

181. *Muttaka'ât rafârif al-'ârifîn:* the obscure Qur'anic term *rafraf,* used at Qur'an 55:77 to describe the "green couches" (or "meadows") of the dwellers of Paradise, was used by Ibn 'Arabî (in his summary of the Prophet's Mi'râj in section II, at III 432.7) to symbolize the angelic "vehicle" employed by Muhammad for the highest stages of his Ascension, after—as described in several other hadith—he was forced to leave Gabriel and Burâq at the "Lotus-Tree of the Limit." There he also adds that "it is like a litter or sedan-chair among us." Its use in reference to the Mi'râj no doubt comes from a hadith explaining Muhammad's vision of *"one of the greatest Signs of his Lord"* (Qur'an 53:13), stating that "he saw a green *rafraf* that had covered the horizon" (Bukhârî, *tafsîr sûrat al-najm,* from 'Abdallâh ibn 'Abbâs). The *K. al-Isrâ',* which contains a long poetic section on *"al-rafârif al-'ûlâ"* *(Rasâ'il,* pp. 45-49, immediately preceding the culminating "intimate dialogues" with God) gives a much clearer idea of the meaning of this symbol for Ibn 'Arabî. There their role in the passage beyond the "Lotus of the Limit" is connected with the voyager's realization of *"the secret of divine theophany in his heart"* (p. 48): on them *"he passed through 300 divine Presences* (hadarât)" (p. 53), until he reached the station *"where 'how' and 'where' disappear, and the secrets... [of the*

Union of God and the traveler] become clear" (p. 49). In the *Shajarat al-Kawn* (note 11 above), the *rafraf*—which is treated there as the fifth in a series of seven mounts used by the Prophet—is more clearly described as a sort of flying carpet "of green light, blocking up everything from East to West" (a description reflecting the above-mentioned hadith), and Ibn 'Arabî associates it with the divine Compassion (*raf'a*). (See Jeffery translation, pp. 152-53; Gloton translation, pp. 100 and 173 [citing another, more detailed hadith also attributed to Ibn 'Abbâs].)

182. The beginning of this sentence echoes the description of the Prophet's revelation and vision of God as "Light" at the Lotus-tree of the Limit, in the Qur'anic verses 53:16-18 and in the hadith discussed just above (note 175)—except that here Ibn 'Arabî himself has *become* that Tree "which is according to the state of Man" (note 178). The "robe of honor" *(khil'a)* here recalls the ceremony of Sufi "initiation" (the bestowal of the *khirqa*), except that here this royal garment symbolizes the spiritual station of the Prophet himself, the *maqâm muhammadî* Ibn 'Arabî attains below (at note 186).

183. This is a Qur'anic expression *(anzala 'alâ)* usually referring to the "descent" of divine Revelation to the prophetic Messengers *(rusul).* For other passages where Ibn 'Arabî applies it to divine inspirations received by the *awliyâ',* see the *Futûhât* II 506; III 94, 181; IV 178. Judging from the context, the "dispersion" or "diversity" of the divine "Signs" mentioned here seems to refer in particular to their division among the various prophets and messengers (and their revealed Books, etc.)—or even to the very multiplicity of the theophanies (God's "Signs in the souls and on the horizons," at Qur'an 41:53) that ordinarily distract us from a full awareness of the divine Unity. See also the similar allusions to the "unity-in-multiplicity" of the prophets and their teachings at the beginning of the key passage from the *K. al-Isrâ'* translated in our article cited at note 13 above.

184. Or "verse," *âya:* since what was revealed to Ibn 'Arabî in this experience was no less than the inner meaning of the true eternal *Qur'ân*—which is also the "Reality of Muhammad"—encompassing all knowledge (including the spiritual sources/realities of all the revealed Books), the phrase could also be read as "all the *verses* in that one verse." Much of the latter part of the *K. al-Isrâ'* (especially pp. 83-92) is particularly devoted to Ibn 'Arabî's detailed explanations of his new, perfect understanding of the spiritual meaning of many different Qur'anic verses, as that revealed insight is "tested" and verified by Muhammad and several other major prophets.

185. *Qarraba 'alayya al-amr:* this translation (taking *amr* in its most general sense) assumes Ibn 'Arabî is referring to his experience of the full eternal reality of the *Qur'an* (the *Umm al-Kitâb*) which is detailed in much of the *K. al-Isrâ'* (see our Introduction and the article cited at note 13). However the phrase could also be construed as referring to his special "proximity" to the (divine) "Command" *(al-amr)* or simply to God—since this experience has many of the features of what Ibn 'Arabî describes elsewhere in the *Futûhât* as the "Station of Proximity" *(maqâm al-qurba)* characterizing the highest group of saints, the "solitary ones" *(afrâd)*: see Hakim, *Mu'jam,* pp. 936-38, Ibn *'Arabî's K. al-Qurba (Rasâ'il,* I no.6), *Futûhât,* chapter 161 (II 260-62) and further detailed references in Chodkiewicz, *Sceau* (index s.v.).

186. Literally, that I was "Muhammad-like in (my spiritual) station"

(Muhammadî al-maqâm), i.e., marked by Muhammad's primordial spiritual condition of "all-comprehensiveness" *(jam'îyya)*, encompassing the eternal Realities of all the prophets (the *majmû'*, "totality") mentioned in the preceding sentence. The similar experience of the unity of all the prophets (and their spiritual knowledge and revelations) in Muhammad (and in Ibn 'Arabî himself) is summarized in the passage from the *K. al-Isrâ'*, pp. 12-14, translated in our article cited at note 13, and is of course carefully elaborated throughout the *Fusûs al-Hikam*. For details on Ibn 'Arabî's conception of the *maqâm muhammadî*, see Hakim, *Mu'jam*, pp. 1191-1201 and especially Chodkiewicz, *Sceau*, chapters IV (on the "Muhammadan Reality"), V (on the concept of the saints as "heirs" of certain prophets) and IX, discussing the many passages of the *Futûhât* and other works concerning Ibn 'Arabî's self-conception as the "Seal of Muhammadan Prophecy." See also the references on the "Station of Proximity" in the previous note: as indicated in the Introduction, note 13, the two stations are certainly very close, and the explicit distinction between them—which depends on Ibn 'Arabî's own role as "Seal"—seems to have developed only gradually in the Shaykh's thought.

187. The verb form here alludes to the celebrated verses (at *sûra* 97) describing the descent of *"the angels and the Spirit"* that marked the beginning of Muhammad's revelation; it is thus an apparent reference to the type of *direct* divine inspiration *(wahy)* uniquely limited to the line of divine lawgiving messengers *(rusul/mursalûn)*. For Ibn 'Arabî's conception of the spiritual insight of the saints as "mediated" or "inherited" through one or more of the earlier messengers, see chapter 14 of the *Futûhât* (I 149-52/O.Y., ed., III 357-62), plus detailed references in Hakim, *Mu'jam*, pp. 1191-1201 and Chodkiewicz, *Sceau*, chapters V and IX.

188. *Jawâmi' al-kilam*: the famous hadith paraphrased in this sentence (see Bukhârî, *ta'bîr*, 11; Muslim, *masâjid*, 5-8; Tirmidhî, *siyar*, 5, etc.) is cited repeatedly by Ibn 'Arabî to summarize the totality of spiritual knowledge or divine "forms of wisdom" *(hikam)* making up the "Muhammadan Reality": that conception is illustrated at length in his treatment of the other prophets (in relation to Muhammad) in the *Fusûs al-Hikam*, and is likewise assumed in his description of a similar revelatory experience in the *K. al-Isrâ'*, translated in our article cited at n. 13 above. (See the related discussions at II 72, 88; III 142; and further references in Hakim, *Mu'jam*, pp. 269-76, entry on *"jam'"*.) The rest of the hadith (translating here from al-Bukhârî) is also important in this context (i.e., regarding the "treasuries" of knowledge enumerated below): *"I was sent with the all-comprehensive Words... and while I was sleeping, I was brought the keys of the treasuries... and they were placed in my hand..."*

189. The text here reads literally "of no community *(umma)* among the communities"—a formulation apparently reflecting Ibn 'Arabî's focus here on the universality of Muhammad's spiritual reality (i.e., as ultimately sent to all the religious communities). It is not clear in this context whether this last phrase refers to six attributes which were not *combined* in one earlier messenger—in which case it might refer back to the revelations of the six prophets who were mentioned by name in the verse 3:84 quoted in the preceding paragraph—or rather to six characteristics which were each completely *unique* to Muhammad. The con-

cluding pages of the *K. al-Isrâ'* (pp. 91-92), for example, discuss several unique qualities of Muhammad that were not shared by Moses, Noah, Zachariah and Yahyâ (John), etc.

190. Or "directions": this sentence involves a play on the word *jiha*, which can mean both "aspect" (in the sense of trait or characteristic) and "direction"—in which sense the traditional "six directions" (i.e., the four cardinal points, plus the vertical axis) implicitly contain all the possible spatial orientations, and thereby again allude to the universality of the Prophet's Reality and divine mission.

191. *Nûr Muhammad:* for the historical background of this term (including early references in hadith and the Sîra literature), see Chodkiewicz, *Sceau,* pp. 80--87. For Ibn 'Arabî, the term is often roughly equivalent—from other points of view—to the "Muhammadan Reality," universal "Intellect," divine "Pen" or "Spirit," "Mother of the Book," etc.: see the references in Hakim, *Mu'jam,* pp. 347-52, and the long list of his synonyms for the "Perfect Man" at p. 158.

192. Or "Him": the pronouns at the end of this sentence, translated here as "It," could also refer simply to "Muhammad" (although in any case the two terms would be essentially identical in this context).

193. We have taken the most literal and obvious meaning. However, this phrase *(hasbî)* is also contained in two Qur'anic verses (39:38; 9:129): "... Say: 'God is enough for me' [hasbî Allâh]... ", and both verses go on to stress the importance of "absolute trust" in God *(tawakkul),* the ostensible subject of this chapter (see notes 2 and 39 on the meaning of the title).

194. *Imkânî:* i.e., everything (including the spatiality and corporality mentioned in Ibn 'Arabî's exclamation here), which had "separated" him from God (the unique "Necessary," noncontingent Being) and thereby offered the possibility of (relative) sin, opposition or conflict with the divine Commands; or in other words, everything that had been an impediment to his new state (or realization) of "pure servanthood," as an unimpeded expression of the divine Will (note 198 below). We may also recall that it was this very "possibility" that made the spiritual journey possible in the first place: see Ibn 'Arabî's mention of his "Burâq of *imkân*" at IV-A, note 84 above.

195. And "Object": *Musammâ wâhid*—the same formula was already mentioned in the schematic discussion of the spiritual journey in section III (at note 6l) above. As indicated there, the "transcendent Unity of the Named (divine Reality)" *(ahadîyyat al-musammâ)* is mentioned at the end of this section (III 354.15-16) in the long list of the kinds of knowledge Ibn 'Arabî "saw" within this experience. There, as throughout his work, he mentions the association of this point (i.e., as an explicit thesis or "doctrine") with the famous Andalusian Sufi Ibn al-Qasî and his book *Khal' al-Na'layn.*

196. Or "One Eye" *('ayn wâhida):* the pun (involving the subject/object of this "vision" or "witnessing": see following note) is certainly intentional here, and is further enriched by some of the other dimensions of meaning of *'ayn,* which is also Source, Essence, etc.

197. *Mashhûdî:* this phrase and the following one *together* carefully sum up the ineffable paradox of this experiential realization of divine Unicity—the very core of Ibn 'Arabî's work—which led to so much subsequent theological and philosophical controversy in the Islamic world (and wherever attempts have been made to treat this realization conceptually as a logical "system"). The first phrase,

taken in separation, states the thesis of *wahdat al-shuhûd*, and the second the position of *wahdat al-wujûd*—while the combination alone expresses the experience and fundamental reality the Shaykh attempts to convey here (and in the above-mentioned key passage from the *K. al-Isrâ'* translated in our article cited at note 13). Note the similar caution in the *K. al-Isrâ'*, pp. 65-66: *"So beware and don't imagine that my conjunction* (ittisâl) *with [the highest divine Presence] was one of identity of essence* (innîya)...," etc.

198. *'Abd mahd:* this formulation (or the related one of *'abd khâlis*), used fairly frequently by Ibn 'Arabî, refers to those rare Knowers who have become wholly devoted *(mukhlisîn)* to the divine *"I"*—i.e., who are among *"My"* servants," *'ibâdî* (alluding especially to Qur'an 15:42 and 17:65)—and not to the totality of creatures, who are all "servants of God" in a metaphysical (but still unrealized) sense. As Ibn 'Arabî explains in chapter 29 (O.Y. ed., III, pp. 228-29): *"Thus every servant of God pays attention to one [or more] of the creatures who has a right* (haqq, *i.e., a claim) against him, and his servantship [to God] is deficient to the extent of that right, because that creature seeks the [fulfillment] of that right from him and thereby has a power* (sultân: *like Satan at Qur'an 15:42, etc.) over him, so that he cannot be a pure servant, wholly devoted to God."* In a revealing autobiographical aside, Ibn 'Arabî adds that *"I encountered a great many of this group [i.e., of those 'seeking freedom from all engendered things']in the days of my wandering,"* and that *"from the day I attained this station I have not possessed any living thing, indeed not even the clothing I wear... And the moment I come into possession of something I dispose of it at that very instant, either by giving it away or setting it free, if that is possible."* At the beginning of chapter 311 (III 26-27), Ibn 'Arabî even more openly "boasts" (to use his expression) of this unique realization: *"Today I do not know of anyone who has realized the station of servanthood to a greater extent than I—and if there is someone [else], then he is like me. For I have attained the ultimate limit of servanthood, so that I am the pure, absolute servant who does not know [even the slightest] taste of Lordship* (rubûbîya)." See also Hakim, *Mu'jam*, pp. 765-778 (*'abd, 'ubûdîya*, and related concepts).

199. Ibn 'Arabî strongly emphasizes the direct experiential *"vision"* of the forms of knowledge he realized in this particular revelation by repeating *"I saw in it..."* before each of the sixty-nine kinds of understanding enumerated in this chapter (III 351-54). (This procedure is apparently unique among the many otherwise similar listings that conclude each of the remaining chapters on the spiritual stations, the *"fasl al-manâzil."*) The "opening of the treasuries" here is an allusion to the famous hadith concerning the special universality of the Prophet's revealed knowledge discussed in note 188 above.

200. These "kinds of knowledge" are, respectively, numbers 12, 15, 22, 25, 28, 45 and 53 in this list. Ibn 'Arabî's descriptions are given here without further annotation, since these principles should be familiar to readers of any of his works and most of them have been discussed in earlier passages of this chapter.

BIBLIOGRAPHY

Abû Tâlib al-Makkî: *Qût al-qulûb*, Cairo, 1961.
Abû Zayd, Nasr Hâmid: *Falsafat al-ta'wîl,* Beirut, 1983.
Addas, Claude: *Ibn 'Arabî ou la quête du Soufre rouge,* Paris, 1989.
Addas, Claude: *Ibn 'Arabî: The Voyage of No Return,* Cambridge, 2000.
Addas, Claude: *Quest for the Red Sulphur: The Life of Ibn 'Arabî,* Cambridge, 1993.
Alchimie, see Ibn 'Arabî: *Futûhât,* translated extracts.
Asin Palacios, M.: *El islam cristianizado,* Madrid, 1931; French tr.: *L'islam christianisé,* Paris, 1982.
Asin Palacios, M.: *El mistico murciano Abenarabi,* Madrid, 1928.
Austin, R.W.J.: *Ibn al 'Arabî: The Bezels of Wisdom*, New York, 1980.
Austin, R.W.J.: *Sufis of Andalusia,* London, 1971.
Balyânî, Awhad al-Dîn: *Epître sur l'Unicité absolue,* tr. M. Chodkiewicz, Paris, 1982.
Bezels, see Ibn 'Arabî: *Fusûs al-hikam.*
Böwering, G.: *The Mystical Vision of Existence in Classical Islam: The Qur'ânic Hermeneutics of the Sufi Sahl al-Tustarî* (d. 283/896), Berlin, 1979.
Al-Bûnî: *Shams al-ma'ârif al-kubrâ,* Cairo, s.d., popular edition in 4 volumes.
Burckhardt, T.: *Clé spirituelle de l'astrologie musulmane,* Milan, 1974; English translation as *Mystical Astrology According to Ibn 'Arabi,* Louisville, 2002.
Chittick, W.: "Death and the World of Imagination: Ibn al-'Arabî's Eschatology," *Muslim World* LXVII (1987).
Chittick, W.: article "Eschatology" in *Islamic Spirituality I,* S. H. Nasr, ed., New York, 1987 (Vol. XIX of "World Spirituality: An Encyclopedic History of the Religious Quest").
Chittick, W.: article "Ibn al-'Arabî and His School" in *Islamic Spirituality II,* S. H. Nasr, ed., New York, 1991 (Vol. XX of "World Spirituality: An Encyclopedic History of the Religious Quest").

Chittick, W.: *Imaginal Worlds: Ibn al-'Arabi and the Problem of Religious Diversity*, Albany, 1994.
Chittick, W.: *Ibn al-'Arabî's Metaphysics of Imagination*, New York, 1989.
Chittick, W.: *The Self-Disclosure of God: Principles of Ibn al-'Arabî's Cosmology* Albany, 1998.
Chittick, W.: *The Sufi Path of Knowledge: Ibn al-'Arabî's Metaphysics of the Imagination*, Albany, 1989.
Chodkiewicz, M.: "Ibn 'Arabî: la lettre et la loi," parts in the collection, *Mystique, culture et société*, ed. M. Meslin, Paris, 1983.
Chodkiewicz, M.: *Le Sceau des saints: Prophétie et sainteté dans la doctrine d'Ibn 'Arabî*, Paris, 1986; English translation as *Seal of the Saints*, Cambridge, 1993.
Chodkiewicz, M.: *An Ocean Without Shore: Ibn 'Arabî, the Book and the Law*, Albany, 1993.
Chodkiewicz, M.: *The Seal of the Saints: Prophethood and Sainthood in the doctrine of Ibn 'Arabî*, Cambridge, 1993.
Corbin, H.: *L'imagination créatrice dans le soufisme d'Ibn 'Arabî*, Paris, 1958; 2nd ed., 1977; New English translation as *Alone with the Alone: Creative Imagination in the Sufism of Ibn 'Arabî*, Princeton, 1998.
Elmore, G.: *Islamic Sainthood in the Fulness of Time: Ibn al-'Arabî's "Book of the Fabulous Gryphon"* Leiden, Brill, 2000.
El-Saleh, S.: *La vie future selon le Coran*, Paris, 1971.
Encyclopaedia Iranica, ed. E. Yarshater, London, 1982.
Encyclopedia of Islam, 1st and 2nd editions (EI^1 and EI^2).
Ernst, C. W.: *Words of Ecstasy in Sufism*, Albany, N.Y., 1985.
Fahd, T.: *La divination arabe*, Strasbourg, 1966; 2nd ed. Paris, 1987.
Al-Farghânî, Sa'îd'al-Dîn: *Mashâriq al-darârî*, S. J. Âshtiyânî, ed., Tehran, 1357/1978.
Furûzânfar, B.: *Ahâdîth-i Mathnawî*, Tehran, 1334/1955.
Fusûs, see Ibn 'Arabî: *Fusûs al-hikam*.
Fut. or *Futûhât*, see Ibn 'Arabî: *al-Futûhât al-Makkiyya*.
Al-Ghazâlî: *Ihyâ 'ulûm al-dîn*, Cairo, 1326.
Al-Ghazâlî: *al-Maqsad al-asnâ*, ed. F. A. Shehadi, Beirut, 1971.
Al-Ghazâlî: *La perle precieuse (K. al-durrat al-fâkhira)* tr. L. Gautier, Leipzig, 1977; *The Precious Pearl*, tr. J. I. Smith, Missoula Montana, 1979.
Graham, W. A.: *Divine Word and Prophetic Word in Early Islam*, The Hague, 1977.
Ghurâb, M: *Al-Fiqh 'inda' l-Shaykh al-Akbar*, Damascus, 1981.
Guénon, R.: *Les symboles fondamentaux de la science sacrée*, Paris, 1962.
Al-Habashî, Badr: *Kitâb al-inbâh*, ed. and tr. D. Gril, *Annales Islamologiques* XV (1979).
Al-Hakîm, S.: *al-Mu'jam al-sûfî: al-hikma fî hudûd al-kalima*, Beirut, 1401/1981.
Halm, H.: *Kosmologie und Heilslehre der frühen Ismâ'îlîya*, Wiesbaden, 1978.
Hirtenstein and P. Beneito, The Seven Days of the Heart, Oxford, 2001.
Hirtenstein, S.: *The Unlimited Mercifier: The Spiritual Life and Thought of Ibn 'Arabî*, Oxford, 1999.
Ibn 'Arabî: *Dîwân*, Cairo, Bûlâq, 1271 h.
Ibn 'Arabî: *K. al-fanâ' fî'l-mushâhada*, tr. M. Vâlsan, *Le livre de l'extinction dans la contemplation*, Paris, 1984.

Ibn 'Arabî: *Fusûs al-hikam*, ed. A. Affifi, Cairo, 1346/1946; *The Bezels of Wisdom*, tr. R. W. J. Austin, New York, 1980; A translation and commentary by Bursevi, I. H., Oxford, 1986; *La sagesse des prophètes*, partial tr. Titus Burckhardt, Paris, 1955.

Ibn 'Arabî: *al-Futûhât al-Makkiyya*, Cairo, 1329, 4 vol.

Ibn 'Arabî: *al-Futûhât al-Makkiyya*, ed. Osman Yahya, Cairo 1392-1413/1972-92 (14 volumes to date, corresponding to one third of volume 1 of *Futûhât* above).
Translated extracts of the *Futûhat*:
—Chapter 167: *L'alchimie du bonheur parfait*, tr. S. Ruspoli, Paris, 1981; partial tr. from the same chapter by G. Anawati, *Revue de l'Institut Dominicain d'Études Orientales du Caire*, Mélanges 6 (1959-61).
—Chapter 178, II 320: *Le traité de l'amour*, tr. M. Gloton, Paris, 1986.
—Chapter 198, *fasl* 9, II 405-420: *Le Coran et la fonction de'Hermès*, tr. C. A. Gilis, Paris, 1984.
—Chapter 262 and 263: tr. M. Vâlsan, *Études Traditionnelles*, July–October 1966.

Ibn 'Arabî: *Kitâb al-Isrâ' ilâ al-maqâm al-asrâ'* (*Rasâ'il* I, no. 13, pp. 1–92), Hyderabad, 1948.

Ibn 'Arabî: *Kitâb al-i'lâm bi-ishârât ahl al-ilhâm;* tr. M. Vâlsan, "Le Livre d'enseignement par formules indicatives des gens inspirés," *Études traditionnelles*, 1967-68.

Ibn 'Arabî: *Kitâb al-istilâhât al-sûfîya;* tr. R. T. Harris, *Journal of the Muhyiddîn Ibn 'Arabî Society*, III (1984); (*Rasâ'il II*, No. 29).

Ibn 'Arabî: *Kitâb al-jalâla;* tr. M. Vâlsan, *Études Traditionnelles,* June, July, August and December, 1948.

Ibn 'Arabî: *Al-kawkab al-durrî fî manâqib Dhî al-Nûn al-Misrî;* tr. R. Deladrière, *La vie merveilleuse de Dhû-l-Nûn l'Égyptien*, Paris, 1988.

Ibn 'Arabî: *Khutbat al-Kitâb* (prologue des *Futûhât Makkiyya); tr.* M. Vâlsan, *Etudes Traditionnelles*, 1953.

Ibn 'Arabî: *Kitâb al-Bâ'*, Cairo, 1954.

Ibn 'Arabî: *Kitâb mawâqi' al-nujûm*, Cairo, 1965.

Ibn 'Arabî: *Kitâb Mishkât al-anwâr fî mâ ruwiya 'an Allâh min al-akhbâr,* Aleppo, 1349/1927; tr. M. Vâlsan, *La niche des lumières*, Paris, 1963.

Ibn 'Arabî: *Majmû'at al-ahzâb*, assembled by Ahmad Diyâ' al-Dîn Kamûshkhânî, Istanbul, 1298 h.

Ibn 'Arabî: *Muhâdarat al-abrâr*, Cairo, 1906, 2 vol.

Ibn 'Arabî: *Rasâ'il Ibn 'Arabî*, Hyderabad, 1948.

Ibn 'Arabî: *Risâlat al-anwâr fî mâ yumnah sâhib al-khalwa min al-asrâr* (*Rasâ'il* I, no. 12, pp. 1–19), Hyderabad, 1948; tr. R. T. Harris, *Journey to the Lord of Power*, New York, 1981.

Ibn 'Arabî: *R. al-ittihâd al-kawnî;* tr. D. Gril, *Le livre de l'Arbre et des Quatre Oiseaux*, Paris, 1984.

Ibn 'Arabî: *Rûh al-quds*, Damascus, 1964.

Ibn 'Arabî: (attributed) *Shajarat al-Kawn*, tr. A. Jeffery, "Ibn 'Arabî's *Shajarat al-Kawn*," *Studia Islamica*, vol. X and XI; tr. M. Gloton, *L'arbre du monde*, Paris, 1962.

Ibn 'Arabî: *Tanazzul al-amlâk min 'âlam al-arwâh ilâ 'âlam al-aflâk*, ed. Ahmad Zakî Atiya & Tâhâ 'Abd al-Bâqî Surûr, 1961.

Izutsu, T.: *A Comparative Study of the Key Philosophical Concepts in Sufism and Taoism: Ibn 'Arabî and Lao-Tz¯u, Chuang-Tz¯u*, Tokyo, 1966.

Izutsu, T.: *Sufism and Taoism*, Tokyo, 1983.

Jâmî: *Naqd al-nusûs fî sharh naqsh al-fusûs*, ed. W. Chittick, Tehran, 1977.

Journey, see Ibn 'Arabî: *Risâlat al-anwâr* tr. Harris.

Kraus, P.: *Jâbir Ibn Hayyân, contribution à l'histoire des idées scientifiques dans l'Islam*, Cairo, 1943 (M.I.E. no. 44).

Lings, M: *Muhammad*, New York, 1983.

Massignon, L: *Essai sur les origines du lexique téchnique de la mystique musulmane*, nouvelle édition, Paris, 1968; translated as *Essay on the Origins of the Technical Language of Islamic Mysticism*, Notre Dame, 1997.

Meyer, F: "Ein kurzer Traktat Ibn 'Arabîs über die A'yân al-Thâbita," *Oriens* 27/28 (1981).

Michot, J: *La destinée de l'homme selon Avicenne: le retour à Dieu* (ma'âd) *et l'imagination*, Louvain-la-Neuve, 1987.

Mishkât, see Ibn 'Arabî: *Kitâb Mishkât al-anwâr*.

Morris, J. W.: "Ibn 'Arabî's Esotericism: The Problem of Spiritual Authority," *Studia Islamica* LXIX (1989).

Morris, J. W.: "Ibn 'Arabî and His Interpreters," *Journal of the American Oriental Society* 106, 3 and 4 (1986) and 107, 1 (1987).

Morris, J. W.: "The Spiritual Ascension: Ibn 'Arabî and the Mi'râj", *Journal of the American Oriental Society* 108 (1988).

Morris, J. W.: *The Wisdom of the Throne: An Introduction to the Philosophy of Mulla Sadra (K. al-Hikmat al-'arshîya)*, Princeton, 1981.

Mu'jam, see al-Hakîm: *al-Mu'jam al-sûfî*.

Murata, *Chinese Gleams of Sufi Light*, Albany, 2000.

Murata, *The Tao of Islam: A Sourcebook on Gender Relationships in Islamic Thought*, Albany, 1992.

Nyberg: *Kleinere Schriften des Ibn al-'Arabî*, Leyde, 1919.

Ormsby, E. L.: *Theodicy in Islamic Thought: The Dispute over al-Ghazâlî's "Best of All Possible Worlds,"* Princeton, 1984.

O. Y., see Ibn 'Arabî: *Futûhât*, ed. Osman Yahya.

al-Qaysarî, Dâwûd: *al-Tawhîd wa'l-nubuwwa wa'l-walâya*, ed. S. J. Âshtiyânî, Mashhad, 1357/1978.

Qushayrî: *al-Risâla*, ed. 'Abd al-Halîm Mahmûd & Mahmûd ibn al-Sharîf, Cairo, 1972-74, 2 vol.

R. al-anwâr, see Ibn 'Arabî: *Risâlat al-anwâr*.

R.G., see Yahya, O.: *Histoire et classification*.

Radtke, B.: *al-Hakîm al-Tirmidhî: Ein islamischer Theosoph des 3/9 Jahrhunderts*, Freiburg, 1980.

Rasâ'il, see Ibn 'Arabî: *Rasâ'il Ibn 'Arabî*.

Râzî, Fakhr al-Dîn: *Sharh asmâ' al-husnâ, wa huwa al-kitâb al-musammâ Lawâmi' al-bayyinât*, ed. Tâhâ 'Abd al-Ra'ûf Sa'd, Cairo, 1976.

Roman, A.: *Etude de la phonologie et de la morphologie de la koiné arabe*, Aix-en-Provence, 1983.

Sakhâwî: *al-Qawl al-munbî*, Ms. Berlin 2849, Spr. 790.
Sarrâj, Abû Nasr: *al-Luma' fî'l-tasawwuf*, ed. R. A. Nicholson, Leiden, 1914.
Sceau, see Chodkiewicz, M.: *Le Sceau des saints*.
SEI: The Shorter Encyclopaedia of Islam, Leiden, 1965.
Sells: *Stations of Desire: Love Elegies From Ibn 'Arabî*, Jerusalem, 2000.
Sha'rânî 'Abd al-Wahhâb: *Al-yawâqît wa'l-jawâhir* & *Al-kibrît al-ahmar*, Cairo, 1369h.
Smith, J. I. & Haddad, Y. Y.: *The Islamic Understanding of Death and Resurrection*, New York, 1981.
Al-Suyûtî: *al-Jâmi' al-saghîr*, in al-Munâwî, *Fayd al-qadîr*, Beirut, 1972.
Vâlsan, M.: "Les références islamiques du 'symbolisme de la croix,'" *Études Traditionnelles*, 1971 et 1972.
Vâlsan, M.: "Le Triangle de l'Androgyne et le monosyllabe Ôm," *Études Traditionnelles*, 1964 to 1966.
Wensinck, A. J. et al: *Concordance et indices de la tradition musulmane*, Leiden, 1936–69.
Word, see Graham, W.: *Divine Word and Prophetic Word…*
Wolfson, H. A.: *The Philosophy of the Kalam*, Cambridge Mass., 1976.
Wronecka, Joanna: "Le *Kitâb al-isrâ' ilâ maqâm al-asrâ*' d'Ibn 'Arabî," *Annales Islamologiques*, XX (1984), containing translated extracts.
Yahya, O.: *Histoire et classification de l'oeuvre d'Ibn 'Arabî*, Damascus, 1964.

INDEX OF QUR'ANIC REFERENCES

Sura : Aya — Pages

1 : 4 — 194.
5 — 163, 166.
7 — 218, 258.

2 : 15 — 58.
18 — 104.
31 — 242.
33 — 242.
42 — 111.
89 — 82.
115 — 120, 291.
154 — 98, 241, 302.
171 — 104.
179 — 195.
188 — 84.
192 — 139.
255 — 222.
272 — 79.

3 : 27 — 32, 238.
54 — 58.
59 — 106.
64 — 227.

66 — 215, 330.
77 to 78 — 84, 265.
83 — 87.
84 — 229, 352.
92 — 55, 143, 144.
97 — 183, 193.
113 — 80.
181 — 313.

4: 18 — 110, 283.
38 — 84.
156 — 154.
164 — 305, 344.
169 — 153.

5 : 20 — 208.
77 — 136.
101 to 102 — 269.

6 : 3 — 321.
5 — 111.
25 — 184.
57 — 110, 282.
74 to 80 — 227.
100 — 121, 239.
125 — 270.

7 : 2 — 270.
28 — 171.
34 — 338.
116 — 307.
143 — 225, 226, 342.
144 — 226, 342.
151 — 224.
156 — 77, 218, 240, 243.
172 — 95, 154, 274, 344.
180 — 58, 328.
185 — 309.
187 — 184.

8 : 17 — 54, 138, 309.
23 — 79.
37 — 37.

9 : 8 to 10 — 338.
79 — 58.

10 : 59 — 170.
62-64 — 215.

11 : 119 — 218.
123 — 60, 105, 163, 188.

12 : 5 — 187.
108 — 73, 110.

13 : 17 — 185.
33 — 61.

14 : 25 — 215.
38 — 321.

15 : 29 — 52.
42 — 354.
46 — 240.
85 — 137, 238.

16 : 2 — 82.
16 — 83.
40 — 192, 244.
44 — 102.
74 — 185, 215, 330.
77 — 114.
81 — 59.

17 : 1 — 61, 131, 201, 209, 212, 213, 314, 322, 323, 347.
20 — 299.
23 — 59, 192, 196, 312, 337.
110 — 61.

18 : 64 — 48.

19 : 31 — 151, 152.
32 — 152, 153.
34 — 154.
56 — 221, 222.
56 to 57 — 336.
57 — 221.
57 to 58 — 336.

20 : 5 — 143.
17 to 21 — 341.
50 — 182, 301, 312.
52 — 153, 165.
66 — 307.
113 — 145.

21 : 1 — 222.
101 — 104.
103 — 240.
107 — 88.

22 : 46 — 104.
54 — 124.
74 — 115, 287.
77 — 139.
78 — 139, 270.

23 : 13 — 169, 177.
56 — 215, 330.
100 — 95, 106.

24 : 35 — 35.
54 — 259.

25 : 53 — 111, 285.

26 : 193 to 194 — 82.
227 — 107, 288.

27 : 16 to 17 — 251.
89 — 240..

28 : 88 — 45.

29 : 46 — 91.

30 : 47 — 70.

31 : 31 — 202, 332.
    29 — 338.

32 : 13 — 346.

33 : 4 — 40, 54, 56, 168.
    12 — 119.
    72 — 36.

34 : 34 — 154.

35 : 15 — 59, 196, 295, 297, 299.

36 : 71 — 245.
    82 — 160, 176.
    83 — 60, 158.

37 : 163 — 79, 80.
    164 — 176.
    180 — 123.

38 : 44 — 145.
    75 — 245.

39 : 3 — 69, 268.
    38 — 353.
    42 — 98, 274, 277.
    67 — 237, 312.
    68 — 279, 343.

40 : 2 — 138.
    7 — 121.
    15 — 300.
    35 — 132, 295.
    60 — 192.

41 : 11 — 36.
    53 — 208, 215, 309, 322, 323, 329, 351.

42 : 7 — 114.
    10 — 32.

11 — 123, 164, 208, 238, 304.
48 — 79.
51 — 74.
52 — 256.
53 — 164.

43 : 32 — 183.
    84 — 208.

44 : 49 — 132.
    56 to 57 — 98, 106.

45 : 12 — 34.
    23 — 184.

47 : 15 — 103, 280.
    23 — 79.
    24 — 184.
    31 — 78.

49 : 11 — 214, 329.

50 : 15 — 237.
    15 to 16 — 322.
    16 — 184, 208, 292.
    22 — 106, 109, 237.

51 : 54 — 188.
    56 — 36, 131, 184, 189, 300, 309.

52 : 4 — 228, 241, 342.
    21 — 88.
    45 — 343.

53 : 1 to 18 — 201, 228, 313.
    3 to 4 — 83.
    7 — 322.
    10 — 325, 348.
    10 to 13 — 348.
    11 — 349.
    13 — 350.
    14 — 228.
    15 — 349.
    16 — 228.
    16 to 18 — 351.
    18 — 325.

54 : 55 — 106.

55 : 4 — 48, 84.
29 — 56, 86, 328.
41 — 84.
77 — 228, 350.

56 : 27 — 218, 237.
61 — 171.
62 — 171, 332.
85 — 184, 292.
95 — 111.

57 : 3 — 43, 241.
4 — 208, 209, 241.

58 : 8 — 136.

59 : 2 — 214, 329.

66 : 8 — 120.

67 : 15 — 130.

70 : 4 — 218.

72 : 19 — 131, 301.

73 : 9 — 312, 319.

78 : 38 — 223.

79 : 10 — 95.
14 — 95, 344.

80 : 1 to 10 — 268.
3 — 87.
22 — 171.

81 : 26 to 27 — 224.

82 : 6 — 295.
6 to 8 — 177.
7 — 297.
8 — 278.

83 : 15 — 215, 226, 344.
20 to 21 — 43.

85 : 3 — 159.

86 : 9 — 78.
16 — 58.

89 : 2 — 135.
97 : 4 — 80, 229.

102 : 2 — 110.

103 : 3 to 7 — 111.

INDEX / GLOSSARY

Aaron : 205, 220, 223-4, 284, 292, 315, 334, 340-341.
'abd : servant : 127, 131, 133, 140, 148, 252, 327, 348;
 —Allâh : 191.
 —*al-mahd* : utter servant : 131, 327, 354.
Abd al-'Azîz al-Mahdawî : 17.
Abraham : 190, 227-8, 322, 346, 347.
Abû Bakr al-Siddîq : 147.
Abû Hurayra : 117, 265.
Abû Madyân : 240.
Abû Tâlib al-Makkî : 236.
'âda : accustomed order : 271, 287, 336.
adab : courtesy : 59, 244, 270.
Adam : 43, 99, 132, 151, 152, 154, 173, 210, 217-18, 222-23, 237, 242, 245, 274, 278, 283, 292, 301, 315, 320, 324, 327, 328, 332, 333, 334, 335, 338, 339.
'adam : nonexistence : 32, 45, 51, 63, 136, 143, 148, 165, 304, 340.
aflâk : see *falak*.
afrâd : solitary saints : 6, 266, 267, 317, 323, 329, 351.
ahad : the One, the Unique : 246, 248, 296.
ahadiyya : Unity : 46, 60, 136, 248, 328, 353.
ahkâm (see also sing., *hukm*) : statutes : 45, 58, 78, 88, 214, 249, 251, 259, 269.
ahl : people
 — *al-batt* : p. of Severance : 186.
 — *al-bayt* : p. of the House : 263.
 — *al-kashf* : p. of Unveiling : 75, 102, 239, 257, 268, 292.
 — *al-nazar* : p. of rational inquiry : 289.
 — *al-rusûm* : p. of exotericism : 15, 195.

INDEX / GLOSSARY • 365

— *al-ru'ya* : p. of vision : 283.
— *al-suluk* : p. of wayfaring : 161.
— *al-wara'* : p. of scrupulous piety : 280.
— of Allah : 302.
— of Qur'an : 302.
ahwâl : see *hâl.*
'A'isha : 73, 244.
ajâl : 338.
âkhira : next, other world : 31, 94, 99, 223, 273, 279, 338, 339.
âkhir : last : 236, 273.
'âlam al-khayâl : imaginal world: 185.
'alâma : mark : 43, 55, 241.
'Alî b. Abî Tâlib : 34, 35, 106, 239, 277, 288, 344.
'âlim (see also pl., *'ulamâ'*) knower : 310.
'amâ' : cloud : 238, 302, 321.
'amal : work : 53, 62, 153, 166, 170.
amâna : responsibility : 109.
'âmma : ordinary people : 85, 115, 122, 123, 173, 242, 307, 339.
amr : affair, commandment, entity, thing : 45, 48, 51, 54, 109, 148, 165, 192, 196, 295, 312, 339, 348, 351.
anbiyâ' : see sing., *nabî.*
Andalusia : 6, 7, 24, 262, 264, 328, 341, 353.
Ansârî : 315.
'aqîda : credo : 120.
'âqil : judicious person : (pl., *'uqalâ'*) : 258, 260, 263.
'aql : reason : 12, 44, 46, 48, 53, 241, 246, 286, 290, 309, 311, 326, 330, 338, 343.
al-Aqsâ (Mosque of) : 322, 347.
'arad (pl. *a'râd*) : accident : 39, 184.
ard : earth : 39, 131.
'ard al-akbar : greater reviewing : 278, 286, 333.
'ârif (pl. *'ârifûn*) : knower : 148, 181, 281, 283, 340, 341, 350.
'arsh : throne : 38, 321.
arwâh (see also sing., *rûh*) : spirits : 158, 240, 349.
asl (see also pl. *usûl*) : root : 33, 63, 159, 193, 236, 269, 340.
asmâ' (see also sing., *ism*) : divine names : 57, 236, 246, 296.
athar : effect : 47, 60, 133, 134, 138.
Avicenna (see also Ibn Sînâ) : 236, 273, 277.
Awhad al-Dîn al-Kirmânî : 170, 286, 306.
awhâm : see *wahm.*
awliyâ' (see also sing., *walî*) : friends; saints : 18, 41, 67, 68, 112, 118, 131, 207, 214, 251, 252, 254, 260, 258, 259, 260, 262, 263, 264, 267, 272, 282, 287, 289, 290, 328, 330, 336, 351;
— *al-atbâ'* : saintly followers : 118, 289.
— *al-fatarât* : saints who lived in periods or places without direct contact with the revealed religious paths : 118, 289, 290.
awwal mawjûd : First Existent : 29.
âya : sign, verse : 351.

a'yân : entities : (see also sing., *'ayn*); 61, 242, 304, 334, 341;
— *al-thâbita* : immutable entities : 51, 55, 324.
'ayn (see also pl., *a'yân*) : entity, essence, self, eye : 35, 55, 73, 128, 147, 160, 182, 183, 188, 196, 217, 281, 286, 300, 324;
— *al-Haqq* : God Himself : 55, 164, 167.
— *al-hiss* : eye of the senses : 286.
— *al-khayâl* : eye of imagination : 113, 286.
— *al-wâhid* : Reality of the One : 137.
— *wâhid* : One Self : 61, 137, 283.
— *al-wâhida* : Single Reality : 284, 300, 353.
— *al-wujûd* : identical with Being : 164.
— *tajalli al-haqq* : the Self-manifestation of the Real : 256.
— *thabita* : immutable entity : 128.
azal : eternity without beginning : 35.
'azama : tremendousness : 153, 159.

badî' : Originator : 248.
Baghdad : 115.
baqâ' : subsistence : 38, 320, 341.
bâriqa ilâhiyya : divine flash : 194.
barzakh : isthmus, intermediate imaginal world : 95, 99, 101, 103, 110, 113, 230, 234, 242, 246, 274, 275, 277, 279, 282, 285, 286, 292, 302, 304, 308, 325, 344, 349.
basmala : 241.
Basra : 194, 305.
Bastâmî : see Bistâmî.
ba'th : resurrection : 110, 284.
bâtin : nonmanifest or inner : 42, 54, 107, 173, 240, 246, 282, 350.
Bishr al-Hâfî : 140, 184.
Bistâmî, Abû Yazîd : 131, 308.
Burâq : 210, 217, 325, 331, 350, 353.

Ceuta : 77, 78.

dalâla : denotation, proof : 60, 131, 144.
Daqqâq, Abû 'Alî : 163, 166, 303.
da'wâ : claim : 143, 164, 191, 313.
dhât : essence : 32, 45, 53, 61, 142, 137, 238, 241, 248.
dhawq : direct, personal experience : 112, 132, 139, 148, 176, 220, 224, 225, 227, 239, 324, 330, 335, 342, 343.
dhikr : invocation : 14, 21, 37, 80, 83, 190, 192, 252, 260, 261, 281, 297.
Dhû'l-Nûn al-Misrî : 115, 286, 287.
Dihyâ al-Kalbî : 172, 306.
dîn : religion : 69, 83, 251, 268, 270.
dunyâ : lower world : 31, 94, 95, 99, 223, 273, 274, 279, 338, 339, 349.

Egypt : 115.
Euphrates : 103, 280, 350.
Eve : 335.

INDEX / GLOSSARY • 367

falak (pl. *aflâk*) : sphere : 29;
— *al-hayât* : sphere of life : 33.
— *al-muhît al-ma'qûl* : all-encompassing intelligible sphere : 33.
fanâ' : extinction, annihilation : 38, 109, 110, 163, 244, 284, 319, 340, 341, 343.
faqr : poverty : 128.
al-Farghânî, Sa'îd al-Dîn : 129, 237.
faqîh (pl. *fuqahâ'*) : jurist : 83, 135, 214, 250, 254, 257, 262, 264, 266, 268, 269, 291, 293.
fath : opening : 177, 190, 232, 296.
fayd al-aqdas : emergence of Names or Realities within the divine Essence : 348.
Fez : 80, 203, 261.
fi'l (pl. *af'âl*) : act : 58, 139, 161, 186; reality : 194, 230.
fiqh : jurisprudence: 19, 250, 268, 293.
fitra : primordial nature : 183, 294.
fu'âd : heart : 349.
furqân : discrimination, division: 234, 253.

Gabriel : 73, 172, 176, 178, 178, 220, 280, 293, 306, 311, 347, 349, 350, 351.
ghafla : inattention, forgetfulness: 155.
ghayb (pl. *ghuyûb*) : unseen : 53, 86, 101, 169, 171, 254, 261,271.
ghayra : jealousy : 138, 143, 238, 299, 312, 313.
al-Ghazâlî : 57, 236, 244, 269, 271, 273, 276, 279, 308, 311, 312.

habâ' : principal substance : 30, 179, 236, 238.
hadd (pl. *hudûd*) : prescription, penalty : 32, 77, 134, 298, 333.
hadîth : 75, 116, 140, 148, 211, 244, 253, 255, 264, 277, 279, 280, 293, 299, 329, 332, 342, 346.
— *qudsî* : 258, 261, 265, 273, 281, 287, 305, 312, 315, 320, 321, 323, 332, 335, 338, 344, 346, 347, 349.
hadra : presence : 46, 171;
— *al-ilâhiyya* : divine presence : 48.
hajj : pilgrimage : 6, 17, 174.
hajjîr : see *hijjîr*.
hâl : spiritual state : 45, 75, 155, 166, 226, 244, 304, 342.
Hallâj : 150.
haqîqa (pl. *haqâ'iq*) : reality : 13, 30, 32, 45, 158, 238, 242, 243, 249, 302, 341.
haqq : Truly Real, God, Truth : 12, 30, 33, 35, 51, 55, 58, 78, 81, 85, 86, 109, 110, 119, 120, 142, 155, 159, 164, 167, 191, 213, 218, 224, 230, 234, 256, 284, 292, 302, 322, 327, 329, 337, 339, 340, 341, 344, 346, 347.
haraka (pl. *harakât*) : movement : 30, 52.
harf (pl. *hurûf*) : letter : 175, 232, 241.
hashr : gathering : 107, 110, 278, 284.
hayba : awe : 47, 182.
hayra : bewilderment : 42, 45, 62, 127, 298, 346.
Haytham b. Abî al-Tîhân : 148.
hayûlâ : hylé, raw matter : 35, 236, 238
hijâb (pl. *hujub*) : veil : 45, 290, 300, 327, 344.

hijjîr : motto, verse used in invocation : 21, 189, 190, 191, 252.
hikma : wisdom : 146, 195.
himma : spiritual intention : 14, 70, 336.
hiss : sensory perception : 39, 52, 171, 172, 187, 244, 286.
hubb : love :184, 192.
hudûd : see *hadd*.
hudûth : temporal origination : 30.
hujub : see *hijâb*.
hukm (see also pl., *ahkâm*) : judgment, authority, command : 35, 44, 59, 61, 71, 79, 81, 82, 135, 148, 219, 230, 251, 252, 259, 260, 267, 268, 269, 332, 333.
huwa : He : 42, 183, 295, 309, 313, 327.
huwiyya : He-ness : 196, 295.

'ibâda (pl. *'ibâdât*) : worship : 12, 19, 62, 128, 153, 191, 247, 249, 312.
ibdâ' : origination : 54, 248.
Ibn 'Abbâs : 73, 131, 295, 309, 349, 350, 351.
Ibn Barrajân : 238, 264.
Ibn Khaldûn : 306.
Ibn Qasî : 264, 328, 353.
Ibn Sînâ (see also Avicenna) : 279.
Idrîs : 99, 220, 221-3, 273, 315, 336-340.
ihsân : perfection : 178, 186, 293, 306.
ijtihâd : judicial : 69, 84, 85, 251, 266.
ikhlâs : sincerity : 252.
Ikhwân al-Safâ' : 263.
iktisâb : acquisition: 45, 169.
ilâh : god, divinity : 8, 30, 43, 44, 48, 55, 58, 112, 128, 131, 137, 142, 143, 148, 158, 170, 177, 179, 190, 191, 194, 236, 237, 238, 244, 255, 295, 302, 303, 327.
ilhâm : inspiration : 184.
'ilm : knowledge, science : 12, 15, 35, 38, 53, 86, 89, 96, 116, 129, 137, 170, 179, 197, 232, 234, 261, 264, 279, 293, 322.
ilqâ' : projection: 8, 75, 82, 255, 263.
imâm : leader : (see also 'Ali, Mahdî) : 69, 71, 72, 79-88, 239, 249, 251-4, 262, 264, 266, 336, 342.
— *al-waqt* : 253, 262.
India : 7.
insân : human being : 30, 164, 188, 260, 278, 291, 322, 331, 349;
— *al-kâmil* : perfect human being : 18, 109, 213, 217, 234, 320, 322.
irâda (pl. *irâdât*) : desire : 34, 192, 282.
Iran : 84, 254.
'Isâ : see Jesus.
ishâra (pl. *ishârât*) : allusion : 11.
ism : (see also pl., *asmâ'*) : divine Name : 60, 61, 144, 290, 291, 295, 303.
'isma : immunity from error : 73, 250, 254, 263, 264.
isrâ' : nocturnal ascent : 201, 280, 313, 314, 316, 318, 322-3, 325, 329, 330, 331, 332, 342, 349.
Istanbul: 287.

istiʿdâd : preparedness : 12, 35, 50, 52, 143, 190, 226, 294, 331.
istihâla : transmutation : 38.
istinbât : deduction : 37, 195.
ittisâl : conjunction : 354.
ʿizza : exaltation, mightiness, might : 57, 131, 244.

Jacob : 187, 228.
jalwa : society, as opposed to *khalwa* : 158, 161, 237.
jamʿ : all-comprehensiveness, union : 162, 309.
jamʿ al-jamʿ : gathering of gathering : 162.
jamâd : inanimate : 36, 52.
jamâl : beauty : 47, 328.
jamʿiyya : all-comprehensiveness : 61, 185, 242, 352.
jasad : body : 300, 301.
jawâmiʿ al-kalim : All-comprehensive words : 242, 261, 352.
Jerusalem : 322.
Jesus : 20, 151-4, 176, 190, 205, 210, 220, 228, 249, 251, 279, 307, 324, 325, 334-6, 343.
al-Jîlî, Abd al-Karîm : 204, 274, 317, 344.
jinn : 36, 70, 73, 79, 131, 184, 189, 195, 239-40, 251, 260, 280, 281, 300, 307, 309, 313.
jism (pl. *jusûm*) : body : 52, 244, 312.
Joseph : 187, 220, 227, 330, 336, 342.
Junayd : 140, 239.

Kaʿba: 8, 222, 227, 241, 322, 338, 347.
kalâm : speech : 48, 63, 161, 194, 255, 256, 290, 304, 319, 322.
kalima (pl. *kalim*) : word : 242, 307, 337.
kamâl : perfection : 32, 43, 238, 241, 294, 335, 341.
karîm : generous: 132.
kashf : unveiling : 42, 53, 62, 75, 91, 102, 118, 119, 120, 177, 190, 237, 239, 243, 257, 268, 287, 290, 292, 330, 331.
kathîb : dune : 117, 283, 345.
kathrat al-ʿilm : manyness of knowledge : 129.
kawn (pl. *akwân*) : engendered existence : 31, 40, 60, 138, 223, 246, 304, 341, 345.
Khadir : 14, 85, 185, 266-7, 281, 310, 336, 342.
khalîfa : vicegerent : 69.
khalq : creation: 11, 29, 51, 110, 143, 230;
— *al-jadîd* : ever renewed creation : 31, 282, 286, 322, 338, 348.
khalwa : spiritual retreat : 37, 157, 158, 161, 318.
kharq al-ʿâda : break of the customary order : 36, 271, 307, 336.
khâssa : elect : 291, 294, 302.
khawâss : elite : 173;
— *al-asmâʾ* : properties of the Names : 155, 175.
khayâl : imagination : 39, 52, 107, 113, 114, 123, 158, 185, 255, 274, 279, 282, 286, 287, 292, 306, 311.
Khidr (see also Khadir) : 48.
khitâb : address : 64, 74, 255, 286.
Konya : 6, 204.

kufr : infidelity : 256.
kursî : footstool : 38, 288.

latîf : Subtle : 240.
lawh al-mahfûz : guarded tablet : 245.

ma'a al-anfâs : see *khalq al-jadîd.*
madhhab (pl. *madhâhib*) : doctrinal position, school : 168, 251.
madhmûm : blameworthy : 40.
Maghreb : 7, 80, 262, 264.
mahall : locus, receptacle : 166, 274.
al-Mahdawî : see 'Abd al-'Azîz.
Mahdî : 67-88, 249-254, 260, 262-64, 267, 269, 270, 275, 335.
mâhiyya : quiddity : 34.
mahmûd : praiseworthy : 40.
mala' al-a'lâ : supreme assembly : 172.
malakût : domination: 158, 307.
malâmiyya : blameworthy : 239, 247.
Mâlik b. Anas : 323, 347.
ma'lûh : vassal of God : 30, 142, 191, 304, 313.
ma'nâ (pl. *ma'ânî*) : meaning : 32, 52, 55, 73, 81, 123, 172, 187, 212, 229, 241, 244, 248.
ma'nawî : spiritual : 52, 53, 213, 244, 260, 262, 263, 318, 325.
mâni' : preventer : 184, 248.
manzil (pl. *manâzil*) : spiritual stage, mansion : 20, 53, 67, 88, 169, 207, 229, 257, 279, 315, 354.
maqâm (pl. *maqâmât*) : spiritual station : 19, 21, 30, 189, 235, 315;
 — *dhâtî* : station of Essence : 142.
 — *al-kamâl* : station of perfection: 335.
 — *al-muhammadî* : spiritual station of Muhammad : 317, 351, 352.
 — *al-qurba* : station of proximity : 317, 322, 351.
 — *al-tawakkul* : station of trust : 320.
ma'rifa (pl. *ma'ârif*) knowledge : 18, 31, 112, 166, 177, 185, 293.
martaba (pl. *marâtib*) : level : 44, 51, 144, 170, 236, 238, 246, 289, 303, 310.
mazhar (pl. *mazâhir*) : locus of manifestation : 47, 112, 128, 133, 160, 167, 241, 296, 303, 324, 340, 342.
Mecca : 6, 17, 232, 240, 280, 322.
Medina (see also Yathrib) : 232, 313.
Michael : 176.
Mina : 104, 280.
mi'râj (pl. *ma'ârij*) : spiritual ascent : 201-207, 210, 212, 217, 225, 235, 249, 254, 276, 280, 283, 287, 313, 314-318, 320, 321, 322, 323, 324, 325, 327, 331, 335, 347, 349, 350.
mithl : likeness, symbolic image : 164.
mizâj : constitution: 101, 123, 171, 293, 294, 302, 337.
Moses : 20, 22, 85, 166, 190, 205, 211, 224, 225-28, 234, 256, 266, 277, 279, 280, 283, 289, 290, 292, 307, 310, 324, 329, 330, 335, 340-345, 353.
Mosul : 174, 306.

mubâh : licit : 267, 268, 269, 270.
mubashshira : dream vision/glad tidings : 307, 324.
mubda' : originated thing : 60.
mudhill : abaser : 296.
muhaddith : faithful transmitter of oral traditions : 293.
muhaqqiq (pl. *muhaqqiqûn*) : verifier, realizer of reality : 15, 112, 151, 207, 271, 282, 283, 292, 293.
muhdath : temporally originated : 138.
muhyî : Life-giver : 296.
mu'în : Helper : 167.
mu'izz : Exalter : 296.
mu'jiza (pl. *mu'jizât*) : miracle : 254, 336.
mulk : kingdom, possession: 34, 71, 172, 262.
mumît : slayer : 296.
munâjât : intimate conversation: 203, 316.
murîd : willing : 310.
mushâhada : contemplation: 183.
mustanad ilâhî divine basis : 236.
mutakallim (pl. *mutakallimûn*) : theologan : 100, 197, 271, 293, 331.

nabî (pl. *anbiyâ'*) : prophet: 118, 221, 223, 239, 260, 266, 270, 272, 289, 289.
nafas al-Rahmân : the All-Merciful breath : 51.
nafs (pl. *anfâs*) : soul, self : 30, 35, 53, 143, 146, 148, 154, 159, 182, 238, 271, 272, 277, 282, 296, 300, 304, 338.
nâ'ib (pl. *nuwwâb*) : substitute : 252.
naql : narration, transmission : 187, 243, 279.
nâr : fire : 275, 282.
nash'a : plane, or realm, of being : 31, 44, 106, 169, 292, 305, 332, 349.
nasr : victorious support : 70, 71, 252, 264.
nass (pl. *nusûs*) : formal text : 269, 263.
nazar : intellectual reflection : 15, 36, 51, 62, 118, 119, 167, 172, 175, 182, 196, 221, 242, 256, 257, 276, 287, 289, 290, 291, 316, 319, 330, 331, 338, 343, 345.
Nile : 103, 114, 280, 350.
nisba (pl. *nisab*) : relation : 38, 62, 132, 160, 165, 166, 242, 248, 334.
niyâba : deputyship : 295; substitution : 299.
nubuwwa : prophecy : 214, 285, 289.
nûr : light : 51, 53, 240, 353.

qâdî : judge : 77-78.
Qadîb al-Bân : 173, 306.
qâdir : Powerful : 184, 310.
qâhir : Triumphant : 184, 238.
qalam : pen : 245.
qalb : heart : 256, 321, 328, 347, 349.
qidam : eternity : 32.
qiyâs : reasoning by analogy : 63, 82, 87, 251, 263, 264, 268, 269.
Qûnawî, Sadr al-Dîn : 8, 129.

Qur'ân : Qur'an : 71, 80, 203, 227, 229, 249, 253, 254, 261, 269, 337, 350, 351.
qurb : proximity : 184, 292, 295, 308, 317, 322, 351.
Qushayrî : 303, 304.
qutb (pl. *aqtâb*) : pole : 189, 221, 252, 253, 262, 299, 336.
quwwa : faculty, force : 35, 38, 39, 60, 62, 155, 158, 172, 179.

rabb : Lord : 8, 57, 234, 237, 300, 321, 334, 343.
rajul : see pl., *rijâl*.
rahma : mercy : 258, 283.
rahmân : All-Merciful : 30, 60, 321.
rasûl (pl. *rusul*) : messenger : 118, 119, 127, 224, 260, 272, 289, 291, 325, 351, 352.
ra'y : personal opinion : 87, 251, 264.
Râzî, Fakhr al-Dîn : 57.
razzâq : Provider : 248.
rijâl (sg. *rajul*) : men, masters : 37, 174-5, 186, 291, 306, 312;
— *al-ghayb* : men of the unseen : 254, 261, 271.
risâla : divine message : 17, 218, 230, 285.
rizq : subsistence : 260.
rubûbiyya : lordship : 128, 143, 170.
rûh (see also pl., *arwâh*) : spirit : 38, 52, 220, 244, 260, 285, 294, 301.
rûhânîya : spiritual reality or entity : 176, 318, 324, 331, 340.
rûhânîyyûn : spiritual beings : 39, 172.
rusul : see *rasûl*.
ru'ya : vision : 108, 113, 116, 211, 275, 279, 281, 283, 287, 291, 292, 325, 343, 345.

sâ'a : hour : 114, 278, 339.
sabab (pl. *asbâb*) : cause : 51, 131, 135, 145, 147, 195, 247, 300, 313, 320, 324.
Sahl al-Tustarî : 238, 273.
salât : prayer : 253.
salb : negation : 45, 60, 132, 246.
sâlik : traveler : 317.
samâ' : heaven : 53, 331.
Sarî' al-Saqatî : 140.
shafâ'a : intercession : 37.
Shâfi'î : 251, 265, 266.
shahâda : formula of profession of faith : 320, 337; visible, as opposed to *ghayb* : 53, 101, 171.
shahwa : desire, passion : 148, 258, 301.
shar' : religious law or way : 4, 32, 46, 63, 81-82, 85, 87-88, 103, 189, 249, 263, 267.
shâri' : lawgiver : 63, 186, 260, 272.
shirk : idolatry, polytheism : 327.
shuhûd : contemplation or witnessing : 330, 331, 354.
sidq : sincerity, truthfulness : 70, 252, 264.
sifa : quality, attribute : 58, 248, 287.
sirr (pl. *asrâr*) : secret, inmost consciousness : 35, 64, 81, 96, 214, 239, 258, 321, 326, 327, 330, 331, 334, 258.
sitr : veil : 327.

siyâsa : policy : 70.
Spain : 6.
sultân : authority : 37, 85, 175, 354.
sulûk : wayfaring : 160, 176, 326.
sûq al-janna : market of paradise : 117, 288, 294.
sûra (pl. *suwar*) : form : 30, 33, 35, 42, 52, 108, 189, 300, 327.

tabaqât : hierarchies, strata : 30, 39, 52.
tafsîr : commentary, explication : 131.
tahaqquq : realization of the essential truth : 131, 140, 140, 143, 170.
tahlîl : dissolution, division : 331, 326, 329.
tahqîq : verification : 10, 12, 17, 97, 108, 139, 239, 299.
tajaddud al-khalq : see *tajdîd al-khalq, khalq al-jadîd.*
tajallî : theophany : 31, 128, 157, 179, 224, 237, 256, 296, 343.
tajdîd al-khalq : constant re-creation : 11, 338.
taklîf : religious prescription : 64, 147, 152, 166, 195, 269, 310.
takhalluq : to assume the character traits of God : 143, 166, 236, 299, 300, 308.
takwîn : formation; engendered existence : 111, 160.
talwîn : variegation, coloration : 51, 127, 328.
tanzîh : incomparability of God : 33, 42, 45, 58, 62, 152, 238, 241, 290, 294, 296, 311, 319, 320, 337.
taqlîd : imitating: 15, 118, 119, 251, 268, 290.
taqwâ : reverence for God : 234.
tarjama : translation : 257.
tark : abandoning : 127, 134, 146, 158, 318.
tarkîb : composition: 52, 153, 326, 329.
tasarruf : free disposal : 138, 172, 184.
tashabbuh : gaining similarity [with God], attachment : 62, 179, 308.
tashbîh : similarity, immanence : 42, 122, 246, 248, 294, 311, 320, 337.
tashrî' : law-giving : 152, 289.
tawajjuh : attentiveness : 53, 245, 301.
tawhîd : divine unity : 221, 222, 337.
ta'wîl : spiritual interpretation : 249, 336.
tawakkul : absolute trust and reliance on God : 207, 319, 320, 324, 353.
thubût : immutability, affirmation : 132, 246, 312.
Tirmidhî : 18, 41, 112-113, 116, 118, 237, 242, 265, 281, 283, 285, 287, 288, 289, 291, 297, 298, 301, 305, 309, 326, 332, 339.
Transoxiana : 85.
Tunis : 17, 38, 90, 235.
turâb : earth : 39.

'ubûda : servitude : 130.
'ubûdiyya : servanthood : 19, 128, 130, 134, 170, 267.
'ulamâ' (see also sing., *'âlim*) : knower : 37, 68, 69, 122, 251, 254, 258, 272, 278, 293;
— *al-dhawq* : men of knowledge through tasting : 139.
— *al-rusûm* : exoteric authorities : 68, 76, 164, 257, 262, 264.
— *bi-Llâh* : true knowers of God : 118, 138, 343, 344.

ulûha, ulûhiyya : divinity : 121, 131, 238.
'ulûm : see *'ilm*.
'uluw : exaltation, elevation : 243.
'Umar (caliph) : 266, 307.
umm : archetype, mother : 302;
    — *al-Kitâb* : Mother of the Book : 350, 351.
umma : community : 230, 338, 352.
ummahât : kingdoms: 40.
usûl (see also sing., *asl*) : sources : 250, 268.
'Utbat al-Ghulâm : 170, 305.

wahdat al-wujûd : Oneness of Being : 128, 354.
wâhid al-'adad : the One : 188.
wâhid al-kathîr : the One Many : 188, 248.
wahm (pl. *awhâm*) : illusion, mental representation : 185, 186, 311.
wahy : [direct] divine revelation : 74, 75, 82, 83, 224, 244, 255, 256, 289, 291, 325, 330, 342, 346, 349, 352.
wajh al-khâss : specific aspect : 326, 332.
walâya : sainthood; authority : 24, 66, 252, 266, 285.
walî (see also pl., *awliyâ'*) : saint : 155, 214, 254, 260, 272, 328, 330.
wâqi'a : visionary experience: 49, 222, 286, 338.
wârid : visionary influx : 241, 274.
wârith : inheritor : 221, 254, 340, 341.
wâsita : intermediary : 119.
wazîr (pl. *wuzarâ'*) : minister : 69, 249, 253.
wujûb : obligation : 296, 343.
wujûd : Being, existence : 32, 51, 53, 55, 58, 114, 128, 137, 158, 164, 193, 239, 279, 292, 304, 340, 354.
Yahyâ (John the Baptist) : 220, 223, 227, 314, 326, 334, 335, 353.
yaqîn : certainty : 108, 111, 282.
Yathrib (see also Medina) : 290, 346.
yawm al-zawr : day of the visit : 116.

zâhid (pl. *zuhhâd*) : ascetic : 131, 190.
zâhir : manifest, apparent : 42, 54, 55, 107, 128, 133, 159, 173, 240, 246, 282.
zamân : time : 40, 98, 250, 278, 284, 304, 334, 338.
zawr al-a'zam : greater visit : 278, 286.
zuhûr : manifestation : 128, 160, 237.
zulm : injustice : 148.
zulma : darkness : 51.

12.95